CHANGING SCHOOLS . . . CHANGING CURRICULUM

Edited by Maurice Galton
Professor of Education, University of Leicester
and Bob Moon, Headteacher,
The Peers School, Oxford

Harper & Row, Publishers
London

Cambridge
Hagerstown
Philadelphia
New York

San Francisco
Mexico City
Sao Paulo
Sydney

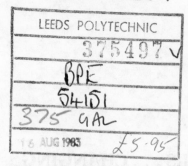
First published 1983

Harper & Row Ltd
28 Tavistock Street
London WC2E 7PN

British Library Cataloguing in Publication Data.

Changing schools . . . changing curriculum.
1. Curriculum planning
I. Galton, Maurice II. Moon, Bob
375'.001 LB1570
ISBN 0-06-318245-9
Printed and bound by Butler & Tanner Ltd, Frome.

CONTENTS

Acknowledgements

INTRODUCTION
Maurice Galton and Bob Moon

Acknowledgements
The Oxford 1982 conference of the Association for the Study of the Curriculum was planned and organized by members of the Shire Counties regional group. Their energy, enthusiasm and imagination is illustrated in the wide ranging ideas and analysis contained within this book. The aims of the association to involve all sectors of education in common pursuit of school and curriculum research and improvement have been vigorously promoted and appreciation to the planning committee is recorded here.

Planning Committee Members
Michael Davies – *Chairman* – Bridgewater Hall School, Stantonbury Campus, Milton Keynes
Martine Moon – *Secretary* – The Open University, School of Education
John Rutherford – *Treasurer* – Hartwell Primary School, Northamptonshire
David Alexander – Bedfordshire C.C.
Pat Atherton – Drayton School, Banbury, Oxon.
Trixie Dacombe – Clipstonbrook Lower School, Bedfordshire
Richard Graydon – Wallingford School, Oxfordshire
David Hill – Northamptonshire C.C.
John Isaac – Oxford Polytechnic
Bob McCormick – The Open University, School of Education
Bob Moon – The Peers School, Oxford
Ann Pennell – Bedford College of Higher Education

Introduction

In 1972 a group of university college lecturers, local authority advisers and teachers met at Exeter to consider the establishment of a standing conference for curriculum study. The declared purpose of the conference was to bring together people with an interest in curriculum study, particularly the practical problems concerned with the implementation of new ideas and courses at school and classroom level. To promote this objective the conference decided that teachers must form the majority of the membership so that they had a major say in the planning and organizing of future meetings. Many people present at the Exeter conference had been actively involved in the curriculum renewal programmes of either the Nuffield Foundation or the Schools Council, as members of the development team, evaluators and teachers in schools taking part in trials of the materials. Among the participants, therefore, was a common awareness that although recent curriculum projects had markedly changed the content of courses and, in some cases, introduced new methods of assessment, they had had a marginal effect on the way the curriculum was taught. The evidence from the Schools Council project for The Evaluation of Science Teaching Methods, presented at the conference, demonstrated that less than one-fifth of the observed teachers adopted practices in their classrooms which were consistent with the aims and objectives set out in the teacher's guide to the various science schemes. Inevitably, there was much heart searching among the conference members and considerable interest was shown in the activities of schools such as Countesthorpe College, Stantonbury and the Sutton Centre, where attempts were being made to 'radicalize' school practice within a programme of school-based curriculum development.

Several years later the expansion of interest in the activities of the standing conference led to the establishment of the Association for the Study of the Curriculum with local branches up and down the country, a journal of its own and its own annual conference. This present volume arises out of papers presented at the recent meeting in Oxford, although, in an attempt to cover a wide range of views, some individuals not in attendance have been invited to contribute.

Something of the history of the curriculum movement in Britain over the last decade can be gleaned from the range of topics which have been discussed at successive conferences. At the inaugural conference, the papers of which were published under the title *The Curriculum, Research, Innovation and Change*, the issues covered included practical curriculum development, the failure of curriculum courses in institutions of higher education, the need for more curriculum research and the growing awareness that change and innovation in schools had to be managed (Taylor and Walton 1973). Mid-way through the decade, 'Power and the Curriculum', the first conference of the reconstituted Association for the Study of the Curriculum, saw a sharp change of emphasis with the potential threat of the accountability movement to the possibilities for curriculum reform, the need to manage and plan for curriculum development in an age of contraction and a growing obsession with the politics of both evaluation and of the wider area of curricular reform (Richards 1977). In their essays the language of the contributors reflected the changing seasons as the spring-like imagery of growth and hope at the inaugural meeting gave way to the more sombre autumnal tones of 'Power and the Curriculum' with its suggestions for preparing the ground for the winter of discontent to follow. Against a background of the setting up of the Assessment of Performance Unit and the dire warnings on the effects of the accountability exercises being conducted in the United States, a strong atmosphere of gloom and despondency developed. Somehow it seemed that the brief flowerings of the curriculum movement during the short summer in between were not thought sufficiently productive to withstand these predicted wintery blasts.

Yet during the intervening period considerable advances had been made. In a reaction to the rather narrow vision of some of the 'hard-line' proponents of behavioural objectives, an alternative paradigm had become strongly established in the field of curriculum evaluation. Arising out of the work of the Humanities and the Ford Teaching projects, the 'teacher as researcher' and the 'action-research' movements became established and flourishing. Attention and interest increased in the day-to-day management of curricular change in schools and in the increasing complex lines of communication between different school departments and the local authority. The Bullock Report, stressing the need of whole school policies for language across the curriculum, gave an added urgency to the need for greater understanding of how the system worked. Increasingly, too, came a strong and growing interest in the processes of teaching, as curriculum researchers began to understand that the problems of curriculum change and the problems of teaching were inextricably linked. The study of the 'curriculum in action' became of central interest, bringing together teachers and researchers and increasing our understanding of the curriculum process. All these gains are described in the late Lawrence Stenhouse's article which concludes the book and in which the legacy of the curriculum development movement in Britain is reviewed.

Curriculum development and curriculum inquiry have become inextricably linked with school reform through these events of the past decade. It was not always so. Many of the early attempts at curriculum change were conceived independently of the social structure and purposes of school. In retrospect it may appear a naïve strategy. Millions of pounds and dollars have been dispensed, particularly in Europe and the USA, in projects and policies aimed at curriculum improvement and modernization. The outcomes of this investment have been the source of considerable debate and controversy. There are many who have been critical of the impact of major national experiments. Too few teachers in too few schools seem ever to have heard of the proposed reform let alone put it into practice. This is a view in England and Wales which has attracted governmental support, as the closure of the Schools Council in its present form illustrates so clearly. For others, however, such an evaluation is far too simplistic. It fails to take account of the rich complexity of influences that surround any curriculum innovation, and it fails to acknowledge that changes occur along a time-scale far different than that envisaged by those active in the early years of the curriculum development boom.

The 1960s and 1970s witnessed a number of growth points for curriculum study and policy. Firstly there were the major national projects, almost always investigating specific subject areas of the primary or secondary school curriculum. Associated with this was the emergence, particularly in university departments of education, of curriculum specialists who proceeded, in parallel with colleagues in the USA, to build a structure of academic credibility around the focus of curriculum theory. In the same period a number of schools used a critique of existing curriculum structures as the base for whole school and whole curriculum reforms, Countesthorpe College in Leicestershire, Stantonbury Campus in Milton Keynes and the Sutton Centre in Nottinghamshire represent three such institutions, each of which has helped establish new boundaries for the development of curriculum policies.

In this same period schools came to have a unity of purpose that had rarely been apparent before. The end of the eleven-plus examination and the publication of the Plowden Report gave primary schooling a new status and a new confidence. The abolition of selective secondary education in most parts of the country was likewise to create a community of interest among secondary school teachers. Such a unity was, however, to attract a political interest of a sort uncharacteristic of education in England and Wales. Cross-party debate (although not agreement) about establishing some common aims in the school curriculum led to a growth of ministerial and civil servant interest and awareness about curriculum issues. One of the first manifestations of this in the 1980s has been the re-assertion of lay governors' influence over the nature of the curriculum in schools.

In the twenty years or so since the first ambitious development projects in science and mathematics, the curriculum field has come to be occupied by a far broader range of interest groups than the early subject specialists and few enthusiastic teachers would ever have given credit for. This trend was anticipated by the establishment of a standing conference on curriculum. Ten years after that first Exeter conference the meeting at Oxford provided an opportunity to look forward to the next ten years of curriculum innovation. Many of those most concerned with events of the previous decade which led to the setting up of the conference were also present at Oxford. Thus the meeting provided a moment both for a balanced retrospective on the ideas and aspirations of the curriculum movement of the past and an opportunity to look forward to the future.

The conference contributions were centred around four inter-related themes which form the main sections of this volume. The first, examining the changing world of schools and teachers, illustrates clearly how curriculum issues are now closely tied to alternative policies for school reform and improvement. The second explores, from a number of different perspectives, new ideas about control of the curriculum, while a third examines the associated industry that has grown up around the twin themes of evaluation and accountability. A fourth section explores the growth of classroom studies and the relevance that this now has to school policies and practice. The contributions represent a rich mixture of theory and practice, polemic diagnosis and prognosis. That, after all, is the reality of curriculum reform and the guiding principles around which the association has developed. This volume, bringing together a selection of these contributions, provides an indication of current thinking and permits an interesting analysis of development over the decade following on from the first Exeter conference. Despite the gloom and despondency associated with economic recession there was a ferment of ideas at Oxford although in very different areas ten years on from Exeter.

Perhaps the most encouraging aspect of the present debate is the growing awareness that the nature of the comprehensive school as an institution needs to be re-thought. In the face of mass unemployment a whole education industry for the sixteen–nineteen age group has been created with little reference to schools or national and local educational authorities. In the past, the comprehensive school appeared to gear itself to meet its main challenge from the pro-grammar school lobby, in terms of the performance of a minority of its pupils in the Ordinary and Advanced Certificates of Education. Now the emphasis is beginning to shift and schools are being questioned about their failure to equip their pupils with sufficient skills to adapt to current uncertainties attached to adult life. David Hargreaves, in his book *The Challenge of the Comprehensive School* (1982), clearly outlines this shift in calling for a curriculum where pupils work together co-operatively in order to maximize the use of their individual talents. Slowly but surely the gap between the pioneering schools of the early 1970s and the more typical comprehensives is narrowing. If schools are beginning to change, then so ultimately must the curriculum which is taught within them. It is to be hoped, therefore, that the essays within this book can make a timely contribution to this current debate.

The need for co-operation and dialogue between all concerned with school improvement (not least curriculum researchers and theorists) is apparent in many of the contributions. Powerful advocacy for new ways forward is linked to a critique of the shortcomings and misunderstanding of old ideas and assumptions; both lead in the direction of new styles of collaboration. It is appropriate that the strongest and most consistent advocate of fusing curriculum research with curriculum practice, Lawrence Stenhouse, should have contributed a final and major retrospective to the Oxford conference. These ideas now appear to have greater chance of widespread adoption. Economic pressures are making closer ties between schools, universities, colleges and local education authorities inevitable. At the same time there is an upsurge of opinion, based on the recent history of curriculum development, that argues for a similar re-assertion of the power of co-operation. It is with this that the contributors to the volume are most concerned.

References

Taylor, P. H. and Walton, J. (eds) (1973) *The Curriculum, Research, Innovation and Change*, Ward Lock.
Richards, C. (ed) (1977) *Power and the Curriculum*, Nafferton
Hargreaves, David H. (1982) *The Challenge for the Comprehensive School:Culture, Curriculum and Community*, Routledge & Kegan Paul.

PART I

CHANGING SCHOOLS

Introduction

BOB MOON

In all the industrialized countries of the Western world schooling is undergoing rapid, and sometimes traumatic, change. The idealism and aspirations of the 1960s (as we now remember them) have been replaced by uncertainty and some disillusion, only a decade and a half later. Economic recession, restricted public expenditure, a sharp downturn in the birth rate and pressures to turn back the clock in educational philosophies have made schools a battlefield of conflicting ideologies and interests. In England and Wales the circumstances have reflected all of these difficulties. The pressures have not been confined to schools. The institutions and agencies supporting school improvement have faced related problems. The wholesale closure of many teacher training institutions, the abolition of the Schools Council, the cutbacks in the advisory service, the dismantling of the impressive network of teachers' centres across the country and increased restrictions on the initiatives taken by educational administrators are now well documented. It is not an easy time. Yet, ironically, in the face of such apparent adversity there are individuals and groups who have thought imaginatively and realistically about future directions for schooling. The two Chief Education Officers, for example, contributing to this volume come from authorities where economic cutbacks have been as acute as anywhere in the country. One education correspondent, reviewing the Oxford conference at which these papers were presented, suggested that 'a consensus is beginning to emerge from the schools that have been bubbling over the last few years, and from the administrators and advisers who have been supporting them'.[1]

What, therefore, is the basis for optimism? It is clear that structural issues are having and will continue to have a major influence on school change. The marked reduction in school numbers has already moved through the primary school, threatened the very existence of middle schools and is now having a critical impact on thinking and development in secondary and tertiary education. Colin Richards, in looking to the future of primary education, gives a very clear summary of the demographic and expenditure trends perhaps to the end of this century. The changing structure of employment with the vast majority of sixteen- to eighteen-year-olds unable to find full-time jobs represents a second issue of great importance. The consequences of youth unemployment are serious but appear as yet to have only just touched the social consciousness of the vast majority of the population, and many teachers and educationalists. Douglas Hamblin details this and the implications for schools. It is clear now, in a way it was not just a few years ago, that the structure of employment is undergoing lasting rather than recessional change. And this will reverberate, not only in the sixteen–nineteen age range, but across the whole adult workforce through to retirement. It has, for example, brought sharply into question the relevance for a national system of examining at sixteen, an issue covered by a number of contributors. Peter Mann, until recently not only a comprehensive school headteacher of long standing but also adviser to the Parliamentary Select Committee on Education, argues for abolition in its present form as does Tim Brighouse.

Alongside these two major issues of birth rate and employment comes a third, the impact of technology both on society as a whole and more specifically on the traditional methods of teaching and learning. The microprocessor, the word processor and other 'processors' as yet undreamt of will eventually transform the traditional form of academic and vocational preparation for life. The irrelevancies in schooling are already there as the host of girls (usually) tapping away at the outdated typewriters of our comprehensive schools will confirm, and as the Cockcroft Report clearly showed to be the case in so much of our teaching of mathematics. David Walton examines the controversial and complex issue of computing which in technological terms is the equivalent of Douglas Hamblin's treatment of employment; issues for the present and the future supporting Tim Brighouse's assertion 'that schools must have a view of the future that anticipates the inexorable march of events so that they may better equip their pupils for such a future'.

Schools will change, wanted or not. Innovation by circumstances regardless of interest is unavoidable and six years after Prime Minister

Callaghan's 'Great Debate' (agenda and minutes circulated in advance, result indifference) there is emerging a well-grounded philosophical debate about future directions. Colin Richards shows how much has been done to clear away the misconceptions about primary schools, misconceptions of the left and the right, which emerged during the ideological periods of Plowden and a decade later the William Tyndale affair. Tim Brighouse, Peter Mann and Peter Cornall, however, each indicate how far there is to go in establishing an identity, perhaps a tradition, in the comprehensive schools to which the vast majority of young people move after their primary education – an identity that is evolved not out of attempts to ape the now antiquated rituals and structures of the grammar schools but is genuinely responsive to the needs, potential and ambition of a generation about to spend the majority of their lives in the twenty-first century.

The moves towards a common curriculum described by Peter Cornall represent one development attracting support across the political spectrum. It is possible that we are witnessing now the beginnings of a genuinely common school of the sort envisaged nearly thirty years ago in one of the first published advocacies for comprehensive schools.[2] Both Peter Cornall and Peter Mann in their argument for a more unified curriculum organization demonstrate that the style of this reform does not imply uniformity or compulsion in all respects. It will, if anything, create more rather than less choice, particularly if, as Tim Brighouse suggests, the richness and potential of a genuinely integrated community programme can enhance curriculum opportunities. Peter Mann links community to curriculum in stressing that 'not only do we need to open schools to the community, but many of our schools need to break isolation within. Where curriculum is planned in entirely separate subject departments, change is not so likely to take root, but where the whole staff of a school seriously set out to serve the needs of their young people, there is an inbuilt dynamism.'

There is no doubt that organizational structures in schools will have to change in responding to new demands. Falling school numbers will undermine inevitably the narrow subject specialist base of much secondary education. Broader groupings of subjects seem highly likely. By the end of this decade the teaching of specialist science, physics, chemistry, biology, geology, zoology will arguably be as much an anachronism as separate algebra, geometry and arithmetic (common not so long ago) may seem to us today. The introduction of design and technology courses and the disappearance of the large proportion of time devoted to the ubiquitous 'option schemes' are further predictions examined in detail in this analysis of change in schools. Peter Cornall, reinforcing Peter Mann's point above, proposes a matrix approach, advocated increasingly in recent years, to look at the horizontal and vertical relationship of subjects and issues within a school curriculum.

If the evidence points towards smaller schools with a more unified curriculum other consequences become apparent. The potential for creativity in adapting schools to social change can be maximized through a real, rather than cosmetic, co-operation and collaboration not only within schools, a point made by many, but also between schools. Ken Shaw and Kay Wood illustrate the problems of continuity in the area of sixteen-plus transfer. A problem familiar but perceived as less relevant at eleven-plus becomes more significant in the examination-conscious period of post-secondary education. And in this paper it is clear that, however neat administrative solutions may be, without a real analysis of the differential perceptions arising from existing structures, the best of intentions may be thwarted. Increased co-operation between teachers within schools may well be matched by the formation of networks bringing together groups of schools in pursuit of specific goals. Colin Richards sees this move as helping provide a more consistent set of experiences for more pupils for a greater part of their time in school, thereby removing some of the extreme curriculum inequalities between schools and furthering the causes of a genuinely comprehensive education in the primary/middle school phase.

Teacher co-operation and development raises the issues of initial and in-service education, not only within the school but also outside in colleges, polytechnics and universities. If schools are experiencing pressures, then the recent restructuring in higher education is every bit as significant. The two papers on teacher education are quite purposefully placed within this section on 'Changing Schools'. John Isaac, from the perspective of the polytechnics, indicates how recent work has reinforced the move towards a more co-operative and school-focused model of in-service work. Recent pronouncements from the DES on initial training have perhaps hardly matched such aspirations and this is explored in some detail by Jim Eggleston.

Yet again a greater degree of co-operation between teacher education and schools seems both desirable and inevitable, although the context created by national policies and restraints worries many looking for the opportunity to create a more flexible interchange between the different sectors.

The sections on control, evaluation and accountability indicate that, whatever intentions to the contrary are, the school and classroom are still the most vital areas for stimulating reform and creating improved and more creative teaching and learning experiences. This is certainly true of England and Wales and perhaps in even the most controlled of educational systems there is far greater room for manoeuvre than many credit. Influencing this individuality, however, is the range of ideas and initiatives that constitute a 'community of discourse' about new directions.

It is a healthy sign that teachers, from schools and higher education, as well as administrators and inspectors are sharing common ground in advocating an optimism about the future of schooling. The different styles of the papers are an interesting reflection on the varied audiences educationalists must address. Together, however, they give a wide-ranging and varied diagnosis of the existing situation matched by an equally diverse series of reform proposals.

Notes

1   O'Connor, Maureen *The Guardian*, 20 April 1982.
2   Simon, Brian (1955) *The Common Secondary School*, Lawrence and Wishart, London.

CHAPTER 1

A GLIMPSE OF THE FUTURE – WHAT SORT OF SOCIETY DO WE WANT?

TIM BRIGHOUSE

There are at least three possibilities for the year 2000. Educators, whether teachers, administrators or advisers, are preparing the young for the future as well as providing for their present needs. Consideration of what the future may hold is inescapable.

The first and least attractive proposition is that no one will be here in the year 2000, that the nuclear disarmers will have been proved right, but will of course have been deprived of the pleasure of saying 'I told you so', and the world will be a wasteland of stunted growth, of strange life forms, of mutants and of disease. It will at best have been seriously depopulated, at worst laid waste. The second possibility – and perhaps more likely than the first – is that the present trends in society will have continued: namely there will be sharper awareness of the growing discrepancy between the rich and the poor both within societies and between societies; increased unemployment; shorter working lives; increased intolerance and violence; less social cohesion in all the recognized institutions, such as the family, the church, marriage, the community, the trade unions, business; more frantic competition; and deeper shades of sadness and distress. Practically the only growth area – and it is interesting to remark how they are growing in our society now – will be ever larger police forces and more and more institutional havens for those who for one reason or another cannot live within a normal society. The third possibility – some would say the least likely – is a world which has learned to harness and develop the co-operative as well as the competitive element of man, a world where man's esteem is measured not only by what he has obtained, whether in riches or employment, but by what he has contributed to the welfare of others, a world where the locally based institutions such as the family and the community have become stronger and where the present growing inequality within society and between societies has been halted, perhaps diminished.

Of these possibilities clearly the first two are far the more likely. Indeed most of our policies and institutions drive us inexorably towards such an outcome. The purpose here, because optimism overcomes realism, is the third possibility. It is not essential to define in detail or chop logic over the compatibility or desirability of the various components of such a society – that after all is for the party politicians – but to describe the broad strategies of how, within the education service and schools in particular, it is possible to set a course so that such an outcome would be more, not less, likely. In particular it is possible to discuss how schools today and tomorrow would look if that possibility were to become more likely and less remote.

A first promise is that schools affect societies. Apart from the fact that to do otherwise is a policy of cynicism and despair, there is now sufficient evidence not merely from the challenged work of Rutter but also from observation of the effects of different schooling systems. For example, in Northern Ireland, no serious observer would pretend that the schools and schooling system are other than a powerful ingredient in the troubles that affect the province.

It is important to start from where we are. These observations – of what schools are like, how they are changing and how they might be – are based on three sets of evidence: the first is the reporting of HMIs nationally and locally, the second is reporting from advisers and the third is personal observation generally over the last twenty years from differing perspectives and especially over the last two years, of spending many days sampling children's school experience.

Until very recently some secondary schools have taken the following stance at the fourth year:

> At our school we are proud of the fact that all our children at sixteen gain qualifications which enable some of them to be employed at sixteen and others – and these are the ones we really value if they stay in the sixth – to continue their studies for two or three years before going on to an institution of higher education, the more prestigious the institution the greater the distinction. So we suggest that you will work very hard for the first barrage of examinations at sixteen-plus. Play is now temporarily behind you to re-emerge at either sixteen or eighteen or later from a hard diet of examinations. There will of course be a few for whom this is too much to

If you do not like our diet you will be excluded and very shortly you iterally excluded but on our terms. Do not however stay away before unless we decide to exclude you because that would set a bad example to others.

This is something but not too much of an exaggerated parody. The use of 'prestigious' is of course apposite, but in different ways some schools even now provide a similar message. It is a message which sees the adult world as one with twin activities, namely work and leisure. The 'work ethic' has been defined to mean 'the higher paid the work the better' and 'leisure' as the reward either for limited hours in boring circumstances or as the occasional extensive release from a stressful activity involving decisions taken from positions of great social importance. It is the contention here that this must change.

Schools exist for three purposes. First they exist to meet the present needs of the students in them at any particular time; often this takes the form of statement such as, 'Childhood is a stage of life in its own right to be enjoyed, not merely regarded as a preparation for later stages'. There is usually little difficulty for primary schools to have such a purpose clearly in mind and often the teachers tell me that their difficulty is in persuading parents not to be too anxious to hasten the maturation of their children. Secondly schools exist to meet the future needs of their students. Here there is a much greater difficulty. At the secondary stage with adulthood beckoning (or threatening depending on the point of view), schools, and teachers in them, face a bewildering range of critical advice and questions such as: 'Why have not the youngsters of today learned how to behave at interview, fill in an application form, talk nicely, dress properly?' or 'Why can't they do simple sums or spell properly?' or again, 'Schools should make their pupils more aware of the world of work, provide better careers advice, train youngsters to be parents, understand the real world.'

More perversely in some parts of the country one hears: 'Youngsters have been blackmailed by their schools into working for examinations on the grounds that these examinations will get them jobs but there are no jobs.'

Paradoxically, in other adjacent areas:'Schools concentrate too much on leisure interests and not enough on the qualities required to get jobs.' As if, incidentally, to concentrate on those qualities has any logical connection with the availability of jobs. So the second purpose, to prepare youngsters for the next stage in their life, is a real worry at the secondary stage and not sufficiently considered at the primary where the first purpose, namely the claims of childhood in its own right, sometimes obscures the need for improvement in preparing youngsters for the difficult period of adolescence which follows.

The third purpose of schools is to be a resource for learning for all those connected with it. This is often overlooked. But to function effectively, all involved, whether teachers, non-teachers, a wider community, students or parents, should join together in the process of learning and share in the defeat of the common enemy, which is relevant ignorance. The phrase relevant ignorance is used because not all ignorance is relevant. Indeed, it is the burden of the thesis here that some of what many still spend our time doing at schools is defeating *irrelevant* ignorance. To take a simple example, if a school spent some time teaching its children to memorize the pages of the 1910 edition of the *Encyclopaedia Britanica*, the children would be learning something, it is true. They would be developing the skill of memory and they would learn a little of what people thought of the world and what history was like in 1910, but it would be generally regarded as a fairly profitless, even dangerously misleading, activity. Much of what is taught today, certainly so far as information is concerned, is similarly destined to be inappropriate, and much more rapidly, than that taught in 1910.

So in the third purpose of the school, as a place for all to share in the defeat of ignorance, it must be asked what, in the light of the first two needs (that of the pupil's childhood and his impending adulthood) relevant ignorance is. Schools must have a view about the nature of adulthood, not their own adulthood but future adulthood. To say that is simple but it does answer another question, namely whether a school should be just one step behind society's needs or one step ahead. When a school is seen to be clearly the former, which is often, teachers are chided for never having left the classroom, being out of touch with the real world; if the latter, the same teachers are accused of being social engineers.

Schools must have a view of the future that anticipates the inexorable march of events so that they may better equip their pupils for such a future. It is not sufficient to answer the question by declaring that students are being prepared for a rapidly changing world and to be flexible. Of course, they must be flexible, but if they are only flexible it sounds as though they might be like a weathercock blown this way or that by the changing winds – the slave of events rather than the controller of the environment. It is a policy of helplessness unless there is something more. For the most important issue, to which schools must now address themselves, is the nature of adult life. Is it a world of 'work' and a world of 'leisure', as mentioned earlier, or is there a need to re-define the notions which have served us for 150 years or more? For what is generally meant by 'work' and 'leisure'? Most honestly this usually means paid – the more highly paid the better – work and leisure to amuse oneself and one's family. That concept, which is hurled at the young by the media, the politicians, economists and their elders, is totally unhelpful. For there is quite simply not going to be paid work for everybody in our society. When Geoffrey Holland addressed a group of educationalists late last year in Oxford he said he was no longer interested so much in the problems of the sixteen–nineteen-year-olds whose unemployment in the space of five years had increased by 600 percent but rather in the problems of the unemployed twenty–twenty-five-year-olds, as he described the projected growth of unemployment, the well-marked decline in manufacturing jobs, the rapid deskilling of whole areas of traditional occupations in the face of microprocessing and robotics, the converse increase in job vacancies in industries and services based on new technology. For the whole of society – not just the sixteen–nineteen-year-olds – faces the prospect of paid employment for ever smaller proportions of life and, unless the politicians tackle the real problem, such employment will be for a diminished proportion of society.

Most sixteen–nineteen-year-olds are not stupid, nor are profit-seeking employers. Both agree that sixteen–nineteen-year olds lack experience, are expensive to employ and have a properly undeveloped sense of vocation. By contrast thirty–thirty-five-year-olds, especially women, are more mature, dependable, experienced and altogether a better investment. Ask any of the secure professional occupations and you will find that whereas ten years ago they had a high proportion of young women in their offices they now have a high proportion of middle-aged women.

Rather than responding to the problem of sixteen–nineteen-year-olds lacking employment by comments such as 'Isn't it terrible? How are we going to provide them with jobs?', shouldn't we acknowledge that we should never have expected them – or, more tragically, falsely led them to expect – that they would have full-time well-paid employment in the first place? They need employment: indeed it is the contention that everybody needs employment – from about fourteen until at least sixty-five – but it should not always be well paid and at least some of it should be devoted to the service of others. And the competitive element (which will always be present in seeking well-paid employment) should and will become inevitably the prerogative of the twenty–fifty-year-olds, perhaps even the thirty–forty-five-year-olds. Nor is it just Geoffrey Holland of the MSC who sees such a change. Most economists and industrialists see the same pattern and prospects for paid employment. Manufacturing jobs are now down to six million from eight and a half million ten years ago: nobody can seriously doubt, that if the country is to be competitive internationally, the new technology, the microchip and robotics will seriously reduce the jobs in the manufacturing sector still further. If allowance is given in addition for an existing figure of ten percent overmanning, the figure declines to well below six million, perhaps to as little as four and a half million. Allow for the new technologies and apply similar overmanning criteria to the service industries (and in particular perhaps contemplate the impact of technology on banking, use of money, the supermarket checkout points) and job losses become significant. It is not unimaginable that the present figure of three million unemployed will be seven or eight million by the end of the decade. Clearly politicians would not wish to allow such an eventuality to happen and will adopt the time-honoured process of the last 150 years: namely that of progressively shortening the week and making retirement earlier. So we can happily contemplate a figure of three or four million as a residual figure of unemployment. Within that, however, there are unacceptable features for society. One is the lack of jobs for the unskilled and semi-skilled; another is the dangerous notion of a hard core of unemployed for whom there is going to be no prospect of employment at any time during their lives; and a third is a sharp difference in prospects between the North and the South of the country.

These problems demand party political solutions. But in the meantime within the education service it is necessary to be political to the extent that steps must be taken to prepare youngsters for an adult world in which they should embrace the concepts not of work and leisure but of:

work for paid employment – not necessarily continuous periods of full-time work, harnessing the competitive and combative features of man;

work for unpaid employment – from the age of about fourteen to around sixty-five and harnessing the co-operative elements of man;

work for oneself (leisure) – co-operative or competitive according to taste.

So that is a personal view of the future – a view which demands some significant changes from the present. It is possible if we acknowledge the competitive *and* the co-operative, and if we encourage, perhaps require, *both* within our society there is a chance that the dismal present can turn into a brighter future: the probable can become less likely and the possible more likely – a society where the family is strong, where there is a strong sense of community, where people feel more in control of their own communal activities and where there is less violence born of envy, frustration and intolerance.

The following steps – small steps – lead one closer. To ignore any of the steps is to make the realization of the vision less likely though by no means impossible. The first step concerns the pre-school years: it is important to build on the successes of the pre-school playgroup movement and establish greater confidence and competence in parents to develop the emotional and intellectual growth of children in their formative and rapidly developing years. During the war years H.C. Dent observed:

> As a result of our neglect of the earlier years of life about one third of children who enter the elementary school at the age of five are by that time suffering from physical defects most of which could have been prevented or remedied. What proportion are suffering from defects of mind and/or character due to the almost universal ignorance of parents concerning the nature of young children, inadequate or improper attention to psychological needs and to lack of proper social training? It has never to my knowledge been estimated but it is certainly very large. It is no exaggeration to say that we allow greater numbers of children to be deprived of any possibility of full development before schooling starts.

Nowadays it is likely that enormous strides have been made as a result of the pre-school playgroup movement, in the expansion of provision for the under-fives. The number of physically impaired and those with emotional or psychological handicaps may well have been diminished in consequence and their lasting effects reduced. Nevertheless the evidence of the Warnock Report and of the Court Report gives cause for concern. School and pre-school agencies need to help harness parental willingness and eagerness to secure the best for their youngsters: the use of television and local radio backed by structural school-based advice could all be achieved at a cost far lower than the social cost later of ignoring it. In more than one authority there seems to be a co-ordinated and purposeful examination of the whole parent/teacher/child partnership with a view to an enormous push towards harnessing the educative potential of that learning partnership both before and during the primary years.

As a second step – in the primary years – real consideration must be given to family-centred learning, an acknowledgement that sometimes the individual needs of one child are less important than the needs of the group of children or than a group of adults or the family. This leads on to embrace the notion of group learning, of parents offering skills to the educational process. For parents have a greater knowledge and love of the individual child, their natural or adopted son or daughter, than the teacher can ever have; but the parent is unskilled in the knowledge of working with groups and lacks the expertise and the experience which working with countless children over many years can bring if the teacher has the eyes to see and the will to learn. All that presupposes a natural progression of good practice in our present primary schools. But it does require positive effort: it is insufficient to adopt an attitude which says 'my door is always open'; parents do not and will not pass through if that is the sole gesture. Indeed it is a wrong and insensivtive gesture. Nevertheless there *are* signs that some schools are moving in this direction: they have the confidence to move on from Plowden, to include Piaget and Feuerstein. But it is a difficult and challenging path. But move on they must. Firstly they must acknowledge that child-centred learning is but a beginning and not a complete philosophy in itself. Secondly they must harness parents in an equal partnership of learning not only for the individual child in his or her individual childhood but for groups of children. Thirdly they must realize that not all learning is experiential just as it is not all abstract or secondhand, and fourthly they must see the group as a means of providing learning through failure – such an important but threatening part of the learning process if individually experienced. These are the four discoveries of schools where the parents are real partners in the learning process. Above all, freed of the eleven-plus, these primary schools have retained pace and rigour in all they do.

The last and greatest step lies in the secondary schools where there will be felt the main impact of the processes which affect the future and changed nature of an adult life. For if adult life patterns are to change as outlined earlier they must bring with them a change in our attitude to the age of sixteen. Sixteen may remain the date of the end of compulsory schooling but it will not be and perhaps never has been a sharp dividing line between childhood and adulthood, between school and work.

If this is correct there are some points that require examination. First, if sixteen ceases to be the leaving age for the majority of pupils why should all examination systems be focused at sixteen-plus? Would it be better to regard the reformed sixteen-plus as a series of modular examinations to be taken when the youngsters are ready for them somewhere over the period of fourteen–plus to seventeen-plus, with those who are able moving to more advanced study at an earlier age? Does the portfolio or the pupil personal record fit more happily with the idea of a leaving certificate to be carried by the students to their next destination after school whether that be work or higher education? Once the notion of the sixteen-plus examination has been dispelled doesn't that free time during the years fourteen-sixteen in order to secure a better balance at any one time between the examination-based activities and activities designed to develop skills, in the broadest sense, and values and attitudes? Does it not also call into question the nature of the secondary school day, week and year? One of the present imperatives of the secondary school is the need to drip-feed for seven or eight periods each day across eight, nine or ten subjects for two years up to the age of sixteen. Such a notion usually affects the whole five years of secondary schooling: but on what evidence is that method of learning thought to be effective or desirable? Remove that sixteen-plus examination imperative – which is possible and accords much more with the theory of pupils progressing at different and individual speeds – and it might be possible to change the pattern of the school day, the school week and even the school year. Indeed think not of years but of 'terms' of sustained experience, study and learning. Breadth within the curriculum – always the worry of the English system which specializes so early – would paradoxically be achieved consecutively by modular courses rather than concurrently. (In any case the notion of the concurrent breadth has of course always been an illusion: the breadth has only been achieved consecutively for the span of a day or a week.)

In the secondary school, however, there is good reason not only to look at the mechanics of the time arrangements within a school but also the hierarchy of posts which sustain what happens within the school. What happens is often described as the school curriculum. Often this is unhelpfully translated into a list of subjects. All secondary schools are good at analysing their subject syllabuses and at curriculum (i.e., subject) development; a smaller but happily increasing number of schools are good at looking at the broader issues, the coherence and balance of school life. This latter activity is sometimes called 'whole curriculum analysis' or school evaluation: the purpose is to examine, for example, homework policies, careers, counselling, use of tutor periods, pastoral systems, language across the curriculum policies, mathematical support for science and vice versa: as well as nowadays perhaps the balance of information and skills elements of the curriculum in the light of the rapid growth of knowledge and the revolution in the means for retrieving the information as the result of the microprocessing advances. Often, however, the enormous effort in discussing such matters is lost in a school because the old structures are not changed to underpin the changes desired. Small wonder that the gains and good intentions of discussions are lost as the old structures reassert themselves. Structures of organizations are less important than people but they can get in the way of good people and good intentions. This is not to argue for the abandonment of subjects but, just as they are convenient if imprecise classifications of knowledge inherited from the past, so it may be necessary to think of other structures designed to solidify classifications of other needs of children such as their skill needs. It is important to do this in order to underpin what everybody should be doing to secure the development of the child's potential. It is a delusion to hold to subject classifications, which incidentally with the multidifferentiated subjects and classifications required by the advance of specialism now bear very little relationship to the world of higher education from which they were originally formed. What for example do biology and history mean to the specialist? It is as precise a compass fixing as saying that you have visited North America when you wish to convey a visit to Yorke Street – and Yorke Street itself is four hundred miles long. But for skills however – skills which are important to the adult – the energy has never been raised to classify even as broadly as the subject information needs. Small wonder that some skills are neglected and the development of others reaches saturation point. After discussion within schools therefore, do the subject posts and hierarchies need a cross-matrix of skill posts? Or would that lead to a similar and undesirable split such as that which occurred between the academic and the pastoral in the early comprehensive schools? For surely every teacher should see himself as the purveyor of information, skills, attitudes and ideas. So maybe all that is required in schools to secure a different match or balance of development between skills and information is a hierarchy and job descriptions and duties that sustain the balance. Some of our existing hierarchical patterns within schools have not yet remarried the pastoral and the academic after their divorce in the post-reorganization years. Perhaps the examination history of that issue will offer telling evidence to the doubters of the subtle influence of organizational hierarchies on schools. If you want change to last, change your organizational structures. And if you want change to be possible make sure that organizational patterns have a limited life.

All this presupposes that there is a need to change and that one of the major shifts will be towards development of skills. Whenever the word skills is used there is a danger of misunderstanding. For some people the word conjures up the notion of reading, writing and arithmetic and one receives a fond and approving 'amen'. And for others it brings to mind hoards of children armed with screwdrivers lying underneath cars or with other utensils cooking and sewing. It is in the area of skills that the pioneering work of classification needs to be undertaken and in this respect all of us should learn from the work taking place in the world of further education. In Oxfordshire skills have been defined in three broad component parts. First there are the time-honoured skills of reading and writing simply because most people understand skills to mean that. The second group of skills is called practical or manipulative, in which group, from a work point of view, there is the need for a shift of emphasis towards the technological and away from the traditional. Although of course for a rewarding adult life many traditional skills remain important. Thirdly, the more elusive area, there are the skills of handling the environment and interpersonal skills, advanced study skills, skills of handling concepts. The theory is well charted in the eleven–sixteen curriculum red book of HMI (1977) and in *The Practical Curriculum* of the Schools Council and in the further education unit publication *Life and Social Skills*. The practice is hard work and requires teachers to devote considerable time to discussion and analysis of the educational process and product. Some of the best schools are tackling this by examining the skill content of their existing courses, designing complementary skill content in new courses, and assessing the contribution that extra-curricular activities can make to skill and attitude development. For example, in one school all children are able to take part in a school production of a play although this means more than one school play in a year and on each occasion the youngsters devote a whole fortnight to the school production in all its aspects. This school has already adopted a modular pattern outlined earlier in this paper. So all can use their skills to produce the costumes, design the set, make the set, act, sell programmes, run the finances, do lighting, etc.

A simultaneous and complementary step within the school is to introduce pupil personal records. It is moreover a step which needs to be discussed very carefully to ensure that the input comes from the pupils rather than the teachers. The teachers, of course, contribute to the ultimate portfolio by an input of profiling and of commenting: but there ought to be a personal pupil record in order that the pupil's view of himself and his activities is seen to be thought worthwhile to the adult world. Don Stansbury has had a significant impact in pioneering this development and there can be few authorities now where there is not evidence of the scheme getting underway.

All this implies a certain stance in teachers – the teacher becomes a different professional from the time-honoured one. His tradition has been the purveyor of information and knowledge and for years he has struggled to change his role in the light of changed circumstances. One hundred and fifty years ago the teacher worked in an environment where there was little information, the possession of which was the legitimate key to power. Information had a fairly long lasting usefulness. There was no television; film was primitive; radio and other printed materials were non-existent. There was no free library system. Now not only is the life outside school transformed for all youngsters and their families but also the microcomputer, computing and microprocessing developments have transformed the means of retrieving knowledge. The teacher knows too that the parent and wider community possess information, knowledge and skill which can enable him to do his job better. For what is the teacher's new role today? It is threefold. Firstly, he needs to be a facilitator – a person who can diagnose and make connections between the learner and the resources so that the learner may develop his potential. Secondly, he needs to be a mediator between the learner and his resources with the skilled eye of a diagnostician of learning difficulties. Finally, and perhaps most importantly, he needs to be an animator who by his inspiration, love of learning and above all his infectious enthusiasm provides the spark from which motivation grows.

A re-orientation of the balance of the curriculum, an examination of the school day and of the hierarchy of posts within the school, a greater but not exclusive concentration on experimental learning through the development of skills within existing courses and development of new courses, especially for the fourteen–nineteen-year-olds involving increased periods outside school, the introduction of pupil personal records – all these factors will facilitate the changed role of the teacher. In such a school, of course, where there is no pretence that the teacher is the fount of all knowledge, the school very naturally becomes a community school providing courses for adults who will join the day-time modules and the evening sessions, which younger members will also be eligible to attend. So it will enlist the support of adults who can contribute both to the learning of the young and of each other: the expertise of each is shared and celebrated by the community. In the truest sense it will have developed family-centred learning to its ultimate conclusion.

At this point there may be doubts. The doubts are not so much that the schooling system described is desirable; more that the steps outlined as a prerequisite of achieving the desirable are feasible. This leads to questions about public opinion, the nature of teachers who are already with us and will remain with us for twenty years, and the availability of resources.

These, of course, are not inconsiderable objections.

First, so far as public opinion is concerned there is no substitute for local discussions by the school with its surrounding community. The community after all is going to be heavily involved in the school and there could be little doubt that a community which sees youngsters obtaining their examinations when they need them – and this may be earlier rather than later – and a community which sees the school harnessing both the competitive and the co-operative is likely to find the prospect attractive rather than a matter for dismay. Moreover it would be surprising if the majority of our society did not accept that there was more to life than paid work and self-indulgent leisure. So the public will share the goal. What of the teacher?

The teacher needs in-service training – by observation, examining courses provided in other schools, by testing the approaches in those settings with other teachers. There are two possible ways of achieving this. The first is for an authority to arrange with local providers of courses such as the university departments and the polytechnics the opportunity for practically based local courses so that the majority of in-service time is spent in school rather than in theoretical study: this step is happening not only in Oxfordshire but in many other parts of the country. The second is for the school to decide to teach more (or reduce their 'formally taught courses' to the minimum four hours each day) and use the time gained to enable the staff to go on planned visits to other schools and to plan curriculum change. Obviously the two are not mutually exclusive and in some authorities there is evidence that both are in operation. By these two methods one cracks the question of the teachers' willingness to adopt a new stance and the time needed to develop it. They do not however provide the time for the initial discussion within the community and the school itself.

For this requirement there is no substitute for school evaluation. There is no avoiding a look at the school and a close analysis of what goes on. Many authorities now have such a scheme in operation.

Finally there is the requirement that the local education authority examines very closely the controls which it exercises over the running of its schools. With the advances in technology and the easier means of retrieving information, there is little justification for the way in which we run our schools. For a community school should be in the hands of the local community. It should have control of nearly all its expenditure. Instead of starting from the basis of what it is feasible to allow a school to control, it seems more productive to begin from the basis that a school should be allowed to control everything 'except . . .

Arguably only the following need not be under the school's direct control: external repairs and painting, long-term maintenance such as boilers and re-wiring and the advisory services. So that would leave within the school's control for decision making such matters as the number of teachers and non-teachers, capitation, cleaning, internal decoration and simple repairs, hiring of premises, telephone, energy costs, playing fields maintenance, school meals. The most impressive steps in this direction are being made in Cambridgeshire.

Such a scheme would fortify the notion of community.

In summary therefore, this glimpse of the future requires the following: Firstly, an acknowledgement by schools of what adult life must be in a sane society and an examination of their practices and processes in the light of that is needed.

Secondly, an examination of the whole curriculum and of its constituent parts, and the organization of the timetable, the school day, week and year. This should lead to an emphasis on skills development, staff in-service training, community schooling and increased periods from about the age of fourteen when youngsters spend periods outside school either in work or a community placement. From this there is a natural transition from childhood to adulthood, from school to the world of work and to the wider community, where unpaid work for others is a part of every youngster's school commitment.

Thirdly, the LEA needs to hand over to the school substantial power over its own resources and to demand occasionally an educational as well as a financial audit and to make local arrangements for appropriate in-service training.

Clearly, missing any of these steps makes the future as described less likely to be realized. There should however be a political will to encourage such development. It may be that the only inhibition comes from bureaucracies which will, of course, be transformed by the reforms suggested. It needs some brave local education authority to take the steps outlined as the third prerequisite. All schools can, of course, take the first two if they have the will and courage to do so.

Inevitably such talk as this can only encompass the small steps towards the vision as a sketch. The detail will require the most careful thought and the help of groups such as the Association for the Study of the Curriculum, Centre for the Study of Comprehensive Schools in York, the Subject Associations, the National Association for Primary Education. They are small steps which together can make a giant stride towards a changed schooling system for a healthier society.

Some schools have travelled far along this road – in Buckinghamshire, Leicestershire (rather more there than in most places), London, Oxfordshire, Hertfordshire, Cambridgeshire, Shropshire, Devon, Somerset, Coventry, Cheshire, Northamptonshire and in Cumbria. It would be possible to go on but here are some characteristics for primary and secondary schools and some areas in which they will have moved, as well as some questions of concern to the local education authorities.

The primary schools which have moved beyond Plowden now have the following characteristics:

The headteacher celebrates the successes of the teachers: he or she finds some pre-eminent strength which is confided to others who visit the school.

The school has learnt interdependence rather than dependence: the teacher is not an island but draws on the expertise or strengths of a colleague or frequently a member of the local community.

There is much structured group work to ensure that failure is a growth point rather than a source of dismay; and to ensure that problem solving has excitement rather than disappointment. Parents are drawn into the school community and vice versa from the date of birth of the child rather than from the age of five. The school has seen the importance of the child's complementary learning stimuli at home whether through television, visits or parent time and love. Its parents meetings on curriculum matters are held more often outside than inside the school. There are parent workshops in school or in twilight sessions. The school realizes that all new parents require individual and long discussion on the aims of the curriculum.

The schools have not seen the abandonment of the eleven-plus as the justification for the removal of all tests and hurdles from learning: the schools realize and use threefold aims of testing – diagnosis, evidence of skills, information or values which have been understood not just encountered.

The schools have pace and rigour: they seek evidence by observation and recording and question whether what they believe is happening is happening.

There is much love but no sentimentality; there is evidence of the urban environment as well as the rural, of modern and ancient, of traditional crafts and new skills.

The schools moving in this direction are taking the following steps:

They have spent hours discussing aims, methods and pupil achievement after school or in the evening, perhaps in a pub, and the staff have covered for each other to enable interschool visiting.

They have invited students or volunteers to watch children and record what happens prior to discussion and monitor their achievements by test, observation and evidence.

They have kept a tally of self-recorded new skills learned by all members of the community; in particular they have involved members of the community in the tasks of the school and all individual parents in the process of their child's learning at *home*, e.g., reading project work. Perhaps they have held in school, and at parents' homes or clubs, parent and child workshops and parent and teacher workshops in which often parents teach teachers. And they have sent home the annual report in a folder of the child's own work, a treasure for the parent and child to hold for the future, full of points of growth and strength.

They change display work of all children's work as the curriculum demands, which will probably be once every three or four weeks rather than at more distant periods. And they have established an opposite environmental link school (i.e., urban to rural and vice versa), and see that as a basis for residential work.

The secondary schools moving towards the changed role described above have the following characteristics:

Much thought about the importance of whole school attitudes to various issues and an enthusiastic subscription to these aims which is evidenced in the tailoring of the curriculum to the needs of the pupil, occasionally to individual teacher or subject disadvantage.

A keen awareness of children's needs which is evidenced by talk about the students and teaching methods and little else in the staff room. Youngsters are treated as individuals who matter in their own right.

Heavy community involvement. School has regularly fifty percent more adults in it than are on the pay roll; children are in the community during school hours.

Very little awareness of rank or station. Tasks are shared to posts in a changeable way so that demarcated hierarchies are only briefly established save in one area – the concern for the individual child or adult which lasts for the duration of that child's stay in the community.

A wealth of plants, fabrics, pictures and artefacts, however unpromising the environmental backdrop, buildings and surroundings.

A willingness to find ways to do things for themselves rather than wait helplessly for 'them' to solve the problem.

Great examination success, few if any suspensions and little talk about either to outsiders. Indeed it is the success of others which is celebrated. Moreover, all are stimulated to question and think. Change is a way of life in a peaceful community.

Schools moving in this direction are taking the following steps:

They have found themselves with a headteacher who, to use Sir Alec Clegg's description, 'is a person with an unsentimental love of children who is specially concerned with the less fortunate. He can win over pupils and staff and kindle a spark in them: he knows the aims and sees to it that all the school's activities contribute to those aims and he can distinguish between sterile and fruitful work. He can manage the administration of the school without foresaking the substance of headmastering for the shadow of management.'

They have examined, if they are large schools, the need for pupils to know teachers and to be known by them and to have adjusted the other constraints of the timetable – rooms, curriculum – accordingly they have reduced the formal timetable to the minimum – 240 minutes – and held a teaching commitment of about eighty-five–ninety percent to this reduced timetable to all save the head and the deputies, all of whom teach too. They see the curriculum however as being far greater than that and, by agreement, all, in groups, and with other members of the community, take another seventy minutes in experiential clubs and societies: the students' involvement in these is an expectation which finds expression in the pupils' portfolio of achievements.

These schools have moved or are discussing a move to a pupil personal record initiated by the youngster at about thirteen or fourteen but not earlier. They are awaiting the sixteen-plus reform for nothing save its removal of the need to take exams at sixteen-plus rather than earlier or later. For these schools choice of subjects at fourteen-plus is a tiresome and temporary irrelevance as they await the ability to introduce modular courses which are examinable in conventional terms, three or four to be taken at a time (i.e., over a year's period).

In these schools the pattern of thought has ceased, or is ceasing to be, the year group or the week. It has become the day, the term's course (or biannual course in some cases), the upper school community and the lower school community. All this may have had its origin in experiments involving a day, week or fortnight devoted to one particular activity such as a school play, an art week or a modern languages week.

Local education authorities with schools moving in this direction display the following characteristics:

They trust their headteachers in schools even when there are incidents to tempt them to do otherwise.

They eschew curriculum policies and encourage instead their schools to examine their curriculum and their aims.

Members of the authority visit the schools in their own area regularly and education officers, as well as advisers, block time to spend in schools.

There is a regular reduction in the number of centrally employed administrators, as tasks and power and responsibility even are passed to schools. Decisions about expenditure are pushed to the lowest possible level.

There is much talk about implication of the new technology on schools, authority and society. Bullock, Warnock, Cockcroft – each report is a new external insight to prompt a search for higher quality. And there is a high commitment to in-service training.

They measure their success as an education authority not so much by their spending level or the frequency of new ventures but by the sense of excitement, of commitment, of interest in what they do, and the size of their application lists, of the success of their staff. To work in these schools is to know that there may be other periods of working life more profitable and successful but there will never be anywhere quite the same.

Some will say that such places do not exist. They do, and it is possible to find at least four or five new schools each term: count them as a collector would a collection of rare flowers. Mark them, observe them, record, make mental bets about when and what the next stop will be in their development and growth.

As they grow and develop whole communities, past, present and future generations within them, will demand and, with appropriate and long overdue constitutional reform, will realize, on a broader front, one of the unchanging characteristics of a civilized society, namely pride and support for the educational system that provides equal opportunity and access for all who need it. For it is only by this, not by deriding it, by starving it, by undermining it, that society will flourish, that wealth will be created and our neighbours will be helped. The reverse process sometimes seen these last ten to fifteen years brings about accelerated disillusion, despair and difficulty. So those are the signs. There are those who share the vision, who can see the steps towards a saner future and a more desirable society. Schools must play their part.

CHAPTER 2

CURRICULUM CHANGE : CONSTRAINTS AND APPROACHES

PETER MANN

In some countries with a traditionally centralized school curriculum, there is now seen to be a need for teachers themselves to be involved in curriculum change. In this country, where the devolution of control appears to have produced an unprecedented diversity of demands on schools, it can seem to teachers that, in spite of their apparent freedom, any change in the curriculum is subject to extremely powerful constraints. In this paper an attempt is made to draw on experience as head of a comprehensive school, as a local authority inspector and as adviser to the House of Commons Select Committee to assess present constraints and possible approaches to curriculum change over the next ten years.

It is often suggested that parents act as a break on the system. They may be anxious to protect their children, to re-create for them the same experiences they themselves have lived through, to safeguard their future by getting them through as many examinations as possible. With the impact of falling rolls on secondary schools, so, it is suggested, many more parents will be able to exercise a real choice of school and therefore directly to influence the curriculum according to their wishes. Most schools will be familiar with such pressures but we do well to remember that there are many other parents who have quite different expectations. In evidence to the House of Commons Select Committee on Education, Mr. D. Cunningham, Vice-Chairman of the National Confederation of Parent–Teacher Associations (with a membership of two million) made it clear that there are 'a lot of parents' who 'are very interested in what the school is doing in the broad ideas of acquiring skills and techniques of learning throughout the whole of the curriculum and not so much in examinations.'[1] In their written memorandum, the confederation showed comparable breadth: 'although schools should take note of employers' needs, they have a wider responsibility. They must also educate for leisure and for the development of all talents.'[2] There is little evidence here of the enormous divergence of outlook so often assumed between teachers and parents.

Too many schools, however, still keep parents at a distance. From one secondary school, for example, an introductory letter to new parents still reads, 'You should not call at the school without making an appointment. You should not telephone the school except for matters of life or death.' It is unlikely that these parents will ever come to understand any new approaches in such a school or that these teachers will ever have much feeling for the concerns of the parents. Instead, curriculum change requires good communication and consultation in both directions. It is likely to be most successful in a friendly, informal atmosphere where teachers and parents come together to share their common concerns. Such a school will seek to ensure that every point of communication is both personal and professional; on the one hand, to extend both the parents' and the teachers' understanding of the individual youngster and, on the other hand, to develop dialogue on the broad educational aims of the schools, sometimes at their own request to discuss their own youngsters, sometimes to work as volunteers in a partnership symbolized by joint use of the staff room. Parents' evenings will include not only the normal review of each child's progress, but an opportunity for parents to see displays of children's work and learning materials. School reports, communicating school aims as well as individual progress, will positively invite parental reactions. So, when it comes to curriculum change, it is not too much to hope that there will be a sense of common purpose, trust and goodwill which will form a cast-iron basis for further staff-parent consultation. Although the school will need to take serious account of parental views, change becomes possible to contemplate simply because there is no chance of uncomprehending deadlock.

Employers are also often regarded as a barrier to curriculum reform. They may be reluctant, so it is said, to accept new ideas and courses. Often without detailed knowledge of public examination procedures, they nonetheless use them as a short cut for recruitment though not uncommonly demanding a much higher level of qualification than the job requires. Many young people then find themselves under pressure to take courses which in terms of their real needs may be quite inappropriate. So far as this view is justified, it presents a challenge to every school within its own community though, once again, it is by no means the whole picture. Large numbers of young people have always been recruited by employers long before their public examination results were known. At national level, the Confederation of British Industry in its evidence to the Select Committee stressed the importance of developing attitudes, skills and knowledge of relevance to adult society. 'There are qualities highly valued by employers which cannot be measured simply by academic achievement or examination success. Practical capability and the application of knowledge and skills to real problems are just as important as intellectual endeavour. . . . Qualities of adaptability, flexibility and a readiness to go on learning will be particularly important in a future in which people can expect to pursue more than one career during their working lives. Initiative, motivation, a positive and responsible attitude towards work and other people, good communication skills and a co-operative approach are indispensable assets at work and in life generally.'[3] Here is strong encouragement for schools and employers to explore common ground. If previously there has been mutual suspicion, now the CBI proposes a way forward with the systematic development of school–industry links and regular exchanges of staff. The organization of work experience for all fourteen- to sixteen-year-olds would provide a natural opportunity for many teachers to visit a number of places of work, though it is equally important for senior industrial staff to spend time within the classroom. In planning curriculum change, teachers and employers would need to consult on the changing skills, knowledge and attitudes required for employment. In implementing curriculum change, they would need to see how far they could pool their resources, both human and material. In promoting curriculum change, they would need together to interpret new developments by preparing for school leavers and local employers a school curriculum statement outlining the main aims of the whole curriculum and of each course. With this degree of involvement, teachers and employers could begin to develop a climate of mutual understanding and support which would actually facilitate curriculum change.

Unhappily, many schools may not grasp this challenging opportunity, because in the eyes of outside observers, the biggest stumbling block to curriculum change often appears to be the teachers themselves. Many move from school to college and from college back to school, thus forming part of the 'closed circle of education'. In their early impressionable years they may come under the influence of heads of department who have

trained up to forty years earlier and, in their turn, they are likely to
influence other young teachers for a further forty years. We can hardly
begin to assess how many come into teaching with the assumption that
somehow the professions are more respectable and therefore desirable
than industry or trade. Lord Taylor of Blackburn made this pungent
comment to the Select Committee: 'The typical school perpetuates those
distinctions which the modern world no longer needs, preserves the
yawning communications gaps which inhibit change. . . . How can it be
otherwise when we still equate education with preparation for the
professions, translate "academic" as "clever" and "practical" as "thick"?
. . . A desperate need is to increase the knowledge teachers have of the
world of industry since they perpetuate old attitudes.'[4] In Sweden, in
an imaginative attempt to open up the teaching profession, students are
not admitted to teacher training until they have gained first-hand
experience of the world of work, and heads, as a condition of their
appointment, must spend time in youth clubs and social services
departments.

Not only do we need to open schools to the community, but many of our
schools need to break isolation within. Where curriculum is planned in
entirely separate subject departments, change is not so likely to take root,
but where the whole staff of a school seriously set out to serve the needs of
their young people, there is an inbuilt dynamism. Both teachers and
pupils conceive of the curriculum as a shared enterprise within which the
youngsters take as much personal responsibility as possible. They are
encouraged to think for themselves, to ask their own questions and to
solve their own problems, to be creative in ideas, skills and relationships.
To meet the varying needs of each individual pupil, the teachers must be
flexible in response. They will probably wish to question the traditional
succession of short thirty-five or forty-minute periods. They will certainly
need to abandon the tradition of teachers working in isolation. Instead,
teams of staff will share together in course planning, preparation of
materials, pupil assessment, course evaluation and perhaps in the teaching
too. Within the strength of the team, individuals will visit each other's
lessons, the more experienced members freely acknowledging their own
weaknesses and problems. In this unthreatening and unhierarchical
atmosphere, ideas will flow from all quarters, including even the newest
member of the team. As each contributes, so each will gain from the
ever-growing pool of experience, skills, knowledge and ideas. Even the
less flexible or the less committed are carried along to the inevitable point

where they catch the attitudes of their colleagues. Within such a school, the obstacle to curriculum change is unlikely to be the teachers.

The HMI Secondary School Survey concluded that the greatest constraint on schools was our system of public examinations. 'The style and ultimately the quality of work in the fourth and fifth years were dominated by the requirements, actual or perceived, of public examinations.'[5] In evidence to the Select Committee, the Society of Education officers extended this analysis to question not only the dominance of the sixteen-plus examinations but, through them, the power of the higher education system. 'The curriculum is moulded by the requirements of higher education, notably degree courses, which only a minority enter. Effective control over the secondary curriculum, especially in the fourth and fifth years, is transmitted through sixteen-plus examinations which prescribe subject-based requirements with an emphasis on factual recall. . . . There are those who challenge an examination system designed to certify the majority of its participants (who still have a lifetime before them) as below par, despite the fact that they have been tailored for it in a very expensive system. It is for many pupils a failure system.'[6] If young people are to stay in full-time education or training well beyond the age of sixteen, then the case at sixteen-plus for anything more than light diagnostic testing may soon appear anachronistic. For the present, however, schools need to recognize the limitations of the present examination framework and to mitigate the potential ill-effects. In place of a curriculum and examination system geared to an able minority, HMI argued in *A View of the Curriculum* that schools should seek to offer 'comparable opportunities and comparable quality, though not uniformity, of education for *all* pupils'.[7] There is an urgent necessity to apply the Norwood principle that 'examinations should follow the curriculum and not determine it'. Schools need to plan to ensure that advantage is taken of the full range of available sixteen-plus examinations and that internal assessment procedures really do reinforce curriculum aims, including the development of understanding and skills. Examinations offering, at best, a seriously incomplete and, at worst, a totally negative picture, need to be complemented by personal profiles, involving pupils, parents and teachers in assessing what *all* young people *can* achieve.

For schools to adapt creatively to social change is a challenge at any time, but especially demanding in a period of falling school rolls and financial stringency. Their combined effects have been documented by

HMI who have made it clear that schools can quickly experience difficulty in maintaining their existing curriculum.[8] There is a danger that random staff losses may lead to a curricular offer depending upon the mere accident of who is left to teach. To meet this threat, every school will need to have a well-thought-out curricular philosophy. What, for example, should all sixteen-year-olds know and be able to do? What should pupils have a reasonable right to expect from their years of compulsory education? This is a far cry from the present option arrangements already described by HMI as 'inherently risky'[9] and resulting in a seriously fragmented and imbalanced curriculum for many young people. Instead of drifting into declining opportunities and morale, schools now need to see the current pressures as a challenge to redetermine their essential curricular framework. Within each subject area, specialists should be considering what the priorities are which ought to be offered within a common curriculum to all young people. This is a powerful basis from which the school can then negotiate with the local authority for curriculum-led staffing. Inside the school the common curriculum will stimulate a productive co-ordination of material resources and a welcome unleashing of human effort. It is still true (though not always apparent) that schools have available to them enormous resources. A quite modest secondary school, for example, could be staffed at a cost of £1 million a year and the estimated capital value of its plant will be far in excess of that. Counted among the resources of any school we must also include that vast army of pupils, parents and interested members of the community who have either past associations or future needs. The test is whether or not all these resources can be harnessed to the pursuit of agreed goals. There can be little doubt that falling rolls and financial stringency could prove a serious obstacle to curriculum change unless they can be countered by the commitment that comes from a whole school and its community discovering a common philosophy and purpose.

We may conclude that the constraints are real but not by any means insuperable. Although the DES has to an unprecedented extent entered the curriculum debate, the tone of *The School Curriculum* is to exhort rather than to legislate. It is still true that the individual school is at the heart of the curriculum debate and that, within the constraints, the leadership of the school can make a decisive difference. The most flexible response is likely from the open school where, in a spirit of partnership, teachers, pupils, parents, employers and community regularly identify and review school aims and objectives. From this openness stems the thinking school – concerned, on the one hand, with individual needs and, on the other, with community tasks, but with examinations never leading to the exclusion of other important objectives. Here, there is a strong commitment to professional development including, for all staff, regular contact with other schools and provision of time and resources for curriculum planning and preparation of materials. Within carefully agreed guidelines, staff enjoy the freedom of modifying their teaching according to circumstances and, encouraged by an atmosphere of mutual warmth and support, they feel the confidence to experiment with new ideas to go on learning themselves. It is then, no matter what the constraints, that things really begin to happen to the curriculum.

Notes

1   *House of Commons Second Report from the Education Science and Arts Committee*, Session 1981-1982, *The Secondary School Curriculum and Examination*, Vol 2, p.538.
2   *Ibid*, Vol 2, p. 535
3   *Ibid*, Vol 2, pp. 116-117.
4   *Ibid*, Vol 2, pp. 523-524.
5   HMI (1979) *Aspects of Secondary Education in England*, HMSO, para. 12.10.
6   *House of Commons Second Report from the Education, Science and Arts Committee*, Session 1981-1982, *The Secondary School Curriculum and Examination*, Vol 2, pp. 234-235.
7   HMI (19801) *A View of the Curriculum*, HMSO, p. 14.
8   Reports by HMI on the *Effects on the Education Service in England and Wales of Local Authority Expenditure Policies 1980-81 and 1981-82.*
9   HMI (1977) *The Red Book*, HMSO, p. 4.

CHAPTER 3

UTOPIA DEFERRED : Curriculum Issues for Primary and Middle School Education

COLIN RICHARDS

Visions

In *Mindstorms* (1980) Papert argues that the classroom is 'an artificial and inefficient learning environment that society has been forced to invent because its informal environments fail in certain learning domains. . . . I believe that the computer presence will enable us so to modify the learning environment outside the classroom that much if not all the knowledge schools presently try to teach with such pain and expense and such limited success will be learned, as the child learns to talk, painlessly, successfully and without organized instruction. This obviously implies that schools as we know them today will have no place in the future. But it is an open question whether they will adapt by transforming themselves into something new or wither away and be replaced' (p.9).

Is this the authentic voice of the educational world of the late 1980s and 1990s or just an echo seemingly more urgent and menacing than the prophecies of the educational technologists or deschoolers of the late 1960s? Education clearly needs creators and purveyors of dreams, though it is the contention here that dreams far removed from realities can provide an escape from current problems rather than a means of confronting them.

In an article called 'School 2000' Benford (1982) argues that the model for a school of the future

> will be the good British primary school admired the world over. Teaching will embrace both the master/apprentice relationship in learning as well as the more usual teacher/pupil relationship. Children and staff will learn from each other. The teachers will be experts in primary education whose

essential qualification is their love for children. . . . The first aims of our educational strategy will be personal and social, with firm but friendly discipline and example – the model of the good parent. Academic aims include the development of intellect and taste, with worth to encourage thoughts, analysis, discrimination and judgement. We believe in capability, versatility and commitment, with trust and responsibility. . . . Teaching will prepare the children for life as citizens, neighbours, friends, parents, colleagues, consumers, creators, leaders and led alike (pp. 8-9).

Is this the authentic voice of the late 1960s when all roads in primary education led to Oxfordshire or to those industrial villages in the West Riding, or is it the voice of the 1990s when children will receive the primary education they deserve rather than the schooling which is all that most of us mortals can provide? While acknowledging the need for idealism, humanism and optimism there is no substitute for the informed painstaking deliberation required to resolve the uncertain practical problems presented by the curriculum today, next year and the years beyond that.

This paper does not deal in curriculum visions nor in uplifting educational sentiment but attempts an analysis of issues and trends which are already developing in primary and middle school education and which seem likely, for good or ill, to have a significant impact on thinking and/or practice between now and 1992. There are dangers in prediction. The Plowden Report (1967) claimed to recognize a number of 'quickening trends' leading to what some would call 'progressive education' on a national scale; the report proved to be mistaken in its prediction. The issues discussed in this paper may similarly not materialize to any significant extent, but they seem to be more firmly rooted in the realities of primary/middle school education than the enthusiastic iconoclasm of Papert or the heady idealism of those who provide a contemporary exegesis of Plowden.

Realities

Compared with 1973 when the first Standing Conference on Curriculum Studies was held in Exeter, discussion about the primary curriculum and its possible development can now take place on a more informed, less conjectural basis. As a result of surveys (DES 1978, DES 1980, DENI 1981) and other researches (e.g., Galton, Simon and Croll 1980, Bennett et al. 1980, Steadman et al. 1979) we now know much more than we did about the state of primary education generally and about the difficult problems of effecting change in curriculum, pedagogy or evaluation. As a result of a decade of financial and demographic contraction and of dissensus rather than consensus in educational policy making at national and local authority levels, we are less naïve than we were and more aware of the socio-political obstacles in the way of transforming schools or the wider society. Greater self-knowledge has brought with it an inevitable sense of discomfort; greater political awareness has brought with it an acknowledgement of the fragility of the education service and of our hopes for its further development.

Since that first Exeter conference we have, for better or worse, witnessed the gradual 'demythologizing' of primary education (Richards 1980). HMI surveys, in particular, have helped to strip primary and middle schools of many myths, both positive and negative. The 'quickening trend' towards enquiry-based approaches detected by Plowden has not materialized on a substantial scale in top infant, junior or middle school classes; 'the primary school revolution' appears not to have been tried and found wanting but never to have been tried at all except in a small number of schools; most teachers have not responded in the 'open', 'flexible', 'experimental' way curriculum developers fondly assumed they would. In retrospect, most proposals for curriculum change made in the 1960s and early 1970s were based on assumptions of teaching and learning which were not shared by the majority of teachers. At present, the curriculum in most schools appears to be a revamped version of the elementary school curriculum – revamped to include some new elements, especially but not only in mathematics, but retaining the same major utilitarian emphases as its predecessor. To describe it so is not necessarily to condemn it. In some classes, the traditional elementary curriculum remains virtually unscathed: reading, writing and ciphering predominate. In a small number of schools, very substantial curriculum changes have presumably taken place, though the experience of such schools has not been documented by those of us interested in curriculum research and development. Judging from the evidence, the major distinguishing feature of primary education during the last twenty years has been organizational rather than curricular change – in particular, the remarkable spread of non-streaming, the introduction of vertical grouping in a substantial number of infant and junior schools, and the resultant changes in internal class organization including a much larger degree of individualization of work. This picture may not be very comforting to those who have worked hard to transform the primary curriculum or still cherish the possibility of its wholesale transformation, but does represent the general situation which curriculum development agencies and agents have to address during the next decade.

This exploration of the next decade is in three parts:

a   a brief examination of certain logistical features which are likely to affect the response that teachers in primary and middle schools make to curriculum issues;

b   a review of major curriculum issues likely to be 'in currency' in the 1980s;

c   a brief discussion of the possible impact of these issues on primary education in the light of the features discussed in (a) and the receptivity of schools to change, as revealed by surveys and researches.

Logistical features

Firstly, the next decade will see the continuance of primary and middle schools as institutions recognizably similar to those which exist at present. This is not as trite a comment as it appears at first sight. Middle schools are under attack from a variety of quarters in the light of falling rolls, sixth-form reorganization and uncertainty as to their effectiveness (Taylor and Garson 1982). Middle schools, however, will still be with us in 1992, not in every local education authority which currently has them but in sufficient numbers to constitute a small but significant minority of schools, catering for children in the middle years. The primary school, too, is likely to come under attack towards the end of the decade by those who will argue that it is an anachronistic institution in the age of the computer-based information revolution. However, Papert's dream of educationally powerful computational environments where learning takes place with LOGO but without a curriculum is unlikely to be realized on a large scale by 1992, nor Stonier's society where most of children's education is via the television screen in their own homes and where primary teachers are replaced by surrogate grandparents (1982). For the next decade at least, the primary school is likely to be more secure as an institution than its secondary counterpart whose existence in its present form seems increasingly threatened by falling rolls (which will continue into the 1990s), the inroads of the Manpower Services Commission, the reorganization of sixteen–nineteen provision and the indifference or even hostility of many of its clients. By 1992 we could be much nearer a scenario where primary education from four to fourteen is the only institutional and compulsory form of schooling, following on from which there is a variety of educational provision on offer with appropriately supported opportunities for would-be students to re-enter the educational system later in their lives, if they so wish.

A second logistical feature is the fall and possible rise of pupil numbers through the 1980s. The primary school population in England and Wales reached a peak in 1973, the year of the Exeter conference, when there were about five and a quarter million children in maintained nursery and primary schools; by 1979 numbers had fallen by about half a million and by 1980 will have fallen by about a further million (Collings 1980). This steep decline presages further school closures and amalgamations, more staff redeployment, smaller schools and more mixed-age classes, and threatens the preservation of the existing curriculum in many primary and middle schools as staff leave or, more likely, retire and are not replaced. But after 1986, what? Certainly a slight rise for a while, but for how long and at what rate? Will the rise be the first step out of the trough of pupil numbers, will it soon level out, or will it be merely a hiccup in a downward trend which will continue into the 1990s? (For one view see Dennison 1981; for another see DES 1982.)

If map projections distort, then population projections distract. They distract us from coming to terms with the period we are now experiencing and will experience till at least 1986. They encourage us to believe that the present situation is temporary, to be endured rather than entered into enthusiastically; with problems which need only be tackled in a makeshift fashion, making the best of a bad job until better times come along; with hopes and ambitions deferred rather than sought or modified in the light of current circumstances. Population projections which are inevitably going to be wrong to some degree are too slender supports to be relied on for the purpose of sustaining developments in primary education or planning personal careers. The possibility has to be faced that pupil numbers may not rise for more than a few years after 1986, or, if they do rise, may rise very slowly and then in a climate unlikely to be characterized by the heady expansionism of the late 1950s and 1960s. Whether we are considering curriculum development or our own careers, we would be wise not to depend too much on a late 1980s equivalent of the 'golden age' of twenty years before.

A third logistical feature which will affect developments is the level of financial support given to the education service, a factor dependent on the state of the economy, the role within it of public expenditure, and the relative importance accorded educational expenditure compared with other forms of public expenditure. Educational expenditure reached a peak in the middle of the last decade and has faltered somewhat since then. To use MacDonald's apt analogy, big spending services such as education 'ground to a crawl as the hare of public expenditure was harnessed to the tortoise of economic growth' (1979, p.28). What about the next decade? At what rate will the crawl proceed? The cynics may ask in what direction? The education lobby has to cope not only with a decline in pupil numbers but also with the effects of an ageing population which means that the claims of rival competitors, especially social services, may prove much more persuasive. The situation might be different with a different political administration but, a Bennite administration apart, probably only marginally so. In the spring of 1982 the White Paper *The Government's Expenditure Plans 1982-3 to 1984-5* was published. During that period, government's expenditure on education is due to increase by eight percent in monetary terms, but this does not allow for the rate of inflation. Assuming an average inflation rate of six percent per year (an optimistic forecast judging from the recent past) overall prices would increase by about eighteen percent during the period. In consequence, on this prediction, real spending on education would fall by about ten percent up to 1984-1985. Based on the figures given in the White Paper, Peston argues that education's share of public expenditure which has fallen steadily since 1977 would stand at 10.4 percent during 1984-1985; his calculations suggest that 'this will take education back to a position similar to what it was in the late 1950s or early 1960s' (p.2). Of course, government expenditure on schools might increase in the latter half of the decade, but by how much and at what rate? It seems almost certain that primary education will operate against a background of continued, if occasionally mitigated, financial constraint, but this does not rule out all developments. After all, during the late 1950s and early 1960s much expenditure was devoted to providing 'roofs over heads', a problem which is unlikely to be particularly pressing during the late 1980s. It should be possible to provide some expenditure for developing or strengthening the primary/middle school curriculum.

Other probable background features to the next decade could have been sketched out. The three featured here have been included to provide some kind of backcloth against which likely issues for the primary curriculum can be discussed. The future is unlikely to be as expansive as we would like nor as retrospective as we fear. It will be a period of restraint, but restraint does not automatically bring with it stagnation or regression. To return to MacDonald's analogy, the hare and the tortoise do not have to remain stationary, nor necessarily need they turn tail and retreat.

Curriculum Issue

Against this backcloth, what curriculum issues will be raised? What pressures will be placed on primary and middle schools? What topics will feature in in-service courses and in future conferences?

Most fundamentally, primary and middle schools will be under increasing pressure from the DES, from HMI and from local education authorities (though not, perhaps, from most parents) to devise intellectually challenging curricula, widely defined and adequately justified. The emphasis on intellectual development, powerfully represented in the primary survey and in the section on the primary phase in *The School Curriculum 1981*, is likely to intensify. It will involve the re-examination of assumptions about what young children can and cannot learn, it will require consideration of the skills, ideas, rules and generalizations underlying areas of understanding, and it will lead to the advocacy of curricula which clearly embody such skills and ideas. It is likely to lead to pressures for the extension of carefully planned programmes of work to areas beyond the basics for younger as well as older children. Support for such a position is provided by White in the final chapter of *The Aims of Education Restated* (1982): 'Children's minds do not develop naturally and in due season like biological entities; conceptual schemes are acquired only in social interaction and can be extended by deliberate intervention. . . . Understanding is a matter of degree, not an all-or-nothing affair. Children of eight or nine may not be capable of a very profound understanding of such concepts as democracy, or the trade balance, or electricity, but there is no reason why they should not have *some* grasp of these things, as well as some purchase on recent world history and current affairs and some capacity to enjoy music, poetry and the other arts' (pp.157,158). As White implies, this emphasis on intellectual development need not be at the expense of the arts (though financial restrictions may put these under increasing strain unless they are protected); it may even add an appreciative dimension to the performance aspect of the arts which is at present dominant in schools. A more challenging curriculum requires deepened understanding of subject matter and of children's learning, greater intraprofessional collaboration and sharing of expertise, and more clearly articulate co-ordination of the efforts of individual schools and teachers.

Increasingly, policies will be required to co-ordinate and reinforce the impact of individual initiatives taken by practitioners within schools and to co-ordinate the work of individual schools within local authorities (Richards 1982).

As part of this intellectual emphasis, schools will be required to refine the nature of 'basic' skills beyond decoding, ciphering and writing for a teacher-audience, so as to include a range of higher-level skills previously considered by many as appropriate for only a small minority of children. The primary survey has already set this in train. Basic to most children's education up to thirteen will be skills involved, for example, in following and presenting arguments, in evaluating various kinds of evidence, in speculating about motives, in approaching the printed word in different ways for different purposes, in writing for a variety of audiences, in setting up different kinds of inquiry and in classifying and generalizing in relation to phenomena encountered in a variety of curriculum areas. It is not, of course, the case that these skills have never before been taught in primary or middle schools; some schools have long redefined what they considered to be basic to a child's education. What is new is the requirement, as outlined in *The School Curriculum*, for all schools to redefine the basics (and incidentally, to re-educate governors and parents to accept, and to demand, the resources to implement the redefinition). It needs to be emphasized how strong the challenge will be to the long-accepted basis of primary education: the 'basic basics', as one observer calls them, are firmly embedded in our assumptions as well as our practices.

Three areas of the curriculum, in particular, are likely to be the focus of considerable activity during the next few years. The impetus to developing primary science will almost certainly continue. The inclusion of primary science in the government's statement of guidance on the school curriculum, the advocacy of HMI, the efforts of LEAs in producing guidelines and providing inset, and the proliferation of published schemes with, at long last, accompanying pupils' materials, will see to that. Getting science of any kind going will be a priority in many primary schools; in others and in middle schools, where science is much more firmly established, more attention will be given to how teacher-directed practical work can be complemented by more open-ended activities where children frame questions based on their own observations, suggest patterns in what is observed, offer explanations of what has caused the patterns and test their suggested explanations. Greater use of the local environment for ecological investigations is likely to be stressed as is the application of science to other areas of the curriculum and the use of mathematics to help children express scientific ideas and relationships.

Craft, design and technology are second areas likely to be increasingly advanced as candidates for development at top primary and middle school levels. At present, in most schools, little demanding work is done in relation to craft, or to design or to technology. The absence of the latter in schools is neatly highlighted in this quotation from Evans, an advocate of primary technology: 'Of nuts and bolts and metal and wires used to conduct electricity, of practical reasoning, of the use of powerful imagination – as distinct from the pixiliated stuff of creative writing – and of the application of science and mathematics in the design of working gadgets, there is rarely a sign' (1980, p.21). Craft, design and technology are intended to give boys and girls skills in the identification and solution of practical problems, including the design and construction of devices which perform practical functions. In tackling such problems, children are introduced to the physical and aesthetic properties of materials such as wood, metal and plastics, and are involved in a variety of processes – defining problems, considering possible solutions, selecting, designing, constructing, operating, appraising, modifying, using, etc. The moves towards establishing craft, design and technology as a central concern of the middle-year curriculum are in their infancy; the next few years should see clearer expectations established as to the skills and capacities to be developed, the range of activities to be included in programmes of work and the material provision required to sustain this work. CDI is likely to be demanding of resources, and there is a danger that its development might be at the expense of the other arts; if so, an important and, in some schools, distinguished area of the curriculum might be put at risk.

Mathematics post-Cockcroft is an obvious focus of attention, though less so than science or CDT. This is partly because primary mathematics received a moderately good press in Cockcroft: 'There has been a general widening of the mathematics curriculum in most primary schools during the last twenty years to include both a greater understanding of number and also work on measurement, shape and space, graphical representation and the development of simple logical ideas. We believe that this broadening of the curriculum has had a beneficial effect both in improving children's attitudes towards mathematics and also in laying the foundations of better understanding' (1982, paragraph 296). Future activity is likely to be focused on the use of calculators and, to a lesser extent, microcomputers, as teaching and learning aids, on the extension and refinement of mathematical language through more extended and considered use of class and small-group discussion, on the application of mathematics to everyday problems and to other areas of the curriculum, and on the planning and co-ordination of mathematics throughout primary and middle schools. Hopefully also, researchers including teacher-researchers may take up Cockcroft's suggestions for studies into the language of mathematics texts, tests and lessons, into children's spontaneous problem-solving activities and into the extent to which strategies and processes for problem solving can be taught.

In addition to curriculum development in science, CDT and mathematics, there will be renewed attempts to introduce three curricular dimensions to inform the planning of the work in different subjects and to provide means of inter-relating such work. The first of these, multicultural education, draws on the experiences of the cultures that make up contemporary British society in order to help children understand the nature of the society and to provide them with a basis for understanding how our society is similar to, and different from, other societies. To achieve this, a multicultural perspective will have to permeate work across the curriculum in all schools, irrespective of whether they have pupils from ethnic minority groups. The second dimension is environmental education, a concept broader than environmental studies, which seeks to develop children's understanding of, and concern for, their own environment and that of others and to help them participate in making informed decisions about environmental issues. Education 'for', 'from' and 'about' the environment are its catchwords; all three aspects will be stressed in the ecologically conscious 1980s. The last dimension is health education, already the subject of considerable curriculum development activity but not yet adequately embodied in curricula. As curricular dimensions rather than timetabled subjects, all three are likely to be overlooked in practice unless there is careful planning and co-ordination at school level. Increasingly, schools will be asked to indicate in what ways their curricula contribute to these three broad areas.

The use of microcomputers is inevitably going to be an important issue for the next decade, not because primary or middle school teachers want it to be but because government, manufacturers and public opinion will make it so. The major question is not whether something called computer studies or the like should be a new area of the curriculum but how far micros can be used to help us in the difficult task of creating that intellectually challenging curriculum described earlier. Micros in primary schools are still news, with all the dangers that newsworthiness brings. In the *Times Educational Supplement* of 19 March 1982, Spencer reported the government's plans to help primary schools buy their own microcomputers as part of a £1000 million boost for new technology announced in that year's budget. The MEP (Micro-Electronics in Education Programme) is also issuing software for use in primary schools.

In line with my other rather conservative predictions, I do not believe that micros are going to transform schooling in general or primary and middle schools in particular over the next decade. As Cockcroft aptly and comfortingly points out, 'we are still at a very early stage in the development of their use as an aid to teaching mathematics. The amount of work which needs to be done before microcomputers are likely to have any major effect on mathematics teaching is very great indeed' (1982, paragraph 403). If that is an accurate reflection of the situation as regards mathematics, then an enormous amount of work has to be done in relation to other areas of the curriculum. At present and in the immediate future, the most important concerns are not to get micros into every primary school but the production of good quality software and the encouragement of careful and *documented* experimentation in a relatively small number of schools (not all of which should be staffed by enthusiasts), on the basis of which local education authorities can devise and implement policies for the gradual introduction and realistic application of micros across the curriculum, not just in mathematics. Such small-scale work should focus particularly on the devising of conceptually based programs, which invite children to tease out possibilities in the situations presented, to speculate about explanations and consequences, to derive generalizations and to formulate and test their hypotheses. Parallel with experimentation in the teaching situation, computer literacy courses for the rest of us in primary education need to be mounted to help us understand the nature of the new technology and to expand our awareness of its potential in the long term and its likely impact on practice in the short term. Micros promise to be an important tool in providing an intellectually challenging curriculum, provided the drill and practice programs common at present are complemented by simulations, by information retrieval and processing and by opportunities for some children, at least, to devise their own programs (see Garland 1982).

This account of curriculum issues likely to be 'in currency' in the 1980s concludes by brief reference to the general issues of continuity and consistency which have underpinned much discussion of the school curriculum since the mid-1970s. Continuity is concerned with the degree to which curricular activities offered children relate to, and build on, their previous experience. Four forms can be distinguished: (a) the continuity which children experience between learning in the home and learning at school, not just at entry age but throughout the primary/middle school phase (see Atkin and Goode 1982), (b) the continuity children experience in any one class in the course of a school year, (c) the continuity they experience as they move from class to class within the same school, and (d) the continuity they experience as they move from one stage of schooling to the next. Up to now most progress has been made in relation to (b), most professional discussion has focused on (d), but as the 1980s proceed, more attention is likely to be paid to (c) through closer co-ordination of programmes of work within schools, and, possibly, towards the end of the decade to (a) as more children have access to data bases through their television sets and personal computers, as more parents have the time and confidence consciously to teach their children the skills and knowledge they value and as the concept of school, particularly at the secondary stage, is called into question by a vociferous minority of parents.

The last six or seven years have seen growing pressures for greater consistency and coherence in the education offered children. Since 1976 the DES has expressed its public concern at the diversity of practice that has emerged at secondary and primary levels. A string of publications from *Educating Our Children* (1977) to *The School Curriculum* (1981) bear witness to this concern. In the primary context, the issue was highlighted by chapter six of the primary survey which reported very considerable inconsistencies in the curricular activities offered primary classes and argued that 'ways of providing a more consistent coverage for important aspects of the curriculum need to be examined' (1978, paragraph 6.9). It would appear that developments towards creating more consistent curricula are taking place at three levels. Through *The School Curriculum* (1981) and a number of follow-up documents the DES is attempting to set out a broad structure for the curriculum at a national level; through the issuing of curriculum guidelines (and the closer monitoring of the work of schools through inspection, testing or other forms of data-gathering) local education authorities are responding to DES initiatives and in the process are devising broad curriculum policies for their schools; through self-evaluation procedures, curriculum reviews and the strengthening of the position of post-holders, schools are being urged to appraise their curricula and to modify these in the light of guidance, whether from LEA guidelines, from evaluation panels or from individual inspectors or advisers. These moves towards greater consistency are not likely to result, by 1992, in the detailed control of the school curriculum by central government, but could result in the removal of some of the more extreme curricular inequalities among schools and could help provide a more consistent set of experiences for more pupils for a greater part of their time in school, which I believe, is necessary if a more genuinely comprehensive education is to be provided in the primary/middle school phase (Richards 1982).

Within the confines of this paper it has not proved possible to discuss issues of assessment and evaluation in any detail. However, for the sake of completeness, some brief comment is necessary. The next decade is likely to witness a decline in the importance at present accorded evaluation and assessment, as the difficulties in this area become more apparent to elected representatives and administrators and as schooling becomes less important as a political issue. It is more than likely that within the next ten years, the APU's ambitious programme of monitoring performance over time will have been replaced by five-yearly surveys of mathematics, science and language performance broadly analogous to the surveys of reading performance carried out since the war but, thanks to the APU, with much more sophisticated tests. I also suggest that there will be a decline in local authority blanket testing as its expense and lack of utility become more apparent, and there will be a parallel disillusionment with school self-evaluation as a means of instituting curriculum change.

Issues and actualities

A number of pressures for change in the 1980s have been outlined, but what of actualities? How far will such pressures be realized in the light of the backcloth described earlier and of schools' proven capacity to absorb and neutralize curriculum innovation?

Generalizing about schools is difficult enough; the difficulty is compounded when generalization is to be accompanied by prediction. Between now and 1992 there will a be considerable number of schools which will provide the kind of challenging curriculum outlined in this paper; there will be a few who will go well beyond this to offer a kind of curriculum of which this imagination cannot conceive. In contrast, there will be schools which will continue to prepare children very adequately for the 1980s and 1990s – as they did for the 1880s and 1890s. But what of the majority of schools?

Two scenarios are offered here. In the first, pupil numbers continue to fall, albeit with a hiccup in the mid-1980s, schools become considerably smaller, staffs become stagnant except for redeployment, local education authorities become increasingly inbred, in-service education is cut back, and isolationism at the class, school and LEA level increases. Only a token response is offered to the issues outlined, and there is an emphasis on the 'basic basics'. In the second scenario, there is some easing of demographic contraction and of financial constraint, greater mobility of staff, more co-operation among schools to share expertise and resources, better co-ordination of curricula among schools in a locality, greater availability of in-service education and a moderate influx of newly qualified teachers, some of whom are particularly knowledgeable in mathematics, science or craft, design and technology. Overall, a genuine attempt is made to respond to the curriculum issues discussed above.

Perhaps the next few years will see a continuing shift towards the realization of the first scenario. Perhaps the latter half of the decade will see developments leading to the realization of the second.

Acknowledgements

The author acknowledges the help received from the following people at an early stage in the preparation of this paper: Norman Thomas, Ron Letheren, Mike Preston, John Burrows, Alan Blyth, Dan Wicksteed and Philip Taylor.

References

Atkin, J and Goode, J. (1982) 'Learning at home and at school,' *Education 3 13*, 10:1, pp.: 7-10.
Benford, M. (1982) 'School 2000', *National Association for Primary Education Journal*, No 5, pp: 8 – 10.
Bennett, S. *et al.* (1980) *Open Plan Schools*, NFEH.
Central Advisory Council for Education (England) (1967) *Children and Their Primary Schools*, HMSO.
Collings, H. (1980) Falling Rolls in Richards, E. (ed) *Primary Education for the Eighties*, A & C Black.
DENI (1981) *Primary Education: Report of an inspectorate survey in Northern Ireland*, HMSO.
Dennison, W. (1981) *Education in Jeopardy: Problems and possibilities of contraction*, Basil Blackwell.
DES (1977) *Educating Our Children*, HMSO.
DES, Welsh Office (1981) *The School Curriculum*.
DES (1978) *Primary Education in England: A survey by HM Inspectors of Schools*, HMSO.
DES (1982) *Pupils and School Leavers: Future numbers*, Report on Education No 97, HMSO.
Galton, M., Simon, B. and Croll, P., (1980) *Inside the Primary Classroom*, Routledge & Kegan Paul.
Evans, P. (1980) 'Science: Pure or applied?' *Education 3-13* 8:1, pp.16-23.

Garland, R. (ed) (1982) *Computers and Children in the Primary School*, The Falmer Press.

MacDonald, B. (1979): 'Hard times: educational accountability in England', *Educational Analysis*, Vol No 1, pp.23 – 43.

Papert, S. (1980) *Mindstorms: Children, computers and powerful ideas*, Harvester Press.

Peston, M. (1982) 'Sir Geoffrey's framework for decline', *Times Educational Supplement*, 12 March.

Richards, C. (1980) 'Demythologizing primary education', *Journal of Curriculum Studies*, 12, pp. 77.

Richards, C. (ed) (1982) *New Directions in Primary Education*, The Falmer Press.

SED (1980) *Learning and Teaching in Primary 4 and Primary 7: A report by HM Inspectors of Schools in Scotland*, HMSO.

Spencer, D. (1982) 'Computers soon for primaries', *Times Educational Supplement*, 19 March.

22   Steadman, S. *et al* (1979) *Impact and Take up Project: A first interim report*, Schools Council Publications.

23.   Stonier, T. (1982) Changes in Western Society: Educational Implications in Richards, C. (ed) *New Directions in Primary Education*, The Falmer Press.

24   Taylor, M. and Garson, Y. (1982) *Schooling in the Middle Years*, Trentham Books.

25   *The Government's Expenditure plans 1982 – 3 to 1984 – 5* (1982) CMnd 8494 – 1, HMSO.

26   White, J. (1982) *The Aims of Education Restated*, Routledge & Kegan Paul.

CHAPTER 4

STARTING FROM HERE : the 'why', 'what' and 'how' of secondary curricular development for the next few years.

PETER CORNALL

Why must we travel?

A professional instinctively recognizes most readily those obligations which spring from the personal morality which he conceives to lie at the heart of his professional commitment, and to regard as secondary such require-ments as are placed upon him and his colleagues by the law. For those involved with the secondary school curriculum, it is still a novelty to face legal as well as moral imperatives, yet there can be no dispute that the terms of *The School Curriculum*, given greater force with the issue of DES Circular No. 6/81, *do* constitute such a legal obligation, even if its precise forms remain somewhat indeterminate and the duties are expressed in the style of opinions and requests. However, the advice of *The School Curriculum* is specifically commended, and the Secretary of State clearly expects all schools to set out their curricular aims in writing, and at a later stage to assess their measure of success. LEAs, school governors and heads are all required to play their important part in making sure that schools conform to the expectations of the Secretary of State; all parties will do well to remember that the circular which contains these unprecedented expres-sions of national policy comes as part of a sequence of events which began some years before the present government took office, and no future change of ministry is likely to cause them to be forgotten. What teachers are asked to do *must* be done, and there is surely everything to be gained by making a virtue of necessity, and taking full advantage of the opportunity for wholesale review presented by the curricular debate of the past few years and culminating in a requirement which comes very near to having the force of law.

The documents which must command attention are by now well known, from the 'red book' (*Curriculum 11-16*) of 1977 to *The School Curriculum* and *The Practical Curriculum* of 1981. About this fascinating sequence, a great deal has been written and spoken, some of it in terms of resentment and anger. At times some may have felt that the more intense critics must have read different publications from those published, so painful has been their experience. For others it is possible only to record a combination of relief and excitement on looking back on what has happened. This reaction is not merely the result of discovering that views held for years now coincided amazingly with a new national orthodoxy. It can also be argued that the challenge which has been given is timely, and certain to do good, once it is accepted as having much to do with the present and future advantage of pupils. From this moment on, I shall assume that acceptance, and ask you to consider with me what appear to be the most important questions to which each school must find the best possible answers.

Both in *The School Curriculum* from the DES and *The Practical Curriculum* from the Schools Council, we discover unequivocal advocacy of a much greater compulsory element in the secondary curriculum than is at present common in our schools. 'There is,' say the ministers, 'an overwhelming case for providing all pupils between eleven and sixteen with curricula of a broadly similar character' (39.2). 'We believe,' says the School Council, 'it is time to agree on a guaranteed curricular offer to every pupil' (p.36). Here then is the first of the principles of action to place before you – that we must consider the case for the largest possible common core, and certainly one much more extensive than is at present usual. Upon what reasoning does this case rest? Upon nothing less than the central arguments in favour of having a comprehensive system of schools. If the abolition of selection at eleven means anything, it simply has to imply the postponement of significant decisions; and if that postponement is to be genuine, there can be no justification for effecting an internal segregation by other means, among which a differentiated curriculum is obviously the most powerful agent. The abolition of selection leads logically to the maintenance within the comprehensive school of the greatest possible degree of similarity between the curriculum followed by all pupils. It will be natural in such schools for the staff to have a very strong perception of the curricular needs which all pupils have in common, because of their common humanity, their common culture and the very great extent to which their future lives will present them with common problems and common opportunities. There will also be a strong disposition to do as little as possible, even within the common-style curriculum, to prejudge the future attainments of the boys and girls; and as a result teachers will put their efforts into finding suitable approaches and methods within the same curriculum, rather than seeking to meet learning difficulties by embracing segregation and supposedly less demanding curricula.

Above all else, it is imperative to seek by every means to preserve, develop or – if necessary – restore, all the pupils' confidence in themselves, their self-esteem, their belief that they have the capacity to make their own individual contribution to society, even if this proves to come about through a different process than traditional employment. To this objective the experience of achievement, related to their own previous efforts rather than ranked too emphatically against those of others, must be extremely important. So too must the school's programme of encouraging, through carefully structured activities, the process of developing self-appraisal, so that many sixteen-year-olds, at the first major moment of choice in their lives, may face their decisions with a confidence which is supported rather than undermined by self-knowledge.

About these principles of action – the large core curriculum and what it implies, and the preservation of self-esteem in pupils – every school has the duty to reach a view. Either virtue in the year four and year five curriculum lies in a supposed à la carte matching of individual 'wishes' through a multitude of options, or it lies in the greatest possible commonness in the curriculum; there must be clarity about the matter, and one view or the other must prevail. As for self-esteem, there is no quality more deserving of 'positive discrimination', particularly in the economic and social conditions of today and tomorrow. Yet of course there may be serious doubt about the best path to follow for its achievement; the views of the present ministers are tending to force the issue upon our attention, by appearing to support a deliberate categorization of students at the age of fourteen into those for whom external examinations, old-style or new, can offer a path to significant success, and the others whose needs are to be better served by embarking on 'pre-vocational' courses. Leaving aside the strong misgivings we felt about these supported 'vocations', it must be asked which plan, the postponement of categorization or its hastening, will do most for self-esteem? There are groups of lower-attainment pupils who find their present work unrewarding in the final two years of compulsory education, and we must accept the objective of improving their morale and their performance;

but it is not self-evident that the solution lies in emphasizing their singularity and in segregating them, against all comprehensive principles, into a special category, rather than asking what changes we must make, in approach, in method, in material, in order to help them enjoy the benefits of a well-thought-out common curriculum, designed to meet needs which they have in common with all their contemporaries and future fellow-citizens. Start from the assumption of common needs, and the nobler conclusion is not hard to reach, even if it spells out a message of professional challenge, and denies us a retreat into the ancient platonic distinction between men of gold, of silver and of iron. But the essential for every school is to debate this issue with the energy and rigour so profound a question deserves, and to reach its answer in the fullest recognition of what is at stake.

A vision of journey's end

It is by now almost a commonplace to present views of the curriculum in terms other than lists of the so-called subjects which appear on school timetables and – perhaps more malignantly – in examination boards' lists of syllabuses. The idea that the curriculum may be looked at in terms of skills or themes or processes is far from new, and the collection of different versions in order to compare and cross-reference them would make a large-scale if tedious piece of research. Is there a secondary school where the traditional curriculum has been completely analysed in other terms? No doubt this has been done somewhere, and perhaps the obvious conclusions – that we throw away opportunities of mutual support while confusing with vain repetitions – have been drawn. Ignorance, however, gives an excuse to make a personal attempt leaving the traditional subjects to one side for a time, and for exploring only such needs of our pupils as may seem self-evidently necessary for them; and to express these needs in terms of (a) skills and (b) knowledge of a sort which is not essentially implied by the possession of a skill. It is helpful to distinguish these two categories, skills and knowledge, while acknowledging how easy it is to become involved in awkward semantic problems. The list will be as subjective, and possibly as idiosyncratic, as others on offer; and is offered rather as an illustration than as a model.

1   Skills associated with language: speaking, listening, writing, reading; and as with all other skills the learning must include an appreciation of the value of the skill acquired.

2   Skills associated with number: computation, measuring, the ability to present quantifiable data in both numerical and non-numerical ways, estimation.

3   Skills in dealing with information: finding it, understanding the forms in which is is available, selecting what is relevant to the immediate purpose, presenting it in the most useful manner. The onrush of information technology gives a very special importance and novelty to these skills, with which few of today's middle-aged managers in education have had the opportunity to become acquainted, more through lack of resources than of imagination. This item is given emphasis by quoting Norman Longworth, Education Officer of IBM: it is taken from a recent paper entitled 'Change and Information – Crucial Ingredients of the Evolving Curriculum', obtainable from the Centre for the Study of Comprehensive Schools at York. 'It *does* require some little imagination to realize what the effects might be of *not* educating *all* our children to sort out the differences between essential and non-essential information, raw fact, prejudice, half-truth and untruth so that they know when they are being manipulated, by whom and for what purpose.'

4   Skills of thinking: logic, analysis, testing theory against experience, the discovery and acknowledgement of error, self-criticism and correction, self-appraisal, conscious redirection.

5   Skills of the eye: thorough and accurate observation.

6   Skills of the ear: careful and attentive listening.

7   Skills involved in making: design, planning, the necessary types of dexterity.

8   Skills prerequisite for the appreciation of beauty: in all forms of 'imagery' – musical, two- and three-dimensional, dramatic, dance, literary.

9   Skills in the exercise and use of the human body as a whole: all types of physical development of the body.

10   Skills of human relationship, inevitably (through immaturity) to an incomplete level, but at least rightly directed by the influence exercised by the school, through the whole of its communal activity.

Turning now from skills to information, acknowledging still that these categories are both arbitrary and imprecise. It is vital to emphasize, however, that the list is intended to contain what is essential for all: it is not put forward as a menu from which selection may be made – here some useful enrichment, and there material of special relevance to this or that career. It is for doubters to argue against the inclusion of items they regard as unjustifiable. Meanwhile there is one further point to be made about the relationship between skills and information; skills can rarely be developed except in a context. The point is interestingly made in one of the quoted submissions to the Cockcroft Report on the *Teaching Of Mathematics*:

> Mathematics lessons in secondary schools are very often not about anything. You collect like items, or learn the laws of indices, with no perception of why anyone needs to do such things. There is excessive preoccupation with a sequence of skills and quite inadequate opportunity to see the skills emerging from the solution of problems. As a consequence of this approach, school mathematics contains very little incidental information. A French lesson might well contain incidental information about France – so on across the curriculum; but in mathematics the incidental information which one might expect (current exchange and interest rates; general knowledge on climate, communications and geography; the rules and scoring systems of games, social statistics) is rarely there, because most teachers in no way see this as part of their responsibility when teaching mathematics.

The point is well made, and applies across the curriculum.

11   The human condition on earth needs exploration, in terms of past, present and future, with a global view. Facts must be given, from the fields of knowledge we know as history, geography, economics and politics; perhaps sociology and psychology should also be drawn upon. The need for communication between different peoples will lead to a consideration of the importance of language learning, and the recognition of foreign languages as a significant area of knowledge, proficiency in which will have value for some.

12   The relation of the individual to society must be examined; facts must be given about the obligations and rights of citizenship, the opportunities which all people have to contribute to society, by one

means or another, and the extent to which they may depend upon the support of others.

13   The essence of being human needs exploration; there must be facts about religious experience and belief, about morality and the heights and depths of human behaviour; and there must be encouragement to reflect upon all these matters in the context of ordinary life.

14   There is also a need to ensure that specific information is provided before the age of sixteen and the possibility of leaving school, on a range of topics, each of which requires careful and detailed expansion:
    Healthy and safe living
    Science, technology and human life (an enormous theme)
    Homemaking and parentcraft
    The maintenance of a house
    The market and the consumer
    Education and training after sixteen; employment and self-employment

A map with better co-ordinates?

Assuming some agreement so far, what are the constraints which lie between them and the realization of any curriculum based on a new formula for the expression of children's needs? First among them must surely be placed each and every individual involved, the limits of their capacity to imagine change, their assumptions about the impenetrable boundaries of traditional specialisms. This brings to mind the prayer: 'Lord, renew Thy Creation . . . and begin with me.' It is important to accept the spirit of that request. Next, perhaps, our minds will turn to the parents of both present and future pupils; what will their response be to news of curricular change, and an atmosphere in which profoundly important questions are being posed about the curricular obligations of the secondary school?

This question brings us to one of the truly critical issues in secondary education today. Can the professionals in education, area by area and school by school, refuse to be mesmerized into believing themselves to be the victims of a consumer-dominated system? Can they be persuaded to see that what the vast majority of parents long for is schools in which their children will be happy, schools which are directed by men and women who speak with authority and conviction, schools which earn confidence because they operate confidently, schools which regard full public explanation of their principles and their action as an inescapable part of their duty to lead and not to follow? Of course the parents we respect share – more acutely but less broadly – hopes for their children's reasonable success, within the limits of their natural endowment, but very few have any wish to dictate to us on issues of educational significance. Those for whom such a wish may be a temptation are more likely to be won over by well-conceived and confident publicity than by hesitation and uncertainty, by open discussion of possibly controversial questions rather than by the policy of Newman's 'safe man . . . who steers his course between "aye" and "no" along the channel of "no meaning".'

However, some may now ask what about examination results, that supposed lynch-pin of consumerism in education, with which every one of us must now be concerned? In the first place, this specific issue does not invalidate the brave assertions already made. The manner will be more decisive than matter in deciding the parental and public response. But there is much more to be said. There are the striking, and surely deeply considered, words of Her Majesty's Inspectors in chapter 11 of *Aspects of Secondary Education*, which reports of the many schools which fail to find the right balance between examination requirements and the achievement of wider educational aims; where a plea is made to continue our endeavours to make examinations serve the educational process rather than determining it. This emphatic message means that it is a duty, now and in the future, to use every ounce of energy and guile to manipulate whatever examination system is wished upon the schools so that it shall serve curricular purposes and never be allowed to dominate them. This is surely possible.

There are major tasks within the schools, where it is necessary to face up to the depth of thinking required in order to reach clearly perceived policies, and sustain the energy necessary to carry into effect the decisions we made about syllabuses and timetabling. It is time to become very practical and work on the assumption that schools can go some way towards a common curriculum, within which emphasis is to be placed upon mutual support between curricular areas, and upon the avoidance of all unintended repetition. About the first steps there can be nothing very revolutionary; specialist teachers are all in post, and most valuably so, yet perhaps they can be convinced of the value of seeing where they can support others, and where others can support them.

The suggestion here is that in each school there should be drawn up a large grid – or a series of smaller sections capable of being assembled or compiled – the one axis (shall we say following the left-hand margin) listing subjects, courses or departments, the other axis (probably along the top margin) listing the skills and topics which the school deems essential as the minimum curricular entitlement of all its pupils. The grid will certainly be a complex one; the subject axis must be subdivided into school years, or possibly even into terms; the skills and facts axis will be broken down into such subsections as the school decides, but inevitably there will be a large number. The grid once established in its final version – undoubtedly after much discussion – each team involved in the teaching of the curriculum will be invited to scrutinize its own syllabuses and methods in order to decide upon those squares on the grid in which it can record a contribution. Then, as both gaps and repetitions become obvious for the school as a whole, careful and detailed discussion can begin with the object of securing, in the most advantageous way, a greater coverage for skills and knowledge which are under-represented in the grid, and the elimination of repetitions which are wasteful or confusing rather than mutually supportive.

The product of this operation should be syllabuses which are better adjusted to the school's curricular objectives, and a staff of teachers which is infinitely better informed about the part their own work plays in the total experience of the young people whom they meet for only a few periods each week. In the longer term it may be permissible to look for a gradual blurring or merging of subject boundaries, a more balanced perception of 'subjects' and 'skills', easier paths into the integration of hitherto distinct categories of study and – above all – for our students a greater sense that their education is all part of a coherent experience rather than a series of discrete events following one another in random sequence, at the incomprehensible whim of the timetabler. Finally, and most important indeed, it is obvious that although a cross-curricular scrutiny of this sort could be of great interest in any school, it will be of special relevance and wider effect where optional subjects, which cannot be depended upon to contribute to every pupil's timetable, form a relatively small proportion of the curriculum.

Setting out – even from here

Following agreement that a curriculum of this sort – perhaps with a core amounting to eighty percent – is best suited to prepare our pupils for their future lives, how is it to be timetabled? Can any generalization be made about where the most difficult problems are likely to arise? What needs to be said about the relationship between this curriculum and the school's policies on pupil deployment (or class formation), which are likely (depending on attitudes among the staff) to include a combination of features such as setting, mixed-ability, banding and streaming? To take this last question first, universal mixed-ability teaching is not being advocated here, even to the age of fourteen, let alone to sixteen, although if a team of specialists wished to teach in this way why prevent them? At the same time, it is impossible to reconcile with a concern for boys' and girls' self-esteem the wholesale transfer of children into streams, bands or sets when they first join a new school at the age of eleven. Between these two extremes all our schools can and should feel their way towards compromises based on highly responsible professionalism and – very important indeed – on the offer to teams of teachers of the greatest possible measure of delegated decision making, within their particular areas of the curriculum. In this way educational ends can be served directly, through the encouraging effects on the children of delayed and essentially subject-based assessment, and also indirectly, through the strengthening effect on teachers' morale when they are trusted to make subject or area-specific decisions for themselves.

For the purposes of this section, a few assumptions must be made:

a   that each pupil's week offers sufficient time for ten separate elements of study, deemed to be of equal significance in terms of time.

b   that one of these elements shall be deemed to consist of religious education together with such other items as are unlikely to figure separately in the timaetable; this category will include health education and careers education.

c   that teachers are ready, if need be, to set aside views about the minimum time required for each 'subject' which are based principally on the demands of existing examination syllabuses, rather than upon any intrinsic needs of the 'subject' itself.

Attempting some curriculum building, starting with a list appropriate for the needs of the large category of pupils clustered in the middle of the ability range, the following items need to have a place:

English (language and literature)   Geography
Mathematics   History
Physical education   Foreign language
Religious education, Health, Careers   A practical subject
Science   An aesthetic subject

If this list is examined in the interest of pupils falling below the central cluster of ability, what modifications may be needed? Perhaps that by the age of fifteen (year four) the foreign language may have become an unprofitable part of the curriculum. In this case, there should be an opportunity to choose an alternative course; such a course could fittingly be designed to reinforce, in an imaginative way, study of the basic skills of language and number. There are other possibilities; although another session devoted to the traditional range of craft subjects, already represented in our list, would seem best avoided. In general, this list as it stands could serve as the medium for those skills and that knowledge which have already been outlined provided that teaching methods and class sizes take proper account of the difficulties encountered by pupils of limited ability.

What if attention is turned in the other direction? In what ways is the list inadequate for the needs of the more able section of a typical student body? The comments will present more taxing problems:

a   It is important that more than ten percent of each week shall be available to more ambitious students for the study of science.

b   It is probable that some of these students will wish to study more than one language other than their own.

What response can be made to these objections, within the constraints of the overall limit on time and the obligation to provide a full curriculum for every student, however talented he or she may be? It is possible, at a sacrifice which may be deemed acceptable, to amalgamate for the more ambitious students the categories of practical and aesthetic, and by so doing create a second ten percent of time for the expansion of science, raising its share in these important years to twenty percent of the week. The further language question is more difficult, and solvable only by a 'contrivance', either (preferably) outside the normal school timetable or else by 'stealing' time from some other place in the curriculum. (One possible solution is to impose upon English and physical education.)

To stop at this point leaves unresolved what for some people will still seem to be a major problem – the wish to make available to year four and five pupils the chance to study three separate science subjects. There is no way of escaping from this dilemma; one must either be content to accept – and persuade others to accept – this limitation, as being in the best interests of the very students who may seem to be handicapped by it; or one must abandon the 'large core' and with it the concept of breadth in the form here. This paper advocates the acceptance of this limitation, and a commitment to the consequent search for a broad science course capable of being taught within the twenty percent of the week allowed, and of serving as a sound basis for post-sixteen study of science. It will be found that such a course will be able to contribute a full share in skills and in knowledge to the curriculum, while alongside it all other elements of importance will be able to do the same.

A final pattern will look like this:

Above Average	**Required**	**Below Average**
	English	
(with 'extra maths?')	Mathematics	'differentiated'?
	Physical education	
	Religious education, etc.	
or an integrated course including politics, economics }	{ Geography History Foreign language }	{ or an integrated course including citizenship or an alternative probably general
	Science	

	Free Choice	
or one of these	A practical subject option	
and 10% more science	An aesthetic subject option	

Second language time
'Found' by contrivance

It is towards some such pattern as this that all schools should be moving, at the best speed that the circumstances of each will permit. If this is too bold a challenge then schools could accept the following challenge: to examine with scrupulous care the case here and to do so with no other consideration than giving its future pupils the most appropriate preparation for their lives in that future which beckons them forward to an incalculable and bewildering climacteric of perils and opportunities. 'We must not strive,' said Ernest Bevin, 'to make giants, but to elevate the human race', and the maxim seems not inappropriate to our business. Has our profession the creative zeal, the courage and – above all – the leadership to achieve renewal today in the cause of tomorrow?

CHAPTER 5

CONTINUITY AT SIXTEEN-PLUS

KEN SHAW AND KAY WOOD

Tertiary, that is, sixteen–nineteen-year education has moved decisively into the area of public interest and political controversy (Naylor 1981, Maclure 1981). The move to create more free-standing sixteen–nineteen colleges is after all but a further step in the reorganization of the maintained system, and the celebrated debate about the Manchester initiative in this area, together with less nationally aired examples at Shrewsbury and Liverpool, show that this is still a hot issue. Indeed the complex relationship between this last phase of structural re-patterning of the maintained system and the comprehensive reorganization of the 1960s and 1970s is still insufficiently explored. The seemingly endless wrangles about examining at sixteen-plus and eighteen-plus and the way these mesh with arguments about curriculum range and content keep tertiary education before the public. Above all, the radical problems of unemployment among school-leavers focus attention as never before on the sixteen-plus phase. There can be little doubt that the New Training Initiative – which if it does not raise the school-leaving age by stealth at any rate raises the work-starting age by a year – is already having washback effects on the secondary school curriculum. The resurgence of interest in vocationalism is only one of the more obvious aspects of this.

It was clearly one of the intentions of the Macfarlane Review, *Education 16-19* (1980), to press home some of the administrative consequences of all this. While terse, realistic and informed, one important reason it appears to have made little impact is that it concerned itself too much with the narrower question of how sixteen–nineteen education should be organized institutionally. Understandably, but regrettably, for there is a big gap in the literature, the review kept to the level of high policy. It had almost nothing to say about local contexts. This chapter is about one small facet, in many ways one of the easiest to deal with, of this large problem, but it does try to take the idea of the local context as a constraint seriously. It is about the way the young people who stay in full-time education move across the discontinuity at sixteen-plus. It is about the articulation of the eleven–sixteen and sixteen–nineteen phases of schooling revealed by the particular arrangements in one town. In a wider sense it is concerned with the choices among institutions and educational styles made by youngsters, parents, local administrators and their political masters. The aim of the project has been to see how larger issues – falling roles, the impact of governmental policies since the Great Debate, the continuing process of comprehensive reform of secondary schools, youngsters' perceptions of their future roles, the effect of reduced resources – are inserted into the specific local context of a provincial town. Using naturalistic or ethnographic methods of research (Shaw 1978, Duignan 1981) our approach has been to get to know the participants, in this case five secondary schools and two colleges, on their ground over a long period of time, and related participants, perceptions and views about how things are to the social political and economic conditions as we understand them, locally and nationally. This involved interviewing a large sample of pupils, parents, teachers, administrators and others and at the same time monitoring developments within the institutions to uncover processes of choice and decision.

In setting out to study transfer at sixteen-plus, then, we are not just concerned with guidance procedures, liaison, common application forms, but equally with trying to get a global picture of what happens when five schools act as the principal feeders to two colleges with very different styles, traditions and public images, all seven institutions forming the maintained provision for a self-contained, well-bounded town. Consequently the research began not with an idea to be tried out or as an 'hypothesis' to be tested but with a situation to be explored. Although the county was largely reorganized, it was not until 1977 that it became politically possible to implement a scheme in the town under which the boys' four-form entry grammar school became the sixth-form college while the girls' grammar school and the four secondary modern schools, appropriately enlarged after some mergers, became six-form entry eleven–sixteen comprehensives. The research originated from a personal project to study the organizational change from grammar school to college. It took eighteen months of weekly all-day visits to set up working relationships, during which it became clear that no study of the college in isolation was worthwhile. Arrangements with the FE College and the feeder schools had then to be worked up. In 1980 the research was funded for one year by the Schools Council as a study of the management of continuity between the two phases, with the active collaboration of the LEA. Its officials had fully supported the project from the beginning.

It quickly became clear that curricular issues were nearer the heart of our concerns than administrative ones. How did the patterns, preferences, opportunities and emphases in the curricula of the feeder schools differentiate the youngsters, pointing them to work (or unemployment), part-time or full-time study? How did the participants understand and appraise the local arrangements? What were the perceptions, beliefs and images they, and the schools and colleges, had of one another which influenced preferences and choices? Some of the most interesting material, inevitably, has to do with the images which people, but especially schools and colleges, have of each other, of where they fit into the system, what each offers, and how they cope. Clearly such appraising perceptions must be expected to influence choices, but it must be borne in mind that they are social constructs by groups of people, not checked on the ground nor based on detailed knowledge (though many staff know each other and each other's work through panel meetings and CSE moderation). They are in the nature of myths, not usually up to date and sometimes very different from the intentions of the institutions they claim to describe.

Though there is still data to be analysed, we can begin to see something of the pattern as it is emerging. Before the new set-up all the institutions could operate with considerable independence. There used to be a small traffic from the secondary modern schools into the separate-sex grammar school sixth forms; but youngsters rejected at eleven-plus were not always keen to present themselves at sixteen-plus so that the FE college was able to develop a large general 'A'-level sixth party drawing on its 'O'-level work. Youngsters went there from a very wide rural catchment area too, as well as from the private sector. But after the reorganization the schools in the town were drawn closer together because of their common stake in the sixteen–nineteen stage. Having given up their right to a sixth form they felt entitled to some say in such matters as admissions policy, courses to be offered, acceptability of Nuffield 'O'-level science or CSE Grade One English as a basis for an 'A'-level course. The schools had practical interests in common enough to draw them into a very loose, informal, unacknowledged consortium. However, as has been stressed by Dawson (1981) and Ebbut (1981), schools so placed are eventually in some measure in competition with each other for subscription and reputation. The requirements of the 1980 Act that schools should specify in detail their curricular offerings and publish their results; the fact that each would be judged by some groups of parents and local politicians on the numbers of youngsters going forward to full-time sixteen-plus education; and in particular, the falling numbers of pupils which by 1982 had already reduced the normal entry to 150 instead of 180, sharpened this up.

To some extent then, the number of youngsters going forward to 'A'-level courses at sixteen-plus would be a test of the success of reorganization and have survival value for the individual school. Continuity was thus a social and political matter, not simply educational and personal. For the schools were not competing as equals: each had its prior tradition, its local image, its catchment, its staffing and facilities, the result of the development of educational provision in the town, and which many parents, politicians and teachers could remember over some twenty years.

The HMI document *Curriculum 11-16: A review of progress* (1981) and some of its sources support the view that schools based on 180 children entering each year, and without a sixth form, are close to the lower limit at which a full-range comprehensive curriculum can be offered. Since the schools studied have fallen below this level, the breadth of the curriculum they can offer, interacting with the quality of their intake, their level of first choice applicants and the characteristics of their catchments is a crucial discriminator. It is the key determinant of flows of youngsters across the sixteen-plus divide, the combinations of 'A'-level (and other) studies they will prefer and the demand for subjects like sociology and psychology which are not available in the schools. To what extent in terms of range, length of specialized course (e.g., not integrated sciences), combinations and level were the schools able to offer similar diets to similar children? There is noticeable variation which stems from the schools' tradition and reflects the catchments served.

In the first year, before curriculum differentiation and segregation has developed, the schools serving the better catchments devote more time to the conventional examination subject areas in the group English, maths, sciences, history/geography and French. Between the school giving most and the one least time, both former secondary moderns, there is a difference of the order of fifteen percent. Since a major single subject usually gets ten–twelve percent this disparity is considerable. Those schools offering less, devote more time to craft/expressive subjects, wood and metal work, home economics, needlework, music, drama. The disparity is not capricious. It relates to the school's history, staffing policies, specialist facilities, former curricular traditions and expectations. The most extreme case is the school which offers six languages while another has to make an effort to keep one second language going to O/CSE and has only two language teachers. This variation in the curriculum offered has been a constant theme of HMI and DES documents which clearly regard it as unacceptable. It is where we examine school curricula in their direct context as historical and social constructs that the reasons for such variation and the difficulties of modifying it become much clearer. It raises very forcefully questions about a comprehensive system without a common curriculum pattern. The central authorities are probably more concerned about the cost-effective use of staff and group sizes as numbers fall; but there is an argument from equity as well.

Within this overall pattern further variation is created by introducing differing curricular patterns available to different groups of children. All the schools are banded and band-related choices are made well in advance of fourth-year options. This has its effects on the flows of pupils which different subject areas perceive themselves to get. As schools evolve into comprehensives, which is more than anything else a matter of extending and remodelling their curricula, yet with different chances to plan ahead, rebalance the staff, adapt or increase the facilities, gain or lose desirable catchments, subjects are differentially penalized or rewarded and their relationship to the post-sixteen-plus phase strengthened or cut down. If a school introduces second languages or brings science into core, re-allocates periods to pastoral care or computing, time has to be reapportioned; there are winners and losers. PE and games, as well as certain down-market crafts, are threatened. As élite upper-band groups emerge marked by second languages or plurality of sciences the obverse are 'sink' subjects defined for the less able or less motivated. Certain subjects are at risk to be used as curriculum 'fillers' (in the HMI usage) to make up a full timetable with for example an extra period of RE here or there. None of this can be separated from the view taken by influential parents, likely to affect their children's preferences, of subjects such as rural science or non-'O'-level crafts. We are able to see clearly how, in Maclure's graphic phrase, the torrent at eleven-plus is cut to the trickle at sixteen-plus.

A final element in this necessary brief and selective account is the problem of CSE and 'O'-level examinations, which relates to school size. Creamed by the independent sector, and with an uneven distribution of abler pupils, some of the town schools are beginning to approach what in *Aspects of Secondary Education* (1980) are called 'restricted range' comprehensives starved of the upper-ability group. On an entry of 150-180 it is usually possible to get an 'O'-level group of twenty-five–thirty in maths and English; in very favourable circumstances even two. But it is frequently the case in other areas to have 'O' and CSE candidates in the same group, as far as the exam syllabuses can be made to overlap, until Christmas of the fifth year. Given the different standing of these two examinations for the youngster hoping to stay on, and the fact that at the margins a mediocre 'O' be preferred to a good CSE for continuity purposes (because of the course content), somewhat edgy choices have to be made about dropping or cooling out youngsters into the more predictable CSE versus encouraging them to stay in the 'O'-level course at increased risk. This problem is compounded if the college proposes that CSE Grade One should be converted to 'O'-level because it has spare capacity or wishes to fill up a course.

Both the colleges admitted students from a wider range of schools than the five feeders in the town. This and the fact that comprehensive reorganization had not worked completely through to the top of the system meant that it was necessary to choose a sample of students representing the feeders as well as other contributors, and take account of the range of subjects as well as both sexes. The main interviews centred on six principal areas: choices at third-year option level, courses followed to O/CSE and results, images of the sixth form and FE colleges, experiences of sixteen-plus transfer, detailed accounts of 'A'-level course experiences and assessments of college life.

It rapidly became clear that it is impossible to separate the difficulties of academic transfer from the social conditions under which learning takes place. The students saw the sixteen-plus step as not only marking a stage in academic competence allowing them to move on, but because of its essentially voluntary nature, as marking a stage in maturity with all the accompanying rites of passage. They had ceased to see themselves as children and expected to be viewed by others, in particular by their parents and college tutors, as young adults. In the route from 'O' to 'A' level the academic and social expectations of the students becomes interwoven, and this had important implications for their view of the two colleges.

The two are very dissimilar in ethos and approach to students. The respondents recounted the steps which had led them to one or the other. The images they had gained were based on visits, talks by official representatives, the influence of teachers, parents, siblings and friends who might already have attended one or other. The pilot interviews suggested that eventual choices were often based not so much on detailed information about courses on offer nor about teacher-student relationships but rather on the relative desirability of the image each institution was able to project. These had assumed sterotypical proportions in the town and were often supported by group solidarities which developed generally or among factions of post-sixteen students. In the main sample respondents were invited to suggest which characteristics would be desirable for students who might be successful in their own or the other institution. It was possible thus to elicit the picture students had of their own and the competing college.

In the sixth-form college the majority of students came from the former grammar schools and independent schools, all single sex. Some fifteen percent of the entry come from the private sector and the numbers are rising. For most of these the passage is smooth, affording few choices or decisions. The boys greeted the mixed-sex college on the whole with enthusiasm, though a few diehards remained. 'I don't like having girls in the class. . . . I think my results showed I did better when I was in an all-boy school. . . . I don't think of it as a college. It will always be a grammar school to me.'

The girls had more disruption, moving to a new site, but the move appeared to be both exciting and a chance to experience something different. But many looked back with nostalgia to a regime they understood and which understood them. 'I don't really mind working with boys. They seem quite friendly but I find the place quite boring. It could be because there are so many rules and regulations. There's a lot of pressure all the time. They don't treat you like a young adult here and you can't talk to the teachers as friends and helpers . . .'

Those from secondary modern schools understandably found the transition often quite difficult, many having had little chance to follow 'O'-level courses except in lunch time, and often lacking experience of languages or separate sciences. For such students entry to the fourth year was a time of real decision at school, and they had some difficulty moving from CSE to 'A'-level work. 'They didn't think I was going to be intelligent enough to go on to 'A' levels; and I think if I'd known I was coming here I wouldn't have taken [T. Drawing]. I think I would have taken geography or history which involves a lot more writing . . .'

By contrast it is difficult to find a representative student among those doing 'A' levels at the FE college, though the numbers were larger than in many school sixth forms. They came from all the feeders including the former grammar and the independent schools but no group predominated and there were a number of mature students. They all had in common the belief that things did not go smoothly and that adjustments were always necessary. The FE college offers 'A'-level business studies, accountancy, law, drama, psychology and computer science; both colleges offer politics and sociology. A few were looking for courses: 'Well my Mum and Dad were a bit disappointed when I didn't pass the eleven-plus so I thought I'd go there [SFC] now. Then I found there was no computing – that was it! I saw accountancy was done in four technical colleges in the country and this was the nearest.'

Some former secondary modern pupils went to the sixth-form college because they felt success at sixteen-plus vindicated their failure at eleven-plus, and for many parental preference influenced their choice. 'I came here because my parents didn't want me to come to tech.' They reflected the idea that the SFC was a place where you went to work and get 'A' levels, the FE college was a place where you went to waste time.

This had disappeared from conversations with second-year students. The FE students were well aware of their image and went to great pains to show the inaccuracy of it. To a person they stressed that the FE college made considerable demands and had high expectations both of the standard of work and degree of responsibility a student would take for him or herself. They saw themselves typically as 'Someone who enjoys studying by themselves, doing a lot of work by themselves. Someone who is responsible, someone who is good at adapting because we are often being put into positions of responsibility. . . . You're just given more responsibility and I enjoy that.'

The majority saw the sixth-form college as for the more emotionally immature who needed extra emotional support to get through the 'A'-level course. Students in both colleges felt they had mastered the transition but by trial and error which wasted time and might have been helped by an introductory learning skills course. All students wanted tightness to be maintained as far as work was concerned, but the confidence and pleasure with which second-year FE students described their college was in contrast to the dissatisfaction which for some sixth-form college students had by then reached serious proportions.

Articulation, then, across the sixteen-plus divide needs to be managed both in respect of contriving greater curriculum coherence and fairness and in promoting more appropriate teacher-student relationships. The tensions and anxieties connected with moving are educative and should be recognized more, in case they are for some a painful initiation rite. The students, parents and even staff are vulnerable to images, myths, rationalizations and fantasies; all would be helped by actually setting foot in the institutions whether they have a direct interest in them or not. It would dispel illusions, deflate misleading images and allow realistic appraisal rather than the distortions of the bush telegraph. Articulation means facing up, also, to the political and social risks which genuine collaboration of institutions with different traditions and preferences would entail. It may well have to be accepted, as Macfarlane foreshadowed, albeit dimly, that there is no school-by-school or college-by-college solution to many of these difficulties. It may turn out that a step on from the comprehensive reforms of the past will come from a recognition that informal consortia or clusters of institutions will have to work together. This may in turn throw up new tasks for LEAs who might by then have lost some old ones to central government.

If it has not already done so, the centre of gravity of the sixteen-plus debate will move away from those who stay on to those who leave with no employment waiting for them. A massive piece of curriculum development is being undertaken – and moreover, on the hoof since the clients are already on the doorstep – for this latter group. Not since the question arose of what was to replace the elementary curriculum has there been anything on this scale. It will certainly not leave the conventional curriculum either pre-sixteen-plus or post-sixteen-plus unchanged. There are strong reasons for believing that the energy and leverage needed to bring about a greater articulation between the eleven–sixteen and the sixteen–nineteen phases of schooling will be generated by this much larger adjustment of the national system.

References

Cronbach, L.J. (1975) 'Beyond the two disciplines of scientific psychology', *American Psychologist, February*.

Dawson, P. (1981) *Making a Comprehensive Work*, Blackwells, London.

Duignan, P.A. (1981) 'Ethnography: an adventure in interpretive research'. *Alberta Journal of Educational Research*, Vol.27, No 3.

Ebbut, D. (1981) 'Types of school and accountability' in Elliott, J. *et al. School Accountability*, Grant McIntyre, London.

HM Inspectorate (1980) *Aspects of Secondary Education*, HMSO.

HM Inspectorate (1981) *Curriculum 11-16: A review of progress*, HMSO.

Macfarlane Review (1980) *Education 16-19*, HMSO.

Maclure, S. (1981) 'Consequences of Tebbitt', *Times Educational Supplement* 12 February 1982, No 3424.

Naylor, F. (1981) *Crisis in the Sixth Form*, Centre for Policy Studies, London.

Shaw, L.E. (1978) 'Understanding the curriculum: the approach through case studies', *Journal of Curriculum Studies*, Vol 10, No 1.

CHAPTER 6

TEACHER EDUCATION IN THE FUTURE

JOHN ISAAC

This chapter focuses on the review of teacher education, both initial and in-service, and comments on the possible advances in the next few years. Those engaged in the work are likely to feel that there are more than enough people giving them advice at present and this, linked with the difficulties of the last ten years, does little to provide a firm basis of institutional strength on which to base any developments. The cuts in intakes, amalgamations of units, redundancies of staff and renewed pressures stemming from the accountability issue, linked with the submission of courses to CNAA validation, all contribute to the position that teacher education has probably gone through more rapid and dramatic change than any section of the education system in our history. As Hencke puts in in his brief review of the period of closures – the country quickly moved from 'Education: a Framework for Expansion' to a 'Framework for Confusion' (Hencke 1978). A recent NUS pamphlet calls for that confusion to be sorted out now. 'The system is a mess, and a radical long-term review is long overdue of how teachers are educated' (NUS 1982). Documents of all kinds are appearing from all quarters discussing the possible changes and reviewing the present position (NUT 1981, CNAA 1982, DES 1981, McNamara and Ross 1982). Working parties are working and consultations are going on. It is a difficult time to suggest what will actually happen in the next phase but it is possible to consider some of the key contributions to the debate and to attempt to judge the views that have the strength to last.

Linked with any consideration of the initial education phase has to be some study of the in-service education of teachers. Here also we are seeing some contributions (Alexander and Ellis 1981), but the real moves seem to be unrecorded except in the minutes of finance committees as professional centres are closed and support provided by advisory teams is cut. In the in-service field the debate mirrors that of initial education as the discussions cover both the quantity and content of the opportunities provided. The real contrast between the two sections is that while initial teacher education is provided on a national basis and students can at present choose which polytechnic or college to attend, the teachers are much more limited to the region where they work and only the Open University is available to all. This variation in provision is considerable and revealed through the uneven provision of advisory teams and then the differences in their funds and activities and the support both human and financial that is available to the teachers. Award-bearing courses have increased dramatically in the last ten years and the new generation of CNAA Master in Education degrees are now providing graduates in the schools. The issue of full-time release from the classroom or part-time courses carried on while teaching is one that may be as much influenced by financial and political forces as by educational ones. Then there is the debate about the content and method of such courses for teachers ranging from the issues of the dissemination of curriculum materials to the provision of advanced study courses. Personal experience makes it clear that the in-service background of the teachers in a region with an extensive take-up for in-service BEd and MEd programmes has a great deal of influence on the response to students working in schools on initial teacher education courses.

To be able to engage in fruitful development in this period of relatively low morale and economic constraint the issues will have to be examined and reviewed rather than all tutors and courses being able to spend time by starting from blank sheets of paper and uninformed discussion groups. The need now is to be able to respond to the need for more primary teachers in the later 1980s with developed courses and programmes that will meet the problems that those teachers will have to react to in as effective and professional way as possible. Initial and in-service programmes have to mesh and build on each other to prepare for the issues that have already been marked out in children with special needs, education in a multicultural society, relations with industry, and the general need to improve the teaching in both primary and secondary schools.

The present position in the teacher education sector has been reviewed by McNamara and Ross (1982) and it should provide a basis from which to forecast the developments for the future. It is a sample taken in 1980 of a number of different institutions engaged in initial teacher education and in a number of aspects it supports other evidence on the state of morale in such institutions. With the high number of closures and redundancies linked with the seemingly random nature of the cut-backs in colleges and intakes, it would be expected that staff would be unlikely to feel that all was well in the teacher education world. There are several matters reported in the study which have important consequences for the development if the sample responses are typical for the scene. They examined three monotechnics, six diversified colleges, six polytechnics and two universities. There were in all 777 staff responses, 1130 student responses, and the team visited the sites.

One of the most important findings was the relationship between the type of institution and the courses. The researchers had expected that there would have evolved a type of course that was typical for a type of institution. They were not able to gain any support for this view and in fact the within-the-category differences were often more significant than those between categories. They also examined various types of course, modular, other forms of interlinked course, three years plus one for honours and other variations. However this study does not provide an answer to the question of what type of course structure is best. 'There are today many types of programme, the information uncovered in this inquiry can certainly not indicate a "best buy" nor can it nominate a model to be avoided' (McNamara and Ross 1982). Although there is no direct indication of that kind there are a number of factors which might be considered in planning the way forward.

The first matter to reflect on is the details that arose about the actual institutions and their background in the 1970s. The report considers them divided into institutional, academic and social features in the context of the dramatic changes of the recent past. It could be considered that this is now history and could be left behind as the polytechnics and colleges recovered from moves that usually took place in the early 1970s. But there have been very recent cases of numbers of staff retiring early and in polytechnics the matter is arising again in attempts to deal with budgeting difficulties, and we are still facing rapid changes. As far as the institutional matters were concerned, the assumption had been widely made that the institutional mergers would result in a real increase in resources. There was no evidence from either staff or students that they felt that resources had improved. Academically the period of growth in size of unit could have resulted in an increased range of courses being available. The study shows no evidence to support this. Socially the effect on communication resulting from amalgamations did not result in a greater social mix of students. In sixty percent of the students in amalgamated institutions the three closest friends were also BEd students. This does not mean that there are no cases in which the resources did improve and the availability of courses increase and clearly there are cases in which this is the result. Working in a multisite pattern was said to produce difficulties in coherence and problems of travel.

The section on modular and interlocked (in which parts of courses were shared with other degrees) degree structures is interesting in relation to some of the recent comments by the HMI on the pattern of courses. But again the results are no real help in clarifying the position in relation simply to the structure. 'It is clear that interlocking and modularization need not in themselves lead to fragmentation but that coherence has to be planned for rather than allowed to happen' (McNamara and Ross 1982).

The section on staff has been much reported. Staff are supposedly largely male, middle aged and with over ten years' experience in the same place and little experience of relevant teaching. However, the figures given for those with no relevant experience in the study show a high figure for nursery and infants and a very high figure (eighty-seven percent) for middle schools. Given the relatively low response rate in some cases, there arise a lot of other questions that require answers before this evidence can be accepted as helpful. For example, seventy-four percent of the sample who responded were men, while most of those teaching nursery courses would be likely to be women and the same would apply to infants courses. Also it does not follow that staff with junior school and secondary school experience cannot successfully teach on middle school courses. The real pattern may not be as bad as the report suggests but there is some cause for concern. As the report suggests, the strength of many college and polytechnic programmes is thought to be in the relevance to primary teaching and there are many lecturers whose experience is secondary. The present swing towards an increase in provision for primary courses is likely to increase this particular difficulty and push staff further along the deskilling continuum.

This, with the general difficulties that education faces and the history of teacher education in the immediate past, may explain the response that the researchers found when examining morale. 'This material conveys the impression that the majority of 'rank and file' staff are worried, angry, frustrated and generally uneasy about the changes in teacher training, their own work and their futures' (McNamara and Ross 1982).

The general conclusions from the report are that there is no prescribed successful way of educating teachers. There are moves towards applied school-focused work but with staff that this study believes lack relevant experience. The relationship of theory and practice has to be planned for carefully as does coherence in modular programmes and assessment should become more experimental. Developments described in the book are being carried out with at least some staff who have low morale and feel that administration is hampering rather than helping. A major item relevant to this section is that the authors report that the retaining of both in-service and initial education in the same institution is an essential feature. *The BEd Degree and Its Future* does provide indicators of the present position. There are features which, while they may reflect the position in those institutions in the sample, are known not to be universal. For example, in several places the restriction of job to teaching is brought out while it is now clear that BEd graduates are successful in gaining many other types of employment. The points for the future are limited in this study and focus on a suggestion that the nature and scope of teacher education should be fixed so that those involved can plan a future both for their institution and themselves. But the McNamara and Ross study has to be looked at in relation to many other contributions to the debate.

There are two closely linked aspects of the position of teacher education which are receiving much attention at present. The first is the debate about the approach to developing the performance of the probationer and experienced teacher in the classroom and the other is the content of the complete programme which should be followed by the student in a BEd or PGCE programme. We have reached a stage of development at which some plans will be made to develop the teacher education system but it remains unclear quite how that will take place.

It seems significant that the NUT's 1981 document on policy for teacher education was titled 'Initial and In-Service BEd Degrees'.

> The Union is concerned that institutions should offer both forms of training as this can help initial training programmes to be related more closely to actual conditions in schools and the needs of pupils as perceived by experienced teachers. (NUT 1981)

This view is, however, linked with that of the then president, Jack Chambers, in a paper presented at a conference mounted by the Teacher Education Study Group (Chambers 1981) in which there is a full development of the concept of advanced courses for teachers which would be linked to the teacher's Vocational Self-Construct. The argument develops the idea of phases in the career of the teacher with the first phase being a training/learning grade that would last for six years and the whole programme being related to a review of the professionalism of teachers and a new structure for the educational system. A main item in the programme is the need for a new type of advanced study for teachers. 'Such a programme of professional enhancement could include school-focused/school-based masters degrees arising from and related to the professional work of the teacher in the school' (Chambers 1981).

This produces the issue of what sort of work would relate to the classroom and brings us into the debate being carried on about initial teacher education and the skills component of the courses. Chambers is well aware of the difficulties.

> Many educationalists have profound misunderstandings as to the nature of skill which, probably, have their roots in a preference for theoretical and academic disputation. All too often this results in a contempt for practical activities which solve problems, and this seems to be manifest throughout the education system. (Chambers 1981)

In 1955 Katz described the three basic developable skills needed by an administrator and these illuminate the ideas of Chambers as he develops his views of skills in the context of teaching. Katz describes his three skills as technical, human and conceptual. It is the technical skill which would include understanding of a proficiency in methods, procedures or techniques. Human skill is used as the category encompassing the ability to work as a group member and conceptual skill is defined as the ability to see the enterprise as a whole. Chambers defines his skills as ways of organizing actions in order to achieve predicted or anticipated results.

Stones, in various papers and books (1972, 1979, 1981, 1982), has, over recent years, developed his views of how pedagogy might be advanced in initial and in-service education and has been able to put his ideas to trial in Liverpool. In a recent paper circulated by CNAA, written originally for the PGCE panel, he explains his position and discusses what he sees as the two main aspects of initial teacher education – the skills of teaching (pedagogy) and the context of teaching. There has been considerable experiment with Competency-Based Teacher Education in the USA and aspects have been incorporated in various courses in this country. However, while micro-teaching and other competency-based approaches are being used the full-scale programmes of teacher preparation designed by some American universities have been subject to criticism and a critical review of these approaches has been published (Stones 1976). The *World Year Book of Education* (1980) also contains a number of papers which consider some of these approaches.

At present a number of polytechnics and colleges are trying out more detailed schedules for feedback to students and assessment, and the CNAA research on School Experience on Initial BEd Degrees (McCulloch 1979) includes examples. There are then programmes such as that developed at Nottingham for the Teacher Education Project which presents a structured course based on a consideration of the needs of PGCE students during their year.

Stones, in *Psychopedagogy* and in a recent paper (Stones 1981), bases his approach on an analysis of the learning processes needed to enable the student to learn. In this his approach is basically psychological but he makes plain that he is suggesting an applied study. 'As with the pupils he teaches, the acid test of his learning is whether he can apply the principles he has learned in practice, in the student teacher's case to practical teaching' (Stones 1981). So that instead of a programme in which the skills needed are analysed from outside and applied to the student, here the student learns to analyse the teaching process and devise action which will aid learning in the individual in the classroom. Assessment of the student then involves assessment of the effectiveness of the learning in the pupil. The example given for the action of such a programme brings us back to the in-service arena as it is carried out in Liverpool by involving teachers on an MEd programme who themselves are studying the process of teaching for learning. Thus, the student has the support of teachers who are aware of the difficulties and advantages of the approach although there still has to be a determined effort to encourage the support of the education system in such a programme. Here, then, we seem to have an advanced course of study for teachers which is focused on teaching and which also forms a basis for a programme on initial teacher education.

The other aspect of the courses which seems important is that termed 'context' by Stones. He suggests that as part of their work in schools the students should carry out ethnographic studies of classrooms and schools in action. An interesting paper by Sarason (1979) puts forward a strong case for the relationship between this type of understanding of the school and job satisfaction. After a study of what his students had gained from a period in school on teaching practice, he comments: 'These students came away from practice teaching almost as ignorant or naïve about the culture and organization of the school as they were when they began' (Sarason 1979). The rest of the paper develops the relationship between motivation and job satisfaction of teachers and their awareness of the context of their teaching. The ethnographic studies suggested would help to contribute to this build-up of understanding. The result would be in the Stones plan that students would actually teach less in schools but study more. As he points out, this would lead to some difficulties with the relationships with the teachers. One of our real difficulties with the institution-based courses is the relative shortage of material that students can refer to that provides some of this context. Even that which is available is sometimes American and is often missing from college and faculty libraries (Smith and Keith 1971, Smith and Geoffrey 1968, Cusick 1973). English studies such as *Inside the Primary Classroom* are relatively rare, or were until recently, and are mostly based on secondary schools (Willis 1977, Corrigan 1979). One of the most encouraging things in the consideration of the future is the way in which some of the studies now available (Delamont 1976, Woods 1980, Barton and Meighan 1979), based on studies of classrooms in action, are encouraging teachers on advanced courses to carry out similar investigations.

One problem for this aspect of teacher education, especially in initial courses, is the complexity of contexts which are now in existence. Students preparing to work with the age range of seven to eleven may meet many different types of school and system structure, and the recent abandoning of middle schools by some LEAs illustrates the way in which such arrangements are changing very rapidly. The micro-classroom scene forming the basis for some of the texts cited above remains relevant, but the total context changes. These changes have to be placed against the present suggestions from the DES that teacher education be much more age-range specific and subject specific as well. At one level this presents no difficulties, as the detailed study of processes in the classroom and the focus on the conceptual learning of the individual child remain common features of probably all subjects and wide age ranges. They do, however, present another dilemma which leads us into the total programme of the initial teacher education course.

A working party on the BEd for primary teachers, established by CNAA, has carried out considerable work reviewing and studying the present position and needs for the future. There was a conference for those involved in such courses and the papers were circulated to all institutions linked to CNAA. A subsequent discussion paper (CNAA 1982) was circulated. During the same period, the DES produced statements about the content of teacher education. The historical perspective here has to be limited but includes the pressure from DES at the time of reorganization of teacher education institutions to eliminate the isolation of their students from the rest of higher education. This was part of the rationale for the move towards polytechnic faculties and interlocked courses.

Placing BEd students in courses that were part of BA or BSc degrees was one response to the criticism that students were isolated and standards suspect. In this move to open up education it was often thought an advantage to offer a wider range of courses of study to these students as part of the liberalization process and this sometimes was effected by setting up or joining modular systems. Here students had a wide range of academic studies open to them and in some cases any subject in the modular programme was accepted, providing as many as twenty-nine different fields of study. The traditional programme for BEd includes the study of education, courses related to the teaching of subjects, teaching experience in schools, and the other component of a course in an accepted degree subject, such as biology. The terms used are interesting in the history of the development, as this last is still sometimes termed the 'main' subject or the 'academic' subject. The developments in the 1970s retained the ideology that this aspect of the course was essential for the development of the student, and although such a subject might be taught in schools, this was not the reason for its inclusion. This followed from a long-standing ideology but also from the need to justify such courses for students preparing to teach very young children. We now have a renewed 'theory into practice' debate which not only encompasses the whole area of the study of teaching and education, but the DES is now suggesting that the other subject component of a BEd degree should be specifically related to the teaching career of the intending teacher. This is linked with the concept of the 'consultant' in primary schools. Another aspect of this debate is the need that there seems to be for teachers to be flexible if primary schools are to continue to operate in cases of falling numbers and static staff, and also in the cases of students attempting to obtain first posts. Clearly, if subject background is to be linked to the teaching position in a specific way we need to enter into manpower planning for teaching in more detail than we have so far. One difficulty that arises is that there is no power to coerce students into courses in particular subjects. We may well need more teachers in primary schools with the equivalent of a mathematics degree but we consistently fail to recruit such students into the BEd programmes in sufficient numbers. Experience of the products of modular degrees with wide-ranging subject courses is that those with degrees involving study of areas not taught in primary schools are equally able to gain posts as those with history or English as a subject and they do quite as well in practical teaching and are successful as teachers.

The CNAA papers ask for a reconsideration of the programmes for those preparing for a teaching career which responds to the needs of the next ten years rather than the last. The preparation aspect of the BEd courses has come under considerable pressure from changes which result in the need for further areas to be introduced in some way. The Undergraduate Initial Training Board has accepted a statement about the place of language in the BEd degrees and all the institutions concerned have copies. Various other subject panels have some form or guideline about the suitable contact hours for various subject areas – termed the bids-for-time approach. There has to be some response in teacher education in general to the issues of education in a multi-cultural society, and the place of children with special needs in the ordinary schools and relations with industry.

In many ways, the time is right for teacher education to change. Pressures on schools and classrooms from those concerned with accountability and effectiveness link with a feeling within the teaching force that all is not right. Schools like Stantonbury seem to need a new type of teacher, just as the Humanities Curriculum Project introduced a new style of teaching. The Royal Society of Arts programme of competitions for the Capability Awards reflects the mood that more can be done to educate in ways that go towards helping the young to be more self-sufficient. New books suggest new approaches to the curriculum that need a more confident and different type of teacher (Hargreaves 1982). Other studies reveal that primary schools may not be as we thought they were in the way that teaching really takes place (Galton 1980). Innovations in teacher education were well reviewed some years ago (Taylor 1978) and the methods described there are still being investigated but the general field of teacher education has yet to build any real common approach or platform for the work. I suggest that we may have reached a stage at which such a development could be based on the literature and transformed into action in this country in a way that would develop a new generation of teachers for the next ten years to deal more effectively with the issues that we already know we face. The basis for such development is already prepared, in that various educators have put forward ideas which, when combined, can form a way to implement such a development. Already there exists a Pedagogy Special Interest Group of the British Educational Research Association which collaborates with the Teacher Education Study Group of the Society for Research into Higher Education.

There are a series of papers which form the basis for a re-thinking of the programmes of teacher education and developments in the programmes of in-service education which link with these concepts. Much of the recent thinking repeats the view that relationships with the schools and the teachers are essential to any real development of schools or classroom-based work in initial teacher education, so the two levels of work have to be linked. The third element is that of the tutors themselves. Taylor (1978) and others have pointed out that there is no form of education for tutors working in courses on the study of teaching in the classroom. The *Journal of Education for Teaching* is established and the interest groups have been mentioned, but the institutions that have made progress in the development of these courses have been involved in internal staff development to enable tutors to con- tribute fully. There are now opportunities to recruit a new generation of tutors into colleges and faculties as primary teachers with considerable study background, and, in some cases, Doctorates, based on the study of classrooms, become available.

A number of contributions to this development have been made in the recent past, both in this country and in America. Bone (1980) suggested, after looking at a number of programmes in many countries, that the theoretical elements had been reduced. 'The general trend, however, is toward some reduction in the theoretical parts of initial training, partly because it has been criticized so much and partly because it is felt that some of it can be provided more relevantly at a later in-service stage.'

Stones has expanded his views of the basis for the education of teachers over a number of years and in the last paper he includes some of the views of Zeichner and Teitelbaum (1982) in which they suggest a programme designed to encourage the development of 'reflective teaching', a concept that they base on the ideas of Dewey. This type of teacher has, they suggest, three characteristics. First, open-mindedness, which refers to the critical appraisal of the rationales of the teaching they observe and undertake. Then there is an attitude of responsibility, which leads to careful consideration of the consequences of the technique of teaching in use. The third attitude is that of whole-heartedness, so that the open-mindedness and responsibility become the central components in the life of the reflective teacher. The course they propose involves reducing the amount of time that a student actually spends teaching and using the time in inquiry-orientated experi- ences that are focused on the classroom. The main purpose of this work, which is followed up in seminars on a regular basis, is to move the student from the position of seeing the school experience as focused on survival.

They put forward a well-argued case that survival-orientated programmes are likely to limit the teacher to that approach for ever, while the reflective teacher inquiry-orientated programme does not exclude the teaching skills element. This approach links well with that suggested by McNamara and Desforge (1978), where they suggest that initial teacher education should be based on a research approach towards the objectification of the craft knowledge of the teacher in the classroom, although many artefacts, such as schemes of work, may be used in the exercise. 'Published schemes, work cards and other materials could be examined, together with critical literature, but the focus of the debate would be the task-under-classroom-constraints.'

The Chambers thesis is extensively developed to include a proposed restructuring of the salary scales and the implementation of regular reviews of teaching staff out of which programmes of study would be developed. An essential feature in his proposals is that of a contract between those involved, so that not only would the trainer undertake to cater for the expressed needs of the teacher, but also the teacher would recognize that a programme might involve him in changing not only his techniques, but possibly his values. He is focusing on courses of advanced study, degree and masters degree. The NUT publication also makes the point that many of the established courses may not really provide what teachers would most value. The requirement of an honours degree for entry to a masters degree also causes some difficulty. The demand for advanced study by teachers remains high, although very uneven, in the country as a whole. There is a suggestion of the need for an award-bearing course which would come between a first degree and a masters.

These ideas of inquiry-based initial courses, linked with teachers' programmes, as described by Stones in Liverpool, can be considered in conjunction with the extensive plans of Chambers to set up a revolutionary approach to salary and progress in the profession. The schools need a class of teacher who is 'reflective' in Zeichner's terms, and providing a school-based support for an initial programme incorporating the inquiry-orientated work. Here student, tutor and teacher would co-operate in work which would move the student beyond the position of survival but also provide a type of research assistant for the teacher on the teaching programme and produce material that would feed back into the tutor-led college-based part of the work, which might also match with the teacher's work. The IT-Inset programme contains some elements of this approach and it is necessary to consider some of the practical issues that would arise.

With the proposed expansion of places for primary education, there might well be difficulties in recruiting a sufficient number of teachers to contribute to such work. The suggestion here is that there would be a diploma in teaching studies that would be completed entirely by course work, which would form the entry to a masters programme in teaching studies which would then be rather more researched based and demanding. The total programme might take four years and the teacher could be engaged with students during that time. This would, of course, mean that those teachers would be working with students for a significant number of years but the classes would probably change and in any case the concept of school experience will have changed to the advantage of the children. This approach would come within the suggestions of Chambers as the course would be very school based, and decided by some form of contract. The school work would involve the ethnographic study described by Zeichner and Teitelbaum and also Stones, and would lead to the reflective teacher. The attitude of the initial student to the programme and teaching is of great importance, and it seems likely that this work in close collaboration with key teachers would contribute to a wide professional view of teaching and lead to an extended professionalism.

There remain two areas of difficulty that can easily be foreseen with such a programme – the tutors and the advisers. Tutors are very largely untrained for their work, although large numbers have recently attained higher degress. This scheme would need skills in analysis and counselling that few higher degree programmes include – a possible exception being the Sussex University MA, described by Hewton in Alexander and Ellis (1981). There are two ways to ameliorate this situation that are available. The first is to train the tutors, and this is the case in those institutions like Ulster Polytechnic and Sunderland Polytechnic, where new developments in teaching skills courses have been introduced. What is needed, however, if the change is to take place in time for the forecast expansion in primary initial education, is a national impetus from a body like the DES to set up intensive programmes that might be modelled on the COSMOS pattern and act as an introduction to some of the skills needed. The other approach is to recruit from those teachers who have already completed MEd and PhD programmes which have detailed studies of classrooms as their focus There are now teachers in primary schools with this kind of background, and although the numbers are few, they continue to grow. The next difficulty would be the role of the advisory teams in the programme, as such extensive work with teachers, students and tutors would clearly be of interest to them, and the place that they would take in relation to the work and the results is a vital element in the improvement of the system. The teachers, after several years' study of this kind, would be best employed as class teachers and part-time consultants on teaching. They would have the background of the study, the skills developed through counselling students, the contact with the research, and the credibility to other teachers. They would in that way extend the advisory service considerably and be a resource that an LEA could use to improve teaching in the teachers' classrooms: a task that the small advisory teams simply cannot carry out in the time they have. What, then, of the advisory teams in this pattern? If the increase in teachers with classroom-relevant higher degrees continues to expand as it is doing at present, with several new CNAA MEd degrees being approved each year, the adviser will need either to become a specialist in a narrow aspect of teaching or qualify through a similar programme of further study. The reason that few advisers at present are attending higher degree programmes is that they find it difficult to gain release from their work, which frequently would cut into the time of even a part-time degree programme with their evening commitments, and also that they cannot usually find a degree programme which is relevant to their needs. The type of programmes suggested here for the attached teachers could be adapted to meet the needs of advisers if it were possible for them to carry out the work. Unless something is done for the advisory teams, they will find themselves in a position where highly qualified classroom teachers with classroom-focused degree courses will need their help less, and their role could become even more administrative. This would be a loss which the system could not afford.

It may be thought that validating bodies are a constraint on the kind of development described. The new degrees approved by CNAA indicate that this is unlikely to be a difficulty in cases where tutors and teachers have really planned a programme carefully. However, the recent papers from the DES and HMI, which seem, at this stage, to propose a restriction on the subject background of students approaching initial teacher education, and to be attempting to fix allocation of resources in courses rather specifically, may be a difficulty. As the proposals do not necessarily require more time in schools than programmes do now, but suggest a different use of the time, fitting the developments into modular or interlocked programmes should offer no more difficulty than is present already. However, the reflective teacher model will permeate the rest of the programme, dissolving the boundary between theory and practice into a course of practical analysis and theory, but this may be more difficult for faculties to get accepted within their colleges and polytechnics than at CNAA. To help in overcoming such resistance there would seem to be a need for some active support from both validating bodies and the DES.

References

Alexander, R.J. and Ellis, J.W. (1981) *Advanced Study for Teachers*. Teacher Education Study Group, Nafferton Books.

Barton, L. and Meighan, R. (1979) *Schools, Pupils and Deviance*, Nafferton Books, Driffield.

Bone, T. (19801) 'Current trends in initial training', in Hoyle, E. and Megarry, J.L. (eds) *The World Yearbook of Education*, Kogan Page, London.

CNAA (1982) 'Initial BEd Courses for the Early and Middle Years: Some issues for discussion', Primary/Middle Working Party discussion paper.

Corrigan, P. and Chambers, J. (1981) 'The role and function of advanced study in professional development', in Ellis, R.J. and Ellis, J.W. *Advanced Study for Teachers*.

Corrigan, P. (1979) *Schooling the Smash Street Kids*, Macmillan.

Cusick, P.A. (1973) *Inside High School. The Student's World*, Holt Rinehart and Winston, New York.

Delamont, S. (1976) *Interaction in the Classroom*, Methuen, London.

DES (1981) 'Teacher Training and the Secondary School', HMSO.

Galton, M., Simon, B., Croll, P. (1980) *Inside the Primary Classroom*, Routledge & Kegan Paul, London.

Hargreaves, D. (1982) *The Challenge for the Comprehensive School Culture, Curriculum and Community*, Routledge & Kegan Paul, London.

Hencke, D. (1978) *Colleges in Crisis*, Penguin, Harmondsworth.

Hoyle, E. and Megarry, J. (eds) (1980) *The World Yearbook of Education*, Professional Development of Teachers, Kogan Page, London.

Katz, R.L. (1955) 'Skills of an effective administrator', *Harvard Business Review*, January – Feburary, pp. 33-42.

McCulloch, M. (1979) 'School experience in initial BEd/BEd honours degrees validated by the Council for National Academic Awards, CNAA, London

McNamara, D.R. and Desforges, C. (1978) 'The social sciences, teacher education and the objectification of craft knowledge, *British Journal of Teacher Education*.

McNamara D.R. and Ross, A.M. (1982) *The BEd Degree and Its Future*, School of Education, University of Lancaster.

Megarry, J. (1980) 'Selected innovations in methods of teacher education' in Hoyle and Megarry *World Yearbook of Education*.

NUS (1982) *Teacher Education – time to sort out the mess*, NUS, February.

NUT (1981) 'Initial and in-service BEd degrees'. A policy statement issued by the National Union of Teachers.

Orlosky, D. (1980) 'Skill training for teachers', in Hoyle, E. and Megarry, J. *World Yearbook of Education*.

Sarason, S.B. (1978-1979), 'Again, the preparation of teachers: competency and job satisfaction', *Interchange*, Vol 10, No 1.

Smith, L.M. and Geoffrey, W. (1968) *The Complexities of an Urban Classroom: An analysis toward a general theory of teaching*, Holt Rinehart & Winston, New York.

Smith, L.M. and Keith, P.M. (1971) *Anatomy of Educational Innovation*, Wiley.

Stones, E. and Morris, S. (1972) *Teaching Practice*, Methuen, London.

Stones, E. (1976) 'Teaching teaching skills', *British Journal of Teacher Education* Vol 2, No 1, January, pp. 59-70.

Stones, E. (1979) *Psychopedagogy: Psychological theory and the practice of teaching*, Methuen, London.

Stones, E. (1981) 'Teacher education and pedagogy', *Journal of Education for Teaching* 7.3, pp. 219-230.

Stones, E. (1982) 'Some notes on practical teaching with special reference to the PGCE course', CNAA.

Taylor, W. (1978) *Research and Reform in Teacher Education*, NFER.

Willis, P. (1977) *Learning to Labour: How working class kids get working class jobs*, Saxon House, Farnborough.

Woods, P. (ed) (1980) *Teacher Strategies, Explorations in the Sociology of the School*, Croom Helm, London.

Zeichner, and Teitelbaum, K. 'Personalized and inquiry-orientated teacher education: An analysis of two approaches to the development of curriculum for field-based experiences', *Journal of Education for Teaching* 8:2, pp. 95-117.

CHAPTER 7

EVOLUTIONARY TRENDS IN POSTGRADUATE INITIAL TEACHER TRAINING

JIM EGGLESTON

When most PGCE students were destined to teach in the grammar schools, in which they had spent seven formative years, and when these schools in terms of their administrative arrangements, curricula, goals and expectations were then as similar as a clone, professional preparation reflected this invariance. PGCE courses typically consisted of a teaching methods component narrowly focused on the discipline with which each student was associated by virtue of his degree and which he would teach. Such teaching 'methods' were rarely if ever presented as a generalizable pedagogy. The theoretical part of the course usually consisted of sociological, psychological and philosophical considerations of schools, their inhabitants and their *raison d'être*. These aspects of the PGCE course tended to have a life somewhat detached from the 'methods' component. The making of connections between the practice of teaching, the profession of teacher, life in schools and the theoretical constructs of supporting disciplines was striven for but difficult to achieve. Few would claim to have achieved a productive symbiosis between theory and practice. Two conflicts resisted resolution. The first was the dilemma faced by the lecturer in a discipline. Should he, in the limited time available, attempt to induct students into its form of disciplined inquiry or limit his contribution to describing those theoretical constructs which relate particularly to the students' experience of schools, teachers and children which they will have during the course and their first year in the teaching profession? The second is the partly logistical problem of giving the students time to reflect on their school experiences in a way which facilitates the use of disciplined theory to give meaning to these experiences.

Such issues as these outlined above were perennial problems before the coming of comprehensive secondary education. Now the PGCE student will typically, during the practical part of the course and later in his first post, be faced with a potentially bewildering diversity of schools which vary in their administrative arrangements, curricular provision, teaching systems, in the kind and amount of pastoral provision and in the methods used to assess and communicate pupils' progress. This increase in the complexity of the professional responsibilities and tasks of teachers is one of the factors which has led to 'widespread agreement that the PGCE course should henceforward focus sharply, perhaps even exclusively, on the *professional preparation* of students for their first teaching appointments'. As the author of the UCET working party document (UCET 1979), Professor Paul Hirst emphasizes professional preparation is not meant to convey 'training of a narrow, routine, mechanical kind'. Quite the reverse is indicated by his description of 'the mark of a professional' which is 'to have a sound knowledge of the circumstances in which he or she is called to operate, the ability to judge responsibly the appropriateness of various possible lines of action, the skills and dispositions to act effectively, the ability to assess the outcome of actions and the capacity intelligently to adapt future practice accordingly'. In order to achieve these professional competences Hirst points to the requirements of 'serious study of what is currently known about the many factors that affect teachers' professional concerns especially those of teaching and learning, and by careful training in the skills and personal qualities involved in the application of this knowledge'. If the PGCE courses are to prepare students for the duties and responsibilities of class teacher, member of a schools' staff and member of the teaching profession, then four 'still very generally expressed goals' must, among others, be achieved, according to the working party. These are:

a An understanding of the subject (taught) and its place in the secondary school curriculum;

b An understanding of the learning of the subject by secondary school pupils;

c The understanding, skills and personal qualities necessary to teaching the subject to secondary school pupils;

d   The understanding, skills and personal qualities necessary to the exercise of the forms of classroom discipline and control appropriate for the teaching of the subject in secondary schools.

Despite the facts that these goals are limited to 'teaching the subject' and they lack the specificity necessary to generate strategies for their achievement they indicate two important features of courses of professional preparation. The first is the diversity of knowledge and understanding required and the second the variety of intellectual and social skills which must be acquired by practice in real teaching environments so that students become progressively disposed to act appropriately.

Under what conditions can students acquire the knowledge, understanding, intellectual and social skills necessary effectively to pursue a career in teaching? What experiences will equip them to develop the dispositions and personal qualities which enable them to apply this understanding and these skills so as to teach their pupils with increasingly beneficial effects? These are the central questions raised by the UCET working party. Listening to lectures, reading appropriate literature, tutorial discussion, undertaking written assignments, all according to prescriptions exclusively determined by the training institution, plus teaching practice(s) conducted largely independent of the institution, are by implication rejected as a potentially effective set of procedures. This is not to deny that each of these elements in the repertoire of training institutions can make a useful contribution to professional training. It is to deny that these elements individually or collectively are likely to be sufficient to achieve the elaborated model of the functioning professional teacher set out in the document. As the author states, 'if the study of educational theory is left dissociated from the development of practice judgements, skills, and personal qualities it cannot be expected to contribute significantly to professional preparation.' It would seem that the kind of teaching strategy nearest to the vision of the working party is one in which the central feature consists of experience in schools, initially limited, possibly including some teaching but under controlled and carefully monitored conditions followed by reflection and analysis. Whatever theory was necessary to give meaning to this experience would be introduced when it was required. Progress through the course would be marked by an increase in the extent and diversity of tasks undertaken by students in schools; by the development of a coherent body of practical knowledge with an increasing willingness to use this knowledge to define and solve pedagogical problems; and the growth of cohesive bodies of theoretical constructs which give forms to educational knowledge and facilitate tests for both the truth *and usefulness* of such knowledge. The orientation of students will thus be empirical. Their tasks will be to define problems, acquire data especially of their own performance and dispositions, to speculate, to theorize, to subject ideas to 'field' testing.

The problems for the course designers and tutors are how to select and sequence the kinds of experiences which facilitate both developments, how to divide the labour between school teachers and training tutors, and the selection of schools and tutors who are willing to engage in professional training when conducted along these lines. Whatever arrangements might be made to use second-hand evidence of classroom behaviour, including video-tape, nothing can replace first-hand experience as a means for developing those skills, dispositions and personal qualities which are goals of professional training as described in the working party's document.

New relationships with schools, a collaborative exploration of ends, means, forms of practical training and pedagogically relevant theories undertaken by tutors and school teachers will be essential if those tentative steps towards new methods of professional training are to be sustained and developed.

The block-teaching practice with its demand for whole-class, whole-lesson teaching almost from the start is perceived by students to be part-training, part-assessment, but mainly a test of their ability to survive. Models of teaching half remembered from their own school days or acquired by unsystematic observation of their qualified colleagues may serve as survival tactics. Organized critical reflection on teaching strategies and tactics and the evaluation of alternative procedures can only be undertaken under conditions which guarantee some measure of security and then only after appropriate training. These conditions do not exist on a typical teaching practice often sandwiched between two 'theory' terms. Many departments are experimenting with various forms of school attachment over a time scale longer than a term, others collaborate with their school teacher colleagues so as to use the school as a 'laboratory' in which to explore pedagogical problems, others conduct some of their method-work sessions in schools with selected classes. There seems to be an increasing awareness of the problems of how to build in to a professional training regime gradualness of exposure, systematic observation, controlled experience, critical reflection, investigation and evaluation and the means for relating practical experience to theory.

The UCET Report considered, rightly, that a 'one year course cannot possibly hope to deal at all adequately with the knowledge, skills and qualities that professional preparation . . . involves.' Furthermore, that 'courses are at present forced to be selective even among . . . obviously necessary topics.' These statements were made with reference to a particular list of topics with which not everyone might agree. However this may be, the time required is less a function of which topics to include than it is a function of the methods of professional preparation chosen. If training is to be centrally the development of professional knowledge and understanding in a way which facilitates the concomitant growth of skills and dispositions to teach effectively and ultimately the achievement of a professional autonomy to implement methods which are theoretically defensibly and demonstrably effective, more time is certainly essential, and furthermore the structure of courses and the roles of tutors and school teachers need to be critically examined.

One of the tasks facing those involved in teacher training may be illustrated by reference to an investigation of the teaching behaviour of student teachers undertaken at Nottingham four years ago (Dreyfus and Eggleston 1980). The incidence of certain kinds of 'intellectual' transactions between student teachers of physics, chemistry and biology and their pupils were monitored on six occasions during the spring term teaching practice. These transactions included different kinds of teachers' questions, classified in seven categories including those demanding recall of information, speculation, observation, experimental design and so on. Similarly the kinds of statements the student teachers made and the directives they gave were recorded. In addition pupil-initiated transactions were recorded such as pupil consultations for a variety of purposes and pupils' questions. In a previous study (Eggleston, Galton and Jones 1976) similar data had been obtained for experienced teachers thus facilitating a comparison. The rather surprising result was that early in their teaching practice student teachers of science, especially of the physical sciences, behaved, as far as the instruments we used could detect, in ways very similar to experienced teachers. Moreover differences in 'style' between student teachers of all three sciences were not significant. As the teaching practice proceeded it became apparent that the student teachers behaved less and less like experienced teachers. The differences progressively made manifest were increases in 'factual transactions', i.e., more questions requiring recall, more factual statements, more directives to find facts, and of the pupil-initiated transaction more consultations and questions directed to the acquisition of information. There was conspicuously less activity in the speculative and experimental design categories. The impression created was that as the teaching practice advanced student teachers increasingly engaged in 'safe' transactions, i.e., those least likely to precipitate problems of management and control of classroom relationships.

These findings could be accounted for if one supposed that the teaching behaviour of student teachers was the result of a modelling process. Students may bring to their training a model of teacher behaviour based on their own experience of teaching when they were pupils. Thirteen years of exposure to teaching, seven of them in secondary schools, had equipped them with models of teaching which provided them with a set of teacher behaviours for emulation, supposing them to represent the key to successful performance.

The observed regression to increasingly fact-acquisition-dominated transactions may be due to the risks evidently involved in the transfer of initiative into the hands of pupils when they are involved in speculation, experimental design, indeed any open-ended activity for which the student teacher may feel unprepared and in which engagement might risk a loss of what they construe as authority or control.

Another interesting finding of this inquiry is the progressive emergence of distinctive styles for physical sciences (chemistry and physics) on the one hand and biology on the other. The former both with experienced teachers and student teachers has a problem-solving but essentially convergent character, the latter is much more dominated by 'factual' transactions. Other evidence suggests that this phenomenon is constant across cultures. Studies in both Canada (Hacker 1979) and Australia (Reid and Patrick 1981) have demonstrated similar differences between physical and life sciences.

If there is substance in these speculations there are serious implications for the initial training of teachers. Students entering professional training may enter their course with a model or stereotype of how teachers behave. During their course they may attend selectively to those experiences which are consistent with this model and which reinforce aspects of it. Their commitment to teaching methods to which they were exposed as pupils (perhaps ineffective or including features which cannot be defended by psychological or pedagogical theory) may result in their rejection of critical theory so as to leave their model intact. It might be that the common phenomenon that students perceive 'teaching practice as the most valuable part of the PGCE course' has precisely these origins.

The difference between the teaching behaviours of physical sciences and biology teachers might be explained in terms of difference between the two disciplines, the former having a convergent problem-solving character related to the rich array of algorithms available, the latter having a more descriptive character being less well endowed with explanatory theories.

Alternatively it may be that the cultural traditions of teaching these disciplines determine how teachers behave. It has been argued that these differences may relate to the nature of demands made in examinations, 'O' level and CSE. If this is the case it would provide powerful homeostatic influence on teaching methods.

Given some measurable success in terms of these goals, i.e., success in public examinations, even if alternative methods might be more effective, considerable professional courage would be required to test them. The resistance of the teaching profession to change has been well documented by those who have studied the dissemination data on curriculum development projects.

These models, transmitted by a sort of cultural imprinting, may have been effective with the pupil groups in which potential graduates found themselves but less successful with other pupil groups. Those same teachers may have varied their teaching strategies and tactics for example, according to the achievement level of pupils. The likelihood is that potential graduates would be denied the opportunity of experiencing adaptive variation of their 'model's' style of interaction.

However this may be, there seems little to commend a process of transmission which does not incorporate critical reflection on professional practice, systematic variation of practice in response to different demands and a rationale which provides both theoretical and empirical grounds for professional decisions.

If the findings of this inquiry and the interpretations placed upon this as generalizable across school subjects are true, it is possible to attempt to account for attitudes of PGCE students to existing courses and to speculate about the effects of evident trends in the evolution of PGCE courses.

It is interesting to speculate how far new and evolving structures of PGCE courses for secondary school teachers are providing for this rational/critical approach to teaching and to try to identify those elements which may still subscribe to or even reinforce the cultural-imprinting mechanism. According to Reid and Patrick, Taylor (1969) raised what seems to be essentially the same question in 1969 when he stated that 'there was very little research evidence concerning the effects of (PGCE) course training methods upon trainee styles. He also argued that it remained unknown whether trainees acquire or use the teaching styles which they themselves experienced . . . in their formative or training years.' These authors also point out that in rather more than a decade which followed there has been both a growth of public knowledge about the contents of PGCE courses and of research into various aspects of these courses. This increase in knowledge has been accompanied by fairly widespread and sometimes fundamental changes in the intentions, content and organization and processes of PGCE courses.

The dimensions along which change has occurred seem to be the theory-practice relationship, and the training institution-school axis.

It would appear that the disciplines which purport to explain the phenomena of institutionalized education are less likely nowadays to be given separate consideration such as they might be given if the intention was to induct students into the concepts and methods of the disciplines. Instead each discipline may be, so to speak, asked to examine a series of practical issues in education from its unique perspective, to show students how through its concepts it can inform judgements on these issues and by reference to its methods of inquiry establish claims to validity.

One can also detect the emergence of another species of theory whose relationship to practice is more direct. This might properly be described as pedagogical theory, an example of which might crystallize out from Bruner's ideas about 'theories of instruction', from Gagne's learning hierarchies, studies of concept formation, classroom interaction studies, or Wragg *et al.*'s work on classroom management. To my mind there is no doubt that many inquiries conducted during recent years contribute to pedagogical theory no matter under what flags of convenience they originally set sail.

The evidence from PGCE courses which I have examined persuades me that the adaptability of tutors in the contributory disciplines of education has yielded approaches which are both academically respectable and professionally relevant.

There is less evidence that PGCE subject method tutors are able or willing to recognize the emergence of pedagogical principles and practices which transcend their subject-bound concerns. My experience, limited to the two universities in which I have worked and the half dozen or so institutions in which I have served as external examiner, leaves me fairly confident that the assignments/essays/dissertations, orthodox products of scholarly endeavour, provide evidence of systematic study which has bases in theory and application in practice. This is less true of either method work or teaching practice. I accept that it is easier to make judgments about work grounded in something like orthodox scholarship but I still wonder why the outputs from method work as presented for examination often seem unsystematic and lacking an explicit rationale. If inquiries have been undertaken in order to examine the effectiveness of teaching strategies or tactics why are accounts of these investigations so rarely included in examined method work? If such inquiries have not been undertaken are methods' tutors either reinforcing the 'cultural-imprinting' to which I referred earlier or simply trying to replace this with an alternative 'model'?

Another puzzling feature of method work is the apparent failure to recognize generalizable features of pedagogical theory, strategies and tactics. The management and control of a class, the handling of mixed-ability groups, matching task demand to cognitive developmental state, assessing the readability of textual materials, establishing a congenial affective climate in a classroom, assessing and reporting achievement and other pedagogical problems are not subject specific. Arguably there would be an advantage in identifying and desystematizing such generalizable pedagogical principles and engaging the collaboration of consultants from appropriate disciplines where necessary, rather than each method tutor being expected to be *au fait* with current developments in all aspects of pedagogy. Current practice may waste precious resources.

Equally worthy of critical investigation is the trend to greater school-based training. Some problems associated with block teaching practice have been referred to earlier but as critical is the extension of school-based experience which may be increasingly under the influence of practising teachers.

A review of thirty-eight PGCE courses validated by the CNAA (Smith 1982) showed that out of a total possible number of 175 course days (35 weeks x 5) courses varied in their provision of school-based experience from sixty (the CNAA minimum) to ninety days; the mean was 78.15 days. We know from a collection of descriptions of both CNAA and university courses included in the SRHE publication *Developments in PGCE Courses* (Alexander and Whittaker 1980) how varied school-based experience can be. The nature of the link established between work undertaken in schools and the college or university depends critically on the nature of the tasks undertaken by students in both and on the congruence achieved between the perceptions of tutors and teachers of the purposes and nature of the training processes. The definition and allocation of tutor's and teacher's roles in the training process requires thoughtful and sensitive negotiation. When Smith allocated the thirty-eight courses which he studied to positions on a continuum responsive-reflexive he was able to point to features of the college-school relationship which appeared discrepant.

On a scale represented as:

a Totally tutor directed

b Student responsive

c Student reflexive

d Totally student directed

he defined **a** as 'highly structured and content orientated with the theoretical input being *determined* by the institution, with at best the practical experience of the student in school being illustrative of theoretical and pedagogic proposition being made by tutors in very general terms'. **d** was defined 'not in terms of content but in terms of process, since such content would change from year to year and from individual student to individual student'. He claimed that no PGCE course validated by CNAA fell into either of these categories. These courses according to Smith could be classified in **b** 'always purporting to be in some sense *responsive* whilst being predominantly structured and college-directed', or **c**, 'always conveying some degree of imposed structure but stressing the *reflexive* student role as content initiation'.

When Smith (1982) examined the contingency between responsive-re-flexive course intuitions and the commitment to school-based training (indicated by time spent in schools) he found the following distribution. (see Fig. 7.1)

Smith points to the apparently incongruous finding that 18.5 percent of courses are apparently committed to 'responsive' tutoring *and* to more than average school-based work; 'these colleges purport to provide the major input yet reduce substantially the opportunity for this, without claiming anything special for the school experience element over [the other responsive group].' As Cortis (1979) has pointed out, 'it should not be accepted as a new conventional wisdom that more school-based work necessarily leads to a better prepared student.'

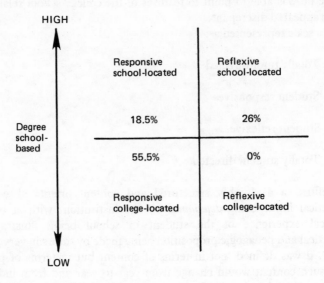

Figure 7.1

Among the necessary conditions for effective collaborative tutelage are,

a   the division of labour between college tutors and school teachers must be made explicit;

b   tutors must understand their own role and that of teachers and vice versa;

c   there must be a large measure of agreement about intentions;

d   co-ordination of engagement with students on professional tasks must be secured;

e   students should be made aware of the hoped for professional outcomes of tasks undertaken in school (as well as at college), the means by which these may be achieved and the kind of support available from school teachers and tutors.

The strengths and weaknesses of different degrees and kinds of collaboration between training institutions and schools may be explored by reference to three examples taken from the SRHE review quoted earlier.

The University College, Cardiff reported a series of pilot schemes in which the 'idea of enlisting external aid in the supervision of PGCE students during their teaching practice' was translated into action by 'asking practising teachers to participate'. Between the years 1968-1969 when six schools participated the scheme has grown so that, in 1979, seventy-five schools were involved.

The duties of heads of schools and numbers of staff selected to act as the school-based tutors include:

the representation to the students of a proper sense of professional responsibility both inside and outside the classroom;

arranging of teaching timetables;

the supervision of lesson preparation;

liaison with school subject teachers;

observation of students' teaching wherever practicable;

collation of reports on students' development as teachers;

recommending grading for students; and

providing material to be included in testimonials.

Headteachers from participating schools and their nominated school-based tutors were invited each year to 'initial meetings held well before the teaching practice began in the spring term'. The purpose of these meetings was 'to agree upon a consistent procedure regarding, for example, form of lesson preparation, number of lessons students were expected to teach, and method of assessment'.

We are also informed that most schools arranged weekly meetings 'where the school-based tutor discussed with the students in his school, as a group, the art of teaching in general and their performances in particular and in turn received the students' views'. Also, 'in addition, talks on school administration, finance, timetabling and pastoral care were arranged.' 'To these meetings the department tutor concerned was usually invited and very good results were achieved as a consequence.'

During this teaching practice, students returned to the college each Friday for 'general tutorials' and 'specialized lectures'. The report explains 'the students . . . had an hour or more with their appropriate general tutor to discuss their teaching during the week . . . [and states] . . . this gave them a sense of belonging even if they were not visited in school by their internal tutor.'

This account is restricted to teaching practice arrangements and therefore it would be inappropriate to compare it with more sophisticated arrangements which often accompany other forms of school-based work. However, with this in mind the reader may be struck by the similarity between this scheme and traditional practice. Teachers though are given greater responsibilities for assessing students' performances which, as evaluations of other schemes have demonstrated, is for teachers, initially at least, a major cause for concern. Also they are committed to a weekly meeting with their students.

But the basis of the collaboration, from this description, seems vague and bureaucratic. It sounds as though teachers had taken over part of the tutor's job but little attempt had been made to connect it with the residual tutorial functions with which it was formerly logically or empirically connected. It may be significant that 'a detailed evaluation' of the scheme in 1976 'emphasized five points' of which the first two are concerned with the beneficial effects of allowing PGCE staff time to undertake other duties. The third was concerned with the value of 'giving schools a stake in the responsibility for preserving standards'.

It seems unlikely that in any future evaluation of this scheme teachers will report that 'the challenge of analysing students' teaching has caused me to re-examine some of my own assumptions about effective teaching'. The growing knowledge which college-based tutors ought to have from researches into teaching or from, for example, cognitive psychology, have no apparently ready means of entry into student/tutor/tutor conversations in the Cardiff scheme.

The second example is one which I have selected partly on the grounds of its apparently full-blown commitment to school-based training, partly because of the kind of evaluation to which it has been subjected. It is the Sussex scheme. A description of 'the first intention' was given by Burrell and Sexton as follows.

The first intention was to associate a student over an extended period with an experienced teacher from whom, it was assumed initially, the student would receive all the professional instruction and support needed. The teacher was contracted to the university to act as teacher-tutor to a pair of students in his care and was paid an honorarium for providing weekly tutorials out of school hours. A university tutor, called an 'E' tutor, acted as personal tutor for the students in a particular curriculum area and conducted a series of seminars concerned with general aspects of teaching in that curriculum area. The seminars were organized for the students, but the teacher-tutors attended half of them, held in the evening. It was intended that the university 'E' tutor should be responsible for selecting the teacher-tutors with whom he wished to work. Once selected, the teacher-tutors had responsibility for the supervision and assessment of the students in their charge.

The second intention was that students should share in the life of a school over an extended period. Thus students were placed in one school for three days a week during school term from October to mid-May and a general tutor was appointed in each school to be responsible for the oversight of the more general aspects of the work of all the students in that school. They too were paid an honorarium to provide fortnightly seminars for the students out of school hours. This aspect of the course has been further strengthened, we believe, by transferring the responsibility for personal tutoring from the 'E' tutor, who was responsible for a number of students in one curriculum area in several schools, to a university tutor appointed to act as personal tutor to all the students in one school. These tutors also have the responsibility for the teaching of 'Education' in the university component of the course. This is part of a more general attempt to help students to relate the theory part of the course to their experience in schools. The structure of the school experience has been modified so that it finishes for most students with a full, three-week block at the beginning of the summer term. This was introduced first for the primary students and subsequently for the secondary students so as to give students experience of a full week in the life of the school. During this three-week period some students may be offered alternative experience in a sixth-form college, a further education college, or at the Urban Studies Centre in Bethnal Green.

A third intention, lying behind the school experience aspect of the course but also related to a second proposition that theory should feed off practice, is that students should collect information and ideas about teaching and the organization of the school which can be used in the theory seminars in the university. Thus, most of the content of the university discussions grows out of the students' experience in the schools. It is hoped that the initial impetus for this dialogue emanates from the student's experience in the school rather than from early inputs of theory.

Here, in Smith's terms, is a reflexive, highly school-based course. It is explicitly based on the belief that 'students learn the craft of teaching best by working alongside experienced colleagues and sharing the life of a school over an extended period.' The danger of this approach is that it may either reinforce the modelling process or precipitate model conflict which will require sensitivity and detachment to resolve. Moreover, this system may not readily accommodate empirical inquiries undertaken by students into curricular or pedagogical problems. The students' role is close to that of apprentice. However, given a careful selection of teachers and schools many of the criteria given earlier might be met even though the effectiveness of the system will be limited by the extent to which its articles of faith are true. The scheme has faced difficulties. Selection of 'ideal teacher tutors' proved to be a problem as LEAs' and universities' financial positions differentiated, forcing 'students to be more concentrated in schools'. Teachers found it increasingly difficult to carry out the major task of supervision 'in the extensive way envisaged' and also discharge their normal professional duties. As teaching posts became more difficult to obtain, the assessment of students' performance became increasingly critical, teacher tutors sought help and advice in this aspect of their work. Also the honorarium paid to teacher tutors lost value as a result of inflation.

Lacey (1974) in an account of an evaluation of the Sussex scheme pointed out some of the problems associated with it, *inter alia* the danger of the 'craft apprenticeship model' and doubts about the school as a place to train teachers. 'However it is clear that schools are not ideally suited to the training of teachers. Examples of this are conflicts between the needs of students and the timetable of the school, or problems of the amount of time school-based tutors can actually spend with students during the school day.'

Another problem identified by Lacey is that of selecting appropriate school teachers as tutors. Initially, when the scheme involved a relatively small number of pupils, it was possible to 'hand-pick the relatively small number of tutors required'. Presumably these teachers would be on professionally open terms with the university tutors with whom they were to work. Later for a variety of reasons other school teachers became involved, not all suited to the task. Placing students in schools depended 'more on negotiation and agreement than upon the selection of the ideal teacher-tutor in the ideal school'. To be a good teacher trainer required security and confidence about one's own teaching, the ability to explain it in terms meaningful to very inexperienced students and, I would add, to allow aspects of it to be observed, questioned and investigated.

The third example which I have selected is one where the commitment to school-based work is far less than at Sussex. It is notable for the attempts made not only to relate experience in schools to other aspects of teacher training in the PGCE year, but also to map out professional (including pedagogical) principles and use this map as an instrument of course planning.

North Staffordshire Polytechnic Education Department PGCE division works closely with eight schools, five secondary, three primary. The professional studies (general) course which occupies nine hours per week in the autumn term was 'planned by teachers in the schools concerned, education tutors and method tutors'. Explicitly the rationale for joint planning was 'to ensure the students will be engaged in relevant and practical acitivies' and to enable students to perform classroom-based tasks which provide opportunities to bring the educational disciplines to bear on problems of immediate relevance to the student; 'also to enable method tutors to design their courses in relation to the core themes and activities.'

Groups of twelve students work with a 'core' tutor for their professional studies and divide their time between college and their 'attachment school'. Teachers are appointed as professional tutors, professional studies tutors are associated with particular schools, so the students operate in a close working relationship with a tutor and a teacher. The 'core' professional studies, with its four themes – the school, the child, the teacher, and the classroom organization – reflects joint planning with teachers and is designed to influence other college-based work. The method work in the secondary school programme, e.g., geography method, will take up the same themes in the same order as the professional studies general course but translate the general principles into geography-specific applications.

This is a genuine attempt to identify general educational/pedagogical principles and to use these in a way which may give the course a degree of cohesion otherwise difficult to achieve. As the author of the account states, this coherence is difficult to achieve, 'problems arise in ensuring that all contributors have a common understanding of the rationale and structure of the course.'

One might not be surprised to learn that teachers' heavy commitments in school prevent their 'attending meetings regularly' and thus being *au fait* with the programme, but the author's main complaint is directed at 'method tutors'. Apparently method tutors are sometimes unable or unwilling to harmonize their contributions with the themes in the professional core. As the author rather nicely expresses the related problem when trying to encourage tutors to use curriculum theory as a basis for method work, 'various subject tutors view the rational planning model in different ways, particularly with regard to the use of objectives and "assessment".'

These three examples indicate clearly that there is some way to go before we can achieve the ideal relationship between teacher training institutions and schools, between tutors and teachers, between students and teachers or tutors in school settings.

Some tasks we are called upon to learn may be learned by watching an expert and copying his actions. Teaching is not such a task; even if it were there are few experts. Teaching is an activity about which it is possible to theorize but one cannot learn how to do it by reading theories. How to teach can however under certain conditions be learned by doing, and it will be learned more effectively if our actions are systematically undertaken and the results of actions observed. Learning to teach requires the growth of empirical knowledge. For such knowledge to grow and be a guide to action it is necessary that schools and teachers collaborate with training institutions not only to provide students with appropriate opportunities to practise but also to provide articulate feedback when engaged in a programme of activities to which both teachers and tutors are committed. Of the twelve descriptions of practice in which schools are significantly involved in teacher initial PGCE training given in Alexander and Whittaker, very few give a sufficient description of the nature of the tutor/teacher/student relationship. Many imply that by doing it (not always specified) in school with tutors and teachers, theory (of what?) and practice are consummated in a fruitful union. This leaves too much to chance.

It is significant that when research and development have been undertaken in professional training, e.g., Wragg *et al.*, with the Nottingham Teacher Education Project, research has involved the investigation of particular problems in classroom settings, the teaching of mixed-ability groups; questioning; management and control. The step from craft knowledge which tends to be specific and non-adaptive to knowledge informed by organizing principles which facilitate appropriate action according to circumstances requires research. By a similar process students may learn how to teach effectively.

References

UCET (1979) 'The PGCE Course and the training of specialist teachers for secondary schools'.
Dreyfus, A. and Eggleston, J. (1980) 'Classroom transactions of student teachers of sciences', *European Journal of Science Education*, Vol No 3.
Eggleston, J.F., Galton, M.J. and Jones, M. (1976) *Processes and Products of Science Teaching*, Schools Council Research Studies, Macmillan, London.

Hacker, R.J. (1979) 'A cross-cultural study of science classroom interation', *British Journal of Education Psychology*.

Hacker, R.J. (1978) 'Cognitive development in science classroom practices prescriptions of theories of learning' (unpublished), University of Western Australia

Reid, Ken and Patrick, Helen (1981) 'The structure and process of initial teacher education within universities in England and Wales' in Alexander, Robin and Whittaker, Jean *Developments in PGCE Courses*, SRHE.

Taylor, W. (1969) *Towards a Policy for the Education of Teachers*, Colston papers No 20, Butterworths.

Smith, Robin N. (1982) 'Towards an analysis of PGCE courses', *Journal of Further and Higher Education* 6 (3).

Alexander, Robin and Whittaker, Jean (1980) *Developments in PGCE Courses*, SRHE.

Cortis, G. (1979) 'An evaluation of school-based training within a PGCE course', *British Journal of Teacher Education* 5 (2).

Lacey, C., Hoad, P., Horton, M. (1973) *The Tutorial Schools Research Project, 1964-73*, SSRC.

CHAPTER 8

LIFE SKILLS IN AN AGE OF GROWING STRUCTURAL UNEMPLOYMENT

DOUGLAS HAMBLIN

The problem

Change in industry is accompanied by growing unemployment which disproportionately affects school-leavers and young adults. Discussion of life skills, if it is to be relevant, must focus on this. The impact of growing structural unemployment is not limited to the post-school situation. Control and order was always the preoccupation of teachers, even in the era of full employment. Today, however, the school master's injunction – 'Work hard, get good 'O' levels and then go to university. This will ensure a good career' – is met by cynicism in pupils. The situation is serious because King (1973) found that middle-class pupils focus on the instrumental values of school. They see it as a means to a valued end – a career. But what will happen to their affiliation to the goals of the school now that a career is doubtful? Sixth-form students are aware that graduate unemployment is now a commonplace.

Unemployment can be reduced to two basic elements:

a   The loss of the indivudal's exchange relationship with society.

b   Erosion of identity and loss of the anchorage to society, which, at least partially, is derived from employment. Employment has provided a structure for life on which many individuals have been dependent.

Moral imperatives and current attitudes foster the feeling of self-blame and powerlessness. Many unemployed individuals feel they occupy a marginal role in society equivalent to that of the handicapped. Warnock (1978) remarked that many handicapped people will have to learn to lead significant lives without work. Many adults will, in the future, have to learn to live meaningful lives without traditional paid employment. Society has tended to treat the handicapped as eternal children, but now the unemployed are in equal danger of being seen permanently as incomplete adults. Employment has given a legitimated and valued relationship with society. Lack of real employment means that many people at the moment feel they are being reluctantly subsidized and their status in society is inferior.

To be unemployed is, to some extent, to run the danger of being depersonalized. Research undertaken by Hamblin (1981) shows that fifth-form pupils feel that unemployment brings the experience of devaluation and becoming an object of blame.

Basic issues and processes

Teachers of life skills must bear in mind the pervasive influence of the Protestant ethic, and the danger of new forms of divisiveness in society. Even in this age, our reaction to unemployment may be shaped unwittingly by subterranean and implicit moral assumptions, e.g., that the linking of men to specific occupational identities is a necessary condition for mental growth and personal integrity. Involvement in work is still seen as a pre-condition for personal worth, even by those who reject the crude assumptions of a Protestant ethic that work roles are tied to the social order by divine sanction.

Life-skills teaching may need to question actively the assumption that identity as a worker is an essential component of mental health. Work and professional identities as social products spring from the organized division of labour. The Marxian concept of alienation seems to suggest that when physical and economic compulsions are removed, then work will be resolutely avoided. In such a period of change, the identities and expectations fostered by traditional socialization will have to be modified, possibly obliterated. The model of man which seems appropriate for the new age is that which Benedict, many years ago, described as Dionysian man. This emphasizes immediate gratification, face-to-face relationships, sensation and spontaneity. Such a model is at variance with many of our in-built assumptions about life. Change of them produces panic or blind adherence to the status quo.

Even if dramatic predictions about the post-industrial society are discounted, there seems to be the danger of a divisive society composed of:

a   A group whose members hold jobs which are functionally necessary for the creation of wealth or are part of essential services.

b   A group who have had jobs created for them as a device for social control or as a palliative for unacceptable conditions.

c   Those who have not had a job, and who are unlikely to get one.

The latter two groups will not be restricted to the less able but will include graduates, 'A'-level holders, and those who would have taken traditional apprenticeships for whom work is an essential ingredient of identity. Neither must it be assumed that all groups will react similarly to the experience of unemployment. The disadvantaged and less able may be the best equipped to cope. Social stresses and financial difficulties are endemic in their backgrounds, while skill has been gained in the use of short-term expedient responses, i.e., the robbing Peter to pay Paul strategy. For them, as Flemming and Lavercombe (1982) show, discovering how to use their enforced leisure is the greatest problem. Their major concern is with money, and training is evaluated in terms of the likelihood of work at the end.

The unemployed who come from homes where the family background is that of the artisan or clerical worker where respectability is stressed present another type of problem. The world view produced within the family may be one which emphasizes threat, stresses the evaluations of others as a major concern, thus making the lack of a job unduly stressful because hard, continuous endeavour is seen as a prerequisite for moral virtue. Paternal redundancy within such families may reinforce the insecurity which is inherent in the family world view, especially if the father's reaction has been one of pained inadequacy. The 'A'-level holder and graduate may have their long-term expectations disrupted. We must then ask what will happen to their previous attitudes of commitment and purpose.

Analysis of life skills requires us to identify the processes to which individuals are vulnerable. It seems that the unemployed individual who feels devalued and rejected is forced into a position of heavy reliance on a peer group which itself has weakened bonds to society. Within these groups, collective identity will be stressed. The consequent suspension of individual identity facilitates the process of de-inviduation described by Zimbardo (1969). Klapp (1972) describes the vulnerability to contagion, and the readiness to indulge in extreme forms of cathartic expression.

Individuals then show a heightened susceptibility to suggestion, leading to a diffusion of responsibility which releases group members from their wider social obligations, allowing them to behave in unrestrained ways. A number of other processes are involved. Blame pinning accompanied by the creation of powerful negative images of the enemy provides one example. Communication is controlled by leaders who have gained credibility within the group. Tensions become formulated as grievances, dramatization occurs and unifying symbols are created, leading to the collective identity taking precedence over other identities.

Life-skills teaching should identify the forces which actually function to reinforce the deprivation and deviant position of the unemployed. Identity can be achieved, either through self-awareness, or through the more primitive mechanism of belonging, as Curle (1972) argues. Awareness implies a sense of consciousness of one's own being. Situations of deprivation and threat facilitate for all of us the growth of identity by belonging, in which we react to others, not as individuals, but in terms of their function and meaning in reinforcing our identity. Curle suggests that low levels of identity through self-awareness are strongly associated with relating to others in terms of threat, and attempting to manipulate them. In combination with the work of Allport (1958) on prejudice, we see the need for life-skills teaching to bring such factors to the forefront. Prejudice, in its negative form, may be described as denigration and gross over-generalization. It is learned, although the basis of the learning is often irrational. Frustration, in conjunction with prejudice, is associated with the displacement of aggression on to a weaker group which is also believed to be inferior. This mechanism of scapegoating does not remove frustration. What is interesting is the fact that unemployed young adults, who themselves often occupy a scapegoat role in society, can cope by scapegoating others.

It is likely that accentuated and new versions of territoriality will develop. These have existed in both urban and rural areas for many generations. What will be different – and of vital importance for those teaching life skills – is that the identities and values fostered within such groups may become primary ones, rather than secondary identities which are restricted to leisure time. Transactions across the boundaries of such groups will then be couched almost solely in terms of hostility. Within the group shared images emerge of the enemy. Periodic abreactive discharges of emotion in intergroup conflicts will foster such images and symbols which have an energizing function. This is equivalent to Durkheim's (1933) rite through which a

collective conscience emerges. Such central symbols are highly imperme-
able to divergent information. Coser (1956), in a reformulation of Simmel's
(1955) propositions of conflict, shows the distinctions between conflicts
motivated by personal goals, and those which are representative of the
needs of the group. Identity by belonging will, of course, facilitate this latter
type of conflict. Returning to Simmel, we see the relevance of his proposition that conflict pursued with a good conscience will be conducted without
mercy. Justification stems in such situations, not from individual conscien-
ces, but from the collective identity and the images of the enemy it has
created.

Strangely enough, Simmel's propositions may have a new relevance in an
age of structural unemployment. His descriptions of the renegade and
heretic illustrate this. The renegade threatens the group by destroying
unity. He becomes a deserter by joining a new group, earning gross
rejection. This explains the disproportionate hostility focused on such
individuals. The heretic creates factions because he delineates an alternative
way of behaving where others wish none to exist. He therefore undermines
the unity of the group. The result, in both cases, is a sharpening of values,
increased vigilance in maintaining the boundary of the group, and harsh
treatment of the deviant. Young people must understand these processes,
although insight alone is insufficient to change behaviours.

What we may not realize is that such conflicts can be useful. Examining
another area we see that conflict centred around school uniform can be a
form of indirect social control. While pupils' attention is directed to that
issue, they are unlikely to focus on poor teaching or lack of participation in
decision making in schools. It may be functional to accept a multiplicity of
small conflicts because they inhibit the appearance of major splits in the
larger society. Therefore, what appears to be solely negative may incorporate an unproductive form of social control – a fact which may not escape
politicians.

Useful life skills
Reaction to the Experience of Unemployment
Predictions cannot be made from the reactions to unemployment of those
who suffered it in the 1930s. The age of full unemployment created expectations which are now being disrupted. Adolescents currently question
society more strongly, while there may be a greater adaptability and
resilience which allows them to cope better than their predecessors. Cas-
uality cannot be assumed to be inevitably in one direction. Unemployed

persons displaying stress or other difficulties may be unemployed because they possess such characteristics, rather than the characteristics being the result of unemployment.

Exchange relationships

It is crucial that we search for new forms of exchange relationship which social anthropologists have shown to be at the heart of social integration. The earlier discussion assumes added significance if we ask, 'What does the unemployed young person have to exchange with society?' New forms of exchange relationships have to be fostered. The direction of change is encapsulated in the statement made at a recent conference that the Youth Service would, in effect, become 'Service by Young People'. This is already happening. What is crucial, and not always achieved, is that the activities convey a positive picture of self of those who undertake them. It is only too easy for so-called remedial measures to reinforce the image of the young person as an incomplete adult.

We must also deliberately set out to stimulate entrepreneurial initiative which leads to self-employment. This, by definition, implies risk taking. The work on achievement motivation shows us that the high achiever prefers the fifty-fifty level of risk, where the chances of failing or succeeding are equally balanced. Risk taking and coping with anxiety are associated with the development of new forms of exchange relationship. Embryonic developments in this field may need to be integrated into the curriculum.

Adjustment to work

Even when they are unlikely to get another job, young people still give up the job they have. Why? It is not because they cannot perform the task but because they cannot make the psychological and social adjustment to the role of the worker. Life skills should focus on this transition. The principles incorporated into the module concerned with adjustment to work might well be:

a *Anticipation* of break-down or stress points;

b *Inoculation* against impulsive reactions;

c *Evolving* coping strategies.

The transition to work is not necessarily difficult, indeed many pupils have anticipated it in a positive way, and are well prepared. It is, however, a less predictable situation because:

a   Authority is less visible, and more variable in its reaction, especially at the level of the charge hand or foreman.

b   A different standard set of values may operate. The school urges pupils towards standards of excellence, but the work group norm may be, 'Do as little as possible for as much as possible'.

c   Stresses exist which are peculiar to a factory or occupation.

Sensible life-skills teaching demands that some teachers from the school should go into local industry, specifically charged with the task of identifying sources of stress for young workers.

Simulations, decision-making exercises and discussion should look at the stresses at the point of entry to work. Usually a young person enters a working group of five to eighteen people with whom he has to interact continuously. Labelling processes are strong, while initiation rituals and other mechanisms serve to integrate the young person into the working group. Initial teasing and joking test the reactions of the young worker. They are still sent for the sky-hook, the tin of striped paint, the rubber-headed hammer and, as I recently found, in the case of some apprentices, for a Fallopian tube. Young workers who have not been prepared for the experience may react by complaining or aggression. This opens them up, not only to further baiting, but to a harsh labelling process. Another practice found in work groups is that of giving all the unpleasant jobs to the newcomer. This is usually temporary and functions as an intuitive personality test of the new entrant. The resultant feeling of being put-on can be dealt with by humour, aggression or whining. The last two responses obviously delay acceptance, and if marked, lead to the irreversible allocation of negative identity. There is then little alternative than to give up the job. Terse and contradictory instructions, the experience of being bawled out by a charge hand, and what workers describe as two-faced foreman also have to be anticipated constructively.

There are certain crucial areas of stress and conflict in which failure to cope brings serious consequences. Fifth-year pupils should be helped to anticipate them and work out their own strategies for coping. This can be done through simple simulations and decision-making activities. The areas to be covered fall into:

a   *The front man position.* The young worker is often the buffer between the customer and other workers in the organization, e.g., on the forecourt of the garage, or as a shop assistant, waitress or junior clerk. They then experience incompatible demands, and as they are at the margin of the organization, they then feel very vulnerable.

b *Coping with mistakes.* Loss of face and the feeling of inadequacy can lead to self-defeating attempts at covering up mistakes. Too high a level of risk is involved in many of these situations. Young workers 'take a chance', and then react aggressively or blame others when the error is discovered.

c *Fellow workers.* The most common source of difficulty is a peer who does not pull his weight. The problem of coping with a workmate who is always missing at the point of real effort is one which disorganizes many young people.

d *Worker-managerial standpoints.* This is often associated with a generational gap. An older worker who may be training the youth puts pressure on him to ignore managerial advice and instructions. Yet the young worker may see the sense of the higher level instructions, especially about safety regulations. Such older workers often phrase their pressures in the following way: 'I've been with this firm – boy and man – for thirty-five years. That lot up in the office don't know what they are talking about! Don't let me find you doing what they told you or else.'

e *Accusations.* Young people often react in an unduly aggressive way causing conflict to escalate. Such reactions convince the accuser of the guilt of the worker, although he or she is innocent of the alleged offence.

f *Expression of the desire to succeed.* Many entrants experience difficulties with maintaining keenness and enthusiasm without acquiring such labels as the 'foreman's boot boy'.

The discussion of the factors influencing successful adjustment to work set out above is merely illustrative and is no sense exhaustive. Attention will also have to be given to the skills of a job search. These will include the mobilization of support from friends, relatives and other adults, telephone skills and interview skills.

Social Anxieties
Adolescents frequently experience social anxieties. Buss (1980) argues that social anxiety is closely related to the perception of being an agent of social

evaluation. Certainly the sense of negative evaluation currently inherent in being unemployed will enhance this. Programmes could beneficially focus on the following aspects of a social anxiety:

a   Fear of creating adverse impressions in authority figures;

b   Fear of the limelight;

c   Fear of strangers and novel situations;

d   Revealing inadequacies;

e   Fear of loss of bodily control in public situations, e.g., voice, sweating or clumsiness.

Social drama, decision making and audio-tapes can be used to develop the ability to cope. Anxiety, itself, can be usefully conceptualized as a signal of danger. Lazarus (1966) shows that anxiety is a response to a situation which contains threat. It can be a cause as well as a response. If too high a level of anxiety is reached – the threshold differs for individuals – then it causes irrational behaviour and ineffective thinking. Social anxiety is obviously linked with vulnerability to negative comparison processes. Individuals then weigh themselves against others, and constantly find themselves lacking. Opportunities for examining their preferred mode of tension reduction, and the mechanisms used in situations where there is a fear of loss of face, should form a salient part of the programme. Prolonged frustration, such as that met in unemployment, induces a state of arousal where minimal provocations trigger off grossly disproportionate responses. Minor situations then escalate into severe conflicts. Adolescents lack the skill of dealing with embarrassment constructively. It is helpful to divide embarrassment into:

a   Coping with unintended impropriety, e.g., inappropriate dress for the occasion or involuntary bodily reactions such as belching.

b   Incompetence in public situations, e.g., inappropriate displays of emotion such as uncontrollable giggling or forgetting someone's name.

A relevant concept is that of learned helplessness, derived from the work of Seligman (1975). The key element is the sense of control of the individual. Learned helplessness exists when a person predicts that any attempt he makes to deal with the situation will be useless. Past experience has produced a sense of impotency, producing the expectation that every effort to change things will be abortive. Learned helplessness probably underlies the increasing passivity seen in the life style of many unemployed persons. In working with the adolescent we must ask, 'Are rewards and change seen as determined by luck or can they be acquired by the acquisition of skills?' Rotter (1966) and Phares (1976) showed the importance of internal versus external locus of control. Few people would be extreme types, i.e., being almost totally internally controlled or completely externally controlled. In situations of threat where self-respect is being eroded, then the perception of where the course of control lies may be vital in determining the individual's behaviour. Phares (1976) shows that when frustration in learning is met, the internally controlled take responsibility for themselves, and begin to modify the way they work. The externally controlled accept failure passively, or more sinisterly, attribute the blame to others, e.g., 'The school is no good. They don't teach you properly here.' It must be pointed out, however, that the relationship between learned helplessness and locus of causality is complex, and not fully understood. We cannot assume that an internal sense of control is necessarily more beneficial in prolonged unemployment than external locus of causality. The depressed, unemployed person who attributes the reasons for his unemployment to personal causes will suffer greater distress and erosion of self-respect than he who is able to attribute his unemployment to external causes such as the recession or current government policies. Life-skills training may well have to work at changing unrealistic personal attributions about the causes of unemployment to more realistic ones.

From the sections above it can be seen that those planning programmes of life skills have to take into account reactions to frustration, complex interaction between predictions and comparisons, and also such factors as learned helplessness and internal versus external control. Failure to do so will lead to concentration on the peripheral rather than the salient.

Family relationships
We have long realized that the family influences the nature of the phenomenon that we call social class. Some elements are highlighted, while others are reduced in importance. Each family creates a symbolic environment for

its members through which meaning is given, to a large degree, to the life events they face. Weight may be given to threat or unpredictability in life, or there may be an over-emphasis on the importance of the evaluations of authority figures. Life skills will have to take this family ethos into account. A young person's reactions to unemployment may be strongly influenced by his father's security in employment, the moral value placed on work within the family as part of a residual Protestant ethic and sex-role stereotypes. The more rigid the views of masculinity and feminity within the family, the greater may be the difficulties experienced in adjusting to the changes stemming from unemployment.

The unemployed father's reaction to the feeling of insignificance which is an accompaniment to unemployment is another source of difficulty. He may attempt to compensate for diminished authority by exercising additional controls over his son or daughter. In some cases, the family becomes an arena in which the father unwittingly provokes rebellion. Many unemployed adolescents believe that adults will blame them for their plight, and in their own words, want to put them down. The problem is compounded by the fact that the redundant father is not necessarily more sympathetic and understanding of his son's or daughter's unemployment. He may cope with his own self-distaste or guilt through condemnation of his children, although he is aware consciously that they are as powerless to change the situation as he is. The anxious mother may further exacarbate difficulties – for she is likely to become the focus of attack. This exemplifies the old adage that each man attacks the thing he loves. Mother and child may then be caught into a self-perpetuating cycle of hostility and recrimination.

Family relationships also incorporate stress when the father – perhaps the father and older son – are jobless, but the younger son or daughter are in work. The employed adolescent can then be provocative, often unwittingly, but the tensions created are very real.

Family communication systems convey messages about the selves of participants, but tensions emanating from unemployment render them liable to gross distortion. The father who is unemployed may take a keener interest in the activities of his son or daughter, especially in their use of leisure time. He may believe that he is signalling concern, but the recipient views them as messages of distrust. These tendencies are reinforced by the life styles which often develop with prolonged unemployment of the young person, e.g., scrounging, late nights and sleeping on become major issues.

Parents often fail to recognize the reality of depressive behaviour in their unemployed son or daughter. Well-meaning parental responses actually increase the sense of helplessness, for the parents urge the unemployed young adult to go out and join friends, rather than mope about. The psychological difficulties of doing this when one feels hopeless are not apprehended by the anxious parent. The well-meant injunctions then become a source of added pressure.

Special attention should be given to females. There is some suggestion that unemployment is currently affecting females more than males. Women have escaped compulsive domesticity, but one could imagine a situation in which moralistic arguments are used to justify economic pressures or as an expedient device in coping with unemployment. Women have a right to employment, independence and a satisfying career.

Tensions develop within families when marriage is in the offing, particularly when an unemployed adolescent shows signs of marrying another unemployed person. Provident, cautious and forceful parents react sharply, creating a tense situation. As yet we have done little to help young people cope with marriage in a situation where both are unemployed, and are likely to remain so. Parents focus on the issue of child rearing, e.g., 'What sort of family is that to bring up children in?' Their reactions force the young adults into premature marriage or co-habitation as a counter-reaction.

A caution

We must not assume that any of the conditions outlined above are inevitable. Certainly, we do not know enough about the long-term effects of unemployment in adolescents and early adult life to make rigid statements. We must, however, alert ourselves to the processes and possibilities without creating self-fulfilling prophecies. We have seen that the disadvantaged may be better able to cope than those from other backgrounds. Disruption of long-term expectations coupled with the orientation produced by the symbolic environment of the family may well be the crucial factor in determining the type and degree of stress which appears.

References

Allport, G. (1958) *The Nature of Prejudice*, New York, Doubleday.
Buss, A. (1980) *Self Conciousness and Anxiety*, San Francisco, Freeman.
Coser, L. (1956) *The Functions of Social Conflict*, London, Routledge & Kegan Paul.
Curle, A. (1972) *Mystics and Militants*, London, Tavistock.
Durkheim, E. (1933) *The Division of Labour in Society*, New York, Macmillan.
Fleming, D. and Lavercombe, S. (1982) 'Talking about unemployment with school leavers', *British Journal of Guidance and Counselling*, Vol. 10, No. 1, pp. 22-23.
Hamblin, D. (1981) *Teaching Study Skills*, Oxford, Blackwell.
King, R. (1973) *School Organisation and Pupil Involvement*, London, Routledge & Kegan Paul.
Klapp, O. (1972) *Currents of Unrest*, New York, Holt, Rinehart and Winston.

Lazarus, R. (1966) *Psychological Stress and the Coping Process*, New York, McGraw-Hill.

Phares, E. (1976) *Locus of Control in Personality*, Morriston, N.J., General Learning Press.

Rotter, J. (1966) *'Generalized expectancies for internal versus external control of reinforcement'*, *Psychological Monographs*, Vol. 80, No. 1, Whole No. 609.

Seligman, M. (1975) *Helplessness: On Depression, Development and Death*, San Francisco, Freeman.

Simmel, G. *(1955) Conflict*, trans Wolff, K., Glencoe, III., Free Press.

Warnock H. (1978) (chairperson) *Special Educational Needs: Report of the Committee of Enquiry into the Education of Handicapped Children and Young People*, London HMSO.

Zimbardo, P. (1969) 'The human choice: Individuation, reason and order versus deindividuation, impulse and chaos', in Arnold, W. and Levine, D. (eds) *Nebraska Symposium on Motivation*, Lincoln, University of Nebraska Press.

CHAPTER 9

EDUCATION AND THE NEW TECHNOLOGY

DAVID WALTON

Impact on society

In the last five years there has been a sudden awareness that rapid changes in technology have a fundamental effect on society. The actual phenomenon is not new – it has been apparent since the industrial revolution. However, one particular development has captured the public imagination – the silicon chip. It is hard to define why the chip has been singled out for this attention instead of, say, the jet engine. It undoubtedly will have an enormous impact on the way we live – some sources claim, with considerable justification, that the effects of the chip will be of the same order of magnitude as those of the printing press. Indeed, both developments have considerable effect on that most valuable of all commodities, information. However, it is impossible to tell why the chip has created such widespread interest; perhaps it is because it is one of the few things whose price is dropping at an even greater rate than the price of other things is increasing; perhaps it is because of the image of the centre of a chip going through the eye of a needle; perhaps it is because they are already appearing in people's homes in everything from video-cassette recorders to hair driers; or perhaps it is the spectre of the widespread use of 'intelligent' robots. In reality it is probably a combination of all these factors.

Employment patterns

A widely expressed view is that the wholesale introduction of microprocessor-controlled machines will lead to massive unemployment – there is an image of just one person walking into a factory, pressing the 'START' button and then going home (or standing back to watch, in the case of

British industry). The huge increase in unemployment in Britain in the last five years has helped encourage this view. However, on further analysis there is little evidence to support this belief; British industry has been very slow to introduce microprocessor-controlled equipment, and there is no relationship between those few areas of industry that have and those where there have been most job losses. However, it is possible to detect a myth in the making here, and it will become increasingly convenient for politicians to blame new technology for high unemployment.

This is not to say, however, that the introduction of automation will not deskill individuals. In the same way that the blacksmith became redundant with the introduction of the railways, and the man wielding a pick and shovel is put out of work by the bulldozer, a machine capable of painting a car will make the man with the hand-held spray gun a potential candidate for the dole queues. However, this development should surely be applauded – human beings ought not to spend their lives doing menial, boring or dangerous jobs. The real problem arises if the human being concerned cannot be retrained or cannot adapt to a new job. It is a mistake however to blame new technology for the length of the dole queues – this is almost entirely the result of economic policy. It is fair to blame new technology (and indeed in the present circumstances, old technology as well) for deciding which people are actually in these dole queues. One of the jobs of education must be to prepare young people for a world where they will need to adapt to new job opportunities, not once, but several times during their working lives.

Priorities in schools
How should schools react to the changes in society which new technology is bringing about? At the moment many schools are introducing computer studies as an option at CSE and 'O' level. This conveniently fits into the structure of schools' timetables, and although there are various murmurings about the relevance, or otherwise, of the actual syllabuses, in general headteachers are quietly congratulating themselves on having reacted to a changing society in the only way they know how – by introducing yet another choice into the fourth- and fifth-year option scheme. A more careful consideration of the reasons for schools getting involved with microcomputers reveals that this in fact is no solution at all. It simply begins to divide society into a technological élite and the remainder who can class new technology along with nuclear physics (and in many cases, the workings of the motor car) as completely beyond their comprehension. This does a

disservice to the large majority of youngsters who will subsequently meet this technology in their place of work and their home. In fact, since there is a considerable question over the content of the average computer studies syllabus, it is quite possible that in isolation it does more harm than good.

Computer awareness course

So, what ought schools to be doing? The first priority should be to address the problem directly, in the form of a computer awareness course for all pupils. In the long term this ought to appear several times during the course of a pupil's schooling, and should form natural units in the curriculum of several existing subjects – humanities, sciences, mathematics, etc. As a short-term step in this direction, a school might think of introducing a course in a single year group – it is important at this stage, however, not to let it become the permanent province of a single department. A typical computer awareness course might consist of between ten and twenty hours of contact time, preferably several lessons per week for a few weeks, rather than one lesson a week for half a year or a year. It is best aimed at second- or third-year pupils. It might contain the following elements:

1   Two or three 'hands on' sessions for every pupil, each lasting about thirty minutes, and illustrating the various facets of the machine. Given a limited number of microcomputers, this would be spread throughout the course, probably outside the lesson time itself.

2   Information retrieval – including a demonstration of a general-purpose information retrieval package and of PRESTEL.

3   Social implications – including data bases, issues of privacy, etc.; implications for jobs for the future; the benefits for the handicapped.

4   Historical perspective – the rate of development of hardware over the last four decades.

5   A *brief* demonstration of the elements of programming, using graphical work as a vehicle, rather than arithmetic. A heavy emphasis on programming is likely to be counter-productive for the majority of children.

6   Word processing and the electronic office – including a demonstration of a word-processing package.

7.   Applications – a look at the range of applications in the world today, from robots making cars, to computers in banking, to farm management with a microcomputer.

8   Control technology – a demonstration of simple control: using the microcomputer to control motors and mechanisms, and reading data from light cells, thermometers, etc.

9   Terms – an explanation of some of the simple terms in computing: hardware, software, input, output, processor, memory, backing store (including disks and cassettes), microcomputer, etc.

Computer-aided learning

A second important development for schools is the use of a microcomputer as a teaching aid in those areas of the curriculum where it is appropriate. At the moment this would include physics, chemistry, biology, geography, history, mathematics, economics and craft, design and technology. There may also be suitable uses in other subjects in due course, although at the moment there is not clear evidence, one way or the other. A reasonable analogy to this application is the use of video-cassette recorders in schools. It is normally a class-based activity, with teachers and pupils able to observe and interact with the program which is running on the machine. This implies one or more large TV/monitors so that all the pupils in a class can comfortably read what's going on. In a similar way to the VCR, the relevance to a particular teaching topic depends entirely on whether an appropriate piece of software is available. However, unlike the TV, software is mainly produced within the educational world, either by individual teachers or groups of teachers working with a programmer. In general, the second of these methods produces the better software. The package of software and a guide for the potential user can then be made available, either through the local education authority, or through a commercial publisher. It is perhaps difficult to imagine the use of such programs, and there is no substitute for seeing and using computer-aided learning packages.

The reasons for introducing computer-aided learning are twofold: firstly it is often the case that the teaching syllabus is a compromise between what is desirable and what is practicable in the classroom. There is evidence that the use of a microcomputer can make it possible to cover some new syllabus topics which in the past had fallen in the category of being worthwhile but not practicable, and also that it enables some existing topics to be taught in a more effective way. The computer is particularly good at simulating a situation, in anything from geography to mathematics, and allowing the class to 'investigate' that environment, by effectively asking the computer 'what if . . .' questions, and allowing the computer to model the real situation. This can often replace the teacher baldly stating 'this is how it is', and can allow the pupils to discover for themselves the relationships in the situation. It is also possible to make use of the computer's power to perform fast and accurate calculations, to display information graphically, in a dynamic way, and to handle large amounts of data. The essential difference between the microcomputer and a video-cassette recorder is that the computer is interactive, responding to the users' decisions and ideas, and using values or real data which come from the user.

A second reason for using a computer in the normal teaching environment is that this can become an opportunity for pupils to see a genuine use of a computer in a context with which they are familiar. This works in both directions, because as computers become more pervasive in the outside world, schools could appear more and more behind the times if they become 'islands of no technology' in an otherwise 'computerate' society.

Microcomputers in primary schools

An exciting recent development is the introduction of microcomputers into primary schools. Initially this has tended to be a cheap microcomputer, using programs such as the 'space invaders' type of games, and so-called 'educational' programs of a fairly crude drill and practice nature. However, with the recent Department of Industry half-price initiative, some primary schools are buying more sophisticated microcomputers, and more worthwhile programs are gradually becoming available. In contrast to secondary schools, this use is almost entirely with individual pupils or small groups. Observing young children using the better quality programs reveals an unexpected side-effect of the specific learning which such programs can help to bring about. In fact, this 'side-effect' is so valuable it ought probably to become a major objective for the use of microcomputers with young children. It is hard to define this effect: it revolves around the non-threatening and relatively predictable nature of microcomputers that allows children to investigate and to learn from their mistakes; it seems able to help with the development of skils of precision, logic and planning – more valuable and fundamental skills than the curriculum topic itself, which becomes a vehicle for this development.

This use in primary schools will have a considerable knock-on effect on secondary schools, as children coming from primary schools gradually become more likely to be experienced users of microcomputers. Again here it is important that primary school teachers make every effort to encourage the widest possible use of whatever hardware is available, at the appropriate level for each individual pupil, rather than concentrating on, say, the more able. Otherwise, there is a danger that the divisive nature of computer studies in secondary schools could come into effect at an even earlier age, with disastrous consequences. Primary teachers will have a difficult job in the next few years as they are expected to gain new skills, both in the use of microcomputers, and in using them as a classroom resource to the best advantage of all their pupils. There will be a temptation to go for many cheap microcomputers with very limited facilities and software; the problem with this strategy is that the quality of each child's experience will be so limited that it is pointless going for such quantity.

Hardware in secondary schools

Secondary schools are faced with a difficult problem in terms of provision of hardware. They will typically have one or two quite sophisticated microcomputers and these will be able to meet the immediate needs of such things as computer-aided learning (unless they have already been siphoned off for use in computer studies). There will be a pressure from the computer studies department to buy a large number of (inevitably) cheap microcomputers to support that course. They might also claim that these machines will meet the needs of the computer awareness course. In practice the latter claim will be a fraud, since the cheap microcomputer will not be able to support a range of applications, so will not be able to offer a broad hands-on experience. The danger is that the hands-on experience becomes a dose of programming, which is just about all that is possible with the cheap microcomputer (other than the 'space invaders' type of game). It is a sad state of affairs that the hands-on experience in a typical computer studies course has degenerated into little more than programming; it will be tragic if the same thing happens with a computer awareness course, with the inevitable consequence that most pupils will be turned away from using microcomputers in the mistaken belief that using computers and programming them are synonymous.

It is not easy for schools to cope with the problem when they are faced with having no additional funds for an area which is crying out for such funds. The problem could be partly alleviated if the priority for use of microcomputers is redirected away from the computer studies course, which gobbles up a disproportionate amount of such resources compared to its ultimate value.

Support from the local education authority

Throughout this discussion of use and hardware, there has been an underlying assumption that two commodities will be available: good quality educational software, and extensive teacher training. Both of these should be the responsibility of the local education authority. The reason for making the second of these the responsibility of the LEA is obvious; the first needs some justification.

It is a sad fact of life that the hundreds of microcomputers on the market are, by and large, incompatible. This is sometimes even true for machines from the same manufacturer, particularly those that come from across the Atlantic. This means that software cannot be easily transferred from one machine to the next, and if it is transferred it does not work when it gets there. There is an optimistic belief that is it possible to produce a clever box through which a program which works on machine A can be made to work on machine B. Unfortunately there is no evidence that this is a practical proposition, particularly since in the time taken to develop such a box, machine B is likely to have changed, and the new, cheaper and better microcomputers C, D and E will have become the target machine. So, at the moment individual schools in search of software have to comb through the hundreds of catalogues looking for worthwhile programs which work on their machine. This will include the educational publishers who at the moment are charging an individual school anything between £12 and £25 for a single program.

The alternative is for the LEA to encourage the development of software within the authority and to exchange this for software from other authorities. This is a much cheaper method of obtaining good educational software, and allows the possibility of further development of such programs. This assumes that the LEA will have indicated to its schools the particular make of microcomputer that it will be able to support in terms of software and training. Having standardized on a particular machine within the authority, schools are then able to share experiences and expertise, and to a limited extent can be mutually self-supporting. The LEA then needs a convenient method for distributing software on demand to its schools and one satisfactory method is to use the public telephone system to connect a school's computer to a large central computer in the authority to get a copy of any program that the school requires. The telephone is only used for the time required to transfer a copy of the program – after that the school is able to keep and use that program indefinitely.

Conclusion

The potential for use of microcomputers in both primary and secondary schools is considerable. Schools have a responsibility to prepare children for a world where technological change will be the norm and where two of the most valuable skills will be the ability to adapt and to use new technology to the full. There are many dangers implicit in such a fast-changing society, much of which will happen by default. An important step towards overcoming such problems will be the widest possible sense of control and understanding of such machines and their effects. The biggest danger will be if a technological élite is able to wield the power that such technology makes possible. This can only be avoided by educating all our young children to be effective and discriminating users of the new technology. In addition, teachers should not be afraid to use microcomputers as a powerful teaching resource within their own classroom.

PART II

CONTROLLING SCHOOLS AND CURRICULUM

Introduction

BOB MOON

Maurice Kogan's interest is in the potential of the school as an instrument of social revival, capable of showing that due process rather than emotive mass movement and reflex actions are the ways in which we can live together. It is an interest and optimism shared by more than one contributor to this volume. Three words characterize the kind of normative model of education he sees schools working towards in the coming decades. *Convergence* illustrates a style that must characterize the purpose of schools; *pluralism* is used in the sense that within such purposes multiple values must be allowed and encouraged; and *permeable* refers to the inevitable need to accept and respond to the influences of the outside world. The directions that the revival might take are not elaborated – that was not the purpose of the paper – although the movement away from the attacks on institutional forms towards a debate which places, for example in education, the school at the centre of concern is noted approvingly.

Barry Taylor looks at some of the issues facing schools and suggests that the concept of a contract between school and parents may well serve to counteract some of the more undesirable pressures that have been exerted in recent years. Such a contract would go beyond the unwritten assumptions shared by most schools, although differently interpreted in practice, about the partnership of parents and teachers within the educational process. Barry Taylor would, perhaps, see that contract as the form of convergence that Maurice Kogan seeks, although some would question the extent to which the associated ideas of pluralism and permeability might in practice be negotiated. Barry Taylor continues by pursuing a theme characteristic of a number of contributions in this volume. He sees co-operation between schools as essential in adjusting to the future. How can you have curriculum development without co-operation he asks? And how can any form of continuity between different types of school be established without co-operation becoming an emotional characteristic of the process. Given the assumption of co-operation the role of the benevolent local education authority in assisting this becomes critical.

Each of the contributors in this section, from different perspectives, re-assert the significance of school-based action in the search for reform and improvement. And this analysis covers descriptions of events that confirm the historical development of school-based control as indicated in Peter Green's and Bob Moon's papers as well as the desirability of the, rather different, focus on the school described by Maurice Kogan and Barry Taylor. Each however indicate new directions that schools might follow to capitalize on their positions of influence.

There has in recent years been a growing interest in questions of control. The most obvious manifestation of this in England and Wales has been the emergence of the evaluation and accountability issues dealt with more fully in Part III. Callaghan's Ruskin College speech, the Assessment of Performance Unit, the attacks on Mode III school-based examining, a resurgence of interest in testing, all represent attempts from different positions outside the school to establish greater control over the activities of teachers in schools. It has been a complex and often unsatisfactory experience. Attempts to tilt the balance of power away from school-focused activity have rarely experienced much visible success. It is not only in the face of apparently threatening developments that this applies. The resistance of schools to curriculum change in the boom years of the 1960s is well documented and if we note Lawrence Stenhouse's contribution to this book it is only now, in very indirect ways, that the real value of the work at that time is becoming apparent.

It could be argued that the survival of school-based influence is a reflection of the traditional structure of education within England and Wales, that here we have a unique system of uncoded and pragmatic checks and balances that leaves decisions with schools rather than officials, administrators or others remote from the classroom. No amount of political interference seems capable of changing this well-established tradition of organization. Peter Green's contribution is almost a celebration of the complexity of curriculum reform within schools. He is critical of those, who perceive, naïvely, curriculum change as based on a simplistic model arising from a coherent overview and an implemented uniformity of purpose. From first-hand experience he reports on the curriculum methodologies of two institutions perceived by many as extreme in their attempt to introduce progressive educational philosophies into secondary schooling, and he illustrates how concepts such as autonomy or control have very differing manifestations in each context. The less-than-straightforward reflection of ideology to reality is emphasized in a discussion of the debates about schooling over the last decade. For Peter Green, a critical conflict, one which gives purpose and institutional individuality, is the opposition between curriculum structure and control and student autonomy. This is a productive tension and one he suggests needs re-establishing as a feature of educational debate. The relations between the papers by Maurice Kogan, Barry Taylor and Peter Green are in certain respects complementary, although noting the differences makes for an interesting analysis.

Taking a different perspective, Bob Moon's examination of primary school mathematics brings into question some of the received wisdom about control at national level in so-called centralized or decentralized systems. He demonstrates how, over the twenty-year period, few of the changes that occurred did so as a consequence of the formal system for reform and control. In France, often cited as the example *par excellence* of central rather than regional (let alone school) control, curriculum reforms were carried out in the 1960s without reference to the formal code or regulations. Teachers did their own thing and when the regulations were finally revised it was more to acknowledge changes that had already occurred. Curriculum development went ahead in many countries while formal regulations gathered dust in cupboards. Other influences outside the formal system became significant: textbook publishers, curriculum developers, the media, especially television, to name but three. And this rarely had any formal integration into the national structure of control. Teachers in school, represented in France by that individualistic re-assertion of rights, *le pouvoir peripherique*, controlled much of what went on.

The experience now of the evaluation and accountability movement shows just how complex issues of control are. Colin Richards refers directly to this in his description of the future for primary education in the chapter on 'Changing Schools'. Barry Taylor in his chapter similarly questions our understanding of how policy is decided and implemented at the level of the local authority. The rhetoric of public debate about education sometimes distorts our observations of real events as both Bob Moon and Barry Taylor suggest. If our understanding of reform is to help improve the style of future reforms then it is important to sweep away some of the misunderstandings, even if, to quote Maurice Kogan, 'we must try harder to make a constructive use of ambiguity, to allow people to follow as many choices simultaneously as can be managed rather than placing them into conflict.'

CHAPTER 10

HOLDING THE MIDDLE GROUND: THE SCHOOL AS A RESPONSIVE INSTITUTION

MAURICE KOGAN

There are two personal motives in giving this paper. The first is political, and the second academic. The political objective is to join or perhaps help start the chorus in favour of public institutions which bring people together and serve the common as well as the individual good. The second is to explore some of what we know about the school as an institution which works within and across its boundaries. At each point in a discussion such as this we come to dichotomies that are often treated as conflicts. But we must try harder to make a constructive use of ambiguity, to allow people to follow as many choices simultaneously as can be managed, rather than placing them into conflict. For presentational purposes, things usually have to come in pairs, as do many of the best things in life, so that we can make our simple little contrasts.

First let us deal with the political concern. This is to repeat a much repeated truth.[1] The school is operating in a world in which the middle ground has collapsed. Traditionally restrictive and authoritarian instit-utions still exist, but just as strong are the demands for freedom, for wider participation and for the destruction of allegedly coercive systems. Pro-fessionalism is invited to share its power with those which advance spontan-eous feeling and passion. Some of these changes derive from changes in value in the wider society, which may be more messy but is certainly more democratic than it used to be, and partly from judgements about what the schools can do.

This becomes clear from some of the titles of the imported American literature of the late 1960s and early 1970s: Everett Reimer's *School is Dead*,

Paul Goodman's *Compulsory Education*, Jonathan Kozol's *Death at an Early Age*, the writings of Ivan Illich and so on. And the attack on institutional forms was not simply of anti-bureaucratic or participative or democratic doctrine, or a discontent with the educative processes. They were dominant themes but they were also mixed up with belief in new social arrangements backed by new technologies. So Goodman advocated an increased involvement in the natural learning patterns of family and community and of the sort of relationships fostered in master-apprentice situations. Reimer argued for alternatives in education of content, organization and finance. Illich and many others paraded the notion that learning patterns could be established along information and learning networks that would somehow break children away from the prisons set for them in their years of compulsory education. It is not the concern here to evaluate these critiques, or remedies entailed in them. They are stated as a phenomenon.

Against all of these radical critiques must be set the more important, but undocumented, fact that most parents and teachers believe in schools. Present discontents are exceedingly difficult to combine into one uncomplicated thought. So, for example, pupils' disaffection (Bird, Chessum, Furlong 1981) is associated with a reluctance on the part of the school to hear what pupils think they need. But at the same time the evidence is surely that parents opt for the more traditional schools, for schools in which skills and examination results are more highly prized, and schools which follow relatively traditional patterns of discipline. The evidence for this is increasing opting for private education, whether of the British traditional kind or of the even more traditional kinds embodied in West Indian and other alternative schools.

So while changes in educational content and education are thought desirable and need to be more strongly pressed for, education will not be put into commission as a free-wheeling activity devoid of institutional formats. It must be affirmed strongly and subjectively, that public institutions need to be stronger rather than weaker. We have lost grip of the notion that there can be continuing public institutions doing good, providing education based on a reasonable degree of consensus. That consensus must always be a product of agreement over ways in which conflict can be resolved, of ways in which pluralism can be encouraged and made to work. But fundamentally and ultimately the school succeeds if it is a strong institution to which both its professional practitioners and its clients have good reason to become committed. If there is cause now to be depressed or to be negatively sceptical we should set to putting things right rather than turning our backs on that which we no longer prize. The present misery must not last for ever. Privatization of the public good, and the break-up of institutions and political parties into small sectarian and conflicting groups, may be part of a needed re-analysis of where we stand and where we ought to go. But sooner or later things have got to be pulled together again. And schools have a place in setting an example.

So much for political bias. Now it is possible to begin, in somewhat more objective vein, to think of the school as an institution, in the middle ground of virtually every value conflict, and able to help express and resolve those conflicts because of the underlying values of democratic education.

In brief, the school is an institution that must be *convergent* if it is going to work properly. At the same time it should encourage and allow multiple or *plural* values.

The school as a convergent institution means several and obvious things. A school evinces its own values. Those that do so as a self-conscious exercise are boring to themselves and those who have to listen to them. The values are expressed best through particular policies that are put to work. And the convergence involves achieving a consensus within the staff group and, increasingly, between the staff, governors, parents and pupils as well. It is difficult to conceive of any way in which a school can be other than convergent and coherent on, for example, whatever it considers to be, and however much it might want to avoid the word, a core curriculum. It is to be doubted whether there has ever been a school without its own core curriculum. And statements about what ought to be in the curriculum might entail statements about the desirable qualities which individuals participating in the curriculum believe in and uphold. Nor can the pastoral, disciplinary, guidance or counselling policies be other than coherent. But here, as in the curriculum, we need not struggle hard to observe that coherence assumes multiplicity rather than singularity. Pastoral systems, however they are formulated in the schools, if formulated at all, embody caring and expressive functions and controlling or disciplining functions. Most people rationalize one by saying that it will enhance the other. Let's hope it does. But most teachers, at all levels, including higher education, would be clear that while at any one time one might be putting a lot of effort into being supportive and caring, and at another time in making sure that rules and implicit moral contracts are kept. Ambivalence is to be avoided.

The relationship between curriculum policies and pastoral policies, or the balance between the cognitive and affective aspects of the school is, again, operated through processes of art rather than deliberative science, but, all the same, the subject is an overall policy rather than what can be worked out individually by teachers and pupils personally. And, again, in relationships with outside bodies, including the governing body, groups in the community and the local authority, the school is expected to be convergent; that is, perhaps, the principal argument for the school having a managerial hierarchy with a head who is visibly responsible for what goes on in the school. Institutions that are not expected to be convergent but rather to be divergent (and that is certainly true of the more prestigious parts of higher education) have collegial rather than hierarchical structures.

At the same time as the school is expected to be a reliable, safe, predictable and coherent institution, it is in the business of *enhancing individuality, personal development and freedom*. The school, while operating convergently and reliably, would be expected to be a permeable and open institution. But, as I already suggested, the simple statement of values in pairs pushes off too easily into unreal conflicts. So we could begin to pull out the theme of convergence, and the kind of institutional arrangements that make for it in such a way as to ensure that the convergence is one in which pluralism and freedom and self-development are equally important norms. But the more values one puts into a system, the more complex the roles within it. So the head in the ideal type of school takes managerial accountability for ensuring that the school works well, but is also a gatekeeper, together with other members of staff, of course, to the values and preferences of those outside the school itself, and the leader not only of a hierarchy but also of a collegial structure. And it follows that the range of values which are then shared are not shared by virtue of being imposed but are shared by virtue of being agreed. That would make for an inherent convergence. Imposed convergences do not lead to good work or good relationships between teachers and teachers or teachers and pupils.

If that is so, and we are talking about ideal types, the same kind of healthy and constructive ambiguity comes about if the school is not only convergent but also *permeable*. And that desirable quality is, as with convergence, a derivation of social and individual needs and not simply a slogan. Just as the school must be convergent because children need a reliable environment in which to work and grow up, as do their teachers, so the school must be permeable because it can't close itself off from the world and so it had better get into the business of regulating and benefitting from the traffic from the outside world. It must be permeable if its curriculum is going to be real enough for its pupils to use while they are going through the school and when they leave it. It has to be permeable, as well, for straight democratic reasons. Teachers' professionality is, or should be, based upon knowledge of how pupils develop and how pupil development and forms of knowledge can best come into alliance with each other. Teachers are not, however, the only arbiters of social values and must, therefore, find ways in which they can conscientiously and professionally interpret the values of those with rights over education but who are outside the school, who are concerned with the outer as opposed to the inner life of the school and can bring those social values into the discussion.

Consideration can be given to going over some of the ground then about the convergence and pluralism characteristics of the school before moving on to think of the school in its institutional forms with boundaries.

Here reference to research undertaken at Brunel on disaffected pupils is valuable (Bird, Chessum and Furlong 1981). This was a quite large piece of research financed by the DES and then largely ignored by them but not, fortunately, by many teachers and others who have been in contact with Daphne Johnson and the rest of the research team.

What that study showed, paraphrasing crudely, is that a school contains multiple groups who shape themselves into very many different social ecologies, that is to say, groups with their own shapings, ways of behaviour, values, preoccupations, peer groups and the like. The field work demonstrated that teachers' and pupils' definitions of particular behaviour seldom corresponded. Different groups of pupils did not place the same consistent meaning on what the teachers might appear to think of as replicated patterns of deviant behaviour, such as truancy or classroom disruption. The researchers concluded that most disaffected behaviour can best be understood as an implied, if inarticulate, critique of schooling. They also concluded that they had comparatively few means of expressing that criticism. They could only behave in a disaffected way.

Now there are various policy implications that one can derive from those findings, none of which will be all that surprising to many people here. The team did conclude that there was such a thing as pupil disaffection, that 'many pupils were behaving in ways which teachers found unacceptable and difficult to deal with'. A larger proportion of pupils who did not share the disaffected behaviour nevertheless shared their implicit disaffection from secondary schooling. Some schools avoided recognizing pupil disaffection and the resulting pupil absences and the like. Others bartered for good behaviour. Or excluded pupils from lessons or school. Or were directly repressive.

In analysing what some schools do and what schools might do, our team gave good examples of what I have attempted to define as the combined convergent and pluralistic approach. There are contextual elements common to all maintained secondary schools. They are compulsory. They deal with large numbers. They have to assess and certify. They have to act as surrogates for the reasonable parent and are bounded by all sorts of educational and professional practice. And apart from the common contextual elements, particular schools have more variable contextual features shaped by their pupil intake, their buildings, their environment and so on.

School must be quite strongly convergent in attempting to deal with disaffection and that does not mean being weak. It means strengthening action by examining more closely the way in which the schools' contexts, many imposed from outside, can be related to the more or less coherent values and theories about pupil disaffection to which schools arrive. So it is necessary to stand firm on principles but those principles have to be lived out on the basis of quite ad hoc, local and contextual work on what in fact is happening with particular groups of children within a particular school setting. This means hearing the pupil voice. And that means paying attention to pluralism. It also means, however, what our team identified as staff coherence and what has been called 'whole school policies'. Again, there is no single model of staff coherence or simple explanation of how it might function. But while the teaching teams must be open and responsive to individual pupils and perhaps defend some of them against the whole school policy where necessary, the whole school policy must happen. So teachers must be hearing their own voices but many other voices as well.

So far the discussion has been mainly about the school operating as an internally consistent but flexible system. All of that was so much easier at a time when the schools had authority which they were expected to use, when there was an implied consensus about the curriculum, although hopelessly parcelled out for the different groups in society, and when the school was not expected to be permeable but expected to be watertight, competent and authoritative.

The factors leading to enforced permeability are well enough known. First, there is the general demographic decline in education. Educational demography has two components. The first is induced by the birth rate and that is taking thirteen percent of the numbers in school out of the market within the next decade or so. The second is demography induced by policies. When the word gets round that higher education opportunities are being clamped down, that maintained sixth forms or sixth-form colleges or tertiary colleges will not be given the resources to cope with the additional numbers, so will demand for education beyond the sixteen age group at least be spontaneously damped down. Those induced or natural reductions in demand lead to insecurity in institutional life. People appointed to schools in the 1970s cannot be sure that the schools will still be there by the mid-1980s. Consortium arrangements or just closure are part of everybody's landscape just now. This means that teachers who could have felt secure in their own schools are now more conscious of being part of a more mobile labour market.

Secondly, as alluded to before, there are all of the pressures on the schools to be far more overt in the curriculum which they are producing and here the whole core curriculum and other curriculum analysis exercises are two obvious examples. At the same time, even watered-down Taylorism is making governing bodies more potent, at least in some areas, while the general drive towards greater participation by clients opens up the schools.

It is a nice question whether those external pressures weaken or strengthen schools. The painfulness of increased exposure and demands to explain oneself are pretty evident. But we are all painfully learning as well that we can't rely upon our public employment systems to keep us secure, to offer security of several kinds. One is job security and that is obvious enough. The other is political and psychological support. So greater strength might come from getting a stronger command of the forces outside the school which in any case are increasingly helping to shape its destiny.

The behavioural details of doing that are too obvious to state at length and in finishing it is important to examine some of the implications. Working hard with a governing body to make it more rather than less knowledgeable about the school so that it can begin to make an effective contribution to discussions is one obvious example. If governors become more knowledgeable about the legal powers and about the working of the school they will want to take a greater part in decision making. But decisions then made about the school are more likely to stick both with the client groups, pupils and their parents, and the governing system above the governing body in the local authority. The curriculum then stands some chance of having been tested not only by teachers' own educational criteria but by the criteria of forces outside the school as well. This does not mean that the school surrenders to external fashion and forces. It means that the teacher group, led by the head, have a more complicated professional task, namely of rendering into educational norms and practices a curriculum that is developed not only by their own knowledge of pupils' development and knowledge systems but also is tuned to respond to if not to conform to messages coming from outside.

Such behaviour would mean a more conscious viewing of the school as a boundaried institution (Richardson 1973, Johnson *et al*. 1980). It is well enough boundaried to be sure. It does have its own physical presence, its rights to be compulsorily attended, its permanent resources of full-time teachers and the like. It does have power over pupils in the references it gives and in the courses it provides, in the preference that it states. It is a very strong institution in terms of the resources that it has. But boundaries are never unilaterally determined. Any social entity can only have the social space made clear for it by those in the rest of society. The school therefore needs to be more conscious of the fact that it has boundaries around it. It needs, therefore, to work more effectively and strongly across the boundaries. And, equally, it needs to become more conscious of the systems and boundaries within itself and these are peer group systems of pupils to which I have referred earlier, as well as for the curriculum and for pastoral functions.

All this is stated as made clear at the beginning, partly because it is a personal occupation to think about the nature of institutions. But there is also a political interest in the school as an instrument of social revival. Everything has taken too much bashing. Social institutions are devalued as if they were the home of pampered beings following soft options instead of the beauties and rigours of the market. Individuals and individuality are also being pushed hard not only by market forces but also by some of the groups who allegedly believe in social revival and redemption. The person with an individual conscience and a belief in his right to exercise it does not get all that much encouragement in some of our political groupings. So we need institutions that will beat out several messages at once. They will be reliable and effective and give people what they have the right to expect for their children. They will give something special because of the expertise that teachers develop about pupils and about the world of knowledge. They will not be impervious to the demands from outside the school itself and be responsive to social need. They will demonstrate that complicated systems can work cohesively. They will demonstrate that whole school policies can be formed. They will also show, and how badly needed this is, that due process rather than emotive mass movement and reflex action are the ways in which we can live together. That is the kind of normative model of education that it is to be hoped that the schools will be working towards in the 1980s.

Note

1   Most recently, *Inspection and Advice*, No 15, Autumn 1981. Conference addresses. Patterns of Advice and Control in Education.

References

Bird, Cathy, Chessum, Rosemary, Furlong, John, Johnson, Daphne (ed) (1981), *Disaffected Pupils*, Department of Government, Brunel University.
Johnson, Daphne, Ransom, Elizabeth, Packwood, Tim, Bowden, Katherine, and Kogan, Maurice (1980) *Secondary Schools and the Welfare Network*, George Allen & Unwin.
Richardson, Elizabeth *The Teacher, The School and the Task of Management*, Heinemann.

CHAPTER 11

CHALK CIRCLES: the curriculum as an area of conflict

PETER GREEN

The theme of this paper is that the current debate about control of the curriculum over-simplifies what actually happens in schools; that the curriculum is created out of conflict: the opposition between a curriculum structure and the opportunity for students to learn for and by themselves. It suggests that we return to the discussions of the 1960s to remind ourselves of this and then seek to restore, in public debate, an awareness of the productive tension between control of the curriculum and student autonomy.

From *The Caucasian Chalk Circle* by Brecht

Enter Shauva with the child.
THE GOVERNOR'S WIFE: It's in rags!
GRUSHA: That's not true. I wasn't given the time
   to put on his good shirt.
THE GOVERNOR'S WIFE: It's been in a pig-stye.
GRUSHA furious: I'm no pig, but there are others
   who are. Where did you leave your child?
THE GOVERNOR'S WIFE: I'll let you have it, you
   vulgar person. (She is about to throw herself
   on Grusha, but is restrained by her lawyers.)
   She's a criminal! She must be whipped!
THE SECOND LAWYER holding his hand over her mouth:
   Most gracious Natella Abashvili, you promised . . .
   Your Worship, the plaintiff's nerves . . .

AZDAK: Plaintiff and defendant! The Court has
   listened to your case, and has come to no
   decision as to who the real mother of the child
   is. I as Judge have the duty of choosing a
   mother for the child. I'll make a test. Shauva,
   get a piece of chalk and draw a circle on the
   floor. (Shauva does so.) Now place the child
   in the centre. (Shauva puts Michael, who
   smiles at Grusha, in the centre of the circle.)
   Stand near the circle, both of you. (The
   Governor's wife and Grusha step up to the circle.)
   Now each of you take the child by a hand. The
   true mother is she who has the strength to pull
   the child out of the circle, towards herself.
THE SECOND LAWYER quickly: High Court of Justice,
   I protest! I object that the fate of the great
   Abashvili estates, which are bound up with the
   child as the heir, should be made dependent on
   such a doubtful wrestling match. Moreover, my
   client does not command the same physical strength
   as this person, who is accustomed to physical work.
AZDAK: She looks pretty well fed to me. Pull!
(The Governor's wife pulls the child out of the circle
to her side. Grusha has let it go and stands aghast.)
THE FIRST LAWYER congratulating the Governor's wife:
   what did I say: The bonds of blood!
AZDAK to Grusha: What's the matter with you? You didn't pull!
GRUSHA: I didn't hold on to him. (She runs to Azdak.)
   Your Worship, I take back everything I said against
   you. I ask your forgiveness. If I could just keep
   him until he can speak properly. He knows only a
   few words.
AZDAK: Don't influence the Court! I bet you know only
   twenty yourself. All right, I'll do the test once
   more to make certain.
(The two women take up positions again.)
AZDAK: Pull! (Again Grusha lets go of the child.)
GRUSHA in despair: I've brought him up! Am I to tear
   him to pieces? I can't do it!

AZDAK rising: And in this manner the Court has established the true mother. (To Grusha): Take
your child and be off with it. I advise you
not to stay in town with him. (To the Governor's
wife): And you disappear before I fine you for
your fraud. Your estates fall to the city. A
playground for children will be made out of
them. They need one, and I have decided it
shall be called after me – The Garden of Azdak.[1]

The chalk circle test

The chalk circle test in Brecht's play is a demonstration of the unconventional wisdom of the anarchic judge, Azdak. He has to decide between rival claims to the possession of a child. On the one hand is the refined governor's wife, who is the boy's natural mother; on the other hand is Grusha, a peasant woman, who has looked after the baby from birth. Which is the real mother? Azdak is suspicious of rhetoric and any claim to be in sole possession of the truth. He is not deceived by the lawyers' legal circumlocutions nor by Grusha's angry bawling. A less wise judge would make up his mind on the basis of what is said but Azdak does not try to resolve the argument on this level; instead he draws a chalk circle in order to explore the real conflict. The governor's wife would happily have destroyed the child in order to claim him as her own. Grusha has more concern for the boy: 'If I could just keep him until he can speak properly. He knows only a few words.' However, in her eagerness to educate the child she will not kill it and so lets go. Azdak does not rush to conclusions: he learns from the conflict dramatized before him.

Analogies are useful, though perhaps as much for their points of contrast as their points of similarity; the purpose of this opening example from Brecht is to help me to make a point. Drawing upon this scene it is to be argued that in making judgements about who should exercise control over the curriculum, it is necessary to be equally wary of rhetoric and equally willing to allow the real issues to emerge in practice, examining the conflicts which make up our experience of teaching. The question, 'Who decides the curriculum?' is one of the key issues for any school; it is most important in helping to determine the school ethos or 'climate'.[2] However, much of the public and some of the professional debate around this question and about what kind of curriculum is imagined is an over-simplification. It often underestimates the problem of turning theory into practice; of translating ideas in curriculum planning meetings into class-room experience. It often assumes too readily not only that schools should work but that they can work to one coherent overview and achieve uniformity of practice. The main theme of this paper is that reality is not nearly so tractable as debate assumes and that we do ourselves a disservice if we do not acknow-ledge just how complex curriculum planning can be and the extent to which the resulting curriculum is a balance of interests, created out of conflict.

At the present time, curriculum discussion is dominated by the vocabu-lary of 'control'. The DES is moving cautiously towards some form of national curriculum and LEAs, it seems clear, will be expected to play a more important role than hitherto in determining the curriculum of their individual schools. Even if we share misgivings about these developments, we have learned to operate with some of the underlying assumptions of the language: schools must evaluate themselves; schools must become more accountable to the public. Is there a challenge to the prevailing consensus? If so, where does it come from? The argument here is that it should come from the classroom and, in order to do so, it is necessary to go back to a different debate, one which was the focus of attention in the early 1970s.

The times are less propitious than they were then. Ten years ago or so, books with titles like *Teaching as a Subversive Activity* or *School is Dead* were well-read challenges to the whole edifice of institutionalized schooling, suggesting that less authoritarian, more open and exploratory forms of learning would lead to a more egalitarian society. It was imagined that control of the curriculum would be in the hands of teachers, at a time when teacher-based assessment was gaining ground, rather than those of the examination boards or local authorities; and, as far as possible, in the hands of students rather than teachers. The emphasis was on 'autonomy' rather than 'control', on the claim that 'the child is the agent in his own learning', on students learning to organize their own work through individual inquiry. One of the key words in what was written about this model of education was 'discovery' – learning by and for oneself. Book titles are mentioned here because texts were often more influential than reality – they ranged from those in the Penguin education series to official publications of the time. A particular model of practice in primary schools is endorsed by the Plowden Report (1967):

> The sense of personal discovery influences the intensity of a child's experi-ence, the vividness of his memory and the probability of effective transfer of learning . . . the teacher is responsible for encouraging children in inquiries which lead to discovery and for asking leading questions. (para 349)

The report recommended this approach particularly for science:

> The treatment of the subject matter may be summarized in the phrase 'learning by discovery'. In a number of ways it resembles the best modern university practice . . . though constant dialogue between teacher and children is an essential factor of the approach we are describing, it would be wrong to picture it all as taking place in a classroom or even a laboratory. Essential elements are inquiry, exploration and first-hand experience which may mean expeditions . . . (para 669)

So pervasive was this view, expressed in this case in the bland, measured and qualified prose of an official document, claiming support from empirical evidence, that it looked for a while as if this model had won the day. Certainly it now looks as if the authors of the first Black Paper, in 1969, thought so – their tone is not one of confidence that the traditional model will survive; it is approaching a cry of defeat from the embattled and embittered:

> Since the war revolutionary changes have taken place in English education – the introduction of free play methods in primary schools, comprehensive schemes, the expansion of higher education, the experimental courses at new universities. . . . Anarchy is becoming fashionable, and in papers such as *The Guardian* and *New Statesman* writers take it for granted that fundamental changes in the student/teacher relationship are inevitable.[3]

'Fight for Education' was published one year after the unofficial six-week student teach-in at Hornsey College of Art, which began on 28 May 1968, and it was really a reaction to student unrest in universities rather than to the school curriculum; unrest which was seen as the result of educational expansion and egalitarianism. Whereas Plowden hoped that university methods of individual research might begin in primary schools, the writers of the Black Paper feared that the influence would work in reverse – that 'free play methods' would be adopted in the universities. Most of the contributors were academics and a significant proportion were English lecturers used to literary criticism. Consequently their views were not, at first, based on anything like hard evidence or first-hand knowledge of schools but on what had been read in books, reports, and particularly in newspapers, which were the texts most quoted and criticized (Wright 1977).

At the end of the 1960s and in the early 1970s, views on education were polarized. At one end of the spectrum was what was written about 'the Hornsey Affair' – probably the most symbolic and therefore one of the most interesting examples of an alternative model of control that we have:

It is patently ridiculous to think that an education in innovation can be carried out in a factory atmosphere where students are conceived of as passive objects being processed along the lines of the system, obediently doing their
prescribed conventional tasks at the appointed hours in the appointed ways . . . education which is not essentially a training in self-education is worthless. And it can only be this if the emphasis is constantly upon the initiative, the free responsibility of the students (both individually and collectively).[4]

We can find the same arguments being put forward in the Plowden Report, published two years earlier. Central to the language here is the idea that the student must learn to learn – to become an innovator able to cope with a rapidly changing environment. At the other end of the spectrum is the six-year series of Black Papers, which articulated some of the main concerns of the period as if they were the consensus views of all sensible, ordinary people. A shorthand for the clusters of attitudes associated with each position is reflected in the words 'autonomy' and 'control' (Hornsey's 'free responsibility' and the Black Paperites' 'structured approach'). See *Figure 11.1*

CONTROL← ————————————— →AUTONOMY

That this basic opposition was a conflict of ideologies is clear. 'Fight for Education' begins from the premise that, 'Children are not naturally good', and goes on to state that, 'You can have equality or equality of opportunity; you cannot have both.' Plowden actually talks of 'a recognizable philosophy of education . . . a view of society, which may be summarized' (para 504).

It is the nature of ideology that it is fictional. While it is expressed through the opinions, attitudes and values which make up our philosophies of education, its relationship with reality is less than straightforward. Louis Althusser (1971) gives a useful definition of ideology as 'a "representation" of the imaginary relationship of individuals to their real conditions of existence'. Ideology attempts to map the real contours of events by turning them into a coherent narrative. However, this sense of completeness or 'closure' (because it excludes the contradictory) is false because reality always escapes definition. This does not mean that a view of education is insincere, but that it is an attempt to clarify real events through language. The accounts of what happened at Hornsey in May 1968, 'The quiet noise of wisdom working', and the Black Papers, are stories about education; 'representations' – novellas with characters and a

TALK WITH US

UNDERSTANDING IS FREE
UNDERSTAND US
WE ARE PART OF ONE ANOTHER
NO MORE THEM AGAINST US
EACH ONE IS INDISPENSABLE
TALKING AND WORKING TOGETHER
WE CREATE AN EDUCATION
EDUCATION MEANS
A LIFETIME GROWING WISER
IS THERE ANYTHING MORE IMPORTANT?
WISDOM EQUALS THOUGHT
ALIVE WITH FEELING
WHAT ELSE CAN ANSWER OUR QUESTIONS?
THE QUIET NOISE OF WISDOM WORKING

THAT IS THE REVOLUTION

ISSUED BY THE ASSOCIATION OF MEMBERS OF HORNSEY COLLEGE OF ART

(8)

AUTONOMY

AND CONTROL

Black Paper Basics

Ten Points

...ities. Without such checks, standards decline. Working-class children suffer when applying for jobs if they cannot bring forward proof of their worth achieved in authoritative examinations.

9 Freedom of speech must be preserved in universities. Institutions which cannot maintain proper standards of open debate should be closed.

(9)

10 You can have equality or equality of opportunity; you cannot have both. Equality will mean the holding back (or the new deprivation) of the brighter children.

...need firm, useful discipline from parents and teachers with clear standards. Too much freedom for children breeds selfishness, vandalism and personal unhappiness.

2 If the non-competitive ethos of progressive education is allowed to dominate our schools, we shall produce a generation unable to maintain our standards of living when opposed by fierce rivalry from overseas competitors.

3 It is the quality of teachers which matters, rather than their numbers or their equipment. We have sacrificed quality for numbers, and the result has been a lowering of standards. We need high-quality, higher-paid teachers in the classroom, not as counsellors or administrators.

4 Schools are for schooling, not social engineering.

5 The best way to help children in deprived areas is to teach them to be literate and numerate, and to develop all their potential abilities.

6 Every normal child should be able to read by the age of seven. This can be achieved by the hard work of teachers who use a structured approach.

7 Without selection the clever working-class child in a deprived area stands little chance of a real academic education.

Figure 11.1

plot which, like all fictional texts, are removed from reality.

This is to over-simplify the complex notion of 'ideology' but it is done in order to point out that these stories express authentic beliefs, whatever their polemical content, but that it would be a mistake to believe that either presented a truthful picture. It would also be a mistake to think that the truth lay somewhere in the middle – between the two. In the scene from Brecht's play, control of the child cannot be shared or he will be torn apart. Until there is a struggle, Azdak is unable to judge where the child's best interests lie.

During the 1970s it was believed that an 'autonomy' model had been implemented upon a large scale and that some kind of balance had to be restored at all levels. Just as it is now accepted that the call for greater public accountability is the result of widespread innovation. Much of what has been written about education since the 1960s has been recruited to this controversy. Thus, Neville Bennet's study of *Teaching Styles and Pupil Progress* (1976) assessed the school curriculum through the language of 'informal' and 'formal' practices – a popular shorthand for our clusters of opposing attitudes. His acceptance of these ideological terms, on the basis of teachers' comments, meant that they shaped the plot of the research: that pupils taught by 'formal' methods were, on the whole, more successful in basic subjects; despite the finding that the most successful single teacher used an 'informal' approach. The book became a bestseller presumably because it was saying something that people liked to believe about the 1960s: that teaching for autonomy, while often inspired, was unsuccessful.

However, practising teachers know that the autonomy model was never implemented to anywhere near the extent claimed by those who supported or opposed it. Brian Simon (1981) argues that, despite what is claimed in the report

> only a minority of primary schools had been transformed along 'modern lines', though an uncertain proportion of others was perceived as following in that way.[5]

The recent ORACLE research project (Galton *et al.* 1980), which claims that by using systematic observations of classrooms it escapes from determining definitions of practice, concludes:

> one thing that does seem clear is that 'progressive' teaching, if by this is meant teaching having the characteristics defined by the Plowden Report, hardly exists in practice.[5]

While unstreaming and individualization have been widely adopted, the main recommendation has not:

> . . . central to the Plowden thesis was the questing, exploratory character of the individual child's actual activity; the stress on discovery methods, on finding out for oneself; while the teacher was seen as stimulating this activity by probing, questioning, guiding – leading the child from behind. It is here that classroom practice, according to our data, does not match the prescripts. Individualized teaching (or interaction) is not 'progressively' orientated, in this sense; it is overwhelmingly factual and managerial. Such probing and questioning as does take place is to be found largely in the whole class teaching situation, one generally to be avoided, according to Plowden, in favour of individualization; and paradoxically, the teaching situation popularly held to be best adapted to didactic teaching (telling).[6]

This research suggests the unreality of much 'progressive' jargon but it also undermines the currently fashionable rhetoric which assumes that the practice in the 1960s has led to a loss of control over the curriculum – a loss of order and of organization. In the ORACLE studies what comes through strongly is the continuing, effective 'managerial' role of the teacher.

Two examples of curriculum planning

This is not to suggest that we return naîvely to the ideals of the 1960s. There have been too many developments in the art of teaching since then to allow this to happen; many of the 'progressive' metaphors of organic growth and the 'child-centred' curriculum seem absurdly romantic to us now. We are more realistic. This realism is reflected in the titles of the books we now read: *Closely Observed Children* and *A Teacher's Guide to Action Research* – which focus on a single classroom and on one or two students; they suggest that, with a greater awareness of how learning takes place, the teacher can make small incremental gains in the quality of his or her teaching. These books no longer claim that we can transform the educational system, or society. Instead, we can improve our skills by learning from each other – we can change our classrooms. The agent of change is no longer the Big Idea, 'individualization', 'unstreaming', 'discovery' . . . but the team of teachers who, by working together, explore the conflict between the need for curriculum control and 'the child as the agent of his (or her) own learning'.

Attention can now be given to two examples of curriculum planning. The first comes from Bridgewater Hall School, Stantonbury Campus, Milton Keynes and the second from Countesthorpe College, Leicestershire. In Bridgewater Hall School on Stantonbury Campus, students aged fourteen–sixteen work for part of the week in each of five main subject or 'faculty' areas: European studies; maths; social studies; science and design technology – all of which are independent units within the agreed curriculum structure. There is no system of option columns, so that students have a compulsory five-subject curriculum. However, although additional examination subjects are made available within these areas for students who can benefit, each area attempts to involve all students in a wide range of 'core' activities. The area called European studies occupies the equivalent of a day and a quarter a week on each student's timetable; 600 fourth- and fifth-years are taught in four half-year groups of about 150 students, in five mixed-ability tutor groups. They follow a broad integrated English course (language and literature – and not just 'English' literature) but one which aims at a European perspective and integrates languages (French and German mainly), drama and music. Most students spend the whole time on the 'core' integrated course; a minority choose to extend their work in particular areas (French and drama are available within the core time and German and music, for timetable convenience, in another faculty's core time). Students work in flexibly designed areas which can be used as large open areas or up to three closed-off spaces. All the teachers involved work as a team, teachers of three adjoining groups as a 'mini-team'.

In order to facilitate shared planning and teaching, integrated work by students and small-group learning, a resource-based, topic-centred course has evolved which is co-operatively structured. At planning meetings everyone contributes ideas and agrees on the broad outline for a half-term's work, then one or two teachers undertake to produce the necessary resources and to organize the activities. In order to make the large number of variables more manageable, the curriculum plan is written out in practical detail – down to the level, for example, of whose job it will be to record, set up and cue a video. This plan is printed and published, with all the resources, within the school: a typographical curriculum. It is not a syllabus but a practical materialization of what is intended and how it could happen. It is a pop-up book of ideas.

This method of consensus planning, which had been one of Stantonbury's aims from the beginning, effectively abolishes the autonomy of the teacher – in the sense that he or she cannot pursue an individual line for long if it has not already been generally agreed. This has produced the major source of conflict within the faculty as the course has developed.

EUROPEAN STUDIES   CURRICULUM PLAN

FOR THE WEEK	MONDAY NOVEMBER 17 TO FRIDAY NOVEMBER 22

TERMLY THEME	IMAGINATION	SUB-THEME	MYTHS

SUMMARY OF THE WEEK: BROWN AND FORDE HOUSES

Mon 2	Mon 4	Thurs 2	Fri 1	Fri 4
TEAM PRESENTATION – MYTHMAKING	MYTHMAKING	+ FAIRY TALES	+ FAIRY TALES	MYTHMAKING

SUMMARY OF THE WEEK: ABBOTT AND COLLINS HOUSES

Mon 1	Tues 1	Wed 2	Fri 2	Fri 3
TEAM PRESENTATION – MYTHMAKING	+ FAIRY TALES	MYTHMAKING	+ FAIRY TALES	MYTHMAKING

TEAM PRESENTATIONS/AUDIO-VISUAL

The work for the week is a groupwork project on 'mythmaking'. The situation should be carefully explained in mini-teams (Forde/Collins in C 214; Brown/Abbott in C 106/7). The situation is explained in the notes and an opening 'script' is provided. You will need to stress the importance of co-operation and of talking quietly. It is an open-ended task, some groups will make false starts but this is part of the learning process. At the end of each session, or at points within each session, the 'reporter' in each group should report to the whole class on the progress being made. This is an opportunity to discuss the process with the class and may help to stimulate the work. Two sessions could be spent on it with the third for the presentations to the whole group (or mini-team?). There are only two extraction sessions this week (the Friday one for French will therefore be a whole session). French and Drama teachers could join in with the project and become more closely identified with the core. Perhaps there could be a direct follow up in the Drama sessions? In the two extraction sessions — read the fairy tales and discuss them. (See notes)

ORAL/AURAL/GROUPWORK

READING

WRITTEN

EXTENSION

CONTINUATION

Ask students to write a brief report on the week's work, focussing on the ways in which the small group co-operated and the final product.

Figure 11.2

The objective, of course, is not to stifle individual initiative or to outlaw spontaneity but to generate good ideas and to enable them to work in practice. Through meetings the printed plan is filled in, amended or extended; students and teachers are encouraged to make connections between different aspects of the course and both are free, despite, or rather because of, the structure to negotiate their own areas of work. Here is a method of curriculum control which aids accountability. Everything is planned and monitored by a team; one teacher could get things wrong but with a group this is much less likely. At a time when schools are required by law to publish prospectuses, here is a way of making the actual curriculum available for inspection or comment in advance. The 'Teacher's Guide' is also a useful diary-record of ideas which work well. It is consensus rather than prescriptive planning.

Planning is open ended and encourages individual students to follow their own ideas. The illustration is from the 'Teacher's Guide' to the course; it shows the page for one week in which it was suggested that students worked in small groups on a particular project – the exact nature of which is not relevant here. This page points to one value of consensus planning: it is a good way to ensure that a wide range of different activities, not just various forms of writing, will take place. It is very difficult to establish co-operative group work, as opposed to groups doing individualized work; group work seems to depend upon careful planning and preparation and rarely arises spontaneously. One of the ambiguities of this kind of curriculum control is that it does rely on most students creating their own curriculum within the framework provided. Usually, students are given a wide range of choices and the plan can accommodate those who reject the 'package' and want to follow an idea of their own. In fact, while the structure is there as a stimulus and a safety net of possibilities, the real interest lies at the point where students engage with, modify or reject what is offered. It is valuable to look further at how a student can be autonomous within this particular example of control.

The example of David Williams and the poetry of Linford Wood

This is a brief description of one project and of one student's active participation. The objectives of the project were to stimulate thought about the images we have of life in the country and the city and to explore their interdependence. We involved, in each fourth-year team, up to ninety students at any one time and, over a period of a week, all 250

Species	Date: 20.3.81 Time	Place	Other features
Magpie	0910	Bushes behind Youth Club	Full black & white plumage
Song Thrush	0910	Path to Linford	Slight albino coloured wing tips
Black-headed Gull	0913	Path to Linford	Not very common in this particular area
Wood Pigeon	0920	Linford Wood	A lot of white plumage
Great Tit & Blue Tit	0920	Linford Wood	These birds are very common in the wood, everywhere you look they are there
Bull Finch	0922	Linford Wood	Beautiful burgundy summer plumage
Wren	0924	Linford Wood	This is a beautiful tiny bird which is hard to spot
Chaffinch	0925	Linford Wood	Like the Bull Finch, a lovely summer plumage
Robin	0926	Linford Wood	Very bright red breast
Coal Tit	0928	Linford Wood	Not too common in woodland areas
Black Bird	0928	Linford Wood	Brightly covered coal-black male
Greenfinch	0935	Linford Wood	Not as brightly coloured as other finches
Starling	0936	Linford Wood	As well as being the so-called scavenger, the starling has a beautiful browny-bronze/blue metallic breast

Table 11.1

fourth-years took part. We began by negotiating with students the terms of an exploratory role play. The result for one team was a drama developed from a social catastrophe in which teachers and students were inhabitants of an area which had been polluted by poisonous chemicals which had leaked out into the atmosphere from a nearby factory on the edge of the city. Important decisions had to be made. Many issues, including political ones, were raised. The government were offering to resettle everybody either in the nearest city or in another, less fertile, rural area. We had to decide which option to adopt. There was a third alternative, which was to refuse to leave and to suffer the alarming consequences of the pollution – disease and sterility. We worked in groups, improvizing appropriate roles – some students were government officials, others formed a closed community opposed to co-operative action, others advocated a united front, each group worked out a different solution; meetings were called and, on the second day when we continued, there was a noisy *coup d'etat*. The students determined the course of the drama and the issues which were raised. Afterwards, in groups, they planned the follow-up, which depended upon their response to the issues and their particular interests. Projects included tape recordings of original plays, a musical presentation, the plans for an ideal community, a video recording of a drama improvized around the same theme and a photographic study of urban and rural life.

Inspired by the drama and discussions with others in his group, David Williams decided to go off to Linford Wood to report on which birds could be seen. His small piece of work is a good example of what happens when a student is able to be autonomous. He returned with a list of birds and some observations upon them.

He then wrote the following account of what he had seen, as if he was still seeing it:

British Birds of Milton Keynes

As Milton Keynes becomes bigger the smaller the countryside becomes. But with Milton Keynes there is a difference as there are places where wildlife can live dotted all around the city, this includes common British birds. One place in particular is Linford Wood and this is an excellent place to go with a pair of binoculars. It is a sunny morning and there is blue sky; it is a moderately quiet time of the day, the best time of all I think. So off I go to spot some birds. And as soon as I am outside the school, a Magpie swoops by some bushes with its beautiful black and white plumage and superbly spread wings and tail. As I approach the wood a Song Thrush scuttles along on the grass on its morning trek for food. I suddenly spot a rare sight, rare for the city – with its very dark head a Black Headed Gull flies overhead. As I start to walk through the wood a pair of Wood Pigeons stand on a branch of a beech tree and as they flutter through the branches I see the very clear white stripes on the tops of their wings. As I go further into the wood, the squabbling sound of Great and Blue Tits can easily be heard; everywhere I look there are these small colourful birds. Also a close relative of the tits are the finches, and I see three, the first two are the Chaffinch and Bullfinch; two birds which are in their full splendour, revealing their beautiful black and red plumages, especially the Bullfinch, as it has a darker burgundy crop and breast than the Chaffinch. Also I see a not-so-bright Greenfinch. A family relation to the finch is the Crossbill, which I have yet to see as its upper and lower bills cross each other to enable them to break nuts and pierce berries more easily, like a pair of scissors. Then I hear the sound of the most beautiful bird I know in the British woodland, its piercing call attracts my attention: the Wren – with its very small size and short vertical tail, it is easily identified when spotted. I stay and watch it amongst the dead leaves, rumaging for food until, suddenly, it darts away. One of the most familiar birds known to most people is the Robin, with its redbreast standing out proudly; it walks from twig to twig amongst the branches of a felled tree. Also near the same spot a Blackbird shrills out its warning call to all the birds around as I approach it. As I begin to make my way back (through the mud!), I see the most common bird around, the so-called scavenging Starling with its blue and bronze metallic breast. This rounded off an enjoyable morning in Linford Wood.

What is interesting about this account is that it is based entirely on David's own observations and pre-existing knowledge, fired by the discussions which had gone on in his group. At this stage he is an ornithologist, collecting the data but in the account he is extending the description to illustrate the wealth of bird life he has discovered. He is beginning to give the experience shape, what is becoming significant for him are the visual qualities of the birds and the sense of movement. In order to focus on these aspects and to further develop his impressions, in the next session he wanted to create a more concise picture of what he had seen. David begins by being an ornithologist for his group but ends by becoming a poet. This is his final attempt, after a few false starts and discussions with others in his group:

LINFORD WOOD

A cold morning air curls around your face
Like the movement of spiralling leaves
When an adder is lose in the early bracken.
It is quiet, apart from the click-clacking

Sound of your feet on the cold-pebbled floor;
The trees are silhouetted against the sun
Which is finding its way through the maze of branches.
A blackbird struts around his ground,
Showing off his bright yellow beak
And the coal-black feathers.
A plum breasted bullfinch warbles
Whilst a timid robin ruffles its ball of fluff.
A tiny wren with its upright tail
Scuttles amongst the undergrowth
Like a bobbing float on the surface of the grass.
On his bright blue-bronze metallic breast
– a starling catches the light.

It is interesting to see how the poem develops out of the original experience: it is not by any means an outstanding piece but it does illustrate how the student begins to transform an experience, in which he was an active participant, into something approaching art. The whole project was worth one line . . . 'a timid robin ruffles its ball of fluff'. In monitoring work over a period of time the real measure of success was the extent to which we generated a conflict between the structure and control we thought necessary for everybody to produce their best work in a happy, purposeful atmosphere and the stimulus for individuals or groups to subvert that control and find the space to organize and shape their own learning. At the present time there should be more debate about which kinds of structures promote autonomy in learning and less about how that autonomy can be controlled.

Countesthorpe College is a series of small schools. The building is circular in shape, which allows quiet access to and from all parts of the college; architecture embodies the idea of learning 'in the round' – making connections between the different areas of experience. Our students aged fourteen–sixteen spend, on average, half their week in a self-contained 'team' area, in which up to six mixed-ability tutor groups are cared for. Students learn English (language and literature), mathematics, social studies, science and art with a team of teachers of these subject disciplines. Each area has its own art space and science laboratory, among its specialist accommodation. There is no distinction between academic and pastoral work: each student has a tutor who will teach him or her for at least one of the related team subjects but the happiness and general welfare of students is the concern of all teachers. Most of the work is individualized; students are encouraged to take equal responsibility, with their tutor, for planning their timetable and how they will tackle the requirements of each subject or topic. Time not spent in the team area is used for work in additional subject areas outside the team base. The team is staffed throughout the week, providing considerable flexibility when tutors are helping students to balance their time between team and non-team activities.

The team was established in order to provide a secure and friendly base in which a valuable corporate identity could be developed to counter the social fragmentation which results when students follow individualized timetables; and in order that one person, at least, could get to know each student very well indeed. Consequently, the experience for the student in one team will be different from that of a student in another team: there is a creative autonomy, despite the common provision, which allows a team to exploit the strengths and interests of its own teachers and students. There can be interesting conflicts at times between the team and specialist subject areas outside, over such matters as staffing for example, and between the interests of each cellular area and the college curriculum as a comprehensive whole. In the first school example, control of the curriculum as a whole is through a compulsory five-subject core and, in the example, through planned activities offered in an attempt to provide a stimulating range of common experiences and opportunities for autonomous learning. At Countesthorpe control of the whole curriculum is through a division into related subjects in team and additional subjects outside; within the team, control is exercised through a process of 'negotiation' between student and tutor. The differences between the two forms of control will become clearer if I look at the work of a student.

Karen Shepherd and the study of society

Ideas for work arise from conversations between students and teachers. There is no attempt at a thematic course although, where examinations are involved, syllabus requirements and course work deadlines act as guidelines and constraints.

Self-Assessment: Work in Team

Once you have decided on your project you usually draw up some sort of plan. You can ask your tutor for assistance if required. One of my choices this term was Mass Media and for this topic I looked at sex stereotypes in children's comics. The idea may be the student's own or it may be a mixture of both the student's and the tutor's ideas and, as with mine, it may be settled by a discussion between the two. This way the student is free to reject ideas which are not suitable. Because my first project was on Poverty, which is a world-wide issue, it was hard to say anything original. It proved a difficult topic to study. My second choice, however, was quite different because it was on sex stereotypes in comics and I was able to include my own opinions and argue them through. I first decided on which material to use and then started to analyse the comics. With the help of my tutor I made a list of headings on what to look out for. Although I made this list I found that points emerged which I hadn't considered and so I was able to add these also. What made this project more immediate than the first was that I was able to write down more of my own thoughts on the subject instead of having to consider a number of difficult international issues.

This was quite a different approach to that of my Poverty project. My tutor put a large amount of literature my way and briefly discussed with me what part of poverty I wanted to look at. When I started I thought I would be studying poverty in the Third World. As my project progressed I went off Third World issues and began to examine poverty in England, which I knew existed but I was unaware of its extent. In order to help me to do this my tutor gave me magazine articles and other sources of information. I also joined Team discussions if they were useful, such as a talk given by a man from Shelter.

A number of points emerged from the projects. With the Mass Media project a number of things came up which I already knew about but I didn't realise how prominently they would be shown. I already knew that girls were encouraged to do the housework while boys were encouraged to go out and play. However, I didn't know how automatically it was all done. In the children's comics a girl is automatically seen with a duster or something equally predictable in her hand, whilst the boy lazily watches telly or plays with his soldiers.

So I discovered how early this minor conditioning starts. Also I saw how the media portrays this idea to the parent and child. My Poverty project produced a more distressing picture. I realized that poverty can be separated into different categories and although there is a large difference between relative and absolute poverty, both are equally disturbing. I also discovered that it is a more complex problem than I had imagined. I realised that I could not do anything to help. All I can do perhaps is to look upon it less emotionally. What also came out of this project was that you do not necessarily have to be without possessions to be poor. I looked at one idea that even if we have luxuries, like a television, washing machine and other goods, which are considered a part of every household, we might still be poor because we lack more important things like jobs and a quality of life.
Karen S.

The student designs his or her own personal curriculum: this account by one student, Karen Shepherd, provides a small insight into part of one term's work in team. The student learns, with guidance, to pace her own work and to evolve a few long-term projects. She is encouraged to value the stages in the evolution of the work as well as the finished product. This kind of learning is exploratory; there is a 'sense of personal discovery'. Learning is not restricted by prescriptions or routines; it can cross subject boundaries and involve different 'areas of experience'. The teachers function as a team and develop a repertoire of strategies and an array of resources for meeting students' requirements as work develops, helping to initiate and sustain ideas. The art of the teacher here is not just to predict the possibilities and then match the students to them but to consider all the options as they arise, shaping plans as they grow out of the learning process. Control of the curriculum is exercised *in situ* by students and teachers together. The teacher has to innovate, to think on his or her feet all the time, but with the support of the team and that confidence which comes from shared expertise. Sometimes there will be conflict: between aspirations for student autonomy and the availability and organization of resources necessary for it to be sustained; between the aspirations for students to organize their own learning and the necessity for an efficient system of recordkeeping – the more flexible the curriculum the harder it becomes to monitor progress; between the autonomy of the teacher and that of the team. It is to some of the productive uses of conflict that I now want to turn.

Alternative structures, innovation and staff development

Within one structure certain things will be practical which are impractical in another. In Bridgewater Hall School, a teacher of European studies teaches three tutor groups in a week and up to three other groups in the sixth year or elsewhere on the campus. In addition a fairly large number of teachers are involved. The method of control which emerged was a response to particular curriculum problems: how to innovate at a time when teachers felt fully stretched by their individual classes. The solution was team teaching and shared planning; an economy of effort. In Countesthorpe, a team tutor is responsible for only one group, although he or she will teach a specialism across the team and may teach a sixth-year group; there is not the same need for detailed consensus planning. Teachers are used to working with each other and can acquire considerable shared expertise through working alongside each other for a two-year cycle. In Bridgewater Hall School, the compulsory core makes it easier to promote integration between subjects within each faculty block and the development of diverse 'core' activities. In Countesthorpe, the close relationship between tutor and student and the integration of key subjects allows the whole timetable to run on negotiation. For example, science is not compulsory; the majority of students learn science, but not because they have to, because they want to. An important choice of this kind is realistic in a supportive and flexible team curriculum; it is even possible for a student who has not chosen science to take it up as a result of becoming interested in the work he or she sees going on in the area.

In the two examples of curriculum planning, the curriculum arises out of the conflict between the constraints of structure and the extent to which students are free agents. Autonomy and control are inseparable. Each school 'climate' will reflect its unique balance of these contradictory pressures. It is not a question of choosing one or the other as the debate at the end of the 1960s suggested. We cannot but choose both, although at a time when the talk is of control it is important to look back with respect at the case for autonomy in learning. In all schools there is a tension between the amount and the type of organization needed for effective teaching and the commitment, large or small, to autonomous, individual development. Curriculum debate should concern itself less with the idea of the coherent, uniform curriculum and more with alternative structures and different models of autonomy and control. There ought to be a creative opposition between the two.

This conflict, however, cannot be the only line of opposition; these two poles generate their own respective opposites: the absence of control and the absence of autonomy. If these two poles become dominant then the school is at risk:

> There is obviously a balance to be struck between too much direction by a teacher, where a child's interest in learning is stifled, and too much freedom allowed to a child, in which his or her interest in learning is never stimulated.

This is from the Auld report (1976) of the public inquiry into the William Tyndale school where it is stated that certain teachers

> failed in general to strike the right balance between direction by the teacher and freedom of choice by the children. Too much freedom was given to children too young and too ill-equipped to take the proper advantage of it. (para 841)

In a case like this autonomy ceases to be beneficial because it is no longer in a creative relationship with the school structure which constrains it.

Diagrammatically we might have:

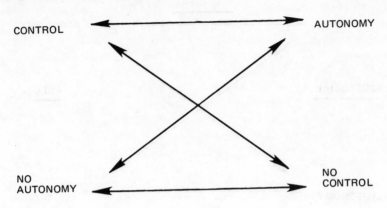

Figure 11.3

The arguments in the Black Papers, or those loudly asserted by one of their contributors, Rhodes Boyson, present the curriculum as a black or white affair: either there is controlled learning or there is anarchy. This is not helpful in evaluating schools. Nor is it true. There are in practice alternative structures and though, if the ORACLE research is right, it may be hard to find schools where autonomy flourishes, structures which encourage this autonomy need be no less concerned with order and organization than schools which are at the other end of the spectrum. The curriculum picture is more complex than is often allowed. The absence of autonomy is as debilitating as the absence of control. The diagram above might give us four types of school: at the top, as a synthesis of autonomy and control, the ideal school; then moving clockwise, the unity of autonomy and no control which might be something like the free school; then at the bottom, the synthesis of no autonomy and no control, where there is little that is positive – perhaps, if we are to believe the Auld Report, this was the dominant opposition at William Tyndale; and finally, the unity of control and no autonomy which would approximate a custodial institution like a prison.[7]

In any school, probably, there will be teachers who would fit into one or other of these types of schools. And schools may well tend to approximate to one or other of these types:

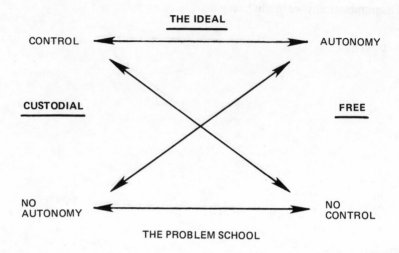

Figure 11.4

This helps to explain why it is so difficult to effect change in schools. Anybody who has been involved in a curriculum development project will know that one significant problem for the staff group is to sustain everybody's co-operation. There are unspoken conflicts and often a subtext to what is spoken. Innovation changes the way the curriculum is structured and affects the balance between control and autonomy, in part because, if only at first, it weakens the teacher's grip on the curriculum. Behind every innovation is the fear that the school will be put at risk. It threatens the ideology with which the teacher 'represents' his or her position in the school. Again, at the risk of distorting his work by over-simplifying it, Louis Althusser is useful. He writes about the way in which ideology can place an individual in position, in particular relation-ships within an institution. The individual teacher is held in a system of social relations, largely determined by the wider social relations outside the school. This means, it would seem, that the teacher involved in innovation must not only help to establish a new reality but must develop a corresponding 'representation' which will make sense of new social relations. Opposition to change may manifest itself in all sorts of seemingly irrelevant objections which are, however, important parts of the old 'representations'. Curriculum change can only occur if programmes or methods of work are devised which challenge the established structure by bringing the old and the new into conflict. Team work with students in the classroom can be the agent of change.

This is the chalk circle test. In Brecht's play, both the governor's wife and Grusha are part of a social structure. They are from opposite ends of the class system. What they say contains a subtext determined by their respective positions. Where individuals refuse to surrender their established beliefs, change will be hard to implement. To find out what is in the best interests of the child, we must see how each woman will treat him in practice. By analogy, we could do the same in our classrooms; that is, judge what lies in the interests of our students, not on the strength of rhetoric but on the evidence of our own eyes. Learning to evaluate what is happening in the classroom and how students use alternative curriculum structures should be the subject of our staff development programmes and the concern of conferences which are discussing the next ten years in education.

Notes

1   The extract from Brecht's *The Caucasian Chalk Circle* is from the translation by James and Tania Stern, with W.H. Auden (1960), Methuen, London.

2   See Rutter, M. *et al.* (1979) *Fifteen Thousand Hours*, Open Books, London:

Outcomes tended to be better when both the curriculum and approaches to discipline were agreed and supported by the staff acting together. Thus, attendance was better and delinquency less frequent in schools where courses were planned jointly. It was not just that this facilitated continuities in teaching (although it did) but also that group planning provided opportunities to encourage and support one another.

3   Cox and Dyson (1969), p. 1.
4   The Hornsey Affair (1968), p. 127.
5   Simon (1981), p. 18.
6   Galton *et al.* (1980), p. 156.
7   I have taken the idea for this kind of diagram from Frederick Jameson's *The Political Unconscious* (1981), Methuen, London. The diagrams are based on the work of A.J. Greimas and are applied by Jameson to literary texts.

References

Althusser, L. (1971) *Lenin and Philosophy*, translated by Brewster, B. (1971), New Left Books, London.
Auld, R. (1976) *William Tyndale Junior and Infants Schools Public Inquiry*, ILEA, para 841.
Bennett, N. (1976) *Teaching Styles and Pupil Progress*, Open Books, London.

168   Changing Schools

Galton, M., Simon, B. and Croll, P. (1980) *Inside the Primary Classroom*, Routledge & Kegan Paul, London, p. 156.

The Hornsey Affair (1969), Penguin Educational Special, London, p. 127.

Simon, B. (1981) 'The primary school: myth or reality?' in Simon, B. and Willcocks, J. (eds) *Research and Practice in the Primary Classroom*, Routledge & Kegan Paul, London, p. 18.

Wright, N. (1977) *Progress in Education*, Croom Helm, London.

CHAPTER 12

LEAS AND THE CURRICULUM: A CASE FOR INTERVENTION

BARRY TAYLOR

Nobody would argue seriously that curriculum design should be in other hands than teachers' any more than that prescription writing should be carried out by other than GPs. It is necessary to go further and assert that the key role in establishing principles as well as detailed practice is rightly the teachers'. Yet in secondary schools, at least, they have been conspicuously unsuccessful, in the main, in evolving curricula to meet changing circumstances. Nor should that be surprising given the, virtually, immovable obstructions to change. Lack of money and therefore time is the obvious one, but equally crucial is the in-built conservatism of articulated public opinion in educational matters. In exploring the constraints bearing upon teachers it is important first to establish that a healthy curriculum is one which is constantly evolving. Consequently the concern is with the management of change. How can schools respond to, for example, the quantum leap in unemployment, or the strict rationing of HE places, when these developments have occurred over a two-year period and the general assumption in the educational world is that nothing substantial can be altered, certainly not the examination system, in less than four or five years?

Moreover statute and practice combine to ensure that the head with governors are responsible for the curriculum. So change, if it is to be universal, must occur in similar ways in hundreds of disparate locations at the bidding of thousands of individuals with differing attitudes. Consequently the conventional model of curriculum planning, involving a cycle of consultations/consideration/design/implementation/evaluation/modification, is extremely unlikely to proceed at a reasonable pace, in good order and similar direction in all schools, even within the area of one LEA, let alone 104. Yet perhaps this does not matter greatly provided there is some evolution everywhere. Let us consider then the constraints upon such evolution.

Why schools find it difficult to change the curriculum

There is the sheer magnitude of the task – heads and teachers like other professionals have to do two things. Firstly, they must carry out day-to-day management, keeping the machine going; they must see that their charges have accommodation, are supervised, fed and watered and also that some teaching and learning occurs, as well as react to the immediate crisis, disciplinary or otherwise. Secondly, they must try to reflect, to plan, to make themselves sensitive to forces and pressures outside the school. How often does the latter responsibility have a chance in the face of the demands of the first? In primary schools almost all teachers teach all week and every week and in the smaller ones so do most heads; deputy heads are often seen as the key curriculum innovators yet customarily either have charge of a class of up to thirty-five under-elevens or a major timetabling or pastoral responsibility for an establishment of up to two thousand pupils. Most heads of departments have no more than one-sixth of normal hours free from class contact and few primary teachers have any 'in-school' preparation or thinking time.

Obviously the official school hours are only a proportion of a teacher's working year, although precisely what proportion is, of course, a matter of dispute and lack of definition between professional associations and employers. Nevertheless it appears extremely unlikely that curriculum development, or its effective control by the professionals in schools, can – or does – occur without a substantial commitment of time and energy outside school hours.

The complexity of the exercise increases almost weekly. The most recent imperative at the primary stage, *pace* HMI's recent publication, is the universal introduction or extension of science. In former times there has been successively, or simultaneously, a collective clamour for French, 'basic skills' (variously interpreted), health education, the world about us (a nicely defined area!), urban or rural studies, preparation for a multi-ethnic and cultural society, combating of sexual stereotypes – and so on. At the secondary stage matters become even more complex – or confused. To the foregoing can be added preparation for the world of work – or leisure – vocational orientation (what vocation and how specific?), more modern language teaching, better maths, political education, more oral English, more technology and science, emphasis on the hidden curriculum and so on. Never does one receive proposals as to what might be left out of the curriculum – ostensible or hidden. Within most schools, large or small, the human resources are likely to be quite insufficient both to run the current operation and to review and refine this vast and growing range of objectives.

In any case how does a school, once it has decided upon a shift of emphasis, achieve it? Primary schools may well wish to tackle science more thoroughly but if they do not have the expertise – and many schools still have only one, two or three full-time teachers – then a substantial investment in staff development is necessary. Yet rather than receive extra staffing resources to permit this, the school is quite likely to face the redeployment of a teacher, justified by declining numbers but really caused by lack of funds. Equally many secondary schools aspire to develop more practical work, particularly in the technologies; but workshops can take only half-classes and redundant history teachers cannot be converted overnight to computer wizards. In other words schools have the combination of staff expertise which they have and within the school's own competence it is simply not possible radically to shift that balance in the course of an academic year or two. So the picture of the typical school which is emerging is of an inert mass. Of course this is only part of the reality. There are, and always have been, individual teachers, whether heads or not, who have broken the existing mould and, indeed, what happens in schools is rarely the same from one year to the next. Yet for the generality of schools the limitations of time, energy and the range of expertise are real and restricting.

It is a truism – but true – that teachers rarely see each other in action. However integrated within the school, only exceptionally are curricula planned with other phases or neighbouring schools of a similar kind. So the innovator, or the innovatory school or department, is likely to be ploughing a lonely furrow. Nor is dissemination of good practice at all easy to manage by an individual school. It may be that the devolution of responsibility for what is taught and how it is taught, not simply to the school but often to individual teachers, has led to a vast expenditure of energy and imagination re-inventing many similar wheels.

Assuming a head with his colleagues wishes to enhance home economics, remove the third, or second, foreign language or abandon Latin then, reading the law, he has to convince his governors. Until recently few heads felt impelled to place such matters before the governing body. The fashion for accountability and the advent of parent and teacher governors has changed all that. Yet the entrenched views of a determined group of governors can be a powerful brake indeed upon progress in curricular matters. Parents too, both collectively and individually, can be potent defenders of the status quo. Woe betide the primary school perceived not to concentrate sufficiently on 'basic skills' or the secondary school flirting with mixed-ability teaching, particularly at a time when schools must compete for increasingly scarce entrants.

Finally, in secondary schools, there is the examination system. What remains to be said? Certainly options and differing styles of teaching can exist within 'O'-level and CSE syllabuses. But the burden of preparing an ever higher proportion of fourteen- and fifteen-year-olds for these tests of knowledge and recall, because only exceptionally, still, are they anything else, militates against inventive teaching, the development of skills and the meeting of needs. Until there is radical revision, and it is by no means only teachers who seek it, then little will change and, as the recent report by the Welsh HMIs has demonstrated again, a large proportion of young people will believe that school has nothing of consequence to offer them. Whatever else an individual school might do it cannot hope to opt out of the examination system. Nor for that matter can an LEA, but at least it, and the 103 others, in alliance with the professional associations and with luck the CBI and the TUC, might move the issue out of the limbo in which it now seems to be suspended.

So the thesis here is that only exceptionally can an individual school, at least within the maintained sector, make a radical shift in the curriculum; and only then by efforts beyond the compass of the generality of teachers acting in isolation of each other. The case for co-operative effort seems to me to be overwhelming. How can it be organized?

What the LEA can do

The fact is, of course, that curriculum development has always been co-operative – nationally and locally. The contributors have been foremost – but not always first – teachers in the schools, but also the training departments, HMI, the Schools Council and, occasionally, the examining boards. Additionally there is the entity we call 'the LEA'. Legally this signifies the corporate membership of a county or district council – not an education committee. But it is not in this precise sense that the term is used here. Nor is it meant simply 'County Hall' or 'the Office' – as in '"The Office" said we couldn't admit rising fives, keep our mobile classroom, be painted'. The elected members are an important part of the whole, as are the administrators, but they are only a part. Some other parts are the advisers and inspectors, the teachers centres, the schools and the teachers. And truly the sum is, or can be, greater than the parts.

Resources

The most direct impact which the LEA can make upon the curriculum is by deciding how to spend its money. It is highly unlikely that primary schools will be enabled to answer HMIs' bidding on science unless LEAs do something to offset the impact of declining rolls on staff, and as well devote money to staff development. If secondary schools are to add City and Guilds 365 or RSA Foundation Courses to their traditional offerings then they can only do so if the LEA is prepared to make the investment.

Perhaps more critical are decisions that money will be withdrawn. The shedding of an LEA's team of instrumental music teachers is hardly likely to enhance music within the total curriculum, even for non-instrumental players. The general tightening of staffing scales is bound to place in jeopardy those subjects in secondary schools which traditionally attract the smallest numbers – classics, the second modern language, perhaps economics. So it is important to realize that few financial decisions, whether positive or negative, do not have curricular implications.

Throughout the financial difficulties of the last few years most, if not all, LEAs have managed to protect or enhance various areas of the curriculum. In Somerset for example the provision for children with special needs has grown modestly year by year while other things have been sacrificed. Investment has been made in county-wide maths guidelines, in primary science schemes, in City and Guilds, and similar vocational courses and in some minimal separate provision for the exceptionally gifted. Obviously there is unlikely to be agreement through-out the county on this or any other order of priorities, but the point being made is that even in hard times the LEA has the means to influence the curriculum – for good or ill – by the decisions it takes about resource allocation both globally and specifically.

Aims and objectives

The received wisdom about LEAs is that the politicians decide policy and the CEO and his senior people advise and implement. It is not, and never has been, as simple as that. Certainly it is not unknown for politicians to take an assertive role in day-to-day management or to follow advice from someone other than the CEO. Equally, the definition of aims, let alone objectives, is, and always has been, arrived at as a result of inputs from a wide spectrum of individuals and groups. Nowhere is this more important than in matters impinging directly upon the curriculum and internal organization of schools. The primary function of the CEO and his political masters is to create a mood or climate in which curriculum development can flourish. For example, in the early 1970s in Somerset, there was a concern that the healthy liberalization of the primary curriculum, which had occurred in the previous twenty years, might have been accompanied by less emphasis, at least directly, on communication and number skills. Secondary and FE teachers expressed anxieties before Callaghan's Ruskin speech and as a consequence there was a general, but obviously not universal, agreement among teachers, advisers and administrators and politicians that this assertion needed attention. Subsequently primary teachers throughout the county developed corporate reading schemes and maths guidelines and co-operated in the introduction of universal testing. Thus, for better or worse a mood was created, or a consensus emerged. Similarly heads of secondary schools have accepted that in the present state of the art it is prudent not to create mixed-ability teaching groups for most subjects beyond the first year of secondary education. This is not an imposed regulation but an agreement – and no doubt there are dissenters.

Of course aims and objectives are easier to achieve if backed by money. In 1982-1983 an additional £600,000 of revenue and £750 million of capital investment, all of it LEA and not MSC money, will go to develop courses for the sixteen–eighteen age group as a response to unemployment, the perceived need for new kinds of courses and for the development of informal educational provision. All schools and colleges, and the community education service, are involved and enthusiastic and, most important, we are learning together. The key point then, and it will be crucially important in the next ten years, is that LEAs can make articulate the needs of their communities and even in difficult times release resources to try to meet them in a way which cannot be managed at the individual school or college level.

Staff development is a phrase much bandied about in FE and HE in recent years but less so in schools. However, throughout the system it is more marked by expressions of need than provision. Currently it is

exceptional and fortuitous for a teacher to be given secondment for one
term every seven years let alone an academic year. Indeed, all too often,
secondment is more a means of making an offering to a potentially
redundant teacher or rescuing an incompetent one than enhancing the
skills of the competent. Yet the basic problem underlying the quickly
forgotten James Report's recommendations remains and indeed becomes
more acute. In primary schools forty percent or more of teachers will be in
the classroom throughout their career and promotion prospects have
worsened and will continue to worsen. Similarly the refreshment afforded
by promotion and new challenges will be significantly less available in
secondary schools and conventional FE now that we are all, for the first
time, part of a contracting industry. Thus if for no better reason than to
maintain enthusiasm or even sanity, it becomes more than ever crucial for
LEAs to create opportunities for teachers to get away from their schools.

But, of course, staff development should go far beyond ad hoc course
attendance. Every teacher should know that his superior reviews his
progress and professional needs with him regularly and then has the means
to deliver those things which will make him more professional, more able
to design and provide relevant curricula. Among them are likely to be, as
well as course attendance, an opportunity to visit other schools and
colleges and to plan the curricula in conjunction with colleagues
responsible for other phases. It is unlikely that any of these can be
facilitated by a school alone. Of course most LEAs also fall far short of
decent provision – of money for courses, for supply teachers, for
pupil/teacher ratios which allow a reasonable amount of time away from
the classroom and so on. But my point is that only by developing the
corporate and political will within an LEA can progress be made. It is
extremely unlikely, for example, that a centralized system will facilitate
local staff development needs more effectively than the LEAs, or be more
receptive to the just demands of teachers in this respect.

Equally, it would be the exceptional school left to its own unsupported
resources which could develop and sustain a programme geared to
enhance the professional competence of its staff. In Somerset, for
example, it was an LEA county-wide initiative which has resulted in the
overwhelming majority of schools now devoting two occasional holidays to
school-based staff development and curricular review programmes. Before
1978 there was always the opportunity for schools to do this; in fact, they
did not do so until it became LEA policy, after full consultation, for all
teachers to be 'strongly encouraged' to participate. As a result school

staffs, both individually and in association with neighbouring or linked schools, have designed and executed a most impressive range of activities. The decisions as to what should happen have been theirs; the education department's job has been to establish the framework, nurture a sense of purpose and then facilitate and fund outside resources drawn from the training institutions, other schools or the local inspectorate.

There is a widespread belief that both staff and curriculum development can only be really effective if firm foundations are laid during the teachers' initial training. There are two crucial aspects of this. Obviously the LEAs collectively must try, as they have done under central government prodding, to relate the numbers of students in training to likely total vacancies. Equally there needs to be a match between, for example, potential maths or science teachers and assessed needs. Curriculum development is a non-starter if a secondary school, in particular, does not have and cannot recruit the appropriate specialists perceived to be necessary to press forward the development. Here we come to the second aspect. During initial training, colleges, and they are largely LEA colleges, must encourage the maximum flexibility of approach, ensure that students are receptive to the idea of later re-training and not wedded undissolubly to a particular specialism. Whether similar principles will take root in university training departments is quite another matter. So the healthy curriculum is seen as dynamic, and the LEA's roll as being to try to ensure that its teaching force is skilful and flexible enough to respond to the need for relatively rapid changes. As the Schools Council recognizes in 'The Practical Curriculum', LEAs 'must recognize that effective teaching demands investment in professional development'.

LEA advisers and inspectors

They are, or ought to be, experienced teachers undertaking a change of role but still retaining the attitudes, commitment and professionalism of teachers. If they are to be effective they must not become distanced from the chalkface. On the other hand, their value to a school lies in their ability to give an external perspective to its day-to-day activities. The inspectoral team must work to combat sterile, or stereotyped, teaching of the type described in 'The Practical Curriculum' where one group of pupils were found to have been presented with work cards at every single lesson throughout a day.

As well as disseminating good practice, the advisory and inspectoral service is now more clearly seen to have a monitoring role, particularly at a time when HMIs are so thinly spread as to jeopardize their collective grasp of detailed knowledge of the system. Many LEAs now have some formal investigative and reporting process. At its most effective this will involve inspections, and with colleagues in schools, make joint assessments and proposals for development. Nevertheless, there is also a key role to identify the inadequate or unacceptable and to detail determined measures to improve matters.

Co-operative curriculum design

'The Practical Curriculum' has remarked on the growth of planning undertaken among a group of schools, throughout an LEA or, occasionally, more widely. In terms of economy of effort and enhancing the variety of inputs, I believe this to have decided advantages, often, over parallel curricular design in, say, an LEA's three hundred primary schools or thirty-six secondary schools.

A basic LEA responsibility identified by the Inspectorate in 'A View of the Curriculum' is to maintain continuity across the breaks at four, eleven, thirteen and sixteen years of age, or whatever. Given that somewhere children start a new school at every age between five and sixteen except, it would seem, six, it is clearly of vital importance that not only do schools have sensible recording and transfer arrangements, but also plan their curriculum, if not jointly with other phases then, at least, in full knowledge of what each other is doing. The LEA must determine when, for example, foreign language teaching should start and share in relation to all curricular areas an 'agreement between schools on whether and how' as HMI puts it. Of course it is not suggested that total uniformity is possible, still less desirable throughout an LEA area; but for any group of children progressing through the system the parts must be seen to make a cohesive whole – and that is the LEA's responsibility

In many areas co-operative efforts have been particularly thorough and detailed in recent years. In Somerset common curricula have been designed by teachers from schools throughout the county brought together, usually by specialist inspectors, in the following areas:

Music in primary schools

Mathematics
Secondary English

Reading

Physical education

Science for middle years, and so on.

In no sense is Somerset exceptional; there is a widespread realization that there is a sensible economy of effort to be achieved as well as that few schools have a sufficient spread of expertise and self-confidence – or arrogance? – to plan their curriculum independently. There is, perhaps, a general anxiety about the evolution of universal curricula, or even a national 'norm' if too rigidly interpreted. It is vital that initiatives are fostered and flexibility and a responsiveness to particular local circumstances assured. It seems unnecessary that a national definition should go much beyond the DES's 'The School Curriculum' – or more practically HMI's 'A View of the Curriculum' or the Schools Council 'The Practical Curriculum'. This then leaves the task of co-ordinating planning between schools, giving the necessary support already described and connecting resource allocation to curricular aspirations where it properly belongs – with the LEAs.

Much is heard these days of the concept of a 'contract' in relation to the curriculum, a guaranteed minimum offering supplemented by optional extras which is, in total, acceptable to parents. Even allowing for the reality that, still, by no means all parents, for whatever reason, concern themselves with the detail of what their child is offered, this approach has much to commend it. In particular when declining rolls combine with financial restrictions it is crucial that LEAs define what is their 'guaranteed offering' at each stage of education and then ensure the resources to provide it – however difficult that may sometimes be. Central government for its part must assist, and not hinder by the insensitive implementation of global financial policies. Finally, LEAs have a key role in determining the respects in which it is – and is not – reasonable to expect individual schools to be 'accountable'. In the first place LEA members and officers must have an explicit policy and must know what is going on in schools, which presumes a regular series of assessments and reports by the LEA inspectorate as well as feedback from HMI. Secondly, the LEA must be ready to support schools and teachers in repelling unreasonable demands of parents or interest groups for intervention in, or determination of, the curriculum. The teachers are the experts in curricular design and implementation. If they are wise they will consult widely and be susceptible to influences from the community at large; but if they are to be held accountable they must have the untrammelled power of determination. The work of schools is too important *not* to be undertaken by the professionals.

In relation to governors, too, the LEA must see that its teachers are not baulked in fulfilling their professional role. Of course governing bodies have a responsibility in general – and ill-defined – terms for overseeing the curriculum. But if this is to be effective and helpful it presumes that the LEA has taken care in forming governing bodies and has ensured that governors have the opportunity to learn of the work of schools and be trained for their proper role.

'The experience each child has at school and what each takes away' (Schools Council, 'The Practical Curriculum')

The LEA has a seminal role in relation to the curriculum, particularly in bringing teachers together, providing thinking time and the means to implement their plans. It is not for the education committee or the Chief Education Officer and his colleagues to determine in detail the nature of the 'experience' referred to above. Nevertheless, it seems sensible that some agreement on goals, both within the LEA and nationally, should be reached.

The most abiding impression left by the recent key publications on the curriculum referred to throughout this paper is the major extent to which they are a statement of what, mostly, happens in most schools. Proposals involve shifts of emphasis rather than a radical restructuring of the educational system, with the possible exceptions of parts of the debate about examinations and sixteen-plus provision. However it has already been said that the curriculum must be dynamic and this assumption underlies all the curriculum booklets, even 'The School Curriculum' (DES). So in what ways might we seek change in the next ten years?

1 A television producer after a brief, but one hopes thorough, examination of our system pronounced recently that we provide 'a counterfeit education for the majority'. This is unfair at least in relation to the primary years. There needs to be a recognition here, as there is abroad, that our primary, first and middle schools have, in general, evolved a broad curriculum which is relevant to children's needs, and to society's, and which also develops the necessary basic

skills for learning. On this basis we can then pay attention to the two main sorts of school where this is often only partially true, those struggling with growing and worsening inner-city problems and those so small as to attract only two or even one teacher to provide for as many as seven age groups. Nowhere is the relationship between effective curricular provision and LEA resource allocation more sharply highlighted. Both breadth and depth of curricula cannot hope to be enhanced without positive discriminatory policies.

2   There may be more validity in the same television producer's assertion that at the secondary stage we have 'produced a mass that have suffered often with remarkable docility (for how much longer?) a schooling that has denied them the practical, useful, marketable and saleable skills that they need and want'. In spite, or because, of the development of comprehensive schools most curricula are still examination orientated and to examinations originally designed for an academic élite. It is time we, i.e., those working in education, considered more open-mindedly the alternatives – profiles, continuous assessment – to the current examination system. It is clear that there are massive forces of inertia within the system and often unreasoning opposition in the community at large to anything which appears to threaten academic standards. Yet if the debate is not opened up – and it is the thirteenth hour – what will happen? It seems critical that the prelude to effective curricular reform in secondary schools must be a radical reappraisal of the examination system, which in spite of the long-running saga of debate in relation to both the sixteen-plus and post-sixteen systems has simply not been held outside a closed circle. Only then can we look to a curriculum for the majority which will be 'practical, useful, marketable and saleable'.

3   In the meantime there is a strong argument for less choice between fourteen and sixteen years of age. Options are expensive as any timetabler knows. If we want a greater emphasis on the technologies, as most of us claim, then to be realistic something must give way. Is it to be the three separate sciences, the option of a third or second modern language, classics or a greater realism about the expense of small sixth forms? We all have an ingrained habit of avoiding harsh choices to the eventual but inevitable detriment of curricular quality.

4   There are hopeful signs at sixteen-plus. The New Training Initiative may provide a genuine one-year educational, as well as training and work, experience for all, *provided* the LEA and college inputs are sufficiently comprehensive – and we can cope with the time-scale for planning as effectively as MSC. It appears desirable that we move as quickly as possible along the road mapped by Mansell's 'A Basis for Choice'. If so, we must not forget to consider the plight of most of the most able, locked in an increasingly outdated 'A'-level system.

These then are just a few of the areas requiring change quickly. Whether or not the directions are the right ones, I am sure, to return to my main theme, that the role of the LEA is crucial. Schools and colleges cannot combat the forces of inertia single handed. They need to be in alliance. Nor can curriculum be imposed nation-wide without sterility and the smothering of initiative. Consequently, within broad national policy guidelines it is the mechanism of the LEA which can best enable teachers to plan and control their curriculum. It is the LEAs' responsibility collectively to see that there is a direct connection made between curricular aspirations and available resources. It is also for the LEAs to open up more widely a consideration of the examination framework within which all post-primary education exists.

CHAPTER 13

MYTHS AND REALITY IN CURRICULUM CONTROL: Two decades of primary school mathematics reform in Western Europe

BOB MOON

Who so ever, in writing a modern history, shall follow truth too near the heels, it may haply strike out his teeth. (From the Preface to *A History of the World*, Sir Walter Raleigh).

The Dutch have a word, *vervuiling*, which graphically expresses the concept of pluralism or separate development. The word is derived from *zuil*, meaning pillar, and is sometimes taken as a reference to the various schools of advice offered by the followers of St Simeon Stylites, hermits who squatted out their lives at the top of pillars. The institutional structure of Dutch education exemplifies this decentralized tradition with Catholic, Protestant and secular pillars of interest more or less balanced in a national framework. Descriptions of *vervuiling* or interest group structures within the different systems of education in Western Europe have proliferated over the years and, in recent times, have come increasingly to the attention of curriculum specialists. An 'accepted wisdom' has grown up which today pervades and influences the national debates about control that have developed in many countries at different times over the last two decades, most recently in England and Wales. If the protagonists sometimes give credibility to the notion of hermits on pillars, this perhaps typifies the inadequate basis of understanding upon which the rhetoric or reposts rest.

A comparative perspective has been implicit in the fears expressed about changes in curriculum control in England and Wales. Terms and phrases have come to symbolize positions, centralized versus decentralized, government- or governor-controlled as opposed to teacher-controlled, to give but two examples. Set out here are 'sketches' of curriculum development in primary school mathematics in five countries. Each description is based on interviews and primary source material collected on visits during the past three years. The evidence accumulated is uneven, and the nature of the sources has varied from country to country and from institution to institution.[1] Each account has, however, been cross-checked by participants in and observers of the events described. Modern mathematics, perhaps more than any other curriculum reform, caught the imagination of the world at large. Controversy was rife. It happened everywhere. For these reasons, investigation may point up the nubs of control and the centres of influence giving a glimpse of the real world of curriculum change.

France

Controversy about mathematics reform continues to flourish in France today, and the French have fought aggressively over the cause in curriculum change. A report from a French weekly of the period reported a speech by one professor saying that, 'Drugs, pornography and modern maths were ruining a generation of young people!' (*L'Express*, February 6th 1972).

This public debate, which, as will be shown later, reached a crescendo of accusation and counter-accusation in the later 1960s, early 1970s, was not merely directed at the formulation of new central directives. In the period from 1960 up until the present time, the changes that occurred (and the evidence suggests these were significant) were carried forward without official sanction or approval. In fact, the dissemination strategies that were applied seem to have more in common with the traditional approaches of, say, Britain or the Netherlands than with what is commonly imagined the Napoleonic formality associated with the French. The reasons for this and current attempts to redress the new balance provide the focus for this report.

Firstly, the formal record. In terms of written instructions or codes, four dates are significant in primary education: 1887 when the first regulations in mathematics were formulated; 1945 when these were reformulated in the wake of the Second World War; 1970 when, after considerable discussion, a programme *transitoire* was published; and 1980 when a new detailed outline was introduced in the most decisive way. Jacques Colomb, *Chef de Travaux*,[2] at the Institut National de

Recherche Pedagogique, caricatured the drawing up of programmes in the pre-1970 period as 'the *Inspecteurs Generaux* taking a pen and paper and writing it at one sitting in front of the fire'. In 1970, the situation was markedly different and a complex series of inter-related discussions were to take place producing ultimately only a provisional programme because of the difficulties in finding a consensus view. In the period up to 1980, much stronger ministerial pressure appears to have been exercised to bring about changes in the formal programme. Inspection of these programmes, however, would give little indication of the upheavals in primary mathematics over the previous two decades. Neither would it reveal the extent of the intensive public debate that was to be carried on through all channels of the media. The origins of the 'modern maths' movement therefore needs elaborating.

A first awareness within the schools has, as in many countries, origins in the university world. France was, after all, the homeland of the *'Bourbakist'* explosion of ideas that was to influence developments all over the world. Geoffrey Mathews, director of the Nuffield Primary Mathematics Project in Britain, has acknowledged the significance of the work that was going forward in France. In the 1950s new concepts were gaining ground in university teaching. The 'academic freedom' experienced by the university teacher was to lead to a strange mixture of ideas. Monsieur Ramis, *Doyen de l'Inspection Generale des Mathematiques* (Chief Inspector), reports on how it was possible, in changing mathematics tutors from one year to the next, to experience a totally different form of study depending on the perspectives adopted by the individual teacher. Increasingly however, the introduction of modern mathematics to university teaching and the claims of the *Grandes Ecoles* was to lead to changes in the upper forms of the *Lycee* and the *classes preparatoires* from which recruits for the *Grandes Ecoles* were selected. Royaumont and other conferences, sponsored by UNESCO in the late 1950s, were to give an added impetus to this.

The official French response to a UNESCO report (UNESCO 1956) for information included the statement, 'No large-scale reform of mathematics teaching appears to be likely in the near future.' Eight years later, following Royaumont at the OECD gathering in Athens (Fehr 1964), the French report read, 'The programmes have been progressively modified since 1957 throughout all school institutions. . . . An important part of the efforts to discover and to present modern mathematics has been realized in France.'

The movement also became significant in the activities of the *Association Professionelle d'Enseignement des Mathematiques* (APEM) which was to play a leading role in the 1960s and early 1970s in promoting the cause of radical change in the mathematics curriculum.

In 1964, the *Institut National de Recherche Pedagogique* agreed to the funding of a research project in primary maths (*Analogue*). The initiative came from Nicole Picard, a university mathematician who, through experience of retraining teachers for maths teaching (*recyclage*), had become interested in the possibilities of reforming school programmes. Experimentation with children of high and low ability in secondary school classes, as well as with her own six children, had suggested that in the new mathematics there were exciting possibilities. The research programme was initially based on a well-known private school *L'Ecole Alsacienne*, which had at that time government permission and funds for the implementation of experimental programmes. The project was to expand and include the public sector so that by 1970, 120 *instituteurs* in over 1000 classes were involved. Additionally, between twelve and fifteen *animateurs d'experience* (research assistants) helped Nicole Picard in the guidance of the project. Interest tended to centre on the university towns where a tradition of work in this area was already established (for example, Lyon, Toulouse, Poitiers, Caen).

Parallel with these explorations, which were to concentrate on the significance of the new concepts in mathematics in, for example, set theory, the textbook market began to focus on the potential for exploiting these ideas. The 1945 programme was by now redundant. Teachers, traditionally, rarely read these and relied on the authority of the *manuel* (textbook) to indicate official thinking. In the period of the 1960s, it was changes in the textbooks, without regard to the guidelines, that was radically to transform the teaching of mathematics throughout France. A number of factors seem significant. Firstly, the *Inspecteurs Generaux* responsible for primary education at the time had little, if any, influence or control over these changes. Traditionally recruited from those with a literary rather than scientific or mathematical background (eighty percent of present inspectorate), often without experience of teaching within the *ecole elementaire* and in a period when teachers were challenging many forms of authority, their power, contrary to popular notions, seems to have been of little significance. Although there is little research to support this, it appears (using, for example, textbook sales figures) that the new mathematics in the late 1960s and early 1970s was to appear in the vast majority of primary school classrooms – a factor which prompted some traditionalists to designate modern mathematicians as *les marchands de mathematique* in view of the associated financial successes. Textbook publishers are reluctant to reveal sales figures to assist inquiry in this area. One leading French publisher,[3] however, did permit scrutiny of the figures, and it was possible to talk with the editor responsible for mathematics at that time.

> In 1968 we knew which way things were going. Sales of our traditional maths book had dropped dramatically. We knew what was being proposed for curriculum changes and so in 1968 we sought out . . . a leader in the teacher association to produce a new series for us. This came in three years before the programme was finally published and the sales figures were quite extraordinary.

A table setting out these figures is given below

Table 13.1

Traditional 'Arithmetic Book'		Modern
No. of copies printed		Sales figures
70,000,	1968-69	35,078
15,000	1969-70	133,229
25,000	1970-71	316,311
12,000	1971-72	217,738
zero	1972-73	168,124
zero	1973-74	139,892

The changes, as has been seen, provoked a quite astonishingly vitriolic public debate and illustrate in the eyes of many observers how neatly modern maths was to become symbolic of some of the deep contradictions in the society, made explicit by the events of May 1968.

This waning, if non-existent, influence of the inspectorate was reflected in the work of the Leibowitz Commission which sat from 1967-1969 to consider mathematical reform. The report was to recommend and lead to the introduction in the secondary sector of a radically different curriculum programme introduced year by year over a six- and seven-year period. The chairman of the commission was a particularly brilliant mathematician of the new school. There was clearly an Inspectorate presence, although as one inspector now points out:

> Perhaps they were getting on a bit and Leibowitz really was a rather daunting man to disagree with, and anyway, everyone seemed to see this as the way forward.

Nicole Picard, who sat on the commission, certainly confirms the heady enthusiasm with which the reforms were approached. Political and social agitation in the country at large, she sees as a more significant influence than, at the time, they were able to appreciate.

There was certainly opposition and increasingly, in the aftermath of 1968, a counter-attack was mounted. The media campaign continued unabated and the programme *transitoire* of 1970 was produced containing little of the content of the new maths that was being taught in the schools. Teachers ignored it. A new mathematics teachers association was formed (UPUM) which originated from a splinter group of the APEM. Attempts by people such as Nicole Picard to write a commentary on the 1970 programme which gave greater importance to new approaches were fought all the way by an Inspectorate increasingly threatened by a loss of authority. Teachers, for example, were refusing to allow the Inspectorate into their classrooms and no actions were taken against them. In fact, one of the leading members of the APEM, a teacher who has to play a major role in the establishment of the regional centres for mathematics education (*Les Instituts Regionaux d'Enseignement des Mathematiques* – IREMS) was to hold particularly strong views on the sovereignty of his classroom against Inspectorate control.

Primary school mathematics reform may have been out of control in the decade from 1964 onwards. Evidence of activity in the formulation of new programmes, firstly in the transition document of 1970 and then the more substantial 1980 reform, indicates that inspectorial and ministerial 'clout' was reintroduced at this formal level of debate.

The 1980 programme cut down the new maths content to a minimum. Nicole Picard has suggested that, when analysed linquistically, a clear bias emerges. When dealing with *calcul* (arithmetic) the instructions use prescriptive words such as *faut* (must); in describing the geometrical components of the course, there is a change towards a more liberal *peut* (may). Jaques Colomb, who worked with Picard and has been involved in the INRP4[4] work on the new programme, accepts this, but points out the political influences which are inescapable. He acknowledges that *les evenements de 1968* were seized upon skilfully, if somewhat intuitively, by curriculum reformers, and now 'the system is fighting back'. The *Inspecteurs Generaux*, for example, and for the first time ever, will be stamping the country to visit regional meetings of administrators, boards and regional inspectors to emphasize the importance of ensuring the new programmes are implemented. The demise of the IREM's (regional mathematics centres) is seen by some as linked to this process.

> The IREM's capacity to circumvent the system by going direct to the teacher and allowing the teacher to go direct to the IREM . . . missing out the hierarchy, was a potential and very powerful way of undermining traditional authority.

This was to have an impact on classrooms. The publishing company referred to above hedged its bets and produced two primary maths series. The first a new edition, new mathematics series that sold so well in the late 1960s and early 1970s, the second a more traditional volume with the title *Mathematiques* but with a descriptive phrase boldly explaining this to mean *Calcul* (Arithmetic). The sales figures speak again

Table 13.2

	New Maths 2nd edition	New publication, direction traditional
1977–78	5,696	2,234
1978–79	15,168	31,796
1979–80	9,966	50,951
1980–81	6,056	52,960

England and Wales

Recent curriculum reform in primary school mathematics reflects influences common in many other European countries. The revolution in university mathematics teaching and the message from the USA and European conferences was seized upon by textbook publishers and the Nuffield Foundation keen to provide a stimulus to change. More importantly, however, at the beginning of the 1960s English primary schools were seen to be leading the world in their development of progressive discovery and activity-based learning which seemed a direct antithesis of the traditional arithmetic. Such methods in mathematics were reflected, for example, in the work of Edith Biggs, HMI, whose evangelical fervour is remembered with freshness even today.

> . . . about that time, the early 1960s, I heard of the work of Miss Biggs –
> running courses up and down the country 2½ day, 3 day, week courses . . .
> to try to get a new approach to maths teaching.

> I remember hearing Edith Biggs on a radio programme; nationally
> something was going on for it to have been on the radio.
> Edith had this enormous car with a very large boot into which she used to
> throw string, cardboard, all sorts of things and set off; a sort of John the
> Baptist of the New Maths.
> (Observations by member of Nuffield project team)

It was the project funders however who were to capture the energies for
curriculum reform, classically set out in the following project specification:

> The Project will follow the general lines of those already started by the
> Nuffield Foundation in other subjects. Teams of teachers will be appointed
> to assist the organizer, who will also be able to seek guidance from a
> consultative committee. An integrated range of teaching resources will be
> prepared, including ample teachers' guides, pupils' materials, and visual
> and other aids. These materials will be subjected to widespread testing with
> pupils of various ages and levels of ability, revised in the light of experience,
> and retested, and finally the resulting range of resources made generally
> available to all who care to make use of them.[5]

The funds were provided by Nuffield, although links with the new
Schools Council were very close. Geoffrey Mathews, appointed with
characteristic British originality after an unknowing interview/lunch at
Nuffield lodge, (he came from the private school sector and had had no
experience of teaching in primary schools) was an inspired choice to lead
the project. Mathews later became the first Professor of Mathematical
Education at London's Chelsea College. Central government had little
involvement in this[6] although Her Majesty's Inspectorate played a
crucial role in negotiation with Nuffield and in helping select the team that
worked with Mathews from 1966 on.

The impetus for projects such as Nuffield was helped by OECD and
UNESCO conferences, particularly the Royaumont seminar, described
elsewhere, as was the success of the Secondary School Mathematics
Project under the direction of Brian Thwaites, then at Southampton
University. Concern about the efficiency of industry and the supply of
trained mathematicians into teaching were significant in creating a climate
in which reform proposals attracted widespread approval. Indeed a leader

in *The Times* of 20 February 1963 was to criticize SMP for a lack of radicalism in suggesting that perhaps the reforms and modernization (the two were seen as synonomous) 'by comparison with some development projects abroad seems a compromise but it is a good first step'. For Mathews the launch of the Nuffield project three years later was an opportunity to put that right. Purity, Profit and Pleasure, the 3 Ps, were to become his catchphrase with Purity indicating the Bourbakist-style[7] ambitions for modernization.

In terms of teacher awareness, Nuffield Primary Maths has been classified as a successful project (Broadfoot 1980) and the reforms were well publicized. In 1967 (30 June) an article in *The Times* was to attract the comment 'a great deal is written about New Maths and it looks attractive in colour magazines' and, in the same article, the author punchingly goes on to say, 'Many teachers use new methods because of sheer boredom with the old and also because they arouse the interest of visitors, television producers and school inspectors.'

As a project it suffered most or all of the trials and tribulations now seen to be characteristic of such an approach; problems associated with staff tenure, publishing schedules, difficulties of relations with the world of teacher training and continued doubts about the advisability or otherwise of publishing pupil materials. The establishment of teachers centres to overcome the problems of ever-widening dissemination problems was a major achievement which had repercussions beyond the mathematics curriculum. Geoffrey Mathews was to play a significant role as a publicist for New Mathematics, appearing, for example, in a number of television programmes. Commercial publishers, however, quickly extended the marketing of new ideas in a direction that the Nuffield project did not wish to follow. The widespread adoption in primary schools of materials written privately by a project team member arguably had greater impact than the project itself (Fletcher Maths). More recently, the extension of the project has been limited to the publication of materials with dissemination through a publishing house, an interesting recognition of the influence of marketing forces.

In England and Wales, university mathematicians seem (with the notable exception of people such as Thwaites) to have been less involved in the cause of new maths and certainly there was no attendance from this area at the UNESCO and OECD gatherings. Similarly media debate, although present, appears to have been muted compared to events in Germany, France and to a lesser degree Denmark. Parents' groups which they did influence appear to have been generally favourable (for example the Advisory Centre for Education, ACE) and the students debate which emerged in the early 1970s was more focused on school organization and structure than issues such as new mathematics.[8] Examination of the newspaper coverage in the period indicates that new mathematics as a phrase only emerges at the point when some public disquiet appears to have become apparent. Modernization, a good 1960s word, excited far less controversy!

Official pronouncements of concern, governmental or inspectorial, did not emerge until the establishment of an official governmental commission on the teaching of mathematics towards the end of the 1970s. Many key inspectors did, after all, have a close involvement with Nuffield although ironically Edith Biggs was to view with disapproval some of the mathematics of the project adopting a more Wiskobas and Freudenthal view of change (see the Dutch case study below). The two, rival associations of mathematics teachers gave differing levels of support with the prestigious Mathematical Association established and dominated by private and grammar school teachers having closer links with Nuffield because of Mathews, own links with the group. The rival, avowedly more practical, Association of Mathematics Teachers, had little contact with the project team and this lack of a primary framed base (and the almost total neglect of teaching training institutions) was to make dissemination problematic.

Geoffrey Mathews today accepts a naîvety in the primary maths reform movement made clear only from the vantage point of a decade or more of attempted change. The integration of publisher dissemination with project development in the latest Nuffield development is one indication of changed ideas and perhaps an indication of a reassertion of the traditional interplay of forces in curriculum development.

The Federal Republic of Germany

The relation between the major social upheavals in the late 1960s and ideas about curriculum reform is well illustrated in this self-parody of a cartoon from the front page of a teachers handbook in the controversial primary maths *Alef* course. The long hair and the mathematical symbol for average stamped on the shirt juxtaposed against the banner-carrying 'Down with Alef' demonstrations. Each of the *Lander* of the Federal Republic of Germany have independent parliaments with control over education

jealously guarded. Controversy about primary mathematics was to range
through the period 1968-1973.

Figure 13.1

> . . . it seemed as if every day there was some new outburst and then
> suddenly in 1977 everything seemed to quieten down. (Professor Heinrich
> Winter, The University of Aachen)

In each of the *Lander* the issue is recorded as being discussed formally in
the parliament, in some cases on more than one occasion.

A chief protagonist in the fight to reform the primary mathematics
curriculum was Heinrich Bauersfeld, the Professor of Mathematical
Education at the University of Frankfurt. He worked in Hessen and,
given the rather different story of each of the *Lander*, attention will be
given to this area. Hessen is traditionally controlled by the SPD
(*Sozialistische Partei Deutschlands*) and support in the early days was given
to the experimentation associated with Bauerfelds 'Project Alef'. Funded
initially by a major teachers' union, Alef was also to obtain substantial
support from the Max Traeger and Volkswagen Foundations covering the
six-year life of the project that began in 1966. The history of the
development parallels that of Nuffield. Success in the early experimental

stage was followed by more circumspection later when increasing numbers of teachers became involved.

> When Professor Bauersfeld was working with the smaller group it was marvellous, very exciting. However, in the latter stages there were many problems. His co-workers didn't have the authority and followed far too rigidly the project guidelines. (A teacher from Hessen)

In an attempt to combat the difficulties, a psychologist, trained in psychoanalysis, was employed to carry out an 'in depth evaluation of the teacher project interface'. Bauersfeld, like Mathews in England, viewed modernization and reform as synonomous. His advocacy of this, however, was in part based on an interpretation of the linguistic work of Basil Bernstein. Like Christiansen in Denmark, he expresses surprise at the limited appreciation of this by English mathematics educationalists. The project saw the purity of the mathematics overcoming social/cultural/linguistic barriers to the development of intellect. This social purpose was to lead to much scepticism among the administration.

Bauersfeld had, for example, to formally sign a contract which said that the children involved in the project would (and this had to be proved by testing) be up to the standards of pupils of the same age following traditional programs. This condition was met, although ironically the 'Alef' materials were not to be given offical approval in the very *Lander* where these experiments had been carried forward.

> . . . in the early 1970s, you had children in Frankfurt who didn't know how to pay for sweets in shops. (An official of the Hessen Ministry of Education

This official, an important figure in the administration, was to be one of the leading opponents of Bauersfeld's work and still speaks scathingly of it today. All the other *Landers* with the exception of Bavaria, which has a markedly isolationist policy with regard to most areas of the curriculum, accepted 'Alef' onto their approved list of textbooks.

'Alef' had to be considered at a time of maximum upheaval in the educational programme of Hessen. Attempts to introduce a more liberal curriculum were to meet with the most fierce of controversies. Debate about mother-tongue and the teaching of social studies were, along with proposals in mathematics, to feature regularly in the headlines. In fact, the controversy nearly brought about the downfall of the regional government and was to lead to the retirement from politics of the then Minister of Education, Von Friedburg (Beattie 1977).

The project workers, following widespread adoption, became overwhelmed by the demands of publishing schedules, although the fact that for every teacher book sold only three pupil texts were sold indicates that an emphasis on the former might have paid greater dividends. This fact backs the views of the Nuffield project team in England who eschewed the production of teacher materials.

'Alef' materials still sell today, although only in a very limited way.[9] In view of the projects' development through a rather turbulent period of reform, it is now useful to place it in the context of the origins and development of modern maths within the country as a whole. Heinrich Winter, Professor of Mathematical Education in the University of Aachen, sees two influences as significant. Firstly, as in many other countries, the introduction of a new tradition of mathematics into the universities and the *Gymnasium* (grammar school) which prepared pupils for higher education. There is an association of teachers of mathematics and science in the *Gymnasium* and active support was given to the introduction of new ideas. At the same time that this groundswell was building up (supplied in part by close contact with experimentation in the USA in the early part of the decade) a particularly significant event was to occur. Dienes, the proponent of a more conceptual approach to mathematics, was, with a colleague, to make a hugely successful tour throughout the whole country. Although not acknowledged at the time, this was to give a tremendous boost to the cause of reform in mathematics education. Dienes lectured to huge audiences using classes of children on the stage (he did likewise on television) and these appearances still seem very vivid in the memory of many teachers today.

The most significant date, however, in development in this area was 1968 when the Conference of Education Ministers in Bonn decreed that modern mathematics should be introduced into all curriculum and that this should happen by 1972. Bauersfeld served on the council that advised the ministers and played a significant role in this promulgation; 1968 represented the height of interest in the development of some sort of national approach to education. The power and influence of this movement was to wane considerably over the years. The agreements and disagreements over primary mathematics were to be just one example. Today, little attempt is made to achieve consensus and repeated 'go it alone' policies are met by counter-measures by different *Lander* on other issues. Political infighting dominated the period after 1968 and New Maths became something of a symbol. Winter reports how, in some *Landers*, such as Nordrheim-Westfalen, it was the conservative Christian Democrats who were to take up the cudgels against the reforms, whereas in other areas (for example, Baden Wurtemberg) it was the left-wing SPD who were opposed. Opposition to the introduction of such changes tended to be located in whichever party was in the minority. This picture presents a more complex interplay of forces than the French or Danish situation where opposition tended to come from the right and support from the left.

It was during this period that a number of *Lander*, led by Hessen, moved away from the word *Lehrplen* or syllabus to the less prescriptive phrase *Rahmenrichtinien*; literally translated this means picture frame, and the English equivalent would be framework. Controversy around the moves towards reforms were less marked in the secondary than the primary sector. Teachers in the *Gymnasium* had in any case been using work in this area for optional courses that could be given accreditation on final certificates. Debates about the transformational as opposed to the Euclidean approach to geometry, for example, were represented in the production of alternative textbooks by some publishers and teachers had almost come to accept this.

The period of the 1960s and early 1970s saw considerable uncertainty about the traditional role of the central state ministry in directing curriculum change. The example of Hessen is similar to many other areas. Prior to this period, the last *Lehrplen* had been introduced in 1957. In terms of New Maths, next to nothing had been included. The life of this *Lehrplen* could only be ten years when, by law, it ceased to have any influence. In 1967 nothing was produced and it was not until 1973 that a new *Rahmenrichtinien* was published. The vacuum created compares significantly with the French and Danish experience.

In Hessen, disillusion with the style of experimentation that had characterized the previous decade led in 1975 to the establishment of an institute to take responsibility for the co-ordination of curriculum development. The *Hessisches Institut fur Bildungsplaning und Schulentwicklung* has an equivocal relationship to the ministry. Some perceive it as the administration's attempt to control what previously they had lost control of, others see it as an innovative agency which has a degree of independence from the ministry and therefore is a valuable counterweight in the struggle for curriculum reform. It certainly experiences considerable financial pressure and it was established when there was less awareness of the need to link in-service education and training with formal curriculum development. The main *Lander* institute for in-service work is situated 250 kilometres away. Left-wing attempts to involve community and parental participation in curriculum change in the 1960s have taken a decidedly different direction than those passing the legislation anticipated. Conservative parent bodies are now preventing the reforms pioneered in part by the *Institut*, in some cases by exercising a statutory delaying power given to them fifteen years before.

Denmark

> We're a very small country and we must therefore pay very careful attention to what is going on around us. This is both a national insecurity and a national strength.

Bert Christiansen, Professor of Mathematics in the Royal School of Educational Studies, captures the style of reform in Denmark, mirrored recently in a speech by the then Minister of Education, Dorte Bennedsen, when she suggested

> A country with five million people and an education system smaller in size than that of many large metropolitan areas needs to look outwards for ideas and inspiration.[10]

This was inevitably true in the area of mathematics reform. Danish education is formally controlled by Act of Parliament and this includes guidelines for curricula content in all the major subject areas. A *Folkeskole* or common school Act in 1958 was only revised in 1975. In between these dates mathematical education in the primary school was to follow a 'pendulum'-like course accompanied by the familiar cacophony of media comment and debate.

Christiansen is concerned to stress an element of continuity in the reform of mathematics education. After all, 'Our Education Act of 1903 introduced the idea of co-ordinates.'

He also expresses the view, repeated by others, that the strong spiritual and community context of schooling (directly descended from the ideas of Grundtvig in the Folk High Schools of the nineteenth century) had a power to defuse polarized and antagonistic controversy. He accepts however, the early complementary and sometimes controversial stimulus of ideas that came from:

a   Changes in mathematics in the universities and consequence changes in the level of gymnasium, b The internationally powerful series of conferences sponsored initially by UNESCO and OECD and later through the International Commission of Mathematics Instruction/Education (ICME) and the lectures of Zoltang Dienes in Denmark during this period.

The first was a significant phenomenon across the whole of Western Europe. The second was to have a particularly important impact on Danish thinking. The Royaumont Seminar was of special significance in awakening Danish educationalists to the importance of reform. Such ideas were incorporated into the teaching of the Royal Danish School of Educational Studies and in the mid-1960s Christiansen was to appear in a Danish television series aimed specifically at educating public opinion. The capacity for modern mathematics to become associated with a 'personality' is at its most significant within the Danish context. Teachers, advisers and inspectors are intrigued to know 'where Christiansen's views are today' almost as if there needed to be a sign for future directions.

The most specific influence however, that brought about major change, without reference to the legislative guidelines, was the publication of new textbooks by authors recently returned from spells of teaching in the USA. Some were translated from Swedish. Jørgan Cort and Jørgan Rydstøm were the first into the market with books for the early years of the folkeskole. The Danish market is inevitably small, with twelve to fifteen series competing for teachers' attention, compared with a figure four times that in West Germany.

Opposition to reform was vigorously expressed, particularly from parents who traditionally in Denmark have a greater degree of involvement in school affairs than has been the case in many other countries (this has been clearly enshrined in the Folkeskole Act of 1975). There is a national parents' association who became concerned about this and played an active part in the protracted debates leading up to the new Act. The influence of the group is apparent in the reading of this legislation where the sections of the programmes concerned with mathematics are all headed mathematics/arithmetic. The arithmetic after the stroke addition came as a result of a last-minute urgent appeal by the chairman of the parents' association direct to the Minister of Education. It seemed generally accepted that in 1980 everyone would accept the designation mathematics without the need for a qualifying word to stress number and basic skills.[11]

In this same period, an active Association of Teachers of Mathematics was established (initially committed to reforms) and eventually becoming incorporated into the powerful Danish Teachers Union. This body is now consulted on all legislative changes. The activities of this association were to be of importance in the modifications made to the second phase of publications produced in the early 1970s. A particular characteristic of the Danish folkeskole is the wide range over which many teachers work. (The folkeskole has a unified compulsory period of schooling from the age of seven to sixteen.) Despite the powerful support of people such as Christiansen, there was in the late 1960s and early 1970s much confusion backed up by particular events which helped sway opinion. The Danes have been generous in the support given to additional 'remedial extraction' programmes within the schools. Christiansen reports on study, carried out by an educational psychologist, showing a high proportion of children being taken out for such programmes in mathematics. This attracted a great deal of attention in the press and on television which, in part, was supported, as in many other countries, by some less than favourable statements by industrialists about the quality of recruits.

The 1974 Act has a more judicious blend of what could be termed the old and the new within the mathematics programme. The textbooks similarly, now in a third generation, reflect this transformation. One successful series is a translation from Swedish of a series called 'Hi!' which one teacher said was, like many of these recent publications, '. . . all new colour, all old maths'.

The Netherlands
On 12 June 1961, the Underminister for Instruction, Arts and Science appointed a Commission on the Modernization of the Mathematics Programme (CMLW).[12] Aimed at the reform of the secondary school curriculum and spurred on by the requests for information from OECD in the wake of the Royaumont Seminar, this commission became a highly influential body. Ten university professors of mathematics out-numbered all other participants and the 'top down' influence to be found in many of the European countries is clearly apparent. CMLW, con-stituted with a sense of urgency, soon extended its brief to primary education and Hans Freudenthal, a leading member, was to propose the establishment of a curriculum development agency to research and develop materials for schools.

Freudenthal was a mathematician of international reputation. A refugee from Germany in pre-war days, he had become a highly respected member of the Dutch academic community. He had played a leading role in the debates about reforming mathematical education and had written widely in response to new materials that were filtering in from other countries during the 1950s[13]. Freudenthal (1979) was not an advocate of 'New Maths' content for content's sake. 'We had to decide if it was teaching modern mathematics or modern teaching of mathematics.' And in a number of articles he was to stress the need for programmes to be strongly related to applications rather than mere mathematical structures void of content (Freudenthal 1978). This viewpoint was to become a major characteristic of the work of the new institute, and is in marked contrast to the experience of many other countries. It helps explain the more muted response reported in the Dutch media.

The *Instituut Ontwikkeling Wiskunde Onderwije* (IOWO) was planned to be the centre of the major curriculum innovations in primary mathematics. Formally established in 1971, with a staff of twenty-three and a budget of six million guilders, it was soon to embark on a formal development project similar in focus to Nuffield Primary Maths in Britain, '*Alef*' in Germany and '*Analogue*' in France. The development style was to continue the experience of CMLW in the previous decade, based on the particular ideas of the staff, especially Freudenthal, as well as a careful study of experience in other countries.

A characteristic theme of IOWO was the need to think in terms of educational development rather than curriculum development, compensating for the rather narrow use of the term curriculum.

> Educational development has three components: curriculum development, in the smaller sense of the word; research; and above all 'change support' which, in part, relates to initial and in-service training. The Wiskobas programme aimed to integrate each of these components. (Adrian Treffers – an IOWO researcher)

IOWO began development work in one primary school in Arnhem in 1971. This decision aroused considerable controversy:

> One famous Dutch psychologist castigated us for drawing conclusions from work in only one school. He wanted us to spread over the country producing representative samples. He had totally misunderstood the way WISKOBAS [primary school programme] was to develop. (Hans Freudenthal)

The experimentation in one school was paralleled by conferences of those responsible for mathematics education in teacher training as well as by in-service courses aimed at developing materials. The attendance at the former was impressively high – in a country the size of the Netherlands, it was possible to bring together ninety percent of such teachers. Involvement had been facilitated by a 1969 conference where the teacher trainers themselves had expressed the need for such a development. In part, this had been a response to the risk of 'New Maths' textbooks from abroad[13] which were being translated into Dutch, and which were causing considerable disquiet.

Treffers (1975) quotes Lawrence Stenhouse approvingly to support the statement that the teacher can no longer pretend to be an expert and has inevitably to cast himself in the role of learner alongside the student. In referring to one project on scale, which used the tale of Gulliver's Travels as a context, he comments:

> The brick 'Gulliver' is therefore neither 'finished', 'teacher-proof' or 'ready to use'. On the other hand, the topic does not only consist of general suggestions. It is rather one example as we might join in saying that 'offers orientation and activity possibilities and offers security to the practitioner without being strictly prescriptive' thus stimulating the teacher's as well as the pupil's initiative.

This style has been termed by one member of the institute staff, Goffree, (1974) 'constructive analysis'. The teacher analyses the material and if necessary constructs a variant that reflects his personal ideas on education and in time revives this variant after the teaching experience.

Such an approach is not answerable to traditional styles of evaluation. No attempt had been made to formally evaluate the Wiskobas project as a whole. There had been links with CITO, the national testing agency, although Freudenthal was dismissive of the value. Specific topics within the different programmes had been evaluated as indicated above in the quotation about development style. Institute staff also made claims about the performance of 'Wiskobas classes' on measures other than those associated with mathematical ability and understanding. Language performance was one area cited.

IOWO appears to have worked closely with ministry officials and inspectors. Wiskobas teacher books were purchased by a third of all primary school teachers and it was, in this respect, more successful than work at the secondary level. The institute, concerned about the proliferation of textbooks on the market, publishes a survey of any publications in the field and it appears publishers and teachers await the IOWO verdict with particular interest. Controversy, however, was to surround the institute's work. The rationalization of curriculum development work into one agency, the SLO,[14] was to leave IOWO as a somewhat expensive anachronism for one subject area. Amid international outcry, the institute was finally closed and development moved to SLO headquarters at Enschede on the German border – only a few of the staff were to make the transition and primary mathematic curriculum development, documented by Freudenthal and the institute for the previous decade, faces an uncertain future.

The international context

This story would be incomplete without some reference to the international organizations that played a role in promoting reform. As early as 1950, UNESCO had published an *Introduction to Mathematics in Primary Schools* (UNESCO 1950). Throughout the decade both UNESCO and OECD were to increasingly become interested in mathematics in schools, pressured in particular, says George Papadopoulos (now deputy director of OECD), by the university mathematics professors concerned about the recruitment of mathematicians from the schools into the universities. OECD, funded massively by the USA, was to be particularly concerned with the issue of training personnel in the technical field. (OECD educational activities at that time came under the Governing Committee for Scientific and Technical Personnel.) In 1959, the consequences of the Royaumont Seminar were to reverberate through European countries. (OEEC 1961).

> There are many unmistakable signs that we are on the brink of important, even radical, changes in a mathematical curriculum which has remained relatively static for a rather long time. In fact, this seminar has been convened because of a conviction that such changes are essential for progress, and that they must be discussed with imagination and discernment before they are put into practice. (from the Introductory Address by Professor Marshall H. Stone to the Royaumont Seminar, 23 November – 4 December 1959)

Although pledged initially to look at elementary and secondary schooling the proceedings were dominated by discussion of the secondary school curriculum. A compulsory one-third attendance of teachers was requested by the organizers and the report of the conference is a student plea to nation states to reform the mathematics curriculum.

The members of the seminar agree unanimously upon the modernization of the teaching of mathematics. In order to realize this modernization it is necessary for the different countries to prepare textbooks and manuals.[15]

It is difficult to imagine such prescriptive recommendations from any international agency at this moment. International conferences followed at regular intervals. Four years after Royaumont, in Athens, conference participants (including many of the same people who had been present in Royaumont) were still optimistic about the pace and direction of change.

The conference of leaders, such as held at Royaumont, Dubrovnik, and now Athens, has stimulated experimentation to a tremendous degree. At these conferences the exchange of ideas, the challenges to do something different (e.g., Euclid Must Go!) and the exhortations of great mathematicians (e.g., Vector spaces should be at the center of the secondary school program) have sent persons back home to do something. It can be said now that all OECD countries have been affected by such conferences and the experiments now in operation promise a new day in school mathematics.[16]

Country reports showed the impact of the reform movement as the French example quoted above illustrates.

Royaumont participants in 1959 pleaded for a revolution in mathematics education. Those in Athens, four years later, proclaimed the revolution accomplished: 'an important part of a reform in mathematics education has been accomplished.'[17]

The next decade, however, was to witness a harsher reality than any contemplating an Aegean winter might have imagined. By 1968, at the first UNESCO-sponsored meeting of the International Commission for Mathematics Education (ICME) in Lyon, Begle (1969), a signatory to the Athens report five years earlier, was to say:

I am convinced that many of the guide posts we have followed in our attempts to improve mathematics education are of dubious value and that the answers we have been given to our fundamental questions about mathematics education cannot be relied upon.

A section (Howson G. 1973) dealing with curriculum design and evaluation was

. . . largely descriptive of the problems that each individual country or project had found in developing its mathematics curriculum, and the steps taken to solve these problems . . .

From there on international affairs, centered around ICME, were to move away from modern *v.* traditional or reform *v.* status quo towards a more diversified assembly of interests and problems. Clearly apparent is the growth of membership from research institutes, departments of mathematics education and curricular projects. In two conferences at Berkeley in California (where more than 2000 participants attended) and at Bielefeld in Germany (a smaller, more specialist gathering) attendance of schoolteachers, a characteristic of Royaumont, was to be reduced to a tiny percentage. In fact, attendance figures for four conferences spread over the decade indicates the increasing dominance of those in higher education (see Figure 13.2). This professionalization of mathematics education, which did not exist until the period of curriculum development and reform, is sustained today within the framework of international co-operation.

Conclusion

Each of these 'sketches' represent a unique constellation of events but, equally, all provide some evidence to question the general assumption made about the nature and style of curriculum control. From these accounts, it is clear that national, regional, local or school control rarely operates within the style that formal processes presuppose.

Centralized or decentralized control represents a contemporary issue as well as classic descriptive categories for educational systems. Centralization is often presented, in caricature form, as a system to be avoided at all costs by any self-respecting Anglo-Saxon. While many now appreciate that the notion of the minister checking the clock to see when French becomes geography across the whole of France is, and always was, a gross distortion, assumptions about centralized power still exist. Distinctions between formal structures and the real world of change are rarely assessed in the hard light of evidence. The story of New Maths in French primary schools suggests that substantial changes occurred all over the country well before any formal modification of the national guidelines. To suggest that 'overall control of the school curriculum in France lies firmly with the Minister of Education'[18] was to be many steps away from the real world of curriculum change. Textbooks were on the market and selling in substantial numbers two even three years before formal changes occurred. These textbooks themselves, written in the period around 1968, anticipated a new programme or curriculum and, in a sense, created the necessity for it. Inspectors played little part in either insisting on implementation of the 1957 code or giving formal approval to the new approaches being adopted in the schools. Textbooks do not have to be

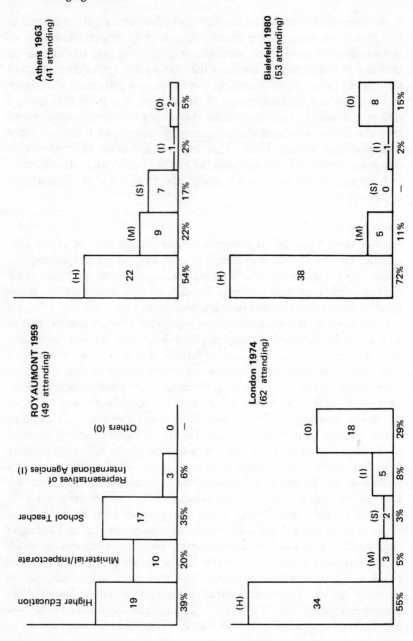

Figure 13.2 Graphs showing percentages of five international conferences concerned with the mathematics curriculum 1959-1980

approved in France as they are in the German *Lander* for example, and this fact alone has a highly significant influence on change. Witness after witness of the French educational scene report that the ministerial programmes are rarely, if ever, read by French teachers, and publishers admit to exploiting the pressures for change by fuelling the need to reform the official programme. Figure 13.2 shows the relationship between changes in the regulations concerning curriculum content and development projects in new mathematics. The three countries with statutory controls maintained outdated regulations throughout this period of significant change.

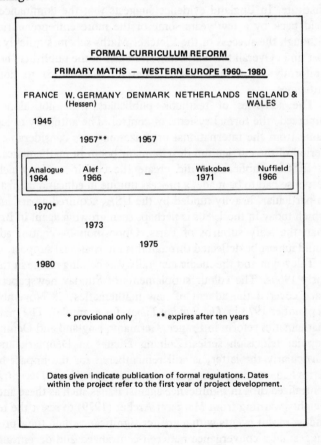

Figure 13.3

In Denmark as in France the story is very much the same with translated books outdating the 1957 Folkeskole Act but still taking over a large share of the market. In Hessen, the centralized regional government maintained outdated formal guidelines (new guidelines could not be agreed) approving textbooks (albeit not 'Alef') which were based on a totally different approach to that laid down in 1957. In the Netherlands, the publishing houses, quick to perceive the possibilities presented by a wholesale renewal of books in one subject of the primary school, translated and introduced French and English texts which created the very uncertainties among teachers that led to the formation of the IOWO Institute. In England evidence suggests that the dominance of Nuffield held back by a few years some of the more entrepreneurial publishers although the success of the Fletcher Maths schemes quickly made up for lost time. Overall the marketing strategies of the publishers houses applied uniformly across historically different systems led to notably similar outcomes.

The activities of textbook publishers were not alone in helping supercede the formal systems of control. The authority to legitimize that came from the international organizations was considerable in the early period of the curriculum development boom in mathematics. OECD and UNESCO publications did create the conditions in which a national response had to be made, a process unique in educational history. OECD, in particular, heavily funded by the USA, acquired a particular influence which today in the 1980s is perhaps seen growing again in Brussels rather than the leafy suburbs of Paris. Opposition by central administration could in part be deflected through this international support.

Television and the media generally was coming of age in the late 1950s, early 1960s. The colour supplements of Sunday newspapers more than once covered the advent of new mathematics (28 November 1976 – 2 September 1973 in *The Sunday Times*, for example). The major figures in mathematics reform in France, Germany, England and Denmark all made popular television series. Zoltang Dienes in Denmark and Germany, particularly the latter, is still remembered for the impact his television series had on educationalists and the public at large. Decentralized versus centralized dips in significance against issues such as these and neither the weighty warning from Margaret Archer (1979) to resist the temptation to endow recent events with a greater significance than their predecessors in suggesting a convergence between centralized and decentralized systems or the strictures of Sir Walter Raleigh, quoted above, can mesh the need to explore further the role of events such as these in the curriculum process.[19]

In looking at the international perspective (of which publishers, the media and organizations such as UNESCO and OECD represent major reference groups) the influence of developments in the USA is also a critical factor, a further dimension transcending the traditional boundaries of control in European nation states. Brian Jackson in a colour supplement digest on mathematics reform explained this.

It was, of course, the Russians who turned our maths classes into fun palaces. When Sputnik 1 circled Europe and American in 1957, its extraordinary wake smashed in one superior act the traditional mathematics which had dominated our schools unchallenged for a century. The maths that grandmother taught was pretty hot at working out how many kippers at a penny three farthings each you might get for £5. But Greek geometry and Victorian mercantile conundrums clearly didn't lead to the stars. (*Sunday Times*, 2 September 1973, p.38)

The notion of the direct transmission from the States across the Atlantic simplifies what appears to have been a far more complex interplay of relationships. What happened in the USA appears to have fuelled rather than initiated change in each of the case studies reported here. In fact, one of the first post-Sputnik initiatives by people such as Begle and Fehr, leading advocates of change, was to propose that studies be made of what was happening in Europe and it was very much in this vein that American participation in Royaumont was launched (see the introduction to the report).

In Europe the oft talked about but again rarely observed influence of the universities on schools was exemplified by the changes in the mathematics curriculum. University changes moved to secondary schools culminating in primary school reform. This was a rapid process, less than ten years, and the involvement of leading university mathematicians in the reform programme is a feature of each of the case studies. Only in the Netherlands was this influence formalized within the structure of curriculum reform although in France there was a significant involvement (in none of the case studies does this appear to be apparent today and in the case of Bauersfeld and Freudenthal hostility seems to have developed between the professors of mathematics and the professors of mathematics education).

It is also interesting to note that the R and D style applied in Europe had least impact in those countries (France and Denmark) where a centralized structure of control would seem more conclusive to such developments.[20]

It is ironic that just as these international forces appear to have, in the examples of primary mathematics, overtaken the traditional controls across a range of specific national systems, so the forces for localized power and authority were exerting influences from a very different base. This has increasingly been a point of investigation for political scientists and a theme pursued by, for example, a number of writers, one of whom, Gottman (1980), under the heading 'The Challenge to Centrality', suggests that

> challenges to the established spatial order result from the dynamic trends of change characteristic of recent decades: technological evolution, economic growth, the redistribution of income, a shifting occupational structure, welfare reforms, and new ideologies, all combined to produce a feeling of relative liberation from old shackles.

Formal central control systems became squeezed between the internationalization of the curriculum debate, fuelled by publishers, the media and international agencies and the forces opposed to this traditional hold on power. In France, Germany and Denmark it would appear that the advocates of decentralization used these international events in opposing the centre. The fervent debate about mathematics reform in France certainly came to symbolize the dichotomy between centre and periphery. The establishment of a unique structure of almost wholly autonomous mathematics curriculum development centres (IREMS) exhibits this *par excellence* and was very much the brainchild of one leading left-wing mathematics teacher, Walusinski, who wouldn't allow any inspectors into his classroom. The power of the periphery was seen by some as a reaction to increasing centralization and not a mere epiphenomenon of it (Sharpe 1979). To stay with France, Eugene Weber (1979) in a marvellous book entitled *Peasants into Frenchmen* indicates how mythical the notion of Napoleonic, centralized and unified France really is. And Theodore Zeldin's parallel work (1980) expresses the view that the history of France's education produces the same conclusion as the history of its politics, that the theories propagated do not provide an accurate guide to what actually happened. Zeldin's amazement at the extent to which, in the period 1848-1945, the rules were disobeyed in schools is matched by recent attempts in political science to understand the process of centralization (Sheriff-Petra 1979, Chevallier 1976).

The study of the state bureaucracy in France has long been dominated by the Faculties of Law with the result that the traditional literature provides extensive accounts of what ought to happen rather than what does happen.[21]

This is a view mirrored perhaps in the curriculum debate about what is meant by control.

These ideas, therefore, seem important to developing an understanding of curriculum change. Recognition of the inadequacy of previous ideas is now beginning to appear in the literature. Patricia Broadfoot, in arguing for research and investigation in this area, asks us to look beyond the rhetoric of control in an education system to the reality that underpins it. In the case of curriculum innovation then, this involves identifying the actual rather than the theoretical controls which affect the impact of research and development.

The story of primary school mathematics development suggests that influences far more significant than governments may underpin the process of control and change. The market economy and the policies of textbook publishers; the role of multinational organizations; the influence, perhaps manipulation, of the media not only by politicians but curriculum developers exploiting particular circumstances and local conditions; and more recently the rise of the professionalized group of mathematics educators have been of critical importance. Above all, the clear inter-relationship of the quest for reform and modernization of new mathematics programmes became inextricably linked with the political and social concerns of those 'pendulum years', clear evidence that the search for ultimate truths, even in mathematics, cannot avoid the ideological assumptions, presuppositions and contradictions of the day. Elizabeth House in the UK, the rue Grenelle in Paris or the remote deliberations of the Kultusministerkonferenz in Bonn each represent very different institutional loci of power embedded in historically or culturally varied national contexts. The events in schools and classrooms in the 1980s may, however, revolve around forces that transcend any national contexts, forces that have much in common regardless of language or tradition and which, therefore, require the closest possible attention if curriculum development processes are to be understood, analysed and made more effective in promoting innovation in the future.

Notes

1   Some of the evidence has been published in the weekly educational press 'Euro-Maths,' Moon, Bob. *Education* 7 August 1981 p.128. 'Wiskobas from Utrecht', Moon, Bob.

Times Educational Supplement 27 March 1981, p.34
2   Roughly translated: Director of Research.
3   Commercial competition between publishers has made the collection of information in the area extremely difficult. All contacts have insisted on anonymity in any publication of comments and statistics.
4.   In the period the INRP was under considerable political pressure with the Director, Louis Legrand, exiled to Strasbourg (he is now back in Paris), and ministerial vetos of some reforms, for example in the teaching of French, excited considerable controversy.
5   Reprinted in Curriculum Bulletin No 1, The Schools Council (1969) *Mathematics in Primary Schools*, third edition.
6   Although in the introduction to a Stationery Office publication in 1959, *Mathematics Teaching in the Secondary School*, the then Minister of Education, Geoffrey Lloyd, was to propose 'We have clearly reached a stage in the teaching of mathematics where our curriculum and methods need to be considered afresh.'
7   Twenty French mathematicians who, up to the present day, have published nearly forty volumes of very pure advanced mathematics under the pseudonym Nicholas Bourbaki. Bourbaki was a rather undistinguished Swiss general. The name was adopted by the group, possibly as an anti-Nazi protection, which later became a 'cult' that continues until today.
8   Although Black Paper Two (1970) published by the Critical Quarterly Society contains one polemic which included innuendo of governmental forces behind the movement

> Officially it was quickly decided that we must keep up with the Russians at all costs, and slowly but surely there came about a revolution in the teaching of number. . . . The first step was to change the name of the subject. Almost overnight the word 'arithmetic' disappeared from the timetable, being replaced by that much more glamorous term 'mathematics'. . . . The opposition to the new maths by sun-loving teachers was . . . quickly overcome. In education if you want promotion you must not question the suggestions from the experts, however dotty they may seem . . . (pp.104-105).

9   Ministry or publishers will not release details of textbook sales.
10   30 October 1980, reception for visiting educationalists.
11   The story of the word 'arithmetic' in each of the major countries is of particular interest. Dutch newspapers, writing recently on the future of mathematical education, had frequently to insert the word 'arithmetic' in brackets to indicate what was being discussed. Denmark and West Germany have only in the last few years experienced a shift towards public acceptance of the word mathematics. A more careful assessment of this transformation would assist in giving an accurate indication of the time-scales of reform on mathematics.
12   Commissie Modernisering Leerplan Wiskune
13   For example, the French *Analogue* materials of Nicole Picard had been translated although sales figures eventually were low.
14   Stichting voor de leerplan ontwikkeling
15   OEEC (1961) pp. 123-124.
16   *Fehr* (1964) p.315.
17   *Fehr* (1964) p.318.
18   See for example Becher, Tony *The Politics of Curriculum Change*, and Maclure, Stuart (1978), Hutchinson, p.25.
19   A need argued strongly in the interesting set of papers on post-war curriculum development – published from the University of Liverpool, forming the proceedings of

the 1979 conference of the History of Education Society.

20 This contrasts with the ideas set out, for example, in *Handbook of Curriculum Development* (CERI, Paris, 1975) pp. 46-49.

21 Sheriff Petra (1979) p.262.

References

Archer, M. (1979) *Social Origins of Educational Systems*, Sage, pp. 789 – 791.

Beattie, N. (1977) *Public Participation in Curriculum Change: a West German Example Compare* Vol 7, No 1, p. 1729

Begle, (1969) *Educational Studies in Mathematics* 2, p. 238.

Broadfoot, P. (1980) 'Rhetoric and reality in the context of innovation', Compare 10:2.

Chevallier, J. (1976) 'La participation dans l'administration francais discours et practique'. *Bulletin de l'institut international d'Administration publique 1 & 2*, pp. 85–119 and pp. 85–142.

Fehr, H F. (ed) (1974) *Mathematics Today*, OECD.

Freudenthal, H. (1978) 'Changes in Mathematics Education since the late 1950's – ideas and realisation', *The Netherlands Educational Studies in Mathematics*, 9, pp. 261 – 270.

Freudenthal, H. (1979) 'New Maths or New Education?' *Prospects*, Vol IX, No 3.

Goffree, F. (1974) Doorkijspiegelingen Wiskobas, *Bulletin*, 3, No 6, IOWO, Utrecht.

Gottman, J. (ed) (1980) *Centre and Periphery: spatial variations in politics*, Saga Publications.

Howson, G. (ed) (1973) *Developments in Education*, Cambridge University Press.

OEEC (1961) *New Thinking in School Mathematics*, Paris.

Sharpe, E J. (ed) (1979) *Decentralized Trends in Western Democracies*, p. 20. Sage Publications.

Sherriff Petra (1979) 'French administration: sanctified or demystified', *West European Politics* 2:2.

Treffers, A (1975) *De Kriekkas van Wiskobas*, IOWO, Utrecht.

UNESCO (1950) *Introduction to Mathematics in Primary Schools* International Bureau of Education, Publication No 121, Geneva.

UNESCO (1956) *Teaching of Mathematics in Secondary Schools*, International Bureau of Education Publication, Geneva.

Weber, E. (1979) *Peasants into Frenchmen*, Chatto and Windus, London.

Zeldin, T (1977) *France 1845–1945* Vol 11, Clarendon Press.

Acknowledgements

Dr Stephen Ball and Professor Tony Becher of the University of Sussex, and the late Professor Lawrence Stenhouse provided valuable advice in the preparation of this paper. The Central Bureau for Educational visits and Exchanges provided funding to support certain aspects of the field work.

PART III

NEW DIRECTIONS IN EVALUATION AND ACCOUNTABILITY

INTRODUCTION

DAVID ALEXANDER AND MAURICE GALTON

The emphasis on school-based evaluation reflected in this section denotes a significant and important change in current thinking on the issue of accountability. Five years ago the pressures for stricter external accounting, similar to that imposed by many school boards in the United States, was a primary feature to be taken into account by any school planning a curricular innovation. Nationally, the campaign of the writers of the Black Papers and the disputed analysis of the NFER reading survey were factors leading to the then education minister, Margaret Thatcher, setting in motion the development of the Assessment and Performance Unit. By the late 1970s, the oft-repeated claims that 'modern teaching methods' were leading to a decline in the standards of literacy and numeracy appeared to receive an added boost from the publication of Professor Neville Bennett's *Teaching Styles and Pupil Progress*, and the note of caution expressed by the author was largely ignored. The National Foundation for Education Research received a massive boost in funds to research into methods of assessment which would allow careful monitoring of standards. They selected as their model an application of latent-trait theory developed by a Danish mathematician, George Rasch. At conferences up and down the country, teachers were told that the 'average' pupil in the school should be expected to improve his or her attainment by two WITS a year. Not surprisingly, there was also a half-WIT and a centi-WIT which represented one day's effort by a pupil on any subject in school. A vision was put before officials of the APU and local authority administrators of a series of item-banks in which every item would be labelled in terms of its difficulty level expressed in these WIT units. So much enthusiasm was displayed by local authorities for these new measurement techniques that plans for blanket testing in schools multiplied with great rapidity. Indeed, it required a stern warning from Shirley Williams, soon after her accession to the Secretaryship of State for Education, to slow down this process when at the annual NFER conference she asked local authority representatives to wait for more evidence from the National Foundation's researchers before beginning to use the new items.

These pressures for some system of external accounting to be imposed upon schools were strongly resisted in several quarters. Researchers, such as John Elliott, working within an 'action-research' model quickly saw that this offered an alternative form of public accounting – one where teachers might continue to exercise responsibility in choosing the curriculum to suit the needs of their pupils while at the same time acknowledging that this power and responsibility should be open to inspection by parents and other outside bodies. Within this style of accountability, teachers, as professionals, exercise their right to choose the type of evaluation most suited to their purpose but there is a need to justify the methods used and make the results available to the widest possible audience within the local community. Through the Cambridge Accountability Project, Elliott has attempted to put these ideas into practice.

In the same period the publication of *Fifteen Thousand Hours*, of which Peter Mortimore was one of the co-authors, helped to demonstrate that judgements about the effectiveness of schooling required more sophisticated evaluative techniques than the mere collection and processing of examination results. Some of these techniques were summarized for the benefit of teachers in Marten Shipman's *In-School Evaluation* and a practical result of these and other initiatives has been the development of school-based accountability schemes by several local authorities, notably Oxfordshire and the Inner London Education Authority. While critics, such as Maurice Holt, have argued strongly against the use of any style of evaluation which sets out to achieve some form of 'objective' assessment of a school's standing, others have argued, as in this present volume, that such schemes have at least given schools the means to fight back against their detractors and have taken some of the pressures off the teacher in the classroom.

More recently, supporters of more formal accounting procedures have received a number of set-backs. Statistical experts have cast strong doubts over the use of the Rasch model as a technique for monitoring standards of performance over a period of time. The leading exponents of the idea within the National Foundation of Educational Research have now left for pastures new. Funding for the main testing programme of the APU may be expected to decline and there is much greater caution about the likelihood of developing sophisticated item-banks of the kind originally envisaged. Part of these successes can be attributed to the development of the school-based curriculum movement in this country. The slight easing of the pressures for external accounting, however, should not be taken as a sign that the battle has been won. Instead efforts must be doubled to develop alternative procedures which are recognized as credible and effective. The three papers in this section take up this theme. Peter Mortimore sets out to describe what has so far been achieved. Elliott argues for a particular way forward which would see accountability not as an end in itself but as a means of a teacher's personal development. In the final paper, Marten Shipman takes up the themes developed in the previous two papers and attempts an evaluation of the present state of evaluation.

CHAPTER 14

SCHOOL SELF-EVALUATION

PETER MORTIMORE

Reasons for self-evaluation

The debate on accountability in education has focused interest on techniques of self-evaluation. Whether or not teachers should be accountable to their heads, LEAs, the Department of Education, the parents of their pupils, local employers or the pupils themselves, the argument is that they can be more critical of their own performance. In many ways, of course, this is what good teachers have always tried to do: to reflect upon their success and failure and, as a result, to modify their teaching. What is new is a more structured approach, and an awareness that there is more to reflect on than just teaching in one classroom. The pioneering work of the ILEA Inspectorate (*Keeping the School Under Review*) and similar exercises opened up questions about the general school environment, resources and parental and community links. The ILEA publication also posed two 'acid tests' for teachers to answer: whether the school should be recommended as a place of work to fellow-teachers, or to friends seeking guidance on where to send their children.

Apart from the acid tests this was the approach (albeit based more on the systematic collection of evidence that reliance on professional judgement) used by the research team working on the *Fifteen Thousand Hours* study. What was different was the attempt to relate what was going on in the school to a set of educational outcomes so that the value of particular aspects of school life could be judged in relation to these. Ignoring the intrinsic value of participation in the communal school life by a large proportion of pupils, the researchers looked to see if it was related in a positive way to one of the chosen outcomes. The advantage of this approach was that dependence on value judgements could be reduced. The disadvantage was that those aspects of school life which could be important without having a *direct* effect on one of a small number of outcomes may have been missed.

Schemes for self-evaluation

It is now nearly five years since the publication of *Keeping the School Under Review* and three years since *Fifteen Thousand Hours* was published. What developments have there been in school self-evaluation over this time?

According to Elliot (1980) approximately seventy local education authorities were involved in some kind of self-evaluation scheme. By 1982 there are undoubtedly many more. If this number of authorities are involved then the number of schools attempting to evaluate some aspect of their performance must be enormous. In London, for instance, all primary and secondary schools are carrying out annual reviews which include some self-evaluation and which are to be reported to governing bodies.

Self-evaluation, however, takes time. If teachers are devoting efforts to this, it is likely to be at the expense of some other activity and they will naturally be anxious that it is time well spent.

The critical conditions for success in self-evaluation rather than in evaluation by inspectors or advisers are, in my opinion, guaranteed confidentiality, the opportunity to develop a trusting relationship with a peer and, within the climate created by those two conditions, honest feedback.

1 *Confidentiality*: Unless teachers are guaranteed confidentiality, self-evaluation will inevitably become dishonest. At a time of redeployment and possible redundancy many teachers will be defensive about their classroom skills. They may also be apprehensive about revealing any deficits to those in authority, who may have to take decisions affecting their future careers.

2 *Trusting relationships*: Human attention is highly selective; it has to be for us to cope with the enormous range of stimuli that impinge upon us. As a result, therefore, honest 'self'-evaluation is extremely difficult

for us to achieve by ourselves for we tend to select evidence that confirms a positive view of our performance and reject any that is dissonant. However, Wigley (1980) has reported improvement in accuracy of self-observation that has come about as a result of working with a peer. Experience suggests that in observing a partner the ability to distance oneself – and thus to observe more objectively – can be developed. Although a similar effect can sometimes be achieved by the use of video-recording, many teachers prefer to work with a partner. The reciprocity of the exercise, whereby each participant takes a time at being observer and observed, helps create the trusting relationship that is so essential. Thus, although the evaluation is carried out by the teacher himself, crucial to the exercise is the assistance of a peer.

3 *Feedback*: Closely related to a trusting relationship with a colleague is the matter of feedback. Novice pairs often have to adjust the giving of information either because it is too bland – and therefore of little use to the observer – or too sharp to be acceptable. Only with time, trust and reciprocality can the appropriate level of feedback be gauged and accepted in good faith. (For those who prefer to work by themselves, the video permits an alternative strategy, though with this aid the participant has to judge for himself how much he can take!)

From what has been argued so far it is clear that self-evaluation cannot be grafted on to other exercises concerned with the identification of incompetent teachers, or any form of inspection. It is something different but something considerably more valuable to the teacher.

Assuming then that these conditions can be achieved, what sort of self-evaluation should teachers carry out?

Quantitative methods

Classroom teachers, in all phases and types of schools and at all stages of education, can gain an indication of the learning taking place in their classes. I have used this form of wording because, quite clearly, monitoring is much easier with some aspects of learning than others. The mechanics of reading can be monitored more easily than reading comprehension and in turn comprehension can probably be monitored more easily than can the enjoyment of a book.

Within a classroom a teacher can focus either directly on their own actions or, alternatively, they can focus on their pupils. If they choose the pupils they will, of course, be observing to a certain extent the consequences of their own actions as well as pupil initiatives. They may wish to compare the amount of time devoted to 'teacher talk' to that of 'pupil talk'. They may decide to chart all the interactions between themselves and their pupils and to note who has initiated these.

Alternatively, if they focus on the class they may try to analyse the incidence of 'teacher talk' or other contact among particular groups of pupils. Thus they could look at the proportion of time they spent talking to boys rather than girls, or certain ethnic groups rather than others. Again they may wish to focus on particular groups of pupils under stress or on those without fluent English. The possibilities are enormous and tasks may be tailored to the concerns of the teacher.

Classroom teachers can also monitor the behaviour of their pupils. Wigley's work has shown that systematic counting of particular incidents can be used to build up a profile of behaviour of particular children. Observation of individuals has also been used by researchers at primary level in studies such as those carried out by the ORACLE team (Simon and Galton 1980), and at secondary level by the *Fifteen Thousand Hours* team (Rutter *et al.* 1979).

In the United States research by Rosenshine and his colleagues has focused on the variation between classes in what they call 'time on task'. Rosenshine argues that this is the most important factor in pupils' learning. Various projects in Bristol, Pennsylvania and in Milwaukee are training teachers to monitor time spent by students in order to enable them to use this resource in the most productive way.

In another American study, Olson (1973) has carried out a large-scale study of nearly twenty thousand school classrooms. Observation data was related to four criteria: individualization, interpersonal regard, group activity and creativity.

Following complex statistical treatment of the data Olson claims to be able to identify factors that are related to high scores on these outcomes. These factors he calls 'indicators of quality'.

Qualitative methods

The quantitative method does not appeal to all. Some teachers will prefer Elliot Eisner's notion of educational connoisseurship. Eisner, an educationalist from California, argues that teachers need a more qualitative –

even an artistic – appreciation of what happens in the classroom. He is much more interested in the processes – or what goes on in the classroom – than in the outcome of education, which in his opinion is little more than 'Knowing the final score of the game after it is over'. The qualitative methods can, however, be applied to both process and outcomes. The problem with this approach is that it needs quite exceptional skills of judgement and a full background of varied experiences. For the novice teachers these are unlikely to have developed sufficiently for confidence in connoisseurship to be strong. However, for inspectors and advisers, this is a common mode of assessment. (Surely the means used to gather the data for *Ten Good Schools*, (HMSO 1977.)

Mixed methods

An approach that seeks to combine both quantitative and qualitative methods has been developed by the Open University 'Curriculum in Action' team. Rather than encourage teachers to use elaborate self-evaluation instruments that have been carefully prepared by 'experts', the OU team asked them to challenge themselves with six very simple questions. The questions are:

1 What did the pupils actually do?

2 What were they learning?

3 How worthwhile was it?

4 What did I do?

5 What did I learn?

6 What do I intend to do now?

These questions are simple yet effective. They force the teacher to examine in some detail exactly what has gone on in the classroom. Pupils may be treated together as a class, a group or as individuals. The questions incorporate monitoring of what was happening, evaluation of its benefit and lead the teacher to think of the implications for further action. Finally, the questions can be asked several times a day for an intensive period, or a couple of times a term as part of a general check. (For those who are interested in following up this work the OU material, Block 1, provides examples of teachers' responses to these questions.)

Schools as institutions

Most of this discussion so far has focused on the individual classroom and the sort of self-evaluation that individual teachers can carry out. Perhaps of greater interest is the concept of 'school self-evaluation'. This is more than an aggregation of the work of individual teachers; it includes the monitoring of the general effects of the institution, the pastoral arrangements, the corporate life of the school and many other areas of school life which do not necessarily take place within a classroom. Many of the indicators that can be evaluated by the school staff can be seen in *Keeping the School under Review*. Others have been advocated by Shipman (1979). He argues that systematic evaluation needs to be carried out and incorporated into the decision making of the school.

Other indications are found in the relevant sections of *Fifteen Thousand Hours*. This research concentrated on five areas of 'process' and four areas of 'outcomes'. The 'process' areas were: academic life; organization of teaching; rewards and punishments; school conditions; and participation and involvement. The outcomes were: examination results; attendance; behaviour; and out-of-school delinquency. These areas do not, of course, represent the whole of school life, but they are indicators of the ethos of a school, and because of the process-outcome relationship, they provide the chance of objective evaluation. Thus it was found that better outcomes were, in general, associated with an academic emphasis, rather structured organization of the teaching, use of rewards but not punishment, pleasant conditions and conscious attempts at developing pupil participation and involvement.

Criticisms of self-evaluation

Both the 'research' approach of the research team and the 'expert' approach of *Keeping the School under Review* have been criticized by Holt (1981). In his view neither approach is able to get to the real heart of teaching.Holt attacks the notion of evaluation, but his definition of it is very limited. Of course test results taken out of the classroom context may be misleading, but within it they must be of great value in informing the teacher. While such information by itself is not necessarily of value, its acquisition does enable teachers to modify their practice and thus improve their teaching.

This is not to make light of the difficulties of assessment. Whether of reading tests or of GCE 'O' level, the difficulties of developing questions that are unambiguous and marking standards that are fair are formidable. However, assessments like those are part of the current educational system and, while we may campaign for change, teachers at present have to learn to live with them. In their own assessments, teachers can overcome many of these difficulties through their knowledge of pupils' skills.

Many heads and teachers see school self-evaluation as a means of reviewing their work in a more systematic way. They will be concerned with indicators of effectiveness. These are not infallible, nor do they tackle every aspect of school life; indeed where there is an absence of a theory of teaching, they cannot be expected to do so. Such opportunities do, however, enable groups of teachers to focus on particular areas and collectively ask questions about aspects of school life. Holt argues that these methods are likely to undermine teachers' confidence. Here the opposite case is argued; that by giving them the skills of researchers and of advisers, teachers will increase their confidence.

The value of self-evaluation

One obvious value of self-evaluation techniques is their flexibility. Individual teachers can use them to gain more insight into their classroom performance. Groups of teachers can use them to gain more insight into their school. In some cases this will enable action to be taken. Thus the staff of a primary school may, after monitoring grouping practices, decide to experiment with a new system. A reading scheme may be replaced following a review of progress through the junior years. A consistent approach to writing may be developed as a result of the systematic study of practice in four or five contrasting classes. Likewise at secondary level, common criteria of marking and of feedback may be developed once the extent of individual variation among teachers in different departments is appreciated. Rules that are unnecessarily punitive may be modified following a review of discipline and systematic collection of data on their effectiveness. Attitudes may be altered once it is realized how frustrating some aspects of organization can be to older pupils.

Changes that are introduced as a result of some form of self-evaluation are far more likely to be maintained than others whose introduction has been negotiated by an outsider. This is not to say that outsiders have no role, but rather that their role should be to help the teachers to increase their own insights. Within the self-evaluation framework, therefore, the relationship of outsiders to teachers must be quite different to ordinary inspections. For this reason it may be better that the usual district inspector or adviser is not used in this role. This is not meant to imply criticism of normal inspection arrangements which can be said to be essential, but rather to emphasize the different nature of the task involved in self-evaluation. For this reason less threatening outsiders, such as wardens of teachers' centres, or fellow-teachers from other schools, can be more valuable in alerting the residents to aspects of school life that they have grown used to, and take for granted as unalterable.

Perhaps one of the most valuable roles for 'outsiders' can be to work with teachers who are members of the school hierarchy. These heads, teachers, deputies, heads of departments and so on may find it easier to discuss their role with this person than with one of their own staff. In this way the threats and jealousies tmay be quite isolated from their colleagues ánd, on the other, that some areas of school life may remain outside the responsibility of any one teacher, may make a self-evaluation exercise especially valuable.

In the United States where schools are fighting to regain public confidence, there are two dominant movements: one is based on a view of accountability through testing; the other has developed around the work of Robert Fox and is concerned with improving school climate. Implicit in this approach is the idea of school self-evaluation. Interestingly, many of the individual areas that Fox's work has described are very similar to items in *Keeping the School under Review*.

For many American educators the limitations of testing has made choice between these two movements simple. The Association for Supervision and Curriculum Development – a large organization drawing its members from all walks of educational life – has backed the school climate work without reservation. In the last year the association has began a project in which a sample of schools will focus on their performance and attempt to find ways to increase their effectiveness.

In England, this is exactly what many schools are also doing. During the last four years I have visited many schools whose teachers are interested and involved in evaluating their own effectiveness. Just gaining information and understanding about their schools will not automatically improve anything, but it is the first step to doing so. If teachers and staff can successfully do this, they will also need to agree an agenda of change. This will not be easy. It is, however, what many heads and teachers have done when they have broken out of a downward spiral of difficulties and pulled themselves up by their boot straps. School self-evaluation merely offers a framework for a more systematic way of doing this. It is not a panacea for all difficulties but is, potentially, the most effective way to improve schools.

References

Berger, M., Yule, W. and Wigley, V. (1980) 'Interviewing in the classroom' *CONTACT* Vol 9,No 13, 12 September.

DES (1977) *Ten Good Schools: a secondary school enquiry*, HMSO.

Eisner, E. (1980) 'The impoverished mind', *Curriculum*, Vol 1, No 2.

Elliot, G. (1980) 'Self-evaluation and the teacher', Parts 1 and 2, Hull University.

Fox, R. *et al.* (1973) *Diagnosing Professional Climates of Schools*, University Associates, La Jolla, California.

Galton, M., Simon, B. and Croll, P. (1980) *Inside the Primary Classroom*, Routledge & Kegan Paul.

Holt, M. (1981) *Evaluating the Evaluators*, Hodder and Stoughton.

ILEA Inspectorate (1977) *Keeping the School under Review*, ILEA.

Olson, M. N. (1970) 'Classroom variables that predict school system quality', *IAR ResearchBulletin*, Vol 11, No 1, November.

Open University (1981) *A Continuing Education Course for Teachers Curriculum in Action: an approach to evaluation*, Open University.

Roshenshine, B. (1970) 'Evaluation of classroom instruction', *Review of Educational Research*, pp. 279-300.

Rutter M. *et al.* (1979) *Fifteen Thousand Hours: secondary schools and their effects on children*, Open Books.

Shipman, M. (1979) *In-school Evaluation*, Heinemann.

Ten Good Schools (1977) HMSO.

CHAPTER 15

SELF-EVALUATION, PROFESSIONAL DEVELOPMENT AND ACCOUNTABILITY

JOHN ELLIOT

Introduction

Many local education authority officials and in-service educators are currently encouraging teachers to engage in something which is variously called 'self-evaluation', 'self-appraisal', or 'self-assessment'. I have recently heard that teachers' centre wardens in Inner London have been directed by their LEA to incorporate a teacher 'self-appraisal' element into all the in-service courses they organize. Numerous LEA-sponsored check-lists have now been produced to assist the staff of schools with self-appraisal. Staff conferences are increasingly being convened in schools to discuss 'methods and techniques of self-evaluation'. It is the very latest innovation, and while in some LEAs or schools it carries the status of recommended activity, in others it is prescribed policy.

Those who recommend the practice of 'self-evaluation' argue that through self-evaluation teachers can identify their own professional needs and develop strategies for meeting them, thereby improving their own professional practice. Now this view is based on the assumption that teachers ought to accept responsibility in some sense for their own professional development. Such an assumption becomes intelligible when one looks at the political context in which self-evaluation is being urged on teachers. It is a context in which they are no longer trusted simply to do a good job at educating pupils. There is political pressure on them to become more publicly accountable. One means of accomplishing this is for

LEA advisers to take on a stronger inspectorial function with a view to identifying and rectifying perceived deficiencies in the professional practices of teachers. In other words there is an increasing tendency to attribute responsibility for the professional development of teachers to their employers: the LEAs. Self-evaluation then, viewed in this political context, appears to be an alternative policy for improving professional practice to one in which agencies external to schools accept responsibility. But why this response to accountability pressures rather than its alternative? A number of reasons can be given:

1   LEAs do not have the resources to monitor and supervise the work of teachers in schools to do an effective job.

2   Self-evaluation is more acceptable to teachers than external monitoring and supervision, since it appears to safeguard their professional autonomy.

3   External monitoring and supervision is inconsistent with the idea of professional development. Teachers can only develop professionally through self-evaluation.

The first two reasons are based on assessments of which alternatives are feasible. The second reason derives from the perception that teachers will perceive self-evaluation as compatible with, and non-threatening towards, their professional autonomy. But it doesn't necessarily imply agreement with this self-construct teachers are perceived to have. It may merely be a pragmatic consideration concerned with what policies teachers will accept. The third is based on a theory of professional development; namely that self-evaluation is a logically necessary means of professional development. According to this theory self-evaluation is not simply one possible way of improving professional practice among others. It is the only way. The professional development of teachers is not something external authorities can possibly accept responsibility for, and the expectation that they can is simply a mistaken one based on a false idea of what is involved in professional development.

Now in spite of these reasons for the desirability of self-evaluation a large number of teachers appear to be very resistant to the idea. Such resistance is rationalized in a number of ways. Firstly, some argue that, given the demands already being made on their time, in circumstances where cut-backs are being made on staffing and other resources, there is simply not enough time to make self-evaluation a feasible enterprise. The assumption by LEAs that schools can make provision for self-evaluation without any additional resources can be a cause of further resistance to the idea, particularly from headteachers.

Secondly, many teachers claim to 'be doing it already'. Policy-makers may perceive such teachers as self-deluded traditionalists. Thirdly, when 'self-evaluation' gets advocated as a matter of policy in a context of public mistrust teachers may suspect an implication that they are incompetent and in need of correction – albeit self-correction – and that the real intent underlying self-evaluation policies is one of subtly increasing external control over their activities to the detriment of their professional autonomy. The fact that many published self-evaluation check-lists of 'questions' to ask oneself are fairly obviously 'loaded', by indicating what teachers ought to be doing, only reinforces this suspicion.

In order to clarify some of the issues at stake in attempts to implement self-evaluation policies for teachers and schools, and in order to provide a conceptual framework for examining policy documents, I shall now try to clarify three rather different types of self-evaluation and explore their implications for professional development and accountability.

Three kinds of self-evaluation and their implications for the professional development of teachers

In this section I want to clarify three distinct kinds of self-evaluation activity and explore their implications for the professional autonomy and development of teachers.

Unreflective self-evaluation based on tacit practical knowledge.

Practical awareness or consciousness can be defined as 'knowing how' rather than 'knowing that'. Much of what counts as teacher education is based on the assumption that the practical knowledge of how to teach ought to be derived from a theoretical awareness of principles governing processes like teaching and learning. Hirst (1966) attacked O'Connor's (1957) influential view that educational theory should be a matter of scientific prediction and explanation, and argued instead that it was a practical theory drawing on a variety of 'Forms of Knowledge'. Nevertheless, as Carr (1980) has recently argued, he didn't question the assumption that sound educational practice is derived from explicit principles of some kind. Prior to Hirst's paper both Oakshott (1962) and Polanyi (1958) had questioned this rationalistic assumption. They claimed that practical knowledge was logically prior to theoretical knowledge of principles. The latter are abstracted from the former, the grounds of which can never be fully articulated and formulated. Practical knowledge is intuitive and tacit rather than explicit. Although its development in the individual depends on their experience of trying things out, it is guided by the accumulated experience of past practitioners embodied in traditions, and transmitted to 'apprentices' by those who have mastered them. The latter get their pupils to observe and emulate the correct ways of doing things, evaluating and correcting their performances by identifying what is right and wrong about them, without necessarily spelling out why a certain aspect is right or wrong, i.e., the principle or theory which explains the performance. Such spelling out wouldn't tell the pupil exactly what to do in order to correct his or her performance. Polanyi provides a nice example of why this is so:

> The rule observed by the cyclist is this. When he starts falling to the right he turns the handlebars to the right, so that the course of the bicycle is deflected along a curve towards the right. This results in a centrifugal force pushing the cyclist to the left and offsets the gravitational force dragging him down to the right. This manoeuvre presently throws the cyclist out of balance to the left, which he counteracts by turning the handlebars to the left; and so he continues to keep himself in balance by winding along a series of appropriate curvatures. A simple analysis shows that for a given angle of unbalance the curvature of each winding is inversely proportional to the square of the speed at which the cyclist is proceeding.
>
> But does this tell us exactly how to ride a bicycle? No . . . Rules of art can be useful, but they do not determine the practice of an art; they are maxims, which can serve as a guide to an art only if they can be integrated into the practical knowledge of the art. They cannot replace this knowledge.

Long before Polanyi, Aristotle in the third century BC argued that, although knowledge of general principles was needed, 'we need the knowledge of particular facts more than general principles' (*Ethics*, book 6, chapter 7). By the former he meant a knowledge of what is required in particular circumstances. He felt this explained why 'men who know nothing of the theory of their subject sometimes practise it with greater success than others who know it' and he provided an illustration which is not unlike Polanyi's.

A man is aware that light meats are easily digested and beneficial to health

but does not know what meats are light. Such a man is not so likely to make
you well as one who knows that chickens are good for you.

Aristotle's essential point is that one develops practical knowledge like
'chickens are good for health' from experience in particular circumstances.
One cannot simply deduce right action from explicit principles. Indeed I
would argue that explicit principles can only be soundly understood if one
already possesses the necessary practical knowledge of the instances to
which they apply. This supports Oakshott's point that theoretical
knowledge constitutes a reflective abstraction from pre-existing practical
knowledge.

Practical knowledge then is grounded in experience rather than
theoretical knowledge. It constitutes the capacity to assess/evaluate what
actions are required in particular circumstances. This capacity does not
necessarily entail an ability to justify assessments/evaluations by reference
to general principles.

Teachers may be regarded as autonomous professionals to the extent
that they possess the capacity to self-evaluate their activities on the basis of
tacit practical knowledge derived from their own and others' past
experience. This practical knowledge constitutes *a tradition*. Teachers can
only possess this capacity for self-evaluation by virtue of that tradition.

The development of this capacity for *unreflective self-evaluation* depends
on the degree to which teachers have mastered a pedagogical tradition.
They cannot therefore develop the practical knowledge necessary to attain
mastery *through* self-evaluation alone. This development only occurs when
they submit their practices to the evaluations and instructions of those
who have mastered the tradition. Until initiates have achieved a satisfactory degree of mastery themselves they will need continuing dependence
on the evaluations of 'master teachers'. Once sufficient mastery has been
achieved they can be counted as autonomous professionals, because they
now possess the power to self-evaluate their own practices.

In the light of this account it is not difficult to see why many teachers
respond to the development of 'self-evaluation policies' by administrators
with 'but we are doing it already'. Indeed the idea of a general policy with
respect to this kind of self-evaluation is nonsensical. If the majority of
teachers employed in schools are reasonably competent professionals, and
one assumes they were judged as such on appointment, then they already
possess the capacity for self-evaluation. If the professional competence of
many teachers is in doubt, and the accountability pressures, which have
stimulated the development of self-evaluation policies by LEAs may

suggest to teachers that this is so, then surely this requires the establishment of stricter systems for supervising and monitoring the activities of individuals; albeit initiated from *within* the teaching profession rather than by representatives of the lay public. Indeed some LEAs may use the term 'self-evaluation' to pick out the latter distinction rather than to indicate an individual teacher responsibility. In which case, what is being urged is the development of policies for identifying and correcting deficiencies in the performance of some individual teachers.

One would reasonably expect any group claiming the status of a profession to develop such policies. But they would not require individual teachers to accept responsibility for their own evaluations. Their major purpose would be to identify the incompetent with a view to correcting their deficient performances.

So the only sense one can give to the idea of a self-evaluation policy for teachers on the view I have outlined is that the latter as a corporate body at national, local, or school level accept responsibility for developing evaluation procedures which identify and correct deficiencies in individual performance. And the only type of professional development such a system can foster is 'development towards competence'. It cannot foster a type of professional development which I shall later turn to, namely, 'development beyond competence'. I will define competence as 'the skilful utilization of existing stocks of tacit professional knowledge'. The merely competent teacher does not operate beyond the tradition he or she has been initiated into. His or her competence consists in the ability to reproduce in his own activities the common stock of tacit professional knowledge. If teachers fail to cope in circumstances for which their existing tacit knowledge provides insufficient guidance, then one would not judge them to be incompetent. The standard of competent practice is the ability to reproduce the traditional wisdom in action. Professionals can intuitively recognize this ability without making the tacit understandings of principles it expresses explicit. In fact requiring professionals to explain the grounds of their judgements always indicates a certain mistrust of their competence to judge well.

The kind of unreflective self-evaluation I have outlined cannot help the merely competent teachers to develop their practical knowledge beyond what they already know, since the latter provides the tacit standards by which they assess present situations and actions. However, there is another sense of 'self-evaluation' which implies precisely this kind of function.

Self-evaluation as practical deliberation

In times of rapid social change the educational situations teachers face will present problems and issues for practice that call for novel and innovatory responses and which the common stock of existing practical knowledge, what Giddens (1979) calls *tacit mutual knowledge*, cannot furnish solutions to. It is when practical social situations like education call for innovation that some mode of conscious reflection and investigation is necessary. Aristotle called the appropriate mode of reflection in this context *deliberation* (see *Ethics*, book 3, chapter 3). The implications of this Aristotelian notion for educational inquiry were outlined in Joseph Schwab's seminal monograph *The Practical: A Language for Curriculum* (1969) and subsequently elaborated by William Reid in his book *Thinking about the Curriculum* (1978). This neo-Aristotelian school of thought has much in common with those who are currently engaged in developing a theory of educational action research (see Stenhouse 1975, Elliott 1980, Grundy and Kemmis 1981a, 1981b, Grundy 1981). I will explore this connection later. In the meantime I shall confine my task to clarifying the Aristotelian concept of deliberation and exploring its implications for teacher self-evaluation. The central features of the concept are:

1   *The outcome of deliberation is a decision or choice about the best means of achieving a certain end in a particular concrete situation (proairesis).*

Proairesis is the act of choosing a course of action, and it implies prior and reflective deliberation. The outcome of deliberation is not theoretical knowledge but a decision to act in a certain way, and it must therefore be distinguished from a type of reflective inquiry which is concerned with demonstrating the truth of beliefs and opinions about things.

2   *The object of deliberation is voluntary human action.*

Deliberation is not a scientific mode of reflection because the object of *proairesis* is voluntary human action, i.e., something which human agents have the power to change and whose existence is therefore not determined by what Aristotle calls 'absolute necessity' or what we can reinterpret as causes and laws operating in the natural world. Aristotle argues that:

No one, however, deliberates about things which cannot be changed, or do not admit of being done by him . . . there can be no science without demonstration, whereas in the case of things whose fundamental assumptions allow of change or modification there can be no demonstrative proof, since in every respect change is possible. (*Ethics*, book 6, chapter 5)

However, Aristotle points out that not all voluntary human action is the outcome of deliberate choice and therefore of deliberation. And I would certainly want to argue that the idea of the teacher as an autonomous professional does not necessarily entail that such a teacher should be constantly engaged in deliberation. The teacher whose actions arise from unreflective self-evaluations grounded in tacit professional knowledge is acting voluntarily, but such actions lack the quality of *proairesis* which stems from deliberation. Of course, Aristotle concedes that human actions can be involuntary inasmuch as they are performed under compulsion or even out of ignorance of the situation. Actions which the agent is compelled to perform, and those which he is not free to choose, are not appropriate objects of deliberation. Effective deliberation must always focus on actions which fall within the agent's sphere of freedom. Applied to the educational practices of individual teachers, this means that activities which they think are desirable in conditions of perfect freedom, but not feasible in present circumstances, are only appropriate objects of deliberative inquiry at the initial stage of determining exactly what freedom of action they have.

3 *Deliberation is an appropriate method of inquiry when human action cannot be regulated by exact technical rules*

Deliberative inquiry is appropriate when it is not possible to generate what Aristotle calls *perfect rules* for choosing means to ends. *Proairesis* goes beyond the mere application of principles and rules and always involves a degree of personal judgement. Aristotle argues that medicine and business methods require greater deliberation than gymnastics because there are less exact rules governing their practice.

When means towards ends can be selected by the strict application of rules they constitute *technical* rather than *practical* activities. Given agreement about ends, disagreements about *technical action* for achieving them can always be settled by reference to the rules. The outcome of deliberation is always open to discussion, and it should therefore always take into account the arguments and views of other practitioners. Aristotle writes:

Deliberation, then, is concerned with things which, while in general following certain lines, have no predictable issues, or the result of which cannot be clearly stated, or in which, when important decisions have to be made, we take others into our counsels, distrusting our own ability to settle the point. (*Ethics*, book 3, chapter 3).

If educational action is an appropriate object of deliberation then it must be a kind of action which cannot be regulated by technical rules. In which case as a form of individual teacher self-evaluation it involves continuous dialogue with fellow professionals about what ought to be done to realize education ends in particular situations.

The current advocacy of the view that teachers ought to take responsibility for research into their practices is made intelligible when educational action is conceived as an object of deliberation rather than technical control. A senior government civil servant visiting the Cambridge Institute of Education recently asked me why the idea of 'teachers as researchers' was receiving such prominence in teaching compared with other careers. One answer might be that teaching is not easily reduced to a technology. But this reason alone cannot account for the view some hold, that an emphasis on reflective inquiry tends to be greater in educational circles than in other *professions* which cannot easily be reduced to technical action, e.g., politics, medicine and the law. Aristotle certainly saw the latter activities as appropriate objects of deliberation. Could it be that the members of these professions find that traditional practice, based on tacit practical knowledge still works for them; that they do not perceive their practical situations to call for novel responses which the tradition cannot handle? Maybe, but I suspect that forms of deliberative inquiry have also developed within these professions to cope with innovation as well. They are simply not labelled 'research'. The reason for this label in the educational sphere can be explained in terms of the way theoretically based research has established itself in teacher training, with the aspiration of discovering theories from which technical rules of teaching can be derived. In order to legitimate a different approach to educationalinquiry in the eyes of its orthodox guardians, and thereby liberate teachers from the dominance of technical prescriptions about what they ought to do, some curriculum innovators and others have tended to use terms like 'action research', rather than 'deliberation'.

4   *Deliberation is guided by ethical rather than technical conceptions of ends.*

Aristotle argued for a distinction between activities which constitute the *making* of a product and those which involve *doing* something well. These different types of activity are guided by different sorts of ends in view.

> . . . the maker of a thing has a different end in view than just making it, whereas in doing something the end can only be the doing of it well. (*Ethics*, book 6, chapter 5)

Making activities are concerned with bringing some concrete object or state of affairs into existence. It is always possible to describe in advance of an activity the objective it is intended to achieve, e.g., in the form of a plan or blueprint, since the ends of *making* or *producing* something can be specified as a blueprint or plan it is possible to develop a *techne* for realizing them; knowledge of the perfect set of rules for producing the required product, and how to apply them.

One of the implications of Aristotle's account of *making activities* for education is that if teaching is largely a matter of producing something, then one will tend to assume that the tacit practical knowledge which governs teachers' judgements about appropriate means to ends can be replaced by the discovery of a perfect set of explicit rules, which when consciously applied will guarantee the production of desired ends. In other words, one will embrace the rationalistic ideal of being able to derive practice from a theoretical knowledge of rules and principles, and thereby change teaching from a craft into a technology. I believe that such an ideal underlies the advocacy of the 'objectives model' as a basis for improving educational practice in schools.

I find it interesting that few contemporary educational philosophers have seriously questioned Paul Hirst's (1974) influential characterization of teaching activities, as 'the intention to *bring about* learning'. From this basic characterization of teaching as a making activity Hirst builds a strong advocacy for the idea of instructional objectives.

Although he has denied any radical disagreement with Hirst's analysis, R.S. Peters (1968) has nevertheless sketched a view of the educational processes which is much more in accord with Aristotle's other conception of *action as doing*. Peters argues that discourse about the aims of education does not appropriately refer to some end state which is external to the process of education. Rather such discourse refers to ends which are realized *in* rather than *by* educational processes, and which indeed warrant their description as *educational*.

According to Aristotle the ends of activities of *doing* are derived from conceptions of the good life and refer to ethical ideals and values. These are qualities to be realized *in* action rather than products to be brought about *by* it. Moreover, it is not possible to define such qualities with absolute precision. They can never be perfectly grasped and understood, and consequently it is not possible to develop a perfect set of rules which will guide their realization in action. This implies that when we select our means we can never be assured that they will achieve the ethical ends in view. For we never possess perfect moral knowledge to guide our doing.

As the appropriate method for determining the means of achieving our ethical ends *deliberation* necessarily involves an element of 'shooting in the dark'. This is why there is always room for personal judgement and discussion on matters of deliberation. Although people may possess common understandings of ethical concepts there will always be some divergence of understanding between them as well, and therefore a measure of disagreement about the best means of realizing them in their *doings*. Also different values may appear to require inconsistent courses of action in a given situation; both of which are equally desirable. In which case, the agent is not simply confronted with an ethical *problem* about realizing a particular end in view, but with a *dilemma* arising out of apparently contradictory ethical requirements.

Through discussion it is always possible to make progress in developing mutual understandings of ethical concepts and their inter-relationships within an ideal of the good life. But the ultimately indefinable nature of 'the good' means that divergence of understanding can never be completely eradicated.

Discussion about the aims of education frequently uses such concepts as 'freedom', 'equality', 'justice', 'personal autonomy', 'self-realization', and 'the growth of understanding'. These educational values are notoriously vague. But it is a mistake to think that clarity comes by attempting to break them down into concrete states of affairs. They cite qualities to be realized *in* the way teachers interact with and treat their pupils in learning situations, rather than extrinsic products of such interactions. To say that a learning situation is 'free', 'equal' and 'just', or that it enables pupils to learn 'autonomously' or 'realize themselves' is to say something about the nature of the conditions for learning established by the teacher, rather than its products. Inasmuch as teachers have a responsibility to *educate* a form of *doing* rather than *making* – then teaching is appropriately conceived as an ethical activity, and a fitting object of practical deliberation.

Such a conception underpins the notion of the teacher as a professional. A professional is not simply someone who possesses practical knowledge; he or she also *professes an ethic*. For Aristotle it would be a mistake to think of the professionals' understanding of this ethic as separable from his or her practical knowledge of how to realize it. I shall now try to indicate why this is so.

5   *Deliberation involves reflecting on both means and ends jointly.*

Although the ethical ends of the professional practice cannot be perfectly understood in advance of choosing means, the latter can lead to a deeper understanding of the former. For in the deliberate choice of a course of action and its reflective implementation practitioners are able to examine how their concepts of ends 'shape up' *in action* and thereby deepen their understanding of how to apply them in choosing the best means. This is why, when asked to define an ethical concept, people tend to cite what they judge to be exemplary instances of their application in action.

A deepened understanding of ends arising from the reflective selection and implementation of means can then be incorporated into the traditional stock of knowledge which guides, rather than determines, a person's future deliberations. Understanding of means and ends develops together through cycles of deliberation and action. In this way professional traditions evolve and change rather than remain rigid and static.

6   *Deliberation is grounded in tacit knowledge of tradition.*

The outcome of moral deliberation, *proairesis*, is not entirely 'shooting in the dark', as Sartre would have us believe. Deliberations can always draw on the professional tradition, a body of general rules which Stenhouse (1978) calls *retrospective* in contrast to *predictive* generalizations. They are retrospective rather than predictive generalizations because they simply represent the common stock of professional wisdom generated from past experiences in similar, if not exactly the same, situations. Present circumstances may require responses which cannot simply be derived from generalizations about past experiences. However, the latter are useful as ways of anticipating future situations; as guides to what actions may be required in them. But they cannot predict what exactly will be required like the perfect rules which define the technical knowledge governing a making activity or craft. As Godamer (1975) argued by way of comment on Aristotle's concept of doing:

What is right . . . cannot be fully determined independently of the situation that requires a right action from me . . .

But he goes on to show how in the thought of Aristotle one doesn't deliberate about a situation from a knowledge vacuum. One always does it in the light of the general rules which define traditional practice. But rather than simply assuming that they can be applied one assesses their applicability. The judgement exercised in *proairesis* always goes beyond the rules even when it asserts that they are applicable. But this judgement is dependent on their existence. If it asserts that certain rules are not applicable the latter's function as guidelines for deliberation is not undermined, inasmuch as they have drawn attention to certain possibilities worth deliberating about.

Moral deliberation may issue in innovation, in actions which are not specified by the traditional rules. This doesn't constitute a rejection of the tradition, but rather a way of developing it to meet changing circumstances. From the collective deliberations of a professional group, what is applicable from the traditional stock of knowledge to present circumstances gets preserved, while this stock also gets replenished with additional rules encapsulating new understandings. Thus through deliberation the traditional stock of knowledge is evolved rather than superseded.

Deliberating teachers may be innovators, but they don't simply cast aside the professional wisdom of the past. Such teachers may be contrasted with those who view innovation as the application of precise rules to clearly defined ends. These rules are derived from the functions of the product they have in mind rather than tradition. And in applying their *techne*, and getting others to apply it, they acknowledge 'the irrelevance' of the traditional store of professional wisdom. This point is forcefully made by Joseph Schwab (1969) when he contrasts innovations derived from theory and those derived from deliberation:

Under the control of theory, curricular changes have their origin in new notions of person, group or society, mind or knowledge, which give rise to suggestions of new things curriculum might be or do. By its nature, this origin takes little or no account of the existing effectiveness of the machine on the consequences of the institution of novelty. If there is concern for what may be displaced by innovations or for the incoherences which may ensue on the insertion of novelty, the concern is gratuitous. It does not arise from the theoretical considerations which commend the novelty.

. . The practical on the other hand, because it institutes changes to repair frictions and deficiencies, is *commanded* to determine the whole array of possible effects of proposed change, to determine what new frictions and deficiencies the proposed change may unintentionally produce.

As a form of self-evaluation deliberation is not incompatible with the kind of unreflective self-evaluation outlined earlier. One cannot deliberate about the whole of one's professional practice. For the most part it will proceed on the basis of unreflective self-evaluations grounded in tacit traditional knowledge. It is only when this tacit knowledge is insufficient to meet new problems that deliberation is required. But even in this context deliberation must proceed from tacit knowledge. From his tacit knowledge of general rules a teacher may, for example, anticipate what is required in a situation but on encountering it intuitively sense that the practice is problematic. He or she may then inhibit further intuitive responses, while the rules which guide them are brought to conscious awareness and their appropriateness to the situation considered. From this deliberative intervention 'new' patterns of behaviour may emerge. In time the new rules they are based on will no longer be consciously followed, but become part of the teacher's tacit knowledge. The changed behaviour is then sustained by unreflective self-evaluations rather than deliberation. Deliberation then is always parasitic upon unreflective self-evaluation and could be defined as a second order self-evaluation of first order self-evaluations.

Earlier on I drew a distinction between professional development 'towards mastery' and development 'beyond mastery', and would argue that deliberative self-evaluation is a necessary condition of the latter. It enables 'autonomous professionals' not simply to reproduce and maintain traditional practice – which I defined as mastery or basic competence – but to develop their practice in ways that are appropriate to changing social conditions.

Whereas the professional development of teachers 'towards mastery' is dependent on the evaluations of those who have mastered traditional educational practice, professional development 'beyond mastery' depends on teachers' capacities to engage in deliberative self-evaluation. The former involves *being developed* while the latter involves a process of *self-development*.

The phrase 'professional development' may additionally be used to refer to the development of the professional group as a whole. And I would claim that, when 'autonomous professionals' continuously improve their practical knowledge through deliberation and discussion with their peers, they not only develop themselves but also help to develop the professional tradition, the common stock of tacit mutual knowledge.

Is deliberative inquiry what policy-makers have in mind when they talk about self-evaluation? If the answer is 'yes' then one can think of few reasons why teachers should resist current policy recommendations. Those that do can be regarded as *traditionalists*, who are not simply concerned to preserve what is worthwhile in the traditional practices of the past but dogmatically believe that they have nothing to learn from the future. However, before we define the problem of teacher resistance as a traditionalist and reactionary response let's examine my third kind of self-evaluation.

Self-evaluation based on an explicit knowledge of technical rules.

Aristotle uses the term *techne* to refer to knowledge of the rules governing the production of a clearly defined object or state of affairs. This kind of knowledge is explicit and self-conscious.

Self-evaluation in the context of *making* rather than *doing* activities will involve consciously monitoring one's activity in the light of the explicit rules (criteria) which govern successful production and competent performance. It is therefore based on a theoretical knowledge of the technical rules for achieving well-defined ends.

Now, although this kind of self-evaluation is one method for improving technical competence or skill it is not a necessary condition of such improvement. An external evaluator who knows the rules can identify technically deficient performances and direct the way in which they are to be rectified. Technical self-evaluation is therefore only an alternative method for improving competence. This is in marked contrast to the relationship between deliberative self-evaluation and professional development 'beyond mastery', where the former is a necessary condition of the latter.

Technical self-evaluation doesn't necessarily diminish external control over performance, although it may make it less overt than that exercised by external evaluation and supervision. This is because the person who engages in it doesn't have to be motivated by a commitment to the ends in view, as the deliberative self-evaluator must. Instead the motivation can stem from a desire to perform correctly in order to please, or avoid displeasing, those who have the power to distribute rewards and punishments of successful and unsuccessful performance. This is why, as Grundy (1981) has pointed out, technical innovations in schools tend to collapse when the power figures who have initiated and 'guided' their implementation depart. It is easy, as Aristotle argued, to 'unlearn' one's technical knowledge, but this is impossible with ethical knowledge (*Ethics*, book 6, chapter 5).

Now I would dispute the view that technical self-evaluation can result in *professional development* if the latter is to be defined in terms of ethical knowledge. For unlike deliberation technical evaluation replaces rather than complements the tacit ethical knowledge of the professional. As a method of improving performance in schools it can only do so by de-professionalizing teachers and making them into technicians whose performances can be politically and administratively controlled. If this is the intent which underlies current policy initiatives, then teacher resistance is not only understandable but, if one is committed to the idea of teachers as professionals, a reasonable response.

At a recent Schools Council conference on self-evaluation at Stoke Rochfort (reported in *The Times Educational Supplement*) it was suggested that self-evaluation for purposes of accountabililty and self-evaluation for purposes of professional development are incompatible activities and should be kept quite distinct in practice. This claim is reasonable if by accountability one is referring to a system of contractual accountability in which teachers are required to perform according to externally prescribed rules. In this context self-evaluation will inevitably be of the technical kind. But implicit in the Aristotelian notion of deliberation there is also a kind of accountability, which takes the form of *moral answerability*. Inasmuch as the outcomes of deliberations are intrinsically problematic, those who engage in them are under a continuing obligation to explain and discuss the reasoning behind them with those who have an interest in the achievement of the moral ends in view. Since the achievement of *educational ends* is a matter of the public interest, then deliberating teachers are under an obligation to provide parents and other external groups, in addition to their professional peers, with opportunities for genuine dialogue about *their decisions*. This kind of moral answerability entailed by deliberative self-evaluation, rather than providing an incompatible context for professional development, provides a facilitating one.

The distinction between *contractual accountability* and *moral answerability* can provide us with strong clues to determining the real intent underlying current self-evaluation policies. If teachers are advised to discuss their self-evaluations with professional peers in collegial and non-hierarchical settings, or with their clients – children, parents, local employers – then it seems to me that the policy indicates a concern with professional development through deliberation. But when self-evaluations are only accessible to those occupying 'superior' positions in the educational hierarchy – to headteachers, LEA officials, or political committees – then one has good reason to suspect that the policy is concerned with increasing political and administrative control over teachers through technical self-evaluation. In practice I suspect that LEAs are seeking a compromise between these two views of accountability.

It would be necessary to study policy documents in some detail before being able to determine which kinds of self-evaluation and accountability are being stressed. The majority stemming from LEAs at the moment take the form of checklists of questions. Most of these 'questions' are 'very loaded', in the sense that they indicate the standards against which teachers ought to assess their activities. But the check-lists tend to constitute a mixture of two kinds of 'standards'. First there are precise rules which leave little room for interpretation and judgement in particular circumstances. Secondly, there are more open principles which leave room for interpretation and judgement. Since the Oxfordshire booklet has been a trend-setter in the self-evaluation field I will draw some examples of both these categories from it.

Precise Rules
'Who ensures that displays in the halls and corridors *are well mounted and frequently changed?*'
'Do I *keep lesson and evaluation notes?*'
'Do I *reply quickly when a report is called for?*'

Open principles
'Do I *prepare properly?*'
'How satisfied am I with my *class control and relationships?*'
'Am I using *appropriate materials and teaching aids?*'

(author's italics)

Now the latter standards can provide a focus for deliberative investigation; as an orientation of where to look for the source of problems and issues in one's practice. The Oxfordshire check-list appears to present a mixture of guiding principles for deliberation and precise rules for technical evaluation. This ambiguity perhaps indicates something of a tension LEA officials experience in trying to reconcile pressure from their political masters for greater social control over the activities of teachers, with a commitment to the idea of teachers as 'autonomous professionals'.

Now I think that at least some LEAs' officials who have tried to implement a check-list approach to self-evaluation are beginning to realize its limitations as a lone stimulus for fostering deliberative inquiry and discussion among the staff of schools. This is because it can only be a useful aid given certain institutional pre-conditions. Check-lists can't foster deliberative reflection independently of attempts to re-order priorities, management styles, and communication networks in schools. Deliberative self-evaluation is time consuming and can't simply be added on to all the other demands on staff time. Priorities have to be re-ordered at the institutional level. Since this kind of self-evaluation also implies free and open discussion between staff, relationships need to become more collegial and less hierarchical, information flowing laterally and 'downwards' rather than simply 'upwards'. The management style needs to become more open and participatory. Deliberation also requires establishing mechanisms for communicating and discussing policies and practices with client groups outside schools (see Elliott *et al.* 1981). Here clients not only need access to information about policy-decision but opportunities to question and critically appraise them.

Now, all this organizational development is unlikely to occur when the staff of a school feel that the traditional ways of doing things still work. It is only when the staff of a school sense that their changing social environment requires changes in customary practice that a motive will exist to implement structures for deliberative self-evaluation.

In schools where staff resist the challenge of a change and cling to tradition the response to check-lists will tend to take the form of a mechanical administrative exercise.

My own view is that schools which are developing institutional structures for deliberation don't require externally produced check-lists anyway. They are creating the contexts which enable teachers to pose their own questions and issues. Currently the London Borough of Enfield is adopting this approach. It is trying to help schools develop organizational structures and procedures that will foster whole staff participation in identifying and deliberating on the practical issues facing them.

242   Changing Schools

An externally produced check-list is more appropriate in a context of technical self-evaluation. Its function is to remind oneself or others of what ought to be done. Moreover, it enables one to quickly check the 'oughts' against actual performance. Check-lists serve an important control function within technical self-evaluation. First, they act as reminders about the prescribed rules, and secondly they enable a teacher to rapidly check his or her performance against them. Check-lists are essentially an instrument for increasing technical efficiency and control rather than the capacity to make reflective professional decisions.

Self-evaluation and action-research

In a previous paper on the 'Implications of Classroom Research for Professional Development' (Elliott 1980) I claimed that:

> It is no coincidence that action research in classrooms tended to emerge in association with the curriculum development movement in the 1960s and early 1970s. Many of the projects which constituted this movement were concerned with shifting the learning context in classrooms from 'memory' and 'routine problem-solving' to 'understanding' tasks. Such innovations tended to articulate this shift in terms of ideas like 'self-directed', 'discovery' and 'inquiry' learning. . . . The problems teachers experienced in initiating and sustaining student performance on 'understanding' tasks generated a whole movement of classroom research. . . .
>
> Interestingly, this research conceptualized the problems of teaching in a radically different way from process-product research. In place of technical problems of selecting causally effective means for bringing about certain pre-specified learning outcomes, the problems were seen as ones of achieving a certain quality of communication with students about the problems and issues posed by learning tasks.

The concept of educational action-research which I described in this and other papers (see also Elliott 1976, 1978a, 1978b) is similar in many respects to the Aristotelian idea of deliberative inquiry. First, it is concerned with developing strategies for realizing educational values which cannot be clearly defined in advance, and independently of, the chosen means. Secondly, it is a process in which practitioners accept responsibility for reflection, and do not simply depend on the analyses of external investigators. The outside researcher's role is to stimulate reflection by practitioners, and the formers' 'accounts' or 'hypotheses' are only validated in dialogue with the latter. Thirdly, and as a consequence of the above points, action-research always proceeds from the perspective of the practitioners ends-in-view. And finally, it is a necessary condition of the professional development of teachers.

In my view deliberative inquiry is an important feature of action-research, which cannot simply be contrasted with theoretical research in terms of having *action* rather than *theory* as its intended result. It also presupposes a certain view of human action; namely, as *ethical* rather than *technical* action. Educational action-research, I would argue, is concerned with the development and testing of strategies for realizing educational values *in* action.

In the UK the action-research movement has tended to develop from curriculum research and development projects based at the Centre for Applied Research in Education, University of East Anglia, under the influence of Lawrence Stenhouse (May 1981). This movement has developed independently of William Reid's work (1978) on curriculum deliberation. Although the latter clearly acknowledges and builds on the ideas of the neo-Aristotelian, Joseph Schwab (1969), the action-research theorists make little reference to Schwab in their writings, tending to spin ideas out of their experiences on action-research projects than any systematic treatment of the relevant theoretical literature. This doesn't mean to say that the writers on action-research have not read or been influenced in their thinking by the neo-Aristotelian theorists.

The links between the UK literature on action-research and Aristotle's view of practical inquiry as deliberation are now being explicitly made by Grundy (1981) and Grundy and Kemmis (1981a, 1981b) who argue there are three types of action-research: the *technical*, *practical*, and *emancipatory*. They see the *practical* kind as virtually synonymous with Aristotle's account of deliberation, and locate the action-research projects directed by Stenhouse and myself in this category.

Grundy's and Kemmis's account of *technical action-research* links with, but does not correspond to, my account of technical self-evaluation. Here the action-research is initiated by a person or group, possessing 'authority' or 'expertise', who wish to get others to achieve certain ends that they have in mind. The aim of this 'action-research' would be to generate the technical rules of how to get others to produce what the 'authority figures' or 'experts' want.

If we relate this to the educational system in the UK, then a group of LEA officials may clearly define an innovation they want to bring about in schools, but are unsure of how they can get teachers to implement it. They select a few 'trial schools' as a context for discovering how to produce the desired innovation. The teachers may even be consulted about what works and what does not, and co-opted as collaborators in the research process. But once the trials are over and more general implementation gets under way, the main role of teachers will be to follow the rules generated from the initial action-research. Within this context they may be required to self-evaluate the extent to which they competently follow such rules.

Within a context of technical control, action-research and self-evaluation are largely carried out by different personnel. Action-research is an approach employed by expert planners while self-evaluation is a task for those who have to implement their plans.

I have a certain reservation about the idea of 'technical action-research'. I cannot see how its function differs markedly from that of the behavioural sciences generally. In its search for the general laws which determine human conduct the behavioural sciences constitute a source of means-ends rules for those wishing to engineer human behaviour in certain predefined directions. If, in a given social context there is not a body of behavioural research to support the necessary social engineering, then some may have to be initiated by the developers themselves. And in discovering how to produce the desired changes they in fact make a contribution to behavioural science knowledge. But researchers have tended to employ the term 'action-research' to pick out an alternative paradigm to the positivism which currently prevails in social research.

The idea of *emancipatory action-research* is grounded in the writings of the Frankfurt school of critical theorists; particularly those of Jurgen Habermas (1971a, 1971b, 1974). According to Grundy and Kemmis it is complementary with *practical action-research*, but goes beyond it. (See also Elliott 1980.)

Grundy writes:

> Although there are many areas where individual professional performance may be improved through the operation of group reflection and action, there are some areas of education that are not amenable to change simply through such action. These are areas where institutional restrictions impinge upon educational practice so that the individual or group, while operating prudently and professionally to initiate change, is powerless to do so because of the strength of the system.

Teachers' capacities to realize their educational ends depend upon the extent to which the institutional structures provide them with the freedom to select appropriate means. But these structures may well impose constraints on their freedom to select the appropriate means, by compelling them to do things which are inconsistent with the educational values they profess. The quasi-causal influences exerted through such structures are maintained by the use of power-coercive sanctions, those who conform to the system being rewarded while those who deviate are punished or deprived in some way. The effective use of sanctions depends on the power which some individuals or groups have over others, access to the satisfactions they desire, e.g., status, financial gain, etc. These motivations, which are extrinsic to the successful performance of the job and often unacknowledged by those who have them, enable people in power positions to compel practitioners to act in conformity with the structures they have an interest in maintaining.

Practitioners are often unaware that their activities are compelled rather than free. And even those who are often claim they are powerless to do otherwise, refusing to acknowledge the roles their own desires and motives play in sustaining the system. Practitioners develop distorted self-understandings which protect them against becoming aware of the inconsistencies which exist between their actions and the values they profess. These distorted self-understandings are sustained by institutional structures which restrict people's opportunities for self-reflection and dialogue.

Emancipatory action-research involves the generation of 'critical theorems', which identify 'distorted' practices and self-understandings, and explain the mechanisms which 'cause' them. The intent is to enlighten practitioners about the ways their activities are subject to hidden constraints, the hidden motives for performing them, and their unintended outcomes. However, Habermas argues that such theorems can only be validated in the self-reflections of practitioners under conditions of free and open dialogue.

Critical theories can therefore be generated by 'outsiders', but they can only be validated through the self-evaluations of practitioners. We have now identified a fourth type of self-evaluation which I shall call *consciousness raising*, and which tends to be dependent on a dialogue about critical theorems with an *external consultant*.

Enlightenment is only one stage in emancipatory action-research. The next is taking action to modify or remove the constraining structures. Such action cannot be undertaken by individuals. It must be collective *political action* undertaken by the practitioner group as a whole. Emancipatory action-research in schools must therefore involve groups of teachers in collective action. It aims to bring about institutional change which will enable individual teachers to develop themselves professionally through deliberation and discussion with each other. Those policy-makers who are concerned that the organizational structures of schools should support deliberative self-evaluation and decision making by individual teachers will need to facilitate procedures by which the staff as a whole can collectively examine the relationship between organizational structures and their activities as individuals. If they resist supporting this 'bottoms up' approach to educational change, then one can be excused for concluding that the real intent behind the policy is one of 'top down' technical control.

I have outlined four types of self-evaluation – *unreflective, deliberation, technical*, and *consciousness raising* – and argued that self-evaluation is a process of action-research when it involves deliberation (practical action-research) and/or consciousness raising through emancipatory action-research. In my view the latter constitute the means by which the professional development of teachers 'beyond mastery' is fostered.

References

Aristotle (1955) *The Ethics of Aristotle*, Penguin Books.

Carr,W. (1980) 'The gap between theory and practice', *Journal of Further and Higher Education*, spring.

Elliott, J. (1976) *Developing Hypotheses from Teachers' Practical Constructs – An Account of the Ford Teaching Project*, North Dakota Monographs on Evaluation, University of N. Dakota, Grand Forks, USA.

Elliott, J. (1978a) 'What is action research in schools?', *Journal of Curriculum Studies*, 104.

Elliott, J. (1978b) 'Classroom research: science or commonsense' in McAleese, R. and Hamilton, D (eds) *Understanding Classroom Life*, NFER.

Elliott, J. (1980) 'Implications of classroom research for professional development' in *Professional Development of Teachers: World Year Book of Education* Hoyle, E. and Megarry, J. (eds) Kogan Page.

Elliott, J. *et al.* (1981) *School Accountability*, Grant McIntyre.

Giddens, A. (1979) *Central Problems in Social Theory*, Macmillan, chapter 2.

Godamer, H.G. (1975) *Truth and Method*, Sheed and Ward, pp. 283–289.

Grundy, S. (1981) 'Three Modes of Action Research' Mimeo, Deakin University, Victoria, Australia.

Grundy, S. and Kemmis, S. (1981a) 'Social theory, group dynamics and action research' in *The Professional Development of Teachers through Involvement in Action Research Projects*, Deakin University, Victoria, Australia.

Grundy, S. and Kemmis, S. (1981b) 'Educational Action Research in Australia: The State of the Art' Mimeo, Deakin University, Victoria, Australia.

Habermas, J. (1971a) *Towards A Rational Society*, Heinemann.

Habermas, J. (1971b) *Knowledge and Human Interests*, Beacon Press, Boston.

Habermas, J. (1974) Introduction, *Theory and Practice*, Heinemann.

Hirst, P.H. (1974) 'What is teaching?' in his *Knowledge and the Curriculum*, Routledge & Kegan Paul.

Hirst, P.H. (1966) 'Educational Theory' in *The Study of Education* J.W. Tibble (ed) Routledge & Kegan Paul.

May , N. (1981) *The Teacher-as-Researcher Movement in Britain* Mimeo, Centre for Applied Research in Education, University of East Anglia, UK.

Oakshott, M. (1962) 'Rational Conduct' in *Rationalism in Politics and Other Essays*, Routledge & Kegan Paul.

O'Connor, D.J. (1957) *An Introduction to the Philosophy of Education*, Routledge & Kegan Paul.

Oxfordshire Education Committee (1979) 'Starting Points in Self-Evaluation'.

Peters, R.S. (1968) 'Must an educator have an aim' in *Concepts of Teaching* Macmillan, C.J.B. and Nelson, T.W. (eds), Rand McNally & Co.

Polanyi, M. (1958) *Personal Knowledge*, Routledge & Kegan Paul.

Reid, W.A. (1978) *Thinking About the Curriculum*, Routledge & Kegan Paul.

Schwab, J.J. (1975) 'The Practical: a language for curriculum', *School Review*.

Stenhouse, L. (1975) *An Introduction to Curriculum Research and Development*, Heinemann.

Stenhouse, L. (1978) 'Case studies and case records: towards a contemporary history of education' *British Educational Research Journal*, 4:2.

CHAPTER 16

STYLES OF SCHOOL-BASED EVALUATIONS

MARTEN SHIPMAN

The justifiable concern of the Association for the Study of the Curriculum over developments in school-based evaluation has an academic as well as a practical dimension. Professional self-evaluation and evaluation imposed as part of the drive for greater accountability can both have a profound effect on curriculum development. But there is also a striking similarity in the way much self-evaluation is being organized and curriculum developments in the 1960s and 1970s. This paper bears a striking resemblance to that delivered almost ten years ago to the association on the relation between school organization and Schools Council curriculum projects.

It would be facile to suggest that the long-term impact and take-up of self-evaluation will be similar to that of the hundreds of Schools Council projects. Much more of it is teacher initiated and school based. Yet the practice of self-evaluation seems to be ignoring the same features in the way schooling was organized that accounted for much of the frustration of curriculum developers. Even the styles of curriculum development are mirrored in those of self-evaluation a decade later. The Research, Development and Dissemination models of the 1960s and the School-Based Curriculum Development models in the 1970s have been repeated a decade later as LEA-initiated evaluation schemes and teacher-initiated school-based schemes have proliferated. There is even the Schools Council GRIDS project (Guidelines for Review and Institutional Development in Schools) providing continuity.

The similarities with curriculum development apply to the many variations in self-evaluation, whether LEA or teacher initiated. It is most obvious in the former which bear most resemblance to the centrally organized projects which schools are invited to join. But even where teachers have worked out their own evaluation schemes there has been a tendency to the same insulation from the procedures through which the school is managed and learning organized. The conception and implementation of self-evaluation still tends to ignore the political give-and-take, the personal and professional interests, the assumptions behind school management that frustrated curriculum project directors.

The close parallels in the two movements are reflected in the papers presented in this volume. They display the variety of interests and assumptions in self-evaluation, as well as exposing similar strengths and weaknesses. Support was based on hopes that self-evaluation would improve professional competence, help schools meet the demands for skills from a high technology economy and support the search for an education promising a brighter twenty-first century. All these motives were present ten years ago.

Scanning the development of school-based evaluation in 1982 shows up the same weaknesses as in evaluations of curriculum development in 1972. First, evaluation is often adopted as an end in itself, not a means to an end. That is where Brighouse is so useful in this book. Evaluation in his scenario is given a central place in the list of characteristics of schools that will restore education to a central place in the twenty-first century of the liberal optimists. The evaluation recommended is not incremental, piecemeal, but concerned with 'whole curriculum analysis'. Evaluation is conceived as part of school organization, not imposed on it or confined to occasional activities. But such breadth is unusual. LEA-initiated self-evaluation in particular tends to contain no model of evaluation in the moving pattern of events.

The second weakness of the school self-evaluation movement follows from this tendency to isolation and incrementalism. Schools are expensive, complicated organizations. A large secondary school has a salary bill of around £1 million. Schools are organized, but this is often taken for granted by those involved. It is this tendency for teachers to ignore school organization when considering evaluation that robs school-based evaluation of much value. Teachers are not often in the right position to see the flow of resources, information and influence. They often only see the hierarchical line of command, the division of labour, the management of external relations or the intentional development of curricula when some crisis occurs. Under these conditions self-evaluation is often organized as an isolated activity, not as part of running of the school. Yet evaluation is inevitably constrained within the procedures in the school and could serve to improve these. A look at the case studies in the Open University's course E364 *Curriculum Evaluation and Assessment in Educational Institutions* (Open University 1982) will show how the organization of evaluation mirrors that of the schools concerned. But evaluation is more concerned with changing procedures than reflecting them.

This situation is exacerbated by the overt prescriptiveness of most LEA self-evaluating documents. This is not a sinister plot to insinuate the procedures approved by advisers into the running of schools. When they sit down with teachers to produce an evaluation scheme they naturally produce questions that have as a hidden agenda their view of the well-run school. 'How many times are register checks made to look at attendance?' is not just a query but a suggestion that this should be done. The questions are also prescriptions. Middle-aged curriculum evaluators will recognize the consequences. Initial enthusiasm evaporates as the evaluation knocks against the entrenched practices of the staff.

The context-bound nature of school-based evaluation leads to a third weakness. LEA-initiated schemes often do not fit the procedures in the school. The parallel with curriculum projects is close. The tissue rejection is likely to recur. But there are other problems. Most LEA-initiated schemes are voluntary. Schools have taken the booklet, attended the meeting in county or town hall, carried out the first review and then self-evaluation has joined all the previous innovations among the stuffed owls and teaching machines in the staffroom cupboard. It is too often the one-shot innovation that dies out prematurely. Hence there is a move to introduce mandatory evaluation. This ranges from the Oxfordshire scheme of four-yearly reports for all schools, to using LEA self-evaluation documents as the basis for in-service courses.

A fourth weakness is that most self-evaluation tends to be pragmatic. There is no model of the school from which hunches can be derived and checked. Selecting aspects such as the pastoral system or public relations can do a lot of good as they are evaluated. It is valuable for staff to review their work regularly. But to produce effective action there needs to be some model of how the various aspects are related, how one influences others and how they add up to the working of the school and relate it to its environment. Such a model is implicit in decisions to evaluate which assume that evidence can be collected to affect improvements. Yet it is rarely explicated beyond a simple aims, objectives, evaluation, feedback systems model.

The fifth weakness is that the activity of self-evaluation remains ill-defined. John Elliott in this book points out that this enables teachers to resist engaging in evaluation despite its obvious benefits. Elliott's four types provide a useful way of sorting out the confusion between those who press the case for self-evaluation because it will lead to more accountable schools and those who support it for professional development. Mortimore's paper in this book illustrates this division. Working for the ILEA which pioneered self-evaluation he is in a position to see it in context. That authority has organized the monitoring of attainment alongside self-evaluation. That enables Mortimore to distinguish evaluation for accountability and for professional development. Indeed, he maintains that confidentiality is essential for evaluation to contribute to the latter.

Each of these weaknesses were detected in curriculum projects in the 1970s (Shipman, Bolam and Jenkins 1974). The debates are recurring. The question whether curriculum development should be a response to external demands for change resulting in tangible changes in timetabled activities or should be mainly concerned with professional development, bedevilled and finally bifurcated the Schools Council. So confusing was this situation that the Council set up its own Impact and Take-up Project and used the criteria that inevitably damned it (Steadman, Parsons and Salter 1980). Yet many project teams started with no intention of producing materials and thought that the Council had set them up to promote professional development among teachers as a priority, not to write textbooks.

It is very easy to pronounce from academia about weaknesses at the coalface. What about the strengths of the movement to self-evaluation? First, as we do not know how schooling changes it is safest to assume that every little helps. Curriculum projects played their part. The project schools after the Keele Integrated Studies Project were not the same after as before. Yet on Impact and Take-up criteria it was one of the least effective projects. Similarly schools are being changed by the evaluation efforts of their staff. A glance through any issue of *School Organization* will show how this is being done.

The second strength is that school-based self-evaluation is indeed likely to promote professional development. Despite Mortimore's caution, it seems to me that the development will come through schemes that are for accountability as well as those designed for internal consumption. The motives for self-evaluation differ but the benefits are similar. The case studies reported at the 1982 ASC Conference illustrate this. The staff at

Faringdon School responding to the request for a report from the LEA benefitted along with those in Rotherham High School developing their own evaluation under the influence of John Elliott's action-research approach. The teaching profession is accumulating professional skills. Part of this comes from blocked promotion which stops the movement of staff into colleges and universities. It results from involvement in the moderation of CSE examinations. It comes from involvement in curriculum projects, in in-service training and attendance on diploma and masters courses. Now it is being strengthened not only by involvement in self-evaluation, but in working out how to evaluate.

The third and most important strength is that evaluation is part of the management of effective schools. This is the concrete base of Brighouse's school for the future. The movement for school-based self-evaluation is an attempt to change the impressionistic, instantaneous judgements that are the basis for management in all schools into something more sustained and controlled. That control avoids what staff like to think is going on from being confused with what actually occurs. It distinguishes the assumptions from the reality. Elliott's support for action-research takes this further, seeing it as the way to professional development through the acceptance of responsibility for reflecting on the nature of learning. School self-evaluation ranges from one-shot judgements of specific aspects to institutionalized consciousness raising.

Thus the range of self-evaluation and the speed with which it has been introduced calls for reflection. It seems to me that there are similar problems in every educational innovation. They arise from the organization of schooling and the network of relations, influences and pressures that bind teachers. These in turn affect developers and evaluators. They have been most fully documented in the evaluation of curriculum developments. But they have affected not only these, but the attempts to introduce the playway, teaching machines and programmed learning, resource-based learning and team teaching. They will be just as influential as microcomputers are unpacked in primary as well as secondary schools. They are also the context of self-evaluation. Yet there are few signs that this has yet been appreciated by those pressing innovations or subsidizing the latest technology.

Fortunately much of the discussion on self-evaluation at the 1982 conference of the ASC was concerned with the methods being used and the social processes that determine impact. Most of the contributors seemed to be confirming the wisdom of seeing evaluation as a form of social research, drawing on a long tradition of going beyond the technical to reflection on the way institutions work. Mortimore's professional development, Elliott's emancipatory action-research and Brighouse's self-critical pied pipers are all in the best social scientific tradition where controlled investigation is combined with critical analysis. The case studies of individual schools reported at the conference were also in this tradition. Encouragingly LEAs arriving later have also learned from those that went before. A look at Stockport's self-evaluation documents in 1982 (Stockport 1982) compared with the ILEA's *Keeping the School under Review* of 1977 (ILEA 1977) will show how far thinking has gone. The former spells out not only ways of asking questions about aspects of school organization and the working of the school as a whole, but about the political nature of evaluation and the cautions that are advisable. The Open University's course E364 also places self-evaluation firmly in the research tradition and in the organizational contexts of schools.

This review of the practice of self-evaluation comes after a remarkable five years of activity. Yet it would be a mistake to ignore the changed context even over such a brief period. The ILEA's *Keeping the School under Review* was published as the Great Debate got started and as Circular 14/77 arrived in LEAs asking for details of LEA arrangements for the school curriculum. DES, HMI and the Schools Council have published views on that curriculum. The Taylor Committee has reported and the 1980 Act has been implemented. The APU has completed the first wave of annual surveys in primary and secondary schools in mathematics, language and science. HMI have surveyed primary, secondary and middle schools. School rolls have fallen, resources have shrunk and the public power base for education has been weakened. In the 1970s self-evaluation could be a marginal, confidential, implicit activity for teachers. In the 1980s it is a defence against attack as well as a launching pad for change.

These defensive and offensive roles for self-evaluation are present in most schemes. They have generated most academic heat. Should self-evaluation be for accountability or for professional development? Should the focus be on outputs or processes? Should it be formative or summative? Mortimore maintains that the two functions should be separated. Evaluation for accountability will disturb the confidentiality that is essential for honest self-evaluation. The ILEA experience certainly supports this caution. But there school-based evaluation is in a context of LEA monitoring programmes. Furthermore, the London teacher unions saw from the first that if you asked a hundred questions, governors and

others would want the hundred answers. Self-evaluation is politically
sensitive. This situation is really a reflection of a major flaw in the
organization of education. It is somehow insulting to suggest that teachers
will only be objective if the information they produce is confidential. Will
accounts rendered always be cosmetic? It is too early to tell, but on the
evidence so far Mortimore's analysis seems to be correct. But confidentiality could be the death-knell of self-evaluation as it joins other defunct
innovations. Somehow information for professional development and
improvements in the organization of learning within the school have to be
made compatible with the production of information to convince the
public outside. The power base has to be restored and consolidated. It
may have been undermined by a reluctance to evaluate and share the
evaluations in the good times. Hopefully school-based self-evaluation can
help increase confidence in the schools and within the schools while the
bad times roll.

References

Inner London Education Authority (1977) *Keeping the School under Review.*
Metropolitan Borough of Stockport (1982) *An Introduction to Self-Evaluation*, Education
Division, Stockport.
Open University (1982) *Curriculum Evaluation and Assessment in Educational Institutions*,
Open University.
Shipman, M., Bolam, D. and Jenkins, D., (1974) *Inside a Curriculum Project*, Methuen.
Steadman, S., Parsons, C. and Salter, B. (1980) *Second Interim Report to the Schools Council*,
Schools Council.

PART IV

CHANGING CLASSROOMS

INTRODUCTION

MAURICE GALTON AND JOHN ISAAC

Studies of classrooms and teaching processes have been an increasing concern of the curriculum movement. The review of such work by Westbury (1978) in the journal of *Curriculum Studies* was largely based on research carried out in America although a few English studies were included. Since that time a number of evaluations have demonstrated that attempts to change classroom practice by producing curriculum materials for the teachers to use have failed to affect teaching methods to any significant extent. As a result of these failures increasing interest has been taken in techniques developed in America for studying the processes of teaching, particularly the kinds of analysis based upon the 'Flanders' system.

During the 1970s a growing number of researchers in the United Kingdom also began to examine classroom process. Some attempted to quantify teacher behaviour while others examined the use of language in the classroom. About the same time interest among some sociologists shifted away from the studies of schools as institutions and from the debate about the sociology of knowledge towards a study of classrooms. These ethnographic approaches, fuelled by work already carried out in the United States, provided an alternative paradigm for the study of classroom events, in sharp contrast to the widely used systematic approach. Inevitably, as researchers debated the validity of their respective methodologies, issues became somewhat polarized and a certain degree of acrimony developed. Happily these conflicts never reached the same level as that in the United States and over the last few years a rapprochement has developed whereby different observational techniques have come to be seen as complementary rather than alternative strategies in the attempts to reach greater understanding of the classroom process.

The papers presented in this section reflect both the growing interest in classroom research in Britain and also the extent to which researchers working from different perspectives are, nevertheless, beginning to reach similar conclusions. Neville Bennett and Andrew Pollard respectively review current work within the existing paradigms of systematic and participant observation. The paper by Galton attempts to meet some of the criticisms of the systematic approach by showing it can be extended and used by teachers to research their own classrooms. In sharp contrast the work of Stephen Rowlands, following on from the pioneering effort of Michael Armstrong, his co-researcher, illustrates how teachers without the help of outside researchers can investigate their own classrooms and increase their knowledge of how their pupils learn. The section is completed by John Williamson's evaluation of the status of current British research. Williamson, an Australian, draws heavily on recent work here, in the United States and in Australia in order to suggest ways in which future classroom studies can be used to support, develop and encourage teachers in the study of teaching.

Early studies of classrooms tended to suggest that researchers were looking for some 'master' model of the effective teacher whose characteristics might be stamped upon future generations of practitioners. The last ten years of classroom research, however, have demonstrated how fruitless such a quest has been. Classrooms have increasingly come to be seen as complex environments whose workings, while governed by external factors, are centrally determined by laws of their own. Research for such patterns demands an immense co-operative effort between teacher and researcher if the pupils are to obtain the benefit of these new initiatives.

Reference

Westbury, I. (1978) 'Research into classroom processes: a review of ten years work', *Journal of Curriculum Studies*, 10, 4, pp. 283-308.

CHAPTER 17

STYLES, TIME AND TASK: CHANGING TRENDS IN RECENT RESEARCH ON TEACHING

NEVILLE BENNETT

My brief is to provide an overview of recent research on teaching. However you should be aware that there are two broad traditions of research in this field which for the sake of argument we will dichotomize into qualitative and quantitative. There was a time in the 1970s when battle lines were drawn and protagonists of both camps lashed each other with liberal doses of epistemological dogma. Like all feuds it was fairly pointless and was based on a totally false premise – that methodology was more important than the problem tackled. As others have noted 'issues of methodology are issues of strategy not of morals. Purity of method is no virtue. That strategy is best which matches research methods to the . . . question being asked' (Patton 1980).

Some researchers have been asking questions which require a quantitative approach, others a qualitative. There is no suggestion that one is of more intrinsic value than the other, simply that they have different purposes. My brief is to deal with quantitative approaches, i.e., investigations which have asked such questions as what teacher and pupil classroom behaviours relate to pupil outcomes.

The last decade or so has seen marked progress in this field, both in developing theory and in providing relevant data. In this period three distinct trends are apparent, although the third is only now emerging, The first trend is represented by a group of studies which have adopted a teaching style approach, beginning in the late 1960s and still continuing. The second trend began in the mid-1970s and is characterized by studies untilizing time variables, and the third emerging trend goes beyond time to concentrate on classroom tasks. Each trend shares the same aim, the improvement of teaching practices, but has been driven by different theories and perspectives. All wish to arrive at the same destination but have decided on different routes.

Each of these trends is considered in turn with greater concentration on research which has used models of time since these are currently in vogue. However the limitations of this approach will be taken up when dealing with the emergent task model.

Most of the research on teaching style has been carried out at primary school level, and can be subdivided into those which have utilized Plowden's model of teaching and those which have adopted a teacher-pupil interaction framework such as the Eggleston and Galton research on science teachers and the recent ORACLE study, although the latter also studied time. Both approaches share the same underlying assumption however: that there is a direct relationship between teacher behaviour and pupil achievement.

The Plowden model of progressive and traditional teaching proved to be a fertile source for a number of studies straddling the 1970s. This began with Barker Lunn's (1970) study, *Streaming in the Primary School*, followed by Cane and Smithers' (1972) *Roots of Reading*; Bennett's (1976) *Teaching Styles and Pupil Progress*; the HMI Primary School Survey (1978) and Gray's work on reading progress in the infant school (1979).

Each of these studies is characterized by the labelling of teachers based on a large number of behaviours to give a rather gross categorization. Most often this resulted in a dichotomy, variously defined and variously labelled, e.g., Type 1, Type 2; Formal, Informal; Exploratory, Didactic, with the consequent danger that teachers are forced into boxes in which they do not really belong.

This is exacerbated by the fact that until very recently the techniques used to classify teachers have lacked a solid base. Different clustering techniques produced different classifications.

Overall it is probably true to say that this body of research has led to more emotive controversy than solid conclusions. Nevertheless the most recent reviews by Gray and Satterley (1981) and Anthony (1982) both come to the same conclusion – that on the basis of available evidence formal teaching does appear to engender increased learning gains. However this bald statement tells us nothing about how to improve teaching, nor does it explain why there are wide differences *within* teaching styles, e.g., why some progressive teachers are good and others poor on the criterion used. Clearly factors other than teaching style are at work and require delineating.

What are those factors likely to be? For me the clues came from the pupil observation studies in the Teaching Styles study. From these it became evident that formal teachers spent more time on the basic subjects, and also that the pupils in such classrooms spent more time involved on the work set than in informal classrooms. These findings fitted in well with models of school and classroom processes being postulated in the United States, originally by Carroll (1963) and developed further by Bloom (1976) and Harnishfeger and Wiley (1976).

These models, which utilize aspects of time as central concepts, dispute the assumptions underlying teaching style research. They do not accept the direct relationship between teaching and learning and instead view pupil activities as the major mediating factor between teaching and learning, i.e., that the total amount of time actively engaged on a particular topic is the most important determinant of achievement on that topic. The teacher on the other hand is, to quote Ian Westbury (1977), seen as the manager of the attention and time of pupils in relation to the educational ends of the classroom. In other words the teacher manages the scarce resources of attention and time.

In order to present a coherent review of this mass of research, much of it American, I have developed a model which is based on recent empirical research in this area. (see Figure 17.1)

Overview

Quantity of schooling is the total amount of time that the school is open for its stated purpose and is defined by the length of school day and school year. The nominal amount may not be the actual amount since the school may be closed for a number of reasons – extra holidays, teacher strikes or building alterations. The actual amount will also be reduced for a particular pupil by his absences. This time is allocated to various curricular activities, curricular used here in its broadest sense to include administration and transition time between activities as well as time devoted to content. The curriculum emphasis or balance achieved varies from school to school and class to class. This element is termed 'curriculum allocation'. The amount of time allocated to a given curriculum activity is, however, unlikely to match the actual amount of time a pupil will spend on it. Disruptions, distractions, lack of interest in the task or poor persistence are all factors likely to reduce the use a pupil makes of

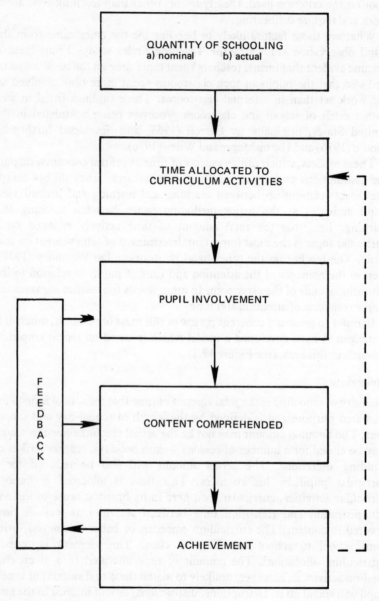

Figure 17.1　A model of teaching-learning process.

the opportunity to study a given content. The next element termed 'pupil involvement' acknowledges this. The underlying assumption here is that the only active portion of the time assigned to a task is effective for learning that task. But whether this active portion is relevant achievement will depend upon a number of other variables subsumed under 'comprehension'. According to this model achievement-relevant time is mediated by a number of factors including the aptitude and prior achievement of the pupil, clarity of instructions, task difficulty and pacing. Thus only that portion of time during which a pupil is actually comprehending the task is effective for its acquisition and thus has a direct link to achievement on that task. The remaining element is feedback since this is assumed to influence both involvement and comprehension and thereby achievement.

Quality of schooling

The exposure of pupils to schooling depends in the first instance on the nominal quantity of schooling defined by length of school day and school year.

The length of the school year in Britain is fixed at 190 days but more flexibility is possible in the length of the school day. The regulations lay down a minimum of three hours per day for infants and four hours for juniors, although in practice primary schools work for longer hours than these regulations require. The evidence available indicates marked variations across schools. A study in Surrey (Hilsum and Cane 1971), recently replicated in Lancashire (Lane 1979), both found that the amount of time the schools were open varied from twenty-two to twenty-seven hours per week. When lunch times, breaks, assemblies and administration are deducted the amount of time remaining for teaching varied from a little over nineteen to twenty-four hours per week. At the extremes therefore some children are exposed to schooling for five hours per week more than others, effectively a gain of one day per week. Over the school year this difference amounts to six school weeks.

These nominal amounts of time are likely to be differentially decreased by such events as teacher or caretaker strikes, structural repairs, use of schools as polling stations and so on. The actual amount of schooling for any individual pupil will also depend on his absences from school. These differences are important. A number of studies have now related the length of school day to pupil achievement and have found positive and significant relationships (Stallings 1975, Wiley and Harnischfeger 1974). Further, studies which have related pupil absence to achievement have typically reported negative relationships (*cf*. Bennett 1978). The latest large-scale study of the effect of pupil absence examined the relationship between school attendance at age seven and fifteen and their reading and mathematics achievement at age sixteen. Their conclusion was 'children with high attendance levels obtain on average higher scores on tests of reading, comprehension and mathematics' (Fogelman 1978). There was also a low but positive link between attendance at age seven and later achievement at age sixteen which could suggest that the effect of early absence persists into secondary school.

Some of the implications of this research are fascinating. The enhanced performance seen in a longer school day could, by inference, question the length of the current school year, particularly since there is evidence of a diminution in performance over the summer holidays, although I doubt if this would be well received by the teaching profession. Such decisions are outside the realm of teachers of course, but the necessity to develop strategies to combat the adverse effects of pupil absence and the possibilities of utilizing homework in a remedial role deserve consideration.

Curriculum allocation

Within the constraints of the actual amount of schooling available the primary teacher subdivides the time by curriculum area and plans and implements corresponding allocations of pupil time either in class, group or individual activities. The curriculum emphasis in primary classrooms is often determined by the class teacher, mediated by school policy, attitudes and aims based on perceptions of the needs of the children and their levels of achievement. The lack of central control of curriculum in Britain is reflected in the large variations found in curriculum emphasis.

A number of recent studies have investigated this and despite differences in methodology and definitions the results are surprisingly consistent (Bennett 1976, Ashton *et al*. 1975, Bassey 1977, Lane 1979, Bennett *et al*. 1980). Two studies have been selected to represent these. The first comprised interviews of nine hundred teachers in Nottinghamshire, and the second utilized direct observation of pupils and teachers in a national sample of open plan primary schools.

The number in the enclosed horizontal column of Figure 17.2 is the

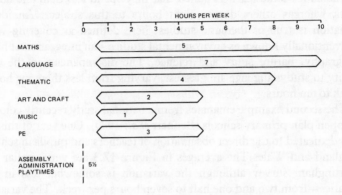

Figure 17.2   Curriculum allocation (Bassey).

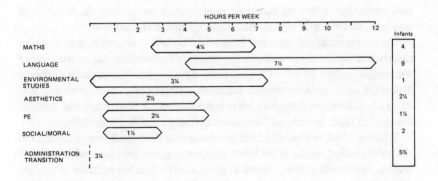

Figure 17.3   Curriculum allocation (Bennett *et. al.*)

average amount of time per week devoted to the subject area for all teachers, e.g., five hours per week mathematics, seven hours per week language. The length of the column denotes the variations found. Thus in mathematics some teachers stated that they spend less than one hour per week whereas others devote eight hours to this subject. An identical variation is true of thematic studies, here defined as covering what is conventionally known as environmental studies – an integration of history, geography, nature study and science. The discrepancies in the opportunity to study language are greatest, varying from less than one hour per week to ten hours.

The second example emanates from a national study recently completed on open plan primary schools (Bennett *et al.* 1980). One year of this study was dedicated to the direct observation of teachers and pupils in schools in England and Wales.The averages in Figure 17.3 are very similar to the Nottingham survey although the variation is somewhat less in mathematics – from two and one half to seven hours per week. The variation in language is four to twelve hours and in environmental studies zero to seven hours.

These observations also allowed a comparison of time allocations in junior and infant classrooms. As might be expected there is more emphasis on language with the younger children. But perhaps the most significant finding is the large amount of time spent on administrative and transition activities. Most of the five and three-quarter hours is in fact spent in transition – here defined as that time between activities – clearing up, moving to a new location, waiting and so on. The fact that such non-curricular activities consume over twenty percent of the week is of concern, and accords with similar findings in the United States.

Other findings of interest from this body of research are that the number of subjects comprising the primary curriculum varies from more than eight to five or less. There are less data on this for secondary schools although case studies would indicate differences across schools, and marked differences between what schools provide and what the Schools Council in their document *The Practical Curriculum* has argued for.

What is clear is that children are receiving quite different educational diets depending on the school they happen to go to, and as in other areas of human functioning, diet relates to growth. The limited number of studies which have investigated this link have shown positive relationships. The largest study concluded 'time allocated to instruction in a content area is positively associated with learning in that content area' (Fisher *et al.*

1978). This was consistent at both infant and junior levels and in both mathematics and reading.

Such a consideration of curriculum allocation leads into the realms of curriculum planning. The evidence indicates that what knowledge the pupil acquires depends on coverage and emphasis of the curriculum adopted. This evidence, together with that drawn from the field of curriculum evaluation (*cf.* Walker and Schaffarzick 1974), indicates that, other things being equal, one curriculum is neither better or worse than another, rather that different curricula result in different patterns of knowledge acquisition (Berliner and Rosenshine 1976). The primary teacher who, in Britain, has considerable influence on curriculum emphasis is thus faced with a set of critical questions. Should the emphasis be on the development of the basic subjects or should there be equal concern with creative expression and aesthetic appreciation? What amount of time should be devoted to each? Should equal time be allocated to pupils irrespective of ability or previous achievement?

Such considerations apply to more people in the secondary sector. The head, who must consider the educational fare in the school as a whole; those responsible for timetabling, in the light of such constraints as staffing, accommodation and resources; the head of department; and finally the individual teacher. This is where the teacher becomes a manager of scarce resources. How much time to allocate to one topic or activity and how much to another? Since the amount of time is fixed, time allocation to one topic necessitates limitations or postponements of time on others. This is no doubt partly why new curricula such as health education and life skills are difficult to implement. Such decisions as these mentioned result in quite diverse emphases and curriculum balance between schools, within schools and within departments.

Such decision making is further complicated by the fact that providing equal amounts of time to each pupil will not produce equal learning. Some pupils require up to nine times the amount as others to achieve the same achievement level (Bloom 1976, Gettinger and White 1979). Thus the teacher faces difficult procedural, organizational and even ethical judgements in relation to her objectives. And an educational system based on age exacerbates this problem.

Pupil involvement

If we conceive curriculum allocation as the opportunity that teachers provide pupils to study a given curriculum content, then pupil involvement can be conceived as the use that pupils make of that opportunity. Here too there is evidence of wide variation.

The problem here is that the answer gained crucially depends on the question asked.

Some researchers have computed a proportion of the time that pupils are actively engaged on the task set in relation to the length of the school day. The question posed in this instance is 'What proportion of the school day is the pupil involved?', and this inevitably includes administration and transition time which serves to depress the size of the proportion gained. Other researchers have posed the question 'What proportion of an identifiable lesson is the pupil involved?', and this obviates the inclusion of much transition time.

In the open plan study we computed both. Here the average proportion of the school day spent involved was sixty-six percent for juniors and sixty-one percent for infants but these averages mask marked divergences across schools. Some schools managed to average over eighty percent, others fifty percent. And if the individual pupil is taken as the unit of analysis the variation was from approximately twenty percent to nearly ninety percent. In other words some teachers were able to keep their pupils involved for nineteen hours per week, others only thirteen hours. If transition time is removed the proportions increase substantially to over seventy-five percent and when these data were further broken down it became evident that involvement was lowest in mathematics and language. That which is allocated most time apparently generates least involvement.

These findings appear fairly general although it is not always clear how different investigations have conceptualized, measured and computed pupil involvement. Deanne Boydell, using the observation schedule that ORACLE later used, found an average of sixty-seven percent in maths lessons and ORACLE found a similar proportion across those subjects taught in the classroom. The largest American study reported a seventy percent average.

The variable here labelled pupil involvement has numerous synonyms – attention, task persistence, active learning time and engagement, but irrespective of nomenclature the central question is whether this variable relates to achievement. Was William James correct when he argued in 1902 'whether the attention comes by grace or genius of by dint of will, the longer one does attend to a topic the more mastery of it one has'?

The short answer is yes. There is clear support for such a view from investigations at all levels of schooling. At nursery and reception level it has been reported that the effect of harnessing and focusing the children's attention is dramatic (Tyler *et al.* 1979), and that interest and task orientation in kindergarten are the best predictors of achievement in infant school (Perry *et al.* 1979). American studies of the attention-achievement link among six (Samuels and Turnure 1974), seven (Fisher *et al.* 1978), eight (McKinney *et al.* 1975), eleven (Cobb 1972, Fisher *et al.* 1978) and twelve-year-old children (Laharderne 1968) have all demonstrated positive and significant relationships.

Supporting evidence from this side of the Atlantic includes the recent ORACLE study which found that pupils categorized as 'solitary workers' performed best and had the highest involvement level. Further, the teaching style which came out best overall, 'class inquirers', had by far the highest proportion of such children and thus the highest pupil involvement of any style.

In the secondary field an analysis of several international evaluation studies on achievement delineated time and opportunity to learn as the most important factors to emanate from these studies (Postlethwaite 1975).

Pupil involvement or attention has been consistently shown to relate to achievement. Marked variations have also been found both within and between classrooms, within different content areas and across ability levels.

The implications for classroom practice are primarily to be found in the area of classroom management since relationships between teacher behaviours and involvement levels have been traced both in relation to whole class teaching and small group work (Kounin 1970). In the former context the most salient teacher behaviours in maintaining involvement were awareness in monitoring classroom events, the ability to maintain a smooth flow of events particularly at points of transition, maintaining the attention of non-responding pupils and the ability to deal with two or more things at the same time.

The effects of these abilities have been supported in recent classroom research. Brophy and Evertson report that successful teachers maintained a smooth flow of events by a system of well-thought-out monitor systems and a good set of classroom rules. This was particularly obvious during transitional periods between activities. In well-organized classrooms transition lasted only a short time and the children seemed to transfer to another activity automatically. In contrast transitional periods in less well-organized classrooms tended to be chaotic with children wandering about, bumping into one another, confused, and needing to ask the teacher what to do. The authors concluded 'student engagement in lessons and activities was the key to successful classroom management' (Brophy and Evertson 1976).

The general principle that increased control of organization and content by the teacher is associated with increased involvement and/or achievement is now well established (Rosenshine 1976, Bennett 1976, DES 1978, Morrison 1979), but differences have been found in what is optimal for differing levels of pupil ability, with lower-ability pupils requiring more structure, as indeed do anxious, insecure children.

As was stated earlier, different managerial skills have been found to be important in small group teaching. Additionally there is evidence to suggest that involvement in groups may be lower (Kounin 1970), which could indicae that, unless well managed, working in groups could depress pupil achievement. This is an important consideration since one of the significant movements in primary teaching in the last decade has been from whole class to small group organization. Partly as a response to this there are now research projects on group work at both Lancaster and Leicester.

The final teacher management competencies considered here relate to transition and queuing. It will be recalled that in the open plan schools study infants spend over a fifth of the week on average in transitional activities and it would be interesting to know the proportion in secondary schools. The amount of transition is regarded by some as a reflection of teacher management competencies as a whole (Arlin 1979). Many investigators have commented on the extent of such time (Brophy and Evertson 1976, Gump 1974, Arlin 1979), and the evidence would suggest that it tends to be higher where the teacher does not have a clear set of rules or a clear signalling system. What must be kept in mind is that time spent in transition means less time on curriculum content. This is also true of queuing, a fairly typical problem which is again brought about by inappropriate classroom management strategies.

Comprehension

But time is not the complete explanation of test differences. It has in fact been called an 'empty box' (Gage 1978) which requires filling with comprehensible and worthwhile content.

Comprehension and feedback are considered separately in the model as it stands but could be joined to provide a more general element relating to structuring the conditions for learning. The cluster of variables of concern here include the manner of presentation of task, the sequence, level and pacing of content and the teacher's level of expectations of pupils as judged by the tasks and activities provided. Unfortunately classroom researchers have tended to neglect this area to date. There is for example no classroom-based research on sequencing content.

Despite this, sequencing has continued to be regarded as central by curriculum developers, and instructional theorists, and some experimental studies have reported that content structure can make a difference in terms of performance and the rate of concept acquisition (Tennyson and Tennyson 1977). But a recent review of this area contended that despite long debates on the issue no satisfactory answer has been developed and no adequate prescription should be expected in the near future. The conclusion was that 'we have very little information based on hard data regarding the consequences of alternative content sequences and will need a good deal more research effort before we are able to satisfactorily report how the content should be sequenced' (Posner and Strike 1976).

Neither has there been much consideration of the sequencing of teacher-produced material. The 'death by worksheet' syndrome, particularly in secondary mixed-ability classes, is well known but the only study on this topic has yet to report although a conference paper on the subject gave no grounds for optimism; indeed gave much ground for pessimism. This is likely to be exacerbated at primary level where such cards are produced by teachers poorly versed in the subject – mathematics being an exemplary case.

Of current concern is the nature of the match between the demands of the task or activity set and the pupils' capacities to undertake it. This is variously referred to as the match or level of difficulty, and was highlighted in the recent survey of primary education undertaken by Her Majesty's Inspectorate. It was their judgement that the top third of pupils in any class were doing work that was insufficiently challenging. Teachers were underestimating these pupils' capacities.

Evidence of poor matching is also available from the United States where, for example, it is claimed that the failure to adjust the material and the instruction to the range of reading capabilities found within the classroom is probably the most important single cause of reading disability (Bond and Tinker 1973).

These assertions about the effect on achievement of poor matching gain limited support from recent classroom-based studies. Support from the HMI survey itself was indirect. They found that exploratory or progressive teaching practices were related to poorer achievement in maths and reading and that matching was least satisfactory there. Direct support is only available from American studies at this stage. One approached the problem by rating the number of errors children made in their work and found that the proportion of time spent on tasks where they have low error rates is positively associated with learning (Fisher *et al*. 1978).

The extent to which children are challenged by the teacher appears to be important. There is research to indicate that increasing the demands made on pupils increases involvement and performance (Block and Burns 1976). This notion of the more you demand the more you are likely to get is supported by other studies. One investigated teachers who consistently gained higher achievement in maths and compared them with those who tended to gain low achievement. They found that the high-achieving teachers typically pushed pupils through textbooks at a much faster rate, covering on average ninety pages of text in eighty days compared to fifty-six pages of the low-achieving teachers. Incidentally, attitudes to maths were also higher in the faster-paced classes (Good *et al*. 1978). A similar conclusion was reached in a large-scale comparative study of the mathematics achievement of British and Californian children. Here the much better performance of British children was interpreted in terms of differing requirements or expectations.

Classroom-based research on the variables included within the comprehension category is fairly limited. Nevertheless, it appears to be consistent in indicating that these factors do have an effect on learning outcomes and that interactions can be expected with pupil ability and attitude.

Feedback

'Feedback confirms correct responses, telling the student how well the content is being understood and it identifies and corrects errors, or allows the learner to correct them. This correction function is probably the most important aspect of feedback, and, if one were given the choice, feedback following wrong responses probably has the greatest positive effect' (Kulhavy 1977).

The effectiveness of the correction function can be shown in recent classroom research. Opportunities for immediate practice of skills, together with opportunity for immediate corrective feedback, have been found to be important particularly with the lower-ability pupil. One report concluded 'the most successful teachers, in terms of pupil gains, conducted group lessons by giving initial demonstrations and then quickly moving around having each student try out what has been demonstrated and providing feedback on an individual basis (Brophy and Evertson, 1976).

An aspect of feedback which has attracted considerable research has been on the relative utility of verbal praise and criticism. Until the early 1970s it was thought that praise was always preferable but research since that date has tended to modify this. The focus or topic of feedback has been shown to be more important than type of feedback (Stallings and Kaskowitz 1973), and interactions with pupil ability have also been found. These would indicate that the most successful teachers of low-ability children motivate primarily through gentle and positive encouragement and praise while the most successful teachers of high-ability children motivate through challenge and a critical demandingness which involved communicating high expectations and criticizing their pupils for failing to meet them (Brophy and Evertson 1976).

The relationship of praise to achievement is thus no longer as clear as earlier reviews suggest. To have pay off in achievement terms, praise has (a) to relate clearly to the topic under consideration, (b) be genuine and credible rather than perfunctory and (c) be used judiciously in relation to individual differences.

A gap which exists in this type of research is the quality of the information fed back. An informal assessment of the types of marking in exercise books or workbooks would indicate that the 'tick, good' or 'four out of ten' is still endemic, a practice which is less than useful in feedback terms. This provision of feedback, even if the feedback is given in an informative way, is insufficient for optimal learning. A pupil must also be given some description of what he can do to correct unsatisfactory results (McKeachie 1974).

Symbolic as well as verbal feedback would seem to be effective. It has been found that the use of symbolic rewards such as gold stars and 'smiling faces placed upon papers to be taken home and shown to the parents, or placed on charts in a room, showed consistent positive association with learning gains' (Brophy and Evertson 1976). Classroom-based experiments on material incentives supports their efficacy (*cf.* Benowitz and Busse 1976).

Research on aspects of time is still flourishing, particularly in the United States, and has been extremely valuable in providing interesting and relevant data, insights and implications. It has also focused attention on pupils and their interaction with classroom tasks, although significantly not on the tasks themselves. It is here where, in common with teaching style approaches, the weakness lies. Intended school learning emanates from the tasks provided by teachers to pupils and yet the quality of these tasks or activities has rarely been investigated. Researchers on teaching have stressed quantity at the expense of quality.

The third trend takes cognisance of this and focuses on task demand. What reviewers of the above research have ignored is that, although pupil involvement does appear to relate to pupil achievement, it does so with marked variations, the correlations ranging from 0.1 to 0.6 and no explanation for this has been forthcoming. However it is clear from observations in classrooms that children may spend a considerable amount of time on tasks that are beyond their capacity, and equally, as HMI found, many children spend considerable time on tasks with which they are fully conversant. Neither of those conditions are likely to lead to learning. Pupil involvement is therefore a necessary but not sufficient condition for learning. It has also been found that correlations vary across subject matter for the primary teacher which could indicate that teachers are more adept at matching task demand to pupils in some subjects than in others. Thus to further our understanding of classroom learning, attention must go beyond time, to task.

This is the direction being taken in our current study entitled *The Quality of Pupil Learning Experiences*. In it objective data are being collected on which to make judgements of quality defined in terms of appropriateness, e.g., the appropriateness of the task to the pupil, of teacher intention to the task, and of the teacher's procedural and management actions. The social context of learning is also being investigated by the recording of group processes in order to ascertain the effect of working in a group on the performance of tasks. The methodology is necessarily complex and is fully described elsewhere (Bennett *et al.* 1981).

A further criticism of other approaches is that they have failed to take seriously the notion of classroom learning. The usual expedient has been to use standardized tests of achievement which have doubtful validity since they rarely reflect the curriculum content taught. It is our experience that no child, even in the same class, experiences the same curriculum. In order to accommodate this state of affairs pupils are interviewed and tested at the conclusion of each task to assess understanding, in addition to undertaking an individually tailored testing programme at the end of each term to assess retention.

Finally it is worth mentioning, as one way in which such research is moving, that the data are being used constructively to develop an in-service course for teachers in a carefully evaluated attempt to improve aspects of the matching process.

Conclusion

The last decade or so has been marked by significant progress and shifting paradigms. Research trends change as theories outlive their usefulness. The broad categorizations of teachers in teaching style research is seen by many to be too gross if the aim of such research is to improve teacher behaviours. Styles are inevitably comprised of a large number of such behaviours and it is never clear which are, and are not, effective. This is further confounded by the relative neglect of the pupil as an agent of his own learning.

Models of time redressed this balance and provided a productive new perspective to bear on classroom processes and their effects. Central to this model is the notion of pupil involvement on task although this is in fact not new. As Philip Jackson noted, much effort was expended on this concept in the earlier part of the century until it was dropped as an authoritarian issue in the progressive post-war era.

Teaching style and time models have both been criticized for reifying quantity at the expense of quality, and for not taking classroom learning sufficiently seriously. Thus the latest initiative on the interaction of pupil and task. However, shifting paradigms should not be seen as an example of researchers being happier to travel than to arrive. The proposed destination does not change, but unlike British Rail we are always seeking more effective routes to it.

References

Anthony, W.S (1982) 'Research on Progressive Teaching'. *British Journal of Educational Psychology* 52, pp.381-385.
Arlin, N. (1979) 'Teacher transitions can disrupt time flow in classrooms'. *American*

Educational Research Journal 16, pp. 42-56.

Ashton, P., Kneen, P., Davies, F., and Holley, B.J. (1975) *The Aims of Primary Education: A Study of Teacher Opinions*, London, Macmillan.

Barker-Lunn, J. (1970) *Streaming in the Primary School*,Slough, NFER.

Bassey, M. (1977) *Nine Hundred Primary School Teachers*, Nottingham, Nottinghamshire Primary Schools Research Project, Trent Polytechnic.

Bennett, S.N. (1976) *Teaching Styles and Pupil Progress*, London, Open Books.

Bennett, S. N. (1978) 'Recent research on teaching: a dream, a belief and a model' *British Journal Educational Psychology* 48, pp. 127-147.

Bennett, S.N., Andreae, J., Hegarty, P., and Wade, B. (1980) *Open Plan Schools: Teaching, Curriculum and Design*, Slough, NFER.

Bennett, S.N., Desforges, C., Cockburn, A., Wilkinson, B. (1981) *The Quality of Pupil Learning Experiences*, Interim Report to SSRC, Lancaster University, Department of Educational Research.

Benowitz, M.L. and Busse, T.V. (1976) 'Effects of material incentives and the classroom learning of middle and lower class children' *Psychology in the School* 10, pp. 79-83.

Berliner, D.C. and Rosenshine, B. (1976) 'The acquisition of knowledge in the classroom' *Technical Report IV-I of BTES*, San Francisco, Far West Lab.

Block, J.H. and Burns, R.B. (1976) 'Mastery learning' in Shulman, L.S. (ed), *Review of Research in Education 4*, Itasca, F.E. Peacock.

Bloom, B.S. (1976) *Human Characteristics and School Learning*, New York, McGraw Hill.

Bond, G. and Tinker, M. (1973) *Reading Difficulties: Their Diagnosis and Correction*, New York, Appleton Century Crofts.

Boydell, D. (1975) 'Pupil behaviour in junior classrooms' *British Journal Educational Psychology* 45, pp. 122-129.

Brophy, J.E. and Evertson, C.M. (1976) *Learning from Teaching*, Boston, Allyn and Bacon.

Cane and Smithers (1972) *Roots of Reading*, Slough, NFER.

Carroll, J.B. (1963) 'A model of school learning' *Teachers College Rec.* 64, pp. 723-33.

Cobb, J.A. (1972) 'Relationship of discrete classroom behaviours to fourth grade academic achievement' *Journal Educational Psychology*, 63, pp. 74-80.

Department of Education and Science. (1978) *Primary Education in England*, London, HMSO.

Fisher, C.W., Filby, N.N., Marliave, R., Cahen, L.S., Dishaw, M.M., Moore, J.E. and Berliner, D. (1978) *Teaching Behaviours, Academic Learning Time and Student Achievement: Final Report of Phase IIIB, Beginning Teacher Evaluation Study*, San Francisco, Far West Lab.

Fogelman, K. (1978) 'School attendance, attainment and behaviour' *British Journal Educational Psychology* 48, pp. 148-158.

Gage, N.L. (1978) *The Scientific Basis of the Art of Teaching*, Teachers College Press, New York, University of Columbia.

Gettinger, M. and White, M.A. (1979) 'Which is the stronger correlate of school learning? Time to learn or measured intelligence?' *Journal Educational Psychology* 71, pp. 405-412.

Good, T., Grouws, D.A., Beckerman, T.M. (1978) 'Curriculum pacing: some empirical data in mathematics' *Journal Curriculum Studies* 10, pp. 75-81.

Gray, J. (1979) 'Reading progress in English infant schools. Some problems emerging from a study of teacher effectiveness' *British Educational Research Journal* 5, pp. 141-157.

Gray, J. and Satterley, D. (1981) 'Formal or informal? A reassessment of the British evidence' *British Journal Educational Psychology* 51, pp.187-196.

Gump, P.V. (1974) 'Operating environments in schools of open and traditional design' *School Review* 82, pp. 575-594.

HMI (1978) *Survey of Primary Education*, London, HMSO.

Hilsum, S. and Cane, B. (1971) *The Teachers Day*, Slough, NFER.

James, W. (1899) *Talks to Teachers*, London, Longman Green.

Kounin, J.S. (1970) *Discipline and Group Management in Classrooms*, New York, Holt, Rinehart and Winston.

Kulhavy, R.W. (1977) 'Feedback in written instruction' *Review of Educational Research* 47, pp. 211-232.

Lahaderne, H.M. (1968) 'Attitudinal and intellectual correlates of attention: a study of four sixth grade classrooms' *Journal Educational Psychology* 59, pp. 320-324.

Lane, R. (1979) *The Teacher's Week: An Appraisal*. Unpublished M.A. Dissertation. Department of Educational Research University of Lancaster.

McKeachie, W.J. (1974) 'The decline and fall of the laws of learning' *Educational Researcher* 3, pp. 7-11.

McKinney, J.D., Mason, J., Perkerson, K., and Clifford, M (1975) 'Relationships between behaviours and academic achievement' *Journal of Educational Psychology* 67, pp. 198-203.

Morrison, T.L (1979) 'Classroom structure, work involvement and social climate in elementary school classrooms' *Journal Educational Psychology* 71, pp. 471-477.

Perry, J.D., Guidubaldi, J., and Kehle, T.J. (1979) 'Kindergarten competencies as predictors of third grade classroom behaviour and achievement' *Journal of Educational Psychology* 71, pp. 443-450.

Posner, G.H. and Strike, K.A. (1976) 'A categorisation scheme for principles of sequencing content' *Review of Educational Research* 46, pp. 665-690.

Postlethwaite, T.N. (1975) 'The surveys of the international association for the evaluation of educational achievement (IEA): implications of the IEA surveys of achievement' In Purvis, A.C. and Levine, D.V. (eds) *Educational Policy and International Assessment* Berkeley, McCutcheon.

Rosenshine, B. (1976) 'Classroom instruction' in Gage, N.L. (ed) *The Psychology of Teaching Methods*, 75th Yearbook of NSSE, Chicago, University of Chicago Press.

Samuels, B.J. and Turnure, J.E. (1974) 'Attention and reading achievement in first grade boys and girls' *Journal Educational Psychology* 66, pp. 29-32.

Schools Council (1981) *The Practical Curriculum*.

Stallings, J.A. (1975) 'Relationships between classroom instructional practices and child development' Paper presented at AERA Annual Conference, Washington D.C.

Stallings, J.A. and Kaskowitz, D.H. (1974) *Follow Through Classroom Observation Evaluation* Menlo Park, California, Stanford Research Institute.

Tennyson, R.D. and Tennyson, C.L. (1977) 'Content structure as a design strategy variable in concept acquisition' Paper presented at AERA Annual Conference, New York.

Tyler, S., Foy, H. and Huff, C. (1979) 'Attention and activity in the young child' *British Journal of Educational Psychology* 49, pp. 194-197.

Walker, D.F. and Schaffarzick, J. (1974) 'Comparing curricula' *Review of Educational Research* 44, pp. 83-112.

Westbury, I. (1977) 'The curriculum and the frames of the classroom' Paper presented at AERA Annual Conference, New York.

Wiley, D.E. and Harnischfeger, A. (1974) 'Explosion of a myth: quantity of schooling and exposure to instruction, major educational vehicles' *Studies of Educative Processes, Report No.8*, University of Chicago.

CHAPTER 18

SOCIOLOGY AND CLASSROOM RESEARCH

ANDREW POLLARD

Introduction

This paper has been written in two parts. The first part introduces the central concerns of sociological studies of classrooms, reviews the development of various types of sociological research on classrooms in the past few years, and attempts to clarify the relationship of such work to two other particularly important approaches – that of systematic observation and of teacher-based action-research. The second part provides an illustration of one type of sociological approach – ethnography – and is concerned with the coping strategies of the teacher and children of one infant classroom as they negotiate to mutually 'accomplish' a storytime.

Part I : Sociological approaches to classroom studies

Sociology can be characterized as being centrally concerned with the problems of 'order' and 'control' in society (Dawe 1970) and as attempting to provide various elements of analysis in answer to questions such as 'how is "society" possible?' and 'what processes and influences are involved in social change?'. These central concerns have generated key concepts such as class, power, socialization, ideology, action, culture, gender, etc., which are used as the building blocks of sociological research and analysis. When applying themselves to the study of education sociologists have been primarily interested in the issue of social differentiation – the ways in which the education system may influence or reproduce patterns of social advantage and disadvantage associated particularly with social class, race and gender. These, and particularly the issue of social class, have been the focal concerns of the sociology of education since the War and, as a branch of the parent discipline, the sociology of education has both contributed to and been influenced by trends in other areas of sociological research and theorizing.

Because of the theoretical underpinning which the links with the parent discipline provides, sociological research on classrooms has always taken a distinctive form vis à vis other work in that same substantive area. In addition, it itself has been subject to considerable changes as the pre-eminence of particular sociological perspectives has changed over the years.[1] Functionalist perspectives, stressing the organic interdependence of various elements of the social structure, dominated sociological thinking in the 1950s and 1960s and were perhaps best represented in a classroom application by Parsons' (1959) paper on 'The School Class as a Social System'. Parsons suggested unproblematically that classroom processes contributed to the socialization of each child for their roles in society, and assumptions about the consensual nature of the social values being transmitted and of the passivity of the participants were not far from the surface of his analysis. The main thrust of functionalist work, however, was at the structural level and it was this, in conjunction with a rejection of the embedded assumptions of value consensus and of passive role enactment, that gave rise to a radical reappraisal of sociological work in the early 1970s which was to have major implications for classroom studies.

The 'new' sociology focused in the first place on the sociology of knowledge and on the ways in which knowledge can be 'socially constructed' through interaction. It quickly became concerned with subjectivity, meaning and action in micro-contexts, using an at times bewildering array of theoretical perspectives such as ethnomethodology (Garfinkel 1967), phenomenology (Schutz 1970) and symbolic interactionism (Blumer 1969). A core assumption of all these approaches was that the participants in social interaction actively create their sense of reality – they are no mere 'cultural dopes' – which placed a considerable importance on the accurate recording and analysis of their perspectives. The umbrella term of 'interpretive approaches' was adopted to describe such work.

In the specific context of the sociology of education Michael Young's *Knowledge and Control* (1971) provided an immensely influential set of papers at this time and an increasing number of sociological researchers began to go 'into the classroom' in attempts to discover the processes operating within schools. This also involved a methodological change of considerable proportions, challenging the previous positivist tradition which had often used forms of input-output design and treated the school as an unexplored 'black box'. The new sociology of education, given its concern with school processes and with the perspectives of the participants, adopted the classic anthropological method of ethnography and undertook various degrees of participant-observation in attempts to inductively 'construct' an understanding of classroom events. Of course, the nature of this new approach was also a reaction against the established and thriving tradition of social-psychological classroom research, not unconnected with functionalism, the modern work of which Neville Bennett reviews in this section. Since the War this tradition had been particularly concerned with teacher effectiveness, had used largely positivist designs and quantitative methods, and in its apparent values and concerns seemed to treat the social context of the classroom as entirely unproblematic. The new sociological studies of classrooms rejected what were regarded as crude and insensitive forms of empiricism and favoured the qualitative methods of enthography as a means of analysing the contextual wholeness, the meaning and social consequences of classroom processes. Keddie's (1971) paper on 'Classroom Knowledge' provides a good example here.

Keddie studied teachers and streamed fourth-year pupils working on a humanities project in a comprehensive school. The focus of her research was a concern with the educational failure of working-class children. Instead of looking for explanations in terms of home background, language and other forms of deficit outside the school, Keddie identified the social organization of curriculum knowledge within the school and the processes by which teachers defined types of pupils from different streams as being central. As she put it

> One use to which the school puts knowledge is to establish that subjects represent the way about which the world is normally known in a 'expert' as opposed to a 'commonsense' mode of knowing. This establishes and maintains normative order . . . and accredits as successful . . . those who can master subjects. The school may be seen as maintaining the social order through the taken-for-granted categories of its superordinates who process pupils and knowledge in mutually confirming ways. (Keddie 1971, p. 156)

From her analysis Keddie argued that the knowledge used in the teacher contexts of the classroom and staffroom has to be distinguished from accounts given in educationalist contexts which may take the form more of professional rationalizations than of bases for routine daily action. It was seen to be crucial therefore for researchers to become fully involved in classrooms and in school life in order to understand what was really going on. A number of collections were published around this time and one might identify those of Stubbs and Delamont (1976) and Hammersley and Woods (1976) as being particularly significant. The Open University course 'School and Society' (E282) also made a great impact.

However, some of the products of this work were quickly criticized by other sociologists for adopting a relativistic view of knowledge and for producing fundamentally idealist analyses which ignored the wider social context within which action at the micro-classroom level occurs and it was not long before Marxist theorists were providing powerful alternative analyses of school processes in structural terms (e.g., Sharp and Green 1975).

The analyses of Bowles and Gintis (1976) and of Althusser (1971) were important at this time but eventually came to be seen as representing economic and ideological forms of determinism respectively. Each saw schools as reproducing the capitalist order and the dominance of particular class interests, and they conceptualized classroom processes in terms of producing docility and acceptance of hegemonic attitudes, values and social relations. Such work largely lacked an empirical base and, when empirical work on classrooms was undertaken by Marxist ethnographers, such determinist analyses, which assumed of the pupils something of the same passivity imputed by functionalism, were quickly amended. Thus the work of Willis (1977), Corrigan (1979) and Anyon (1981) conceptualized pupil deviance as forms of 'resistance' to the dominance of teachers and ultimately of the social order.

Meanwhile grounded ethnographic work with its origins in the 'new' sociology of education had continued and case studies have been steadily accumulated to the point now where a degree of generalization and theory construction from a strict empirical base is proving possible.There have for instance been a cumulative series of studies of teacher coping strategies in classrooms (Westbury 1973, Woods 1977, Hargreaves A. 1978, Pollard 1982) on which I will draw in the second section of this paper.

The present situation is an interesting one. While interpretive studies continue to be produced but also criticized for their lack of structural referents, so Marxist theorists have been criticized for the quality of their empirical work and for the values and assumptions which are embedded in their studies (Hargreaves A. 1982). The necessity now is to link different levels of analysis, for there seems little doubt that as forms of *sociological* analysis studies which focus on either macro or micro poles alone are ultimately weakened in consequence. Sociology in any sphere of application has to attempt to relate the individual to society if it is to fulfil the promise of the 'sociological imagination' (Mills 1959) and this applies to research on classrooms as much as in any other substantive area.

Of course it is in this respect that sociologists studying classrooms tend to part company with others also researching on classrooms but approaching their study from other perspectives. The basic aim and focus of sociology is particular and perhaps seems overly abstract to some. Both work in the systematic observation mode, reviewed in this volume by Neville Bennett,[2] and in the teacher-research mode, represented by Stephen Rowland's paper,[3] seems to take the 'improvement' of education and the educational system as unproblematic though they differ in that where one appears to orientate to 'results' the other appears to orient to the 'quality of learning experiences'. Sociologists would have to question the nature of 'improvement' itself – improvement in whose interests and with what social consequences? In this context concerns such as time-on-task and self-evaluative inquiry seem to be rather peripheral and to miss the sociological point. Such a statement is not intended to diminish other perspectives for each has its own terms of reference, but, in that sociological studies have clearly defined areas of study and clearly delineated focal concerns, then there are limitations to the degree of integration with other perspectives which is possible. At the same time it is the case that very little integration has been attempted and this could legitimately be regarded as a failing of academia. The reasons for this failing seen to relate to a curious cross-cutting over aims and means by the three perspectives which are indicated in a simplified way below

AIMS		MEANS
'improvement' of education	⎰ Systematic observation	Quantitative methods Positivist paradigm
analyse the relation between the individual, society and education	⎱ Teacher-based research ⎰ Sociology of classrooms ⎱	Qualitative methods Humanistic/interpretive paradigm

There are significant philosophical issues and deeply engrained prejudices embedded here.

For instance, there are different points of view about the analysis of findings, particularly concerning validation and interpretation. Systematic studies appear to be the most rigorous in terms of 'scientific' procedures but sometimes seem to be atheoretical to the point where accumulative descriptive empiricism frustrates attempts to *understand* the wider relationships between factors involved in classroom processes. Sociological studies of the ethnographic variety have tended to be based on relatively discrete case studies and thus, despite procedures such as the constant comparative method suggested by Glaser and Strauss (1967), sociological work has faced difficulties over generalization. Thus the 'generation' of theoretical models has been emphasized and the need for refinement of such models prior to claims of 'verification' has been accepted. Teacher-based research often takes yet another view which reflects the concern with the immediate utility of the analysis and the links with self-evaluation which exist. Given these interests the generalizability of the findings is not necessarily important; thus Stephen Rowlands can argue that as a 'teacher-inquirer' he can adopt the role of 'critic' to child-artists with all the scope and idiosyncracies in the relationship which that allows. Different purposes clearly tend to call for different methods and to produce different types of results which are interpreted in different ways. It will be interesting to see how these approaches to classroom research develop in the next few years. The area of classroom studies is certainly ripe for some kind of rapprochement but whether it will come and what form it might take remains to be seen.

The study on which I will draw in the second part of this paper is intended to illustrate one type of interpretive analysis of classroom processes. It cannot be taken as part of the rapprochement alluded to above for it is clearly sociological in orientation. Yet it may be of interest that it was undertaken while I was an infant school teacher and it was supported with a certain amount of quantitative data particularly on the range and type of teacher-child contacts (Pollard 1976). For the purposes of this paper I have re-analysed the data in the context of the work on teacher-pupil coping strategies cited previously.

Part II : Coping with storytime: an interpretive analysis

The concept of 'coping' is dependent on two elements – that of social context, which defines the situation which has to be coped with,

(Hargreaves A. 1978) and that of self-image which determines the criteria by which any individual will define what coping means to them personally (Pollard 1982). The concept can thus provide the necessary sociological linkage between society and the individual and between macro and micro levels of analysis.

The social context can be seen as important at at least four levels and I can apply them to the case in point – a class of six – seven-year-olds on the edge of a council estate in a northern town taught by Mrs Rothwell. Firstly there is the macro level, the level of the national and international socio-economic and political system. Clearly Mrs Rothwell's classroom could not be isolated from economic conditions, government expectations, cultural values, etc., and nor did she anticipate that the expectations, pressures and constraints which they placed on her would be consistent. She thus faced certain dilemmas. For instance, we might identify the contradition between the individualistic, materialistic and competitive ethos generated by the nature of our capitalist society with the particular caring, co-operative ethos emanating from Mrs Rothwell's strongly held religious beliefs. The children faced similar contraditions when trying to relate such factors as the 'message' of 'Incredible Hulk' cartoons with the moral injunctions of their teachers. Macro factors perhaps took a slightly more tangible form at the second main level of social context – that of the community in which the school was situated. Here the scale and nature of economic conditions, local government policies, parental expectations, etc. were different but probably no less diverse. Should Mrs Rothwell have 'taught for understanding' which the LEA advisers told her was needed for the flexible world of the twenty-first century or 'just teach 'em 'ow to get it right' as many parents in the school catchment area demanded with half an eye on the depressed local textile economy and the problems of future employment for their children? The third layer of social context – the school – in a sense provided a buffer between Mrs Rothwell and the children and society at large. The headteacher acted as a protective front while teachers' culture and professional solidarity represented resources on which Mrs Rothwell could draw to develop strategies for classroom action, to resolve dilemmas, and to 'let off steam'. At the same time though the school was also a constraint. Both the headteacher and staff peers had expectations and the school ethos was as constraining as it was facilitating. The school had a strong headteacher with rather traditional views of infant education and the intake, predominantly from a large council estate, were regarded by the staff somewhat unfavourably as being 'deprived' in cultural and moral values and as coming from 'difficult homes'. From the children's point of view the school represented constraint in the form of the adult-controlled organization in which they were relatively powerless but this was balanced in the informal life of the playground by the generally facilitating cultural resources of their peers. The fourth, and final, level of social context was the most tangible and immediate to the participants. Their classroom provided the routine social context of daily life. The material provision, its organization, its overt and hidden curriculum were crucially important for their coping were they alone and powerful, as was Mrs Rothwell, or one of a crowd but officially powerless, as were the twenty-seven children in her class at the time of the study. The classroom in question was in fact set out formally with two long tables in the middle of the room on which were seated the 'Top', 'Middle' and 'Bottom' groups of children. An unusual amount of class teaching for children of this age was undertaken and the children were concerned to 'get things right' and 'do well'. This rather 'traditional' classroom was highly structured and had a happy and ordered atmosphere.

We can now look at a specific instance of the classroom process – a 'sitting together' session on the carpet in which some leaves which a child had brought in were 'shown' and the Bible story of Zacchaeus was read to the children. From the sociological point of view the *content* of this episode illustrates Mrs Rothwell's aim to provide a necessary 'moral education' for the children while the *form* which her management of the session took illustrates her more immediate skills for coping with the flow of the lesson and the crowd of children. Thus both the content and form of the session relate to aspects of Mrs Rothwell's coping concerns. These were closely related to those of the children – an almost inevitable relationship given the reality-defining power of the teacher. The children in this session are also seen striving to cope though in different ways. The ways in which they contributed to discussion and answered teacher questions can be seen as attempts by them to negotiate favourable identities with Mrs Rothwell in the flow of classroom events. As we shall see, one child, Nigel, was particularly successful. I shall argue that to a significant extent the 'coping' of the teacher and the children was interdependent and the main sociological point to draw attention to is the process of incremental accumulation of child identities. This would have likely consequences for social differentiation in the long term if the cross-sectional case study which this is could be verified as reflecting more enduring basic processes in classrooms at other levels of the educational system.

The example is presented in the form of an unedited transcript of instruction plus an analysis of negotiating moves. The example occurred at the beginning of a work period. Mrs Rothwell had turned her chair sideways to her desk while the children sat cross-legged on the floor in front of her. Child speech is indented, teacher speech is not.

TRANSCRIPT		ANALYSIS OF NEGOTIATION
Lee has brought some leaves for us to see	1	Mrs Rothwell introduces item for 'showing'.
Brown	2	A child anticipates a question about colour.
Brown leaves, Lee knows what sort of tree it comes from, don't you, let's see if the others know?	3	Child's contribution accepted but Mrs Rothwell has already formed question.
. . . .	4	No response
Anyone know?	5	Encouragement
. . . .		
This time there's just one leaf on each stalk with just one point, it's called a 'simple' leaf.	6	Mrs Rothwell reminds children of a previous discussion about leaves.
. . . .	7	Still no response
One there look, one there.	8	Cue to specific criteria for identification
. . . .	9	No response
It's beech, copper beech and any autumn time when the tree grows a layer of cork there (points) to stop the leaves getting any water and food, these leaves go very brown and dry, and at my house I have a hedge of these sort of trees, and when the wind blows the leaves crackle and rustle because they are so dry, and they make rather a nice noise in the winter time when the wind blows on them and rustle and crackle in the night	10	Mrs Rothwell gives the answer and attempts to give more facts about leaves and to make it interesting.

that's when it's blowing dry leaves up and they're blowing away

Thats right, just like that, and at night time when you lie in bed you can hear this rustling, crackling sound, it sounds very nice. Right, I've found a picture for you this morning, who can guess what the picture is about?
  Jesus.

Yes, which one do you think is Jesus in the picture

  him in that tree
  in that tree
  (Jane points)

You think that one's Jesus do you Jane?

And who do you think this is up in the tree?
  a guard
Well I'll give you a clue . . .

  God
  Zacchaeus

We sang a song about him yesterday . . .

11 Child supplies feedback regarding experience of hearing leaves. No feedback sought on explicit knowledge.
12 Restructures the content of session.

13 Poses question, gives opportunity for someone to excel.
14 Mass response, cue from style and colours of art work or Bible picture leads to a frequently correct response.
15 Mrs Rothwell seeks specific evidence that children have identified main character.
16 A child leads a mass response which is the wrong answer but the most exciting-looking part of the picture.
17 Mrs Rothwell ignores wrong answers, picks out a child sitting in a 'devotional' position who has indicated correct answer.
18 Frames question to clarify confusion over other characters.
19 A child envisages a TV plot?
20 Mrs Rothwell considers children need clue for progress.
21 Guess, the first was often a right answer, the second was right this time, but Mrs Rothwell is in the process of giving a clue and continues.
22 Clue

Zacchaeus
. . . ccheus
Zacchaeus, there's Zacchaeus up
in the . . .

23   A child realizes answer, rest of
     class join in.
24   Mrs Rothwell acknowledges
     correctness, asks an 'infil'
     question which refers back to
     previous discussion of trees.

. . . .
What sort of tree . . .

25   No response
26   Mrs Rothwell makes question
     explicit.

. . . .
. . . did Zacchaeus climb in?

27   No response
28   Mrs Rothwell reminds of context,
     this is a clue.

(Nigel) a sycamore tree
A sycamore tree, there's
Zacchaeus up in the sycamore
tree, and he's looking down at
Jesus. Can we remember that
song to sing today – Duncan, is
Duncan here – no, are some other
people here, who also know that
song?
    (some children nod)
Well you'll have to sing up,
ready?(sings) now, Zacchaeus was
a very little man . . . .
    now Zacchaeus was a very little
man . . . .
(Three verses of song sung, it tells
the Zacchaeus story).
Why was Zacchaeus in the
sycamore tree?
    because he wanted to see Jesus

29   Correct response from one child.

31   Refers to song learnt at hymn
     practice the day before
32   Considers whether the children
     will be able to remember it
     without a key child. Places her
     trust in others.

33   Mrs Rothwell leads singing, class
     sing together for first verse,
     become more dependent on
     teacher's lead by third verse.
     (This is clear on tape but
     impossible to show in print.)
34   Mrs Rothwell restructures session
     in terms of picture again.
35   Gets correct response and
     continues story.

And he couldn't see, could he,
because all these people were
standing near
Alan come and sit here, face the
front.
(changes tone of voice)

36   Child from peripheral position
     brought forward

He couldn't see because he was small, like me, and he couldn't see through the crowd, so he had to climb up the tree so he could look down and see Jesus – but Jesus spotted him in the tree.	37 Story continues
No one liked Zacchaeus, why didn't they like him?	38 Question
because he was so small	39 Wrong answer, but the child who gave this has understood the type of answer required but picked up wrong cues at 37.
No it wasn't because he was small because he took money, and he took too much when he shouldn't	40 Child gives answer (song told whole story) which contains correct moralistic flavour as well as content.
Yes, he collected taxes from the people and he took more than he should from the poor people, and kept it for	41 Response reinforced.
	42 Infil question.
Him . . . self self	43 Cue given, children en masse pick it up.
He was dishonest.	44 Mrs. Rothwell makes point explicit and continues story
And Jesus knew all about this and said 'come along Zacchaeus, come down from that tree, I want to have a talk with you . . . and they went away and they had a meal together, and Zacchaeus decided to kill the lion of . . .?	45 Infil question.
(Nigel) greediness	46 A correct response, cue was given in the phrase "kill the lion of . . ." which referred to a story told earlier in the week.[4]
Yes, . . . and . . . laziness	47 Asks for more.
	48 Get 'a lion' but it is inappropriate, child has followed only the cue, not the context of usage.

Dis . . .
  honesty
  honesty
Dishonesty.
Jesus persuaded him to do that, to
kill these wretched lions that
caused him so much unhappiness
and he became honest and good
and he didn't take money from
people any more
  'cos that's naughty

I'll read it to you in the words
which we have in the Bible,
they're very hard to understand
but see if you can try it . . .
'And he entered', that's Jesus,
'and was passing through Jericho
and behold a man called
Zacchaeus, and he was a chief
publican and he was rich, and he
sought to see Jesus who he was,
and he could not for the crowd
because he was little of stature,
and he ran on before and climbed
up into a sycamore tree to see
him, for he was to pass that way.
And when Jesus came, into the
place, he looked up and said to
him . . . 'Zacchaeus, make haste
and come down, for today I must
abide at your house' and he made
haste and came down and received
him joyfully. When they saw it' –
that means the crowd – 'they
murmured saying – he's gone to
lodge with a man that is a sinner,

49 Mrs Rothwell gives cue, children
    follow her lead.

50 Reaffirms correct answer.
51 Continues moral

52 Child recognizes type of
    behaviour and responds to Mrs
    Rothwell's intentions with use of
    common constructs.
53 Mrs Rothwell again restructures
    lesson, prepares children for
    difficult task.

54 Reads from a children's Bible, in
    fact this version is very close to
    that in a King James Bible, Luke
    19, verses 1-10.

and Zacchaeus stood and said to the Lord – 'behold Lord the half of my wealth I give to the poor and if I have wrongfully exacted ought of any man, I restore it fourfold' – and Jesus said to him 'today is salvation to come to this house, for as much as he also is a son of Abraham. For the son of man came to seek and to save that which was lost'.

It's very hard to understand that sort of writing isn't it? But you understand the story, people were very upset because Jesus had chosen a man they didn't like, Zacchaeus . . . he'd chosen him . . .

55 Mrs Rothwell acknowledges difficulty of listening, and draws out the points in the story which she wishes to stress.

   because he was . . .

56 Child keen to 'infil' in a pause, when in fact not required.

. . . to go to his house, they couldn't understand it, they said 'why has Jesus chosen this horrid little man, he's horrid, we don't like him, he takes money from us'.

Why had Jesus chosen him, why did Jesus choose Zacchaeus?

57 Mrs Rothwell ask the question which a child had anticipated at 56, and for which the answer has been stressed from 40-50.

   (Nigel) because he were stealing their money.

58   Correct response obtained.

That's right, good boy – because he knew that Zacchaeus was dishonest and greedy – he knew that Zacchaeus had a lot of lions to . . . kill. 'So he thought I'd better have a word with him, and he did, and Zacchaeus paid all the money

59 Mrs Rothwell acknowledges response, fills in more detail, and relates it all to previous story on 'lions'.

60 The happy ending.

he had stolen back again four
times over, so he gave the people
four times more than he'd actually
taken from them and then he
didn't do those nasty things any
more – and that's the story of
Zacchaeus.

I'll leave that, on the reading table	61	Mrs Rothwell makes book
open at that page, I hope your		available for reinforcement.
hands are clean because this book	62	Reminds children of rules for
doesn't belong to us so it has to be		using books.
cared for. Nigel put it on there		
. . . thank you.	63	Child entrusted with book.

This transcript illustrates several aspects of Mrs Rothwell's coping
strategies. The content shows her emphasis on standards of behaviour and
the religious source of such emphasis. This provided clear aims for the
sequence which she then planned carefully. For instance, the topic builds
on a previous story (Lions) and a song learned the day before. Mrs
Rothwell also overlaps the discussion on leaves with her main purpose.
The sequence is structured: firstly (from 12 to 32) Mrs Rothwell reminds
the children of the Zacchaeus story, then they sing the story, this is
followed by questions and instruction intended to check on understanding
(35-53), then the story is read from a Bible (54). Mrs Rothwell then selects
and re-emphasizes the points which are salient to her aims and makes links
with the 'Lions' theme which had been maintained during the week in
question (55-61): finally the story is made available in the reading corner.

This teaching sequence has its rationale in Mrs Rothwell's, and the
school's, assumptions about learning and knowledge. It provides for the
repetition of the content several times and in different media, and is
clearly instructional comprising the transmission of explicit knowledge
and attitudes which the children are believed to lack. It is thus accountable
both personally, institutionally and of course in terms of wider ideologies.

Mrs Rothwell held the initiative throughout the sequence, controlling it
by defining relative content, by checking on attentiveness and learning
with questions, and by reminding children of setting rules with a desist.
The children's degree of acceptance of the institutional definition of the
situation is indicated by their conformity to their ascribed learning role, by
the skill with which they picked up cues when a mass response was

possible (14, 23, 49), and by eager attempts at 'pleasing teacher' answers, which lacked other attributes of a 'correct answer' (21, 39, 52, 56). 'Correct answers' were supplied by individual children and one (Nigel) earned the privilege of carrying the book to the reading table.

A very important point to note is the fact that the children could only cope successfully in this situation by accepting and adopting the moral teaching and values embedded in the story. This can clearly be interpreted in terms of education as an ideological process, indeed from some perspectives it can be argued that child-centred education is essentially a manipulative form of social control. It is certainly the case in this example that the manipulative basis of interaction undercut most potentially oppositional attitudes from the children, so that they competed to be the 'good child' who supplied correct answers and actively picked up cues with which to overtly show attention and understanding of the particular values and content being taught

Mrs Rothwell accomplished this sequence with confidence, strength and security deriving from her institutional role position and from her taken-for-granted knowledge of the suitability of this type of content and pedagogy for children from poor homes. There is evidence that she felt her coping to be threatened only once, when she moved an inattentive child from the periphery.

Apart from this, she had order, she maintained the momentum of her instruction and appeared satisfied at its transmission. It is significant though to notice the means by which she maintained this momentum. At 16 she glides over a mass-produced wrong answer by picking out Jane who has got it right, at 31 she calls for Duncan who can sing and remember words reliably and at several points (29, 46, 58) she is enabled to proceed by Nigel's ability to provide the right answers. Because the momentum of instruction was maintained and the moral theme appeared to have been transmitted effectively, Mrs Rothwell regarded the session as 'successful' and it is certainly the case that her personal perspective of her role, purposes and duties was being enacted – she had coped well with the session.

The crucial point which has to be made is that the success of her coping strategies was intimately connected with the process of the social differentiation with child identity formation and with child coping strategies. The children accomplished the sequence by working to produce the responses valued by Mrs Rothwell. Their strategies appeared to be alert to weaknesses in her interpretation of acceptable responses.

Thus they used cues of intonation, indexical expression and gesture to interpret acceptable responses and some children appeared well satisfied that other children should give a response and thus relieve them of the obligation (58). As we have seen Mrs Rothwell in fact encouraged such strategies by continuing to give cues (49, 20), by actively seeking out 'clever' children (32) and, most importantly, by her interpretation of such responses as indicating more general understanding (58, 30). Thus the coping strategies of the teacher and the children were meshed together. Mrs Rothwell coped by calling on certain children to maintain the flow of the session and to lead the children in the required ways. These children were interpersonally rewarded while less successful children were not. The successful children coped and negotiated a favourable identity for themselves precisely by helping Mrs Rothwell at these key points and are thus likely over time to evolve a committed form of positive compliance with school life. The children who could not provide answers and so are not well represented on the transcript had no such incorporative basis for their coping available to them and it is likely that over time they would develop alternative and possibly oppositional value systems by which to preserve their self-esteem and 'cope' in their own terms. There is a great deal of ethnographic work available to support this type of analysis.[5]

Conclusion

I have suggested in this short illustrative analysis that social differentiation starts in crucial ways at the level of face-to-face interaction in classrooms. In terms of social consequence the point is that all of us as teachers are helping to reconstitute society in our daily practice – be it in terms of class, gender, race, ideologies or other factors. As individuals we are *in* society and just as we cannot escape from the pressures and constraints which it places on us so we cannot escape from the knowledge that by our routine actions we help to re-create society in new forms. Attempts to specify these processes represent the particular contribution which sociological ayalyses are attempting to provide regarding classroom research. There is a great deal of work yet to be done, for sociological work at the moment remains mainly at the stage of generating models of relationships. Hopefully at some point in the future a satisfactory level of clarification and verification will be established so that generalizable analyses will become available to teachers and policy-makers. However long this may take, the issues being raised are too important to ignore and demand attention on a day-to-day basis. Education can never be 'neutral', and everybody involved in it inevitably bears some responsibility for making it whatever it in fact becomes in their particular context.

Notes

1   See also Hammersley, M. (1980) 'Classroom ethnography', *Educational Analysis*, Vol 2, No 2.
2   See also McIntyre, D.I. (1980), 'Systematic observation of classroom activities', *Educational Analysis*, Vol 2, No 2.
3   See also Elliott, J. and Whitehead, D. (eds) (1980) *The Theory and Practice of Educational Action Research*, Bulletin No 4, Classroom Action Research Network, Cambridge Institute of Education.
4   The 'lions' story was a means of portraying various attributes or attitudes, which were disapproved of, in a way which would interest the children – thus they were to be 'hunted' and 'killed'.
5   Studies such as Hargreaves (1967), Lacey (1970), Woods (1979) and Ball (1981) are all relevant here, as are many others.

References

Althusser, L. (1971) 'Ideology and ideological state apparatuses', in *Lenin and Philosophy and other Essays*, New Left Books, London.
Anyon, J. (1981) 'Social class and school knowledge', *Curriculum Inquiry*, Vol II, No 1, pp. 67-92.
Ball, S. (1981) *Beechside Comprehensive*, Cambridge University Press, Cambridge.
Bowles, S. and Gintis, H. (1976) *Schooling in Capitalist America*, Routledge & Kegan Paul, London.
Blumer, H. (1969) *Symbolic Interactionism*, Prentice Hall, New Jersey.
Corrigan, P. (1979) *Scholling the Smash St Kids*, Macmillan, London.
Dawe, A. (1970) 'The two sociologies', *'British Journal of Sociology*, Vol 21, No 2.
Garfinkel, H. (1967) *Studies in Ethnomethodology*, Prentice Hall, New Jersey.
Glaser, B.G. and Strauss, A.L. (1967) *The Discovery of Grounded Theory*, Weidenfield & Nicholson, London.
Hammersley, M and Woods, P. (1976) *The Process of Schooling*, Routledge & Kegan Paul, London.
Hargreaves, A. (1978) 'The significance of classroom coping strategies' in Barton L and Meighan R (eds) *Sociological Interpretations of Schooling and Classrooms*, Nafferton.
Hargreaves, A. (1982) 'Resistance and relative autonomy theories: problems of distortion and incoherence in recent Marxist analyses of education,' *British Journal of Sociology of Education*, Vol 3, No 2, pp. 107-126.
Hargreaves, D.H. (1967) *Social Relations in a Secondary School*, Routledge & Kegan Paul, London.
Keddie, N. (1971) 'Classroom Knowledge' in Young, M. (ed) *Knowledge and Control*, Macmillan, London.
Lacey, C. (1970) *Hightown Grammar*, Manchester University Press, Manchester.
Mills, C.W. (1959) *The Sociological Imagination*, Oxford University Press, New York.
Parsons, T. (1959) 'The school class as a social system', *Harvard Educational Review*, XXIX, fall.

Pollard, A.J. (1976) *Classroom Interaction Processes towards a grounded sociological model of cultural, structural and experiential factors*,Unpb.MEd Dissertation, University of Sheffield.

Pollard, A. (1982) 'A model of coping strategies', *British Journal of Sociology of Education*, Vol 3, No 1, pp. 19-37.

Schutz, A (1970) *On Phenomenology and Social Relations; selected writings* Wagner, H. R, (ed) Chicago University, Chicago.

Sharp, R. and Green, A.G. (1976) *Education and Social Control*, Routledge & Kegan Paul, London.

Stubbs, M. and Delamont, S. (1976) *Explorations in Classroom Observation*, Wiley, London.

Westbury, I. (1973) 'Conventional classrooms, "open" classrooms, and the technology of teaching' *Journal of Curriculum Studies*, 5, pp. 95-121.

Willis, P. (1977) *Learning to Labour: How Working Class Kids Get Working Class Jobs*, Saxon House, London.

Woods, P. (1977) 'Teaching for survival' in Woods, P and Hammersley, M. (eds) *School Experience*, Croom Helm, London.

Woods, P. (1979) *The Divided School*, Routledge & Kegan Paul, London.

Young, M.F.D. (1971) *Knowledge and Control*, Collier-Macmillan, London.

CHAPTER 19

CLASSROOM RESEARCH AND THE TEACHER

MAURICE GALTON

When I started teaching I was told by my older colleagues not to worry about the latest educational theory because, like the buses, it didn't matter too much if you missed it as another would follow within five minutes. Given the depressing list of earlier researches which failed to make an impact on classroom practice – (is anyone still using those programmed learning auto-tutor machines of the early 1970s?) – you may be sceptical about whether studies of classrooms will have any lasting effects upon practice in the next decade. Nevertheless I believe that recent classroom research has much to offer teachers.

The opposite view has certainly been expressed vehemently in one or two quarters. Reviewing a recent book on classroom research, *Focus on Teaching* (Bennett and McNamara 1979), a well-known headmaster disputes the editors claim that 'Studies in classroom observation have much to offer to students in sharpening their perceptions of the educational process and in the longer term of providing coherent theories on which to guide practice.' The headmaster believes that 'teachers know when they are teaching effectively . . .' and 'have their own checks. General class response, individual pupil interest, the work pupils produce, the progress they make, all indicate whether things are going well' (Spooner 1980). The same reviewer also argues that 'by and large teachers acquire their skills pragmatically. They learn to vary their approach to meet different types of problem.' Thus, according to this particular headmaster, 'the aim of researchers to focus on the analysis of actual classroom processes should be regarded as unnecessary, and even ludicrous.' The idea that from an analysis of effective practice 'a science of teacher craft' can be constructed is seen as 'ridiculous'. The reviewer concludes that fortunately 'there are rich elements in our heritage which should protect us from the worst excesses of educational research.'

The master teaching model

As a classroom researcher looking to effect changes in classroom practice, I have a certain sympathy for the sentiments which provoked the headteacher's attack on current classroom research. I would, however, disagree with his view that teachers have built-in antennae which inform them when they are at their most effective. Part of his antagonism towards classroom research arises from the attempts of the earlier workers in the field to produce a blueprint for a 'master teacher'. In aptly named teaching laboratories student teachers were wired up for sound to their tutors through a small earpiece. From time to time the student would receive a message to the effect that they should move from category four to category two because they weren't showing enough warmth or interest in the pupils' ideas. The approved behaviours were those previous research showed to be important. The studies mentioned earlier by Bennett, whereby formal teachers were compared with informal ones, 'progress-ives' with 'traditionalists', 'streamers' with 'non-streamers' were, to a certain extent, part of this tradition. It was thought that there was a 'best buy' and if only the practice of the best of these teachers could be itemized then the next generation of students could be fashioned in the same mould.

It is this scenario that Headmaster Spooner, in his review, reacts against so forcibly. Before taking sides in this argument it is well to remember that classroom research in Britain is a relatively new phenomena. At the beginning of the 1970s, only a handful of observation studies had been reported but as more and more classroom observation systems were developed and participant observation studies hinted at the complexity of the classroom process the search for a 'science of teaching' has come to be seen by many researchers as a pious aspiration rather than a realistic goal. Researchers now set themselves more modest objectives. Almost any aspect of practice which is studied will be seen to have both positive and negative effects on some pupils. The researchers main task is to describe and document these effects in ways which teachers can recognize. The teacher then attempts to interpret these findings in the context of his or her own particular classroom so that decisions relating to particular pupils are better informed. Teachers who seek to use the research in this way also then become their own researchers.

Teachers as researchers

As an example, let us consider the attempts of researchers to describe various types of pupil so that teachers having identified such pupils in their own classroom can take action to encourage or prevent certain behaviour. In the past descriptions of pupils have been based on broad personality descriptions – anxious, introverted, conformist – and it is repeatedly claimed that such children do less well in informally organized classrooms. Since teachers are not provided with valid ways of identifying such children there is little they can do to discover why such pupils have difficulty. In contrast, recent descriptions of pupils in studies such as ORACLE (Galton *et al*. 1980) are based on what the pupils actually do in the classroom. For example, there are children who are described as *intermittent workers*. These pupils pay close attention to what the teacher is doing when he or she is elsewhere in the classroom. When the teacher's eye falls upon them they give the appearance of concentrating on their work while as soon as she becomes engaged with another pupil they go back to their private conversations. Overall, it was estimated that such conversations, relating to matter not connected with the work in hand, occupied nearly one day a week. Such practices more often occurred in classrooms where attention was individualized because, in such situations, these pupils were out of the teacher's line of vision more often. Yet such children made approximately the same amount of progress as those who worked on their tasks for longer periods. It would, therefore, appear that these were not pupils who lacked powers of concentration. Rather the strategy of *intermittent working* seemed to be a response to the rather routine activities which were set by the teacher in order to keep the class busy. In mathematics, for example, where such pupil behaviour was very prevalent, it is usual for children to be grouped on different tables according to ability (HMI 1978). Children in the same ability group are then given similar tasks at the same level of difficulty. In the ORACLE study it was observed that if some children finished the work quickly the teacher would be reluctant to set them on to a new topic until the others on the table were also ready. The usual reaction, in such circumstances, was to set the pupils who finished additional examples, either from worksheets or exercise books, until the remaining pupils caught up. Thus the reward for pupils who complete the work quickly and correctly was to be given more work of the same kind. Inevitably some of these children chose to reject the offer and found ways of making the original examples last until it was time to change to a different activity.

A teacher who wishes to look at his or her own classroom practice in the light of such findings has to face questions concerned with the choice of curriculum material, the organization and grouping of children in the light of factors relating to the classroom environment such as open-plan areas, vertical grouping and so on. Whether to accept the pupils' behaviour or try to change it will depend primarily, however, on who the *intermittent workers* in the class are. No teacher would expect children to work continuously. Some teachers may conclude that the balance of four days' work and one day of social interaction is about right, particularly if the children come from deprived home backgrounds. Other teachers, however, may decide that some *intermittent workers* were under-achieving and needed a more demanding mathematical diet.

The perception gap in teaching

Before looking at one or two important classroom issues which might profitably receive closer scrutiny from teachers, it is necessary to refute the view expressed by Spooner, and those like him, that teachers know intuitively when they are effective and when things are going to plan in their classroom. If this is true, how does one explain why throughout the evaluation of various curriculum development projects in the 1960s teachers who supported the aims of the projects consistently failed to practise in accordance with these aims. The evidence from the evaluation of science teaching methods, for example, produced teachers who consistently claimed to observers that they were 'out-performing Nuffield' yet belonging to styles characterized by highly didactic directive teaching (Eggleston *et al.* 1976). Similar findings emerged from the Humanities Project and the follow-up study using the 'RACE Pack' testified to the difficulties teachers had in evaluating their classroom style with respect to particular suggested teaching strategies. Even more dramatic evidence has come from the Ford Teaching Project (Elliott 1976) where teachers whose aim was to encourage inquiry-based learning among the pupils were surprised and even shattered to listen to the tape recordings of their lessons. One teacher told researchers that

> I had no idea how much discussion was dominated by me, how rarely I allowed children to finish their comments, what leading questions I asked, and how much I gave away what I considered to be the right answers.

Similar experiences have come to light in the follow-up study of ORACLE where teachers continually express surprise at the gap between their perception of what is happening during a lesson and the evidence provided from live or recorded observations.

A detailed exploration of some of the transcripts of these lessons shows clearly that this gap between intention and practice arises unconsciously rather than from a deliberate decision by teachers to offer over-optimistic accounts of their teaching. In class discussion, for example, although the teacher may intend that pupils should develop their own ideas about how to organize and carry out a particular topic, he or she will nevertheless have an interest in seeing that the pupils choose lines of inquiry which are likely to be productive. In a school where 'pollution' has been chosen as the theme for topic work the teacher may hope that some of the children will get round to investigating the quality of pond life in various rivers and pools around the neighbourhood. When a pupil does mention the possibility of looking at water, the teacher's face or voice may unconsciously register tacit approval and the pupil's answer will be repeated. At times some pupils' answers will be rephrased to fit in with the particular idea while other suggestions from pupils will be considered as either too difficult or time consuming and will therefore receive less enthusiastic approval or may be ignored in some cases.

While the teacher's perception of this discussion may be such that she will tell the observer that 'the class was getting somewhere' and that 'the children produced some good ideas' the reality for the pupils will be altogether different. Some will remain silent because 'in the end the teacher always lets us know what she wants us to do' and will therefore refuse to take part in the discussion until the teacher has given enough clues by the way she repeats and rephrases certain answers in preference to other responses. Thus for much of the time during class discussion the pupils may be trying to guess what it is the teacher wants of them and if the correct suggestions are slow in coming the teacher is forced to dominate the discussion more and more to give additional clues. In the ORACLE study nearly two-thirds of the class generally remained passive listeners during class discussions of this kind. Many of these were slow-learning pupils whose subsequent progress appeared to indicate that they remained silent while not understanding what was being said (Galton and Simon 1980).

There are many examples in psychology of the perception gap whereby we see the things we expect to see and ignore any information to the contrary. White lettering on dark paper is seen by most people as a series of irregular dark shapes because they normally expect written stimuli to be in heavy type against a light background. In the same way a teacher may see a group of pupils talking and will assume, if they are talking again five minutes later when he looks, that these two episodes are part of a continuous discussion. Yet the ORACLE research shows that most exchanges between pupils rarely last beyond a half minute and when concerned with work generally have to do with routine matters such as borrowing pencils or rubbers or checking each others' answers. It is easy to see how this perception gap might enable a teacher to assert that his classroom is more productive than it might be. A teacher who therefore wishes to evaluate practice may find it difficult to do so on the basis of casual observation, general class response, individual pupil interest, or the work that pupils' produce, as Spooner suggests in his review. It is for this reason that those interested in teacher-based research encourage the use of triangulation procedures which allow the events, as perceived by the teacher, to be checked against those of both pupils, colleagues or outside observers.

Some crucial classroom issues

For this next section I have chosen to highlight three issues which emerged from the analysis of the observation of primary and middle school teaching during the ORACLE project (Observational Research and Classroom Learning Evaluation). This choice should not be taken to imply that ORACLE deserves special attention compared to other classroom research. A feature of ORACLE, however, was that it focused on aspects of a teacher's classroom organization which appear a crucial factor in influencing what pupils and teachers do and say to each other during the course of a lesson. The Plowden conclusion that because 'individual differences between children of the same age are so great that any class, however homogeneous it seems, must always be treated as a body of children needing *individual* and *different* attention' (Plowden 1967, paragraph 75) now appears to be an undisputed article of faith on which much initial and in-service training of teachers is based. In ORACLE, a typical teacher spent eighty percent of the time spent interacting with the class involved with a single pupil. This individualized approach to teaching had important consequences for the curriculum, the quality of the interaction and for the behaviour of the pupils.

ORACLE and the curriculum

The ORACLE study found that, typically, a teacher spent about two-thirds of each day talking and listening to individual pupils. With this pattern of individualized working, considerable management problems arise in finding things for the other children to do when they are not getting the teacher's attention. Although many teachers in our study placed great emphasis on communication skills and creative writing, we found that, in practice, children in the junior school classrooms which we observed spent about eigthy percent of their time working on their own on formal written assignments (punctuation and grammar exercises, comprehension, descriptive story writing, etc.).

In mathematics particularly, where children were organized in ability groups, and some finished an exercise before the others, teachers tended to give additional examples for pupils to do until the others had caught up. This was particularly true when worksheets were used. As a consequence, a large proportion of the child's day was spent working alone on routine, and, at times, fairly undemanding tasks, without any real involvement with either the teacher or other pupils. The HMI (1978) survey reported similar findings. Thus although many schools spend considerable effort in developing curriculum guidelines it would seem that for individual children the curriculum is much more restricted, because of the use of these organizational strategies.

ORACLE and the quality of teacher-pupil contact

The HMI (1978) report called upon teachers to engage in more challenging conversations with pupils. However, the ORACLE study showed that this rarely happened when teachers were engaged with individual children. There simply wasn't enough time for such conversations to take place because there was often a queue of pupils waiting to be seen by the teacher. As a consequence, much of the teacher's time was spent in giving directions about tasks and in providing information. One teacher in the study spoke for many when she said, 'I find that the pressures on my time are such that I have to let the worksheet do my thinking and challenging for me.'

Another aspect of the problem concerned the amount of time available to the teacher for talking with pupils about their work (giving feedback). In general, teachers looked at the mistakes but rarely had time to discuss with the child work which was correct. Indeed many teachers engaged in marking without the child being present or would read the work, put a tick and write 'good' at the end. Yet the ORACLE study showed that talking to children about their work, particularly work which was well done, was one of the major factors influencing pupil progress. It not only gave the teacher an insight into the ways in which children tackled problems but also increased pupil motivation because the child felt the teacher valued what they had done.

ORACLE and pupil behaviour

As a consequence of the individualized pattern of working described previously, children find ways of coping with the problem that some of the work is not sufficiently challenging. This gives rise to the following styles of behaviour.

Intermittent workers are pupils who tend to break up their work pattern by working hard when the teacher is looking at them but chatting to each other when the teacher is engaged elsewhere. The ORACLE study estimates that the time that the children spend on non-work-related conversations, on average, amounts to one day a week. This means that some pupils spend more of the week in this way. The ORACLE study also suggests that some of these pupils are not lacking in powers of concentration. Some of the *intermittent workers* were among the most successful on the various tests which were given to measure the pupils' progress.

Easy riders are a little like *intermittent workers* except that they give the appearance of working for most of the time but take as much time as possible to complete each task. They take twice as long to find their pencils, the page in the book or draw a margin. Some children were observed deliberately breaking their pencil point in order to have a genuine excuse to get up from their seat and walk over to the sharpener.

Attention seekers were pupils who took up more of the teacher's time. Some of these were 'naughty' pupils tending to wander around the class causing a disturbance from time to time. They always seemed to have an explanation when challenged by the teacher so that dealing with them took more than normal time and effort. When certain practical activities take place, for example, in mathematics or science where pupils have to move freely around the classroom collecting data, such children have a perfect excuse for not being in their place. To minimize the possibility of disruption, teachers tended to cut down on such activities and to increase the amount of time when children were working in their place on exercises. This appears to be a further factor resulting in a restricted primary curriculum dominated by workcards, exercises and story writing.

Relating research and practice

If these research findings and their interpretation are to influence classroom practice, their legitimacy must be recognized by teachers themselves. Thus, the prime requirement for classroom research is to establish face validity, in that teachers recognize something of their own practice in the descriptions of classroom behaviour provided. Contrast, for example, the descriptions given here of *intermittent workers* and *easy riders* with those supplied by a recent American research where,

> Children in this cluster score low on prior achievement and other cognitive skills (creativity, inquiry skill, and writing quality). They were relatively lacking in self-confidence, and tended not to value interpersonal equality or to be concerned about the welfare of others. They did not believe that they exerted much environmental control, had little intrinsic motivation, and expressed a value on compliance. They were however, moderate with respect to autonomy, self-direction and achievement motivation. . . . Focusing on the most salient aspects, this cluster represents children who are *low prior achievers who value compliance, lack self-confidence and intrinsic motivation, and feel powerless.* (Solomon and Kendall, 1979 pp.141-142).

To make use of such information the teacher must first make a subjective assessment of the personality characteristics of the pupils, their degree of self-confidence, their compliance and so forth. Recent classroom studies of such assessments suggest, however, that the process can be circular. Teachers often rate pupils as poor students because they are less busy and require more attention than others in the class. Since schools attach great importance to busyness (Jackson 1968) teachers sometime register disapproval if a pupil takes up too much time and prevents them from getting round to see the other children in the class. Thus, when Solomon and Kendall (1979) labelled pupils as unconfident because they reply 'yes' to questions of the kind 'do you feel worried when you have to go out and see the teacher?', they may be merely reflecting the nature of the classroom interaction between the teacher and the pupil and not revealing some underlying personality trait. Because this type of pupil may express a yearning for a more structured class setting where they can remain silent and largely undetected it does not necessarily follow that teachers should adopt such a style in order to overcome the particular child's difficulties. Instead schools could, Jackson suggests, re-evaluate what constitutes 'busyness' and success within an informal setting so that the source of disquiet can be removed.

In contrast descriptions of pupils, based upon objective measures of typical classroom behaviour, should be immediately recognizable by teachers who may take comfort from the fact that the behaviours of certain 'problem' children are not a special feature of their classroom and thus a reflection of their personal failure as teachers. All classrooms in the ORACLE study had the kind of troublesome *attention seeker* described earlier. Teachers prepared to study the effects of different teaching strategies on pupil behaviour can therefore be confident that they are involved in activities which will benefit not only their own classroom practice but that of their fellow-teachers. Hopefully, this awareness of common problems results in less defensive attitudes towards existing practice and a greater preparedness to be innovating.

Sustaining classroom-based research

Certainly teachers involved in in-service work related to the ORACLE study have shown their 'openness' to new ideas but it has not always been possible to sustain these innovative activities within the existing school system. One of the earlier in-service programmes run by Jasman (1979) required groups of teachers to work on a series of classroom-based exercises which were designed to provide more accurate subjective assessments of children's class work in a variety of areas. The skills to be assessed included those skills of independent study which are commonly thought of value for topic or thematic work at primary level. All the teachers in these groups became highly committed to the activity, attending meetings regularly and carrying out work in their own classrooms. They all testified to the usefulness of the enterprise, many claiming that it had made them rethink their approach to teaching.

The following year the attachment of a visiting fellow to the project provided the opportunity to evaluate the success of this scheme (Leith 1981). Leith visited all the teachers involved in Jasman's group. Not one of them was using the new techniques which they had developed during their course. All, however, continued to testify to the usefulness of the experience and claimed that it had changed their approach to teaching.

Two main reasons were given for their failure to continue with the innovation within the school. The first centred on the degree of support which the head was prepared to give for the inactivity. In some schools teachers had simply been diverted from the innovation under pressure of other activities. When they described the experience to the headteacher he or she would reply 'very interesting' but then continue, 'I'd like you to take on the revision of the mathematics guidelines.' Other teachers, however, did get the support from the head and attempted to interest other members in the work. They too found that without the immediate motivation which came from taking part in the original course they were unable to interest their colleagues sufficiently when describing their recent experiences secondhand.

This experience is not an isolated one to judge from general comments or reports from other research projects. For example, the IT-INSET project reported that when the team went back in the following year after the withdrawal of Open University support only one of the participating schools was still attempting to make use of the materials and ideas. Thus, to create the conditions where the results of classroom research are utilized by teachers themselves, it would seem essential to bring about the active participation of the headteacher within the programme and not just obtain his or her general goodwill. To change teaching it is necessary, above all, to change the notion of 'busyness' within a school and the headteacher is the greatest influence at the primary level on deciding what constitutes effective practice.

School-based in-service and the role of the headteacher

An effective headteacher can transform a school with an average staff but it would seem doubtful whether even an enthusiastic staff can change a school without active leadership on the part of a headteacher. In a recent survey for ORACLE over nine hundred teachers were asked whether they would institute changes in their classroom practice, such as increasing the proportion of time given to collaborative group work, without being assured of the support and permission of the headteacher. Nearly seventy percent of the teachers questioned said that they would not initiate such changes unless they had first sought and received the headteacher's approval, whereas when their headteachers were asked the same question the majority replied that changes in classroom practice were the responsibility of the teacher.

Both the ORACLE and HMI (1978) survey hint at a climate in the typical primary school where the effective teacher is thought to be one who runs a busy and efficient classroom with high levels of work involvement by pupils and a degree of quiet orderliness within the room. In the ORACLE study seventy-five percent of the teachers taking part said that they preferred their pupils to be silent for most of the day. Other factors by which teachers can demonstrate their quality include the frequency with which displays are changed and mounted on the wall together with progress on tests of reading, writing and numerical computation. It was noticed by the ORACLE observers during the period of the fieldwork that testing increased from year to year. Some headteachers told us that 'I am prepared to give my staff total responsibility for what they do but I make certain that I test the children regularly to check that the teachers don't go too far.' Teachers in the ORACLE study who use schemes of individualized work appeared to find that the only way to meet these self-imposed standards was to have children writing or doing exercises from worksheets for the greater part of the day. Writing dominates the primary curriculum in the junior school because it provides the pupil with tasks which require little attention from the teacher and thus frees her to deal with children who have genuine difficulties. It appears also to have become the main indicator of an effective school in the eyes of many parents who on open evenings go straight to the child's exercise books in order to see if the teacher has missed any spelling mistakes! Even children have learned to think of work in terms of writing. One teacher described how after a morning's discussion a little girl came to her and said 'when are we going to do some real work Miss?'

A headteacher who wishes to bring about more than a superficial change in the primary school curriculum requires a determined will and strong nerves. Inevitably, there will be moments of crisis when the staff appear less than enthusiastic about the changes or parents are openly critical. This is one of the main reasons why any approach at in-service work connected with changes in classroom practice must involve the headteachers at an active level. This not only secures their agreement to the aims of these courses but provides mutual support and counselling in the times of crisis which are bound to occur. School-based in-service, envisaged in this way, differs radically from the 'teacher-researcher approach' discussed by Rowlands in this volume. There the teachers who attempt to research their own classroom meet regularly to discuss and help evaluate each other's attempts at modifying practice in the light of a number of working hypotheses derived from earlier observations. The importance of establishing, through the headteacher, between-school networks, however, is that it includes the possibility of involving all teachers within the institution and not just those who are 'open' to innovation or who share the ideology of the 'action-research' promoter. In the latter case there is always a danger that the shared openness of the participants in the project leads to a situation where the members become so committed to supporting each other that they close ranks against any individual who questions or disagrees with the ideological framework in which the classroom research is based. Outsiders are particularly at risk, for example, in the debates between teacher-researchers concerning ethical problems which can arise when conducting the investigation.

ORACLE and in-service training

In one other respect the in-service approach used in the ORACLE project differs from that which has been developed by other workers who are directly concerned to raise issues which are important to a particular teacher so that they can be challenged to evaluate their own practice. For example, the Open University Curriculum in Action materials begin by asking teachers to question what the pupils did, what they learned, how valuable it was and so on, whereas in the ORACLE approach, which is more prescriptive but less personal, the teachers begin by discussing issues which generalize the problem. A number of headteachers in the study have argued for this approach in that they feel it is less threatening to individual teachers and therefore produces a less defensive response by the staff. One account of this style of in-service is provided by Johnson (1981) who made use of the Progress in Learning Science film loops (Harlen *et al.* 1977) to get staff to question the value of the mathematics curriculum for the slow-learning pupils. The film loop shows a slow learner, Benny, who writes badly but can draw and describe how a car engine works. Johnson begins by getting the staff to discuss the problems of Benny before zoning down to the more crucial issue of how in their school the Bennys are identified and provided with a suitable curriculum. Crucial in such an approach is the status of the conclusions that the staff may reach during such discussions. In Johnson's case the staff decided that the Bennys in the school were best served by being setted in classes for mathematics. Johnson, as a headteacher, was opposed to setting within his school but rather than override the staff and undermine the new-found degree of co-operation, he allowed this scheme a trial on condition that it was properly evaluated by means of classroom observations. Thus the staff found themselves in a position where to have their ideas implemented required them in turn to display more 'openness' and to subject their practice to the critical scrutiny of others.

In the same way schools participating in the ORACLE project are led by the headteacher to look at video-tapes which illustrate the problems of working with individual children, developing collaborative group work, holding class discussions and so on. The tapes for such sessions are prepared in advance by the research team. The discussions following the viewing of the tapes are guided by the use of certain discussion points already agreed between the headteachers in advance. For example, when examining the issue of individualization and the manner in which the curriculum often becomes constricted by the demands of managing such a classroom environment, three discussion points are listed:

1   How do you keep the other children in the class busy while dealing with the needs of an individual pupil?

2   Individual attention is important, particularly for developing children's skills and comprehension for reading. Some studies show, however, that the attention the child receives at any point of the day is very short although cumulatively it may add up to a sizable proportion of the teacher's time. How can the class be organized to allow a teacher to spend more uninterrupted time with individuals?

3   Under pressure of dealing with large classes, teachers may not realize just how restricted the children's curriculum has become. Assignment cards can show the amount of work done but say nothing about the quality of the various learning experiences. What ways would it be possible to monitor such experiences to see that a broad and balanced curriculum is achieved by each child?

Other groups may look at related problems connected with intermittent working, solitary working and other pupil behaviours. As each group develops its own ideas about how to solve the problems these are tried out in classes, discussed, first on a school basis, and then between the schools taking part in the work. Finally, when the ideas have been refined a programme is developed whereby the schools involved undertake to work alongside a new group of teachers in order to extend and develop the programme. The development of the second phase programmes of in-service, run by teachers for teachers, is important because it helps to concentrate the minds of those involved in the first stage of the programme. It is important however that such follow-up in-service courses are not presented as a group of 'expert' teachers attempting to pass on their knowledge to a number of less experienced colleagues. The stress must always be on the tentative nature of the ideas developed within the group so that the role of the participating teachers in the follow-up in-service course is to act as hypothesis testers and to contribute from their own practical experience ways of refining the programme even further.

Many of the ideas developed here are not new and are similar to those of other workers such as Elliott in the Cambridge Accountability Project. The major difference here is that the in-service work is linked to a large body of systematic classroom research about what goes on in schools and it is this that provides the foundation for making decisions about which problems the groups should look at during the course of the in-service development. If these programmes can succeed and draw in teachers of all levels within a school, as happened in Johnson's case, then the implications for teaching and learning in our schools are much wider than merely introducing new ideas into the profession. The links between an in-service programme and the training of new entrants to the profession should be very clear. If the new generation of teachers are to be encouraged to be critical and to self-evaluate what they do then they will need to be taught and helped to do this by experienced teachers in our schools who are already familiar with the techniques and have the courage to put them into practice.

References

Bennett, N. and McNamara, D. (eds) (1979) *Focus on Teaching*, Longman, London.

Eggleston, J.F., Galton, M.J., Jones, M.E. (1976) *Processes and Products of Science Teaching*, Schools Council Research Studies, Macmillan Education, London.

Elliott, J. (1976) 'Preparing teachers for classroom accountability', *Education for Teaching*, 100, pp.49-71.

Galton, M.J., Simon, B. and Croll, P. (1980) *Inside the Primary Classroom*, Routledge & Kegan Paul, London.

Harlen, W., Darwin, A. and Murphy, M. (1977) *Match and Mismatch: Raising Questions, Leader's Guide*, Oliver & Boyd, Edinburgh.

HMI Survey (1978) Department of Education and Science, *Primary Education in England: A Survey by HM Inspectors of Schools*, HMSO, London.

Jackson, P. (1968) *Life in Classrooms*, Holt, Rinehart, New York.

Jasman, A. (1979) 'Developing teacher-based assessment for primary schools', *British Educational Research Journal*, Vol 5, No 1, pp.125-134.

Johnston, D. (1981) 'Curriculum change and research in a middle school' in Simon, B. and Willcocks, J. (eds) *Research and Practice in the Primary Classroom*, Routledge & Kegan Paul, London.

Leith, S. (1981) 'Project work: an enigma' in Simon, B. and Willcocks, J. (eds) *Research and Practice in the Primary Classroom*, Routledge & Kegan Paul, London.

Plowden Report (1967) *Children and their Primary Schools* (2 vols) Report of the Central Advisory Council for Education in England, HMSO.

Solomon, D. and Kendall, A.J. (1979) *Children in Classrooms – An Investigation of Person Environment Interaction*, Praeger Publishers, New York.

Spooner, R.T. (1980) 'Teacher Craft', a review of *Focus on Teaching*, Bennett, N. and McNamara, D. (eds), *Education*, June 27.

CHAPTER 20

TEACHERS STUDYING CLASSROOM LEARNING

STEPHEN ROWLANDS

Six years ago Michael Armstrong put forward a research proposal which was accepted by Leicestershire LEA to conduct fieldwork in order to gain some understanding of the quality of children's intellectual activity as it is evidenced in the classroom. His plan was to work as both a teacher and a researcher alongside another teacher and thereby gain access to the details of the children's work as it progressed. After considering various schools, he decided to spend most of the year working with me in my class of eight-to nine-year-olds in Sherard Primary School, Melton Mowbray. Although we taught and 'researched' together, he, as 'teacher researcher' took the major responsibility for the research, while I, as 'host' teacher, undertook the day-to-day running of the classroom. The results of this year's work were then written up in the book *Closely Observed Children*.

The purpose of this article is to describe some of the developments that have taken place since then, the ideas behind this type of inquiry and the problems and possibilities it raises.

Taking children's work seriously

After that year together, it became clear that the value of two experienced teachers working together to teach and research into classroom learning did more than increase the 'teacher-researcher's' understanding about the quality of children's thinking – most important though that is. It also provided the 'host' teacher with a unique opportunity to increase his own awareness of the complex relationship between what he does as a teacher, the subject matter being studied and the resulting changes in the children's skills and abilities.

The central idea behind this work – one might say a research assumption which the evidence appeared to support – was that children's work is worth taking seriously not merely as reflecting the fits and starts towards the ultimate goal of adulthood, but as a contribution in its own right. For example, if one considers the painting of a child in the same light as one would that of an adult artist, or their philosophical puzzlings as one would the thoughts of a philosopher, then, granted the limitations in experience which are bound to constrain the child more than the adult, one finds children to be artists, philosophers.

Such a notion may sound somewhat fanciful, romantic and 'unscientific'. How could one set about verifying such a claim? Is it not just another bit of progressivist myth? But such criticism misses the point. This claim is not made as a statement of objective fact, but as describing an approach, a stance from which one might view children's endeavours. Only by doing so was the research able to make sense of children's work and account for its development. Without an approach which conceives of the child as a rational and fully human being, their intellectual activity could only be explained as being the combination of arbitrary behaviour and mechanistic responses to the world in which they learn.

One could pursue the philosophical discussion of this point endlessly – and indeed it has been a central issue of the project as it is now developing in Leicestershire – but it may be more interesting here to look at the implications for adopting such a stance as far as teachers doing research is concerned.

There is a wealth of research evidence which makes it quite clear that few classrooms provide the type of environment which is in any way similar to that in which we would expect the adult writer, mathematician or whatever to function in. Those who have tried (against all the odds recently) to provide an 'informal' or 'open' education have seen the need to provide an intellectual space in which students can reflect, make choices and develop a critical awareness of their own activity. Only when the classroom atmosphere includes an element of this can teachers or researchers begin to 'get into' the child's thinking. Only then can the rational human that is so easily submerged in the hectic teacher-centred institutions that many of us feel constrained to operate be perceived for what he is.

It was in the hope of finding such an informal classroom that Armstrong selected the 'host' for his inquiry and, two years later this 'host' decided to work in the 'teacher-research' role with Chris Harris in his class of nine- to eleven-year-olds at Merton School, Syston. There, with the support of the LEA and Leicester University (who accepted these proposals as appropriate for a research MEd), the aim was to continue the inquiry from where Armstrong had left off. Of particular concern was to gain a clearer understanding of how children can provide a structuring of their own work, how their skill can develop in response to their perceived need for development, or, in general terms, how children are able to exercise a degree of control over their own learning (Rowland 1980). Clearly, the exploration of such matters required a classroom in which the children were encouraged by their teacher to work independently to some extent, to value the contribution which they could make and to use their initiative. It was apparent that children working exclusively on programmed work schedules or on other activities rigidly structured by the teacher were unlikely to provide much valuable evidence about the abilities of children to plan and organize their learning.

At this point what the research was trying to do might be criticized as being merely to select a 'cosy' and informal classroom where the pedagogical assumptions upon which the research was based were liable to be supported, to staff it with two experienced teachers (teaching and researching together) and, hardly surprisingly, the children would be found to be working imaginatively and making responsible use of the autonomy offered them. The necessarily subjective nature of the analysis of the children's work left open to question whether the interpretations and findings would be supported by other teachers working under more normal conditions. In question here was not only the 'truth' of the findings (are children really as depicted?), but their value (if they are, how does it help the teacher?).

'Pure researchers' might only be expected to meet the first of these objections; it would be up to others to decide upon the value of the findings. But for 'teacher-researchers' who were committed teachers it became vital to explore these ideas with other teachers not only as a check to their plausibility, but also to see if others found them useful. Furthermore, it was felt that the process of gathering and analysing work from the classroom had led to an increase of professional awareness. Might not others benefit from such experience?

Sharing ideas

It was in order to meet these criticisms and explore these possibilities that a research consultative group was set up in 1978. This group of about fifteen (now grown to thirty) classroom teachers met together once or twice a term out of a common interest in the work. Initially, the 'teacher-researchers' would present material gathered from the classroom – a child's painting, a series of stories, a description of a scientific investigation, etc. – together with a tentative analysis of it. Invariably these presentations were well received. People seemed to think the analyses were plausible enough. At first such agreement seemed to confirm what was being found out about children. But underneath this comfortable agreement there emerged an increasing unease about these meetings. This unease was rarely articulated and took nearly two years of the group meeting before it came fully to light. It then became apparent that general agreement with the 'teacher-researcher's' interpretations of children's work was not sufficient. Any descriptive account of what happens in a classroom is made in the light of a particular theoretical perspective. This problem of the impossibility of theory-free data is not only applicable to qualitative or descriptive analysis. It applies equally, though this is too rarely recognized, to quantitative data. Even if accurate measurements are made, rather than a form of analysis which relies on judgement, the question still remains, 'Why were those particular measures made?' which, to be answered, must lead back to a statement of theory or value. The particular problem here was that unless the other teachers in the research consultative group themselves contributed material which they had selected, described and analysed, the issues of the theoretical underpinning of our work could not be confronted. Up till that point people had agreed with the 'teacher-researcher's' analyses largely because no alternative was available to the 'reality' of the classroom as viewed from their own theoretical perspective. Had others worked with the same children, they would have seen a different 'reality'. Only then could conflicting 'realities' lead to critical consideration of the theoretical perspectives themselves.

But all this is no simple matter. Like the question of the approach to children's learning, it has been the subject of hours of discussion among those in the group, and is never likely to be finally resolved. However, as far as this research and the professional development of teachers were concerned, it was clear that a more active part needed to be taken by all those involved. And so, in 1980, the local authority agreed to support the enlargement of the scheme. The consultative group was doubled in size, with four full-day meetings per year during term time. Also, support was given for other teachers who might be interested to obtain secondment from their schools so that they could also work for a year alongside a colleague, teaching and researching together. Leicester University has also been supportive in this, offering places at the School of Education so that these studies could be incorporated into research MEd degrees. While the encouragement and practical assistance that the LEA and the university has been able to provide have been vital to the development of the project, it has also been fortunate in being allowed the autonomy to develop according to the wishes of its participants. So far, five teachers have taken up the opportunity to conduct their own 'teacher-research' studies on secondment, and others hope to start next year.

Researching as teachers

Let us now look in a bit more detail at the work that has been done, its methods and its concerns. A central idea behind the project is that teaching itself involves an element of research – finding out how the student is thinking, what is important to him and so on, in order that the teacher might be able to respond appropriately. It is this aspect of teaching which, as 'teacher-researchers', the project seems to capitalize upon. Compared with more traditional forms of research, it does not have a highly developed array of techniques distinct from those strategies which teachers would use. Were 'teacher-researchers' to enter the classroom armed with sophisticated recording devices, the danger is not so much that they would disturb the classroom which they are studying (their presence as teachers does that anyway), but that their relationship with the children as one of their teachers would be threatened. It is upon a relationship of mutual confidence and proximity that the 'teacher-researcher's' access to data depends. In general, the principle has been held that only those research techniques should be used which can be justified on teaching grounds and pose no threat to the open relationships involved. Thus the 'teacher-researcher' is not concerned to 'bug' the 'host's' classroom, but to try to record activity in a way which helps the learning he is studying. For example, it has often been found that audio tapes, photographs and fieldnotes made in the classroom as work progresses become transformed into a valuable teaching aid when played back or read to the students involved. Moreover, their response often increases the value of such records as research material. This access which students have to the 'teacher-researcher's' material and thoughts on their work has been found to be crucial especially with secondary school students who might otherwise become suspicious of his activity.

As far as the work in the classroom goes, the activity of the 'teacher-researcher' would appear to differ little from that of the 'host' teacher. Ideally, both would equally teach together, using the additional human resource in order to follow the children's work in much more detail than would normally be possible. In practice, however, the 'teacher-researcher' takes the responsibility for the research and so it is important that he is able to work with the children in a way which is unpressurized, free as much as possible from the minute-to-minute and external demands that occupy so much of the normal classroom teacher's time. Some have described the 'teacher-researcher' process as being one in which they have been able to work as 'ideal' teachers, interacting with their students whenever this appears to be valuable and for longer stretches of time than is often practicable in the normal way.

For those conducting fieldwork on secondment, this daily teaching is followed in the evening by making detailed notes describing the work they have been involved in and analysing it. The object of this analysis will depend upon the focus of the particular investigation, but it will normally be concerned to uncover the purposes that students have in their work, the ways in which they interpret the various environmental 'inputs' and the ways in which growth in understanding takes place. As has been suggested, any such analysis is bound to be highly inferential and subjective, and so it is most important that these notes are discussed as widely as possible. Normally, the 'host' teacher will take an interest in this, perhaps contributing his own notes or comments on the fieldnotes. The co-ordinator of the project would also read and comment on the notes, and at times university supervisors will also add their comments. In addition, all those on secondment meet once a week to discuss certain fieldnotes in more detail, and there are occasional opportunities to share them with the wider consultative group at its meetings. These opportunities to share the descriptions and interpretations of children's work not only provide the possibility for the 'teacher-researcher' to check his own ideas about the work, but also provide a forum in which further analysis takes place. However full his description of, say, a child's painting or mathematical investigation, it is difficult, on his own, to provide a very full or coherent analysis. It is often other teachers, with perhaps quite different teaching experience, who provide the odd clues, the missing pieces, by which he can grasp a clearer idea of what the particular work signifies. For this reason, the weekly meetings of the seconded teachers and the meetings of the consultative group have not been so much vehicles for disseminating the work (although they do have that function) but have become primarily a forum in which analysis takes place.

This integration of analysis and dissemination is an important characteristic of the project. Traditionally, it is the job of professional researchers to gather the material and conduct the analysis, then produce the 'findings' for the consumer. The consumer (often the teacher in educational research) can then make use of these findings, or ignore them (as is often the case). But in this project, the teacher is also the researcher: the roles of consumer and producer are combined. The teacher is no longer presented with a package to be acted upon or left, but is himself involved in its production. While an individual teacher may not agree with a particular 'teacher-researcher's' interpretation of a child's work, or the implications which are drawn from it, such disagreement becomes a positive and active attitude, one from which he can learn and from which he can contribute his own ideas into the dynamic of analysis. As this suggests, analysis is not a process which ends at some point, or one which is right or wrong in its entirety (though mistakes as well as insights are frequent). So often it has been found that a particular piece of work has been written about and discussed with different groups of teachers, but then, in the light of a further teacher's experience, it becomes seen in a new light. In this way, the valuable resource of each teacher's experience is exploited in the process of research.

A forum for analysis

As suggested earlier, this critical reflection upon the research 'findings' ('concerns' might be a better word here) becomes possible only when the 'audience' are also involved in the research process. Among the group of teachers seconded to do a year's fieldwork, this involvement is absolute. But increasingly, the teachers in the consultative group – who represent a wide range of primary and secondary schools in county and inner city areas – have begun to conduct their own studies. The 'fieldwork' for this is sometimes done within the normal teaching routine. At other times it requires a colleague to stand in and take care of the minute-to-minute needs of the children while the teacher, as 'teacher-researcher', concentrates on some particular aspect of the children's work which is to be studied in more detail. Discussion, and often some form of written documentation, of the work may then lead to a presentation at a meeting of the consultative group. In this way the meetings of the consultative group have changed from being a forum in which the results of full-time 'teacher-researchers' are scrutinized, to one in which the members of the group present and analyse material from their own classrooms. But as these small-scale studies get under way, so the meetings of the consultative group become less central to its members, and the school itself becomes the place where discussion and analysis takes place. A teacher once described the consultative group meetings as providing what the ordinary staff room should provide – an opportunity and an atmosphere in which teachers can seriously discuss the work of their students. Many would agree that staff rooms do not at present provide this opportunity (if they ever did), and that increasing pressure in terms of teacher/pupil ratios and curriculum demands make it less likely that they will do so. But if more teachers can begin to conduct their own small studies, based upon the needs of their own classrooms as they see them, then perhaps this trend could be reversed. As this begins to happen – and it is only just beginning – then the consultative group will change again from being a centre in which research ideas are generated, to a group which provides a supportive structure and meeting point for a wide variety of school-based research projects. This is perhaps the final objective of the project: to stimulate and support school environments in which educational research – that is, the serious and disciplined study of learning and teaching – can be generated to meet the needs of the schools. Only then will the artificial distinction which has been made between 'researcher' and 'teacher' be eliminated with the result that educational research becomes meaningful to teachers and its results affect their practice.

Focus on learning

So far little has been said about the content of the studies. Since it has been important that teachers pursue their own interests, the topics cover a wide area. One study attempts to describe the ways in which adolescent students, in writing from their own personal experience, seek at once to gain a greater sense of their own identity and at the same time to explore the broader social world. In another, a tentative model is suggested for describing the pre-scientific activity of young children in a primary school. Yet another examines in detail the ways in which scientific concepts are developed both through the science curriculum and through work in the humanities. Small-scale studies conducted by classroom teachers in the consultative group cover such areas as the ways in which the social relationships of one child in a primary classroom effect the quality of her learning; the use that a group of young children make of a tape recorder as a medium for composing their own stories. One might wonder how it is possible to achieve a sense of unity with such a decentralized and wide-ranging collection of studies.

Part of the answer to this lies in the research approach that is adopted, that is, to view the child's activity and work as the starting point of the investigations, rather than the teacher's teaching. I know it would be facile to view teaching and learning as separate phenomena, as though one can exist independently of the other. However, almost all classroom research has focused on the teacher's teaching rather than the child's learning. It is often assumed that learning follows directly from teaching. Studies that have sought to correlate the pupil's achievements with the teacher's performance (e.g., ORACLE and Bennett 1976) invariably use forms of standardized testing to measure the former – tests whose value is suspected by many teachers and which can reveal little of the quality, rather than the quantity, of what is learned. Even the growing trend towards 'action-research' (The Ford Teaching Project, The Schools Council Action Research Network), which has many similarities with this project – in particular the way in which the teacher has the role of researcher – normally sees the teacher as the main subject of study whose performance is to be improved through his own research. The risk that such studies run is that, without sufficient analysis of the learning process itself through close examination of the children's work, unjustifiable assumptions are made concerning the relationship between the teacher's behaviour and the child's learning. On the other hand the studies of this project, with its focus upon the children's work, run the risk of taking insufficient account of the teacher's influence in generating learning. There has been an awareness of this danger, and much time in the consultative group meetings is now spent trying to articulate the complex relationship between how the teacher teaches and the learner learns. The group is in fact approaching a view in which learning and teaching are seen as inseparable activities. The view that knowledge is not a commodity which is 'passed on' from teacher to learner – and is thus not readily quantifiable – leads to an understanding of learning as some kind of active construction or reconstruction which both the teacher and learner are engaged in each time they together confront 'a community of subject matter which extends beyond the circle of their intimacy' (Hawkins 1974). Perhaps it is the significance attached to the child's contribution to this 'community of subject matter' which leads the project to adopt such a 'constructive' – rather than imitative – view of learning, one according to which child learning is, in principle, no different from adult learning.

Towards a shared language

From what has been said, it should be clear that the consultative group, in its meetings, is largely concerned to articulate a framework which underlies its studies of children's work. But its attempts to develop a rationale for 'the nature of learning', 'the research methodology', 'the purpose of education', and other such grand issues which must underlie any research endeavour – and they must – inevitably prove to be frought with difficulties.

The first difficulty is evident in any discussion of an abstract and highly ideological or value-laden nature. The participants soon feel that they are, yet again, tackling the same old unresolved question and getting no further with it. Alternatively, the question is not tackled because the terms of the discussion cannot be agreed upon – hours are spent discussing these terms and one ends up in a semantic bog. This problem is most evident when the participants do not share central beliefs and values. But matters can be just as bad when they do share (or think they share) such understanding, for then the assumptions upon which they are working may not be brought into the open to be challenged. The consultative group has found this type of difficulty to be most evident when the starting point for discussion is a theoretical issue – for example, 'What is the value of student autonomy in the classroom?' It seems that, to some extent, the problem can be overcome if the theoretical issue is no longer seen as the starting point, but actual material from the classroom (work samples, descriptions, etc.) is seen as the focus of the debate. While consideration of such material and its analysis inevitably leads to the discussion of theoretical concerns, teachers at least have the concrete material before them to refer to in order to clarify and illustrate the meanings that develop in the course of the discussion. Looked at in this way, presentations of classroom material may be seen not so much as providing evidence to support a particular theory about learning or teaching, but as a reference point from which a variety of theoretical perspectives might be developed. It is, I think, by this means that teachers can increase their level of awareness; by using specific instances of learning in order to develop a greater articulation of the theoretical ideas that underlie their practice. They thereby bring to a conscious level what had been unconsciously assumed, transforming intuition (so often held to be the chief resource of the 'good' teacher) into deliberation which is thus open to change.

The second difficulty confronted when it comes to sharing teaching and research experience concerns the extent to which values are shared between teachers. On the one hand the project would not want to develop a doctrine which would necessarily exclude many teachers. On the other, too wide a divergence would make it impossible for communication and a sharing of understanding to take place. What has been attempted is to develop a language for talking about classroom experience, a language rooted in the activity of the child, a language which permits the individual teacher to extend his own ideas rather than uncritically to take on board or reject the ideas of others. Careful observation of children at work can provide the start to developing such a language. But just as we can never absolutely share experience, so we can never absolutely share a language. This is the problem teachers will always face as they learn together. It is also the problem they and their students confront in their classrooms as they strive to share experience of the world.

References

Armstrong, M. (1981) *Closely Observed Children*, Writers and Readers, London.

Bennett, N. (1976) *Teaching Styles and Pupil Progress*, Open Books, London.

East Anglia, University of Centre for Applied Research in Education (1975), Ford Teaching Project.

Elliot, J. (1981) *Action Research: A Framework for Self-Evaluation in Schools*, Working Paper No. 1 of the Schools Council Programme 2 'Teacher-Pupil Interaction and the Quality of Learning' Project.

Galton, M., Simon, B. (1980) *Inside the Primary Classroom*, and *Progress and Performance in the Primary Classroom*, Vols 1 and 2 of the Observational Research and Classroom Learning Evaluation project, Routledge & Kegan Paul,

Hawkins, D. (1974) *The Informed Vision: Essays on Learning and Human Nature*, Agathon Press, New York.

Rowland, S. (1980) *Enquiry Into Classroom Learning*, unpublished MEd thesis, Leicester University.

Further examples of the qualitative analysis of children's work may be found in:

Rowland, S. (1979) 'Ability matching: a critique' in *Forum for the Discussion of New Trends in Education*, Vol 21, No 3, p. 82.

Rowland, S. (1981) 'How to intervene: clues from the work of a ten year old', *Forum*, Vol 23, No 2, p. 33.

Rowland, S. (1982) 'Progressive education: a reformulation from close observation of children, in Richards, C. (ed) *New Directions in Primary Education*, Falmer Press, London.

CHAPTER 21

CLASSROOM AND CURRICULUM RESEARCH: SOME NATIONAL AND INTERNATIONAL EXAMPLES

JOHN WILLIAMSON

Introduction

While most of the chapters in this section were delivered as papers at the 1982 ASC Conference, the present chapter had its genesis in the plenary session of that meeting. There it was suggested that an attempt should be made to draw together some of the broader threads that had been raised at the conference and to do so in such a way that comparisons with issues in a similar area of research or development which were being conducted and reported in the United States and Australia were possible.

The intention of this chapter is not, of course, to review all of the issues canvassed at the 1982 ASC Conference, nor is it designed to serve as a compendium of classroom or curriculum research. The aim is much narrower and more idiosyncratic than this. Indeed, it seeks only to select from these broader fields a few of the recent research or development activities which seem to the author as indicative of a worthwhile area of research and development. Readers will undoubtedly recognize in such an attempt a more than usual degree of 'bias' in selection and presentation, especially when these pieces of research and/or development are taken from the United Kingdom, Australia and the United States and dealt with so briefly and generally. However, the intention is to highlight certain issues and developments and not review the field.

In the chapter there are four sections. The first three sections report briefly and descriptively several issues that have been the focus of research and development work in various countries. The first section is concerned with the United Kingdom work and several of the issues which were raised at the plenary session are mentioned before two are discussed in greater detail. The second and third sections extend the issues to a consideration of North American and Australian research in the same or similar areas. The final section presents an overview and summary of these research and development activities which have been outlined.

Research in the United Kingdom

Introduction

In the plenary session at the ASC Conference a panel chaired by John Eggleston, and comprising Michael Armstrong, Neville Bennett, John Elliott and Maurice Galton, was invited to answer questions submitted by conference participants. As expected, there was a plethora of questions presented to the panel. Also, not unexpectedly, the questions reflected the educational uncertainty of the 1980s, as they extended over a large number of issues, from teacher morale and teacher 'burnout', through instructional strategies, to action-research and accountability. In the remainder of this section, two issues have been chosen for consideration. They were chosen on the basis that they present a positive aspect of research by showing teachers and schools in a constructive approach to the present educational context, and they also present research which is breaking new ground.

Teacher as researcher: No longer a methodological issue

In many recent discussions of methodological issues in classroom and curriculum research, there has been a timely recognition that no single research methodology is likely to provide answers to all of the questions that might be asked in these contexts. The debate over methodology when it is expressed merely in terms of 'qualitative' versus 'quantitative' has been shown to be overly simplistic. It is now accepted by many that the nature of the research problem and the research questions that relate to that problem also must be considered as contributing factors to the choice of methodology. In brief, it is now widely agreed that methodological pluralism is in fact vital to examining a research question appropriately. As Patton (1978) suggested: 'If we only want to know the number of words a child can spell or the frequency of interaction between children of different races in designated schools, then statistical procedures are appropriate. However, if we want to understand the relevance of the words to that child's life situation, or the meaning of interracial interactions, then some form of qualitative methodology . . . may well be more appropriate' (pp. 213-214).

The 1982 conference reflected the tempo of the times. The methodological issues that were debated were no longer at the paradigm level (Kuhn 1972). The participants focused instead on the use of an action-research approach to investigate some of the particular needs and problems in the classroom.

Many participants saw the key task as one of helping teachers to develop a professional role as researcher so that the teachers could conduct programmatic research in their own classrooms. This approach to research in the classroom has undoubtedly proved popular with teachers. In seeking to understand why it has proved so popular, Corey (1954) pointed to the difficulties that would arise when the outside expert, the professional investigator, began to study the problem and to propose solutions which the practitioner is then expected to implement. He commented, as a practitioner, 'In the first place, the professional investigator can never study our problems in any strict sense. They are unique to the situations in which we are working, and we ourselves are part of the problem. A second limitation is that, even when the recommendations make sense to us as we read them, we have great difficulty getting these recommendations into our behaviour patterns' (p.376).

It is not quite thirty years since Corey wrote his article but in that time there have been attempts to deal with the problems he outlined. Recently Michael Armstrong in *Closely Observed Children: the diary of a primary classroom* presented an excellent account of action research which focused upon classroom life and the development of children's understanding.

Armstrong wished to study the process of learning of children but aimed to do this in such a way that the findings reflected the relationship between observation, analysis and teaching. The integration of these three elements is problematic, but for Armstrong, 'it seemed to me that the study of intellectual growth and its enabling conditions demanded a more intimate relationship between the activities of teaching and observation than has been common in educational research' (p.3). Armstrong was clearly taking the view of a practising teacher when he argued the need for an 'authentic' view of the classroom world. On this matter he quoted

David Hawkins: 'A Lorenz swims with his goslings, a Schiller lives with mountain gorillas, ethnologists live the life of the peoples they would study. To expect more from the ethological study of young children, for a lesser effort, seems naïve indeed. The fine scale of such observations is very clearly not the day or the week. The transitions and transformations of intellectual development may be rapid indeed, but they are statistically rare and must be observed in context to be given significance' (p.4). Hence, to follow his argument, it can *only* be through actually teaching the children that a researcher can gain any real insight into the intellectual growth of children. The dilemma for the teacher, of course, is how to cope with a full teaching load and at the same time maintain the detachment of an observer while recording the intellectual experiences of the pupils. The solution adopted by Armstrong was to work in conjunction with another teacher in one classroom. This approach allowed for a shared respon- sibility for the teaching and curriculum material and freed enough time for Armstrong to have periods of quite extraordinarily sustained observation.

Armstrong's work provided many examples of the practice-based and action-orientated focus advocated by teacher-researchers. Consider too the following examples. In his notes as an observer, Armstrong drew attention to the apparent discrepancy between the children's ability to express themselves in conversation and their poor attempts to capture this liveliness in their writing. He commented: 'Writing is not like telling it anyway, especially not if you're at the beginning of learning to write' and then posed himself the question: 'How . . . can you give children a sense of something worth saying in writing, or, more than that, of something worth saying that can *only* be said in writing?' Armstrong then moved through several stages of 'progressive focusing' until he had stripped side-issues away and revealed the essence of the problem. As is often the case, the problem lay with the teacher (Armstrong), who misunderstood the children's intentions and their achievements. It was after a series of classroom incidents and examples of children's work that Armstrong asserted, '. . . it makes good sense to interpret the thought and action of eight-year-old children – their early writing, art and mathematics – as an appropriation of knowledge' (p.131). It is the outcome of these successive appropriations of knowledge, over long periods of time, that he described as intellectual growth. The intensity of effort as a child grappled with his/her own intellectual constraints and the manner by which this dynamic experience served as the precursor to new levels of mastery and skill was evidenced to Armstrong in his teacher-research role. And it is perhaps only through such a rich methodological approach that we can gain insights into such aspects of classroom life.

Certainly the more quantative approach of time-on-task serves only to indicate the opportunity to learn, it provides no information about the quality of the learning. In his classroom, Armstrong looked beyond the concern for 'busyness' on the part of children (as shown by the orderly flow of activity and the covering of a particular amount of content), and focused on the growth of a pupil's understanding. The emphasis was upon comprehension and reasoning, rather than on the learning and recall of information.

Accountability: To be or not to be is no longer the question

The issue of 'accountability' in the schools of the United Kingdom is one that has generated much interest. At the ASC Conference the concerns surrounding 'accountability' and the 'accountability movement' focused upon the role of external authorities in an evaluation of the educational process or system. There was, however, no debate at the conference on the question whether or not schools should be accountable to the wider community. Unfortunately, the issue was dichotomized into 'internal' and 'external' accountability with the former being seen as 'good' and the latter 'bad'. As is often the case in education, however, a simple dichotomy may not be the most appropriate formulation. The presence of an external monitoring authority may, in fact, achieve positive changes in the educational process and practices.

A number of simple examples to support this view can readily be found in the Assessment Performance Unit (APU) report. If the APU, for example, decreed that in science the skills of observation were to be assessed, and the APU also required that pupils must demonstrate observation in a variety of contexts, then the classroom teachers would have to ensure that pupils could conduct observations. Or if junior school science assessment were only concerned with student recall of presented information, that is, the most basic form of cognitive skill, then an external monitoring authority that established assessment procedures which involved other higher cognitive abilities might influence teachers to address other cognitive skills. In these simple illustrations, what might be seen as 'teaching to the text', could in fact promote a change in the school system that would be seen as desirable. The argument here is not to suggest that an externally developed assessment procedure is the panacea. Rather, it is presented to indicate that the simple dichotomy of 'internal' or 'external', when viewed as 'good' and 'bad' respectively, is too simplistic to be useful.

One project which has moved the discussion of accountability away from a reflexive negative reaction into a consideration of issues is that of John Elliott and his colleagues on the Cambridge Accountability Project (CAP). Elliott *et al.* have provided much valuable information about the processes which teachers, schools and the local community could develop and use to conduct a self-evaluation. In the context of the new Education Act which makes it obligatory for local authorities to publish the examination results of their secondary schools in such a way as to allow comparisons to be made between schools Elliott wrote, '. . . the evidence we have gathered of parental opinion in CAP schools suggests that a considerable number of parents value the *human qualities* of schools above their technological efficiency in maximizing examination success' (p.40). This parental view, with its emphasis upon interpersonal relationships, was developed by Elliott in his initial document. This was circulated to LEAs and outlined the research approach the project team would be adopting. Elliott contrasted this humanistic view which emphasized interpersonal relationships with another that would put emphasis largely upon product criteria: 'Currently there appear to be two main views of school accountability representing different ideas about how schooling might be improved. One view is that improvement comes with greater public control over decisions about school organization, teaching methods and the curriculum. The other view is that schooling is more rapidly improved when the school retains control over decisions but becomes more responsive to those whose interests are affected by those decisions' (p.xiii).

In the same document he indicates that the project team would focus on this latter 'responsive-school' approach rather than what might be termed the 'bureaucratic-school' approach. In the study, many parents indicated that they wished to see a balance struck between academic results and the child's satisfactory personal and social development. One consequence of this desire would be some confounding of attempts to use examination results as a way of moving schools into line with the 'productivity ethic'.

What then did a school conducting its own accountability exercise look like? One example described a comprehensive upper school which conducted a self-evaluation with assistance from the local advisory team. The main aim was to examine the work and organization of the subject departments. There was joint observation and consultation between each head of subject department and local adviser with the outcome statement being written jointly by these two. In turn the separate statements and reports on other aspects of the school, e.g., the pastoral system, were all drawn together in a report which was written jointly by the headmaster and heads of departments.

In the example which is described, several features of the evaluation should be noted: the school proposed the self-audit, teachers examined their own practice in a team atmosphere, and the evaluation was viewed as a process, rather than as an event. One important nurturant effect that Elliott *et al.* demonstrated was that when the school began a self-evaluation there was a dialogue between the members of the school and its local community which, in turn, was reflected in the nature and quality of the relationships.

Related research in North America

Introduction

At the conference, in both formal and informal discussions, a number of issues and themes constantly arose. As was appropriate at a major conference concerned with the study of curriculum, one recurring topic was the problematic nature of curriculum implementation. The concern was often voiced in terms of the difficulties experienced in having curricula adopted by schools or teachers.

One line of research from the United States that has also attempted to grapple with this issue and a consideration of which might prove useful in the British context is the study of both the 'change process' and also the tactics involved in the successful 'take-up' of curricula. The most comprehensive research in this area has been conducted by Gene Hall and his associates, of the University of Texas at Austin.

Another theme that emerged in conference discussion concerned the choice of teachers' instructional strategies. While statements from such sources as the Black Papers and several politicians would lead one still to believe that there is one global and 'right' way of teaching, even a slight familiarity with recent research in the United Kingdom indicates that this is far from being the case. A similar conclusion must be drawn from research emerging from the United States. The work of Bruce Joyce, for example, has indicated that there is no overall superiority that can be claimed for any one of a number of teaching strategies. Thus, the task of the teacher is not to adopt any single teaching strategy, as a general panacea, but rather to choose suitable strategies on the basis of variations in subject matter, pupil characteristics and teaching objectives.

Each of these issues, the change process and teaching strategies, will be examined below to give some indication of the nature and direction of this research.

The change process: The forgotten dimension in evaluation studies

In the field of evaluation studies, the statement that 'there were no significant differences between the extremes of curriculum x or y or project x or y' is seemingly all too common. For many in the lay public it provides yet another instance for them to wonder why such curricula were developed in the first place, especially when the exercise was mounted at a cost of many thousands (or millions) of pounds or dollars and it still had no measurable impact. Gene Hall and his colleagues have studied the problems of implementation and they argue that on many occasions this 'no difference' conclusion arises because the change process itself has been ignored in the project evaluation. Hall and his colleagues (1975, 1977, 1979) have worked extensively in an attempt to understand this change process. The model that these authors propose is the Concerns Based Adoption Model (CBAM).

The CBAM is predicated on five assumptions. In brief outline, these are, firstly, that change is viewed as a process, rather than a particular event or decision. For example, the passage of legislation to implement a curriculum does not guarantee change. Secondly, it is the individual who decides to change even though the decision may be made within a group context. Thirdly, the individual's feelings, purposes and perceptions must be examined. Fourthly, changes in the individual's feelings about the innovation and his skill in using the innovation are necessarily viewed in a developmental framework. Fifthly, for an innovation to be adopted some individual or group of individuals must assume the role of 'change facilitator'. The change facilitator role is crucial as it is the encumbent of this role who must assist those involved in the innovation to become more confident and competent in their use of the innovation. (The concept Stages of Concern (SoC) is used to describe the changes in the individual's feelings about his work, and Levels of Use (LoU) is the term used to describe the individual's skill in using the innovation.)

Hall *et al.* have used the earlier research of Fuller (1969) as the basis for their operational description of Stages of Concern. The three-stage taxonomy outlined by Fuller has been extended to seven stages by Hall *et al.* and they are shown in Figure 21.1.

Figure 21.1   Stages of Concern

Fuller	Hall *et al.*	
I m p a	6 Refocusing	– User seeks alternatives to innovation which would save time/materials, etc. User wishes to maximize impact upon clients/students.
c	5 Collaboration	– User concerned to tie innovation into colleague's work to increase impact upon clients/students.
t	4 Consequence	– User concerned about organization and problems involved in implementation.
T a s k	3 Management	– User concerned about organization and problems involved in implementation.
S e	2 Personal	– User examining own role and determining how it would change if used innovation; what commitments are required.
l	1 Information	– User wishes to learn more of the general nature of the innovation. Requests details of how to use, etc.
f	0 Awareness	– User unaware of innovation. Expresses no concern about it.

It is apparent that the more unusual the innovation then the more supportive needs to be the context in which it is introduced. We know from classroom observation, for instance, that teachers, when unsure of academic content, or when the content is more difficult, move much more slowly over the material. To be effective, the support should not be just hierarchically arranged from headmaster-(down to)-teachers-(down to)-parents, but also laterally, in a collegial model, from teacher-to-teacher. For success in adoption of the innovation there needs to be a maximum opportunity for communication between interested groups, and the establishment of a 'support network', so that encouragement or assistance can be provided.

Figure 21.2   Levels of Use of the Innovation

Levels of Use		Definitions of Use
O.	Non-Use	User has little or no knowledge of innovation and is not becoming involved with it.
I.	Orientation	User is aware of the innovation and is exploring its demands upon user and user system.
II.	Preparation	User preparing for first use of the innovation.
III.	Mechanical Use	User concerned with short-term day-to-day use of the innovation. Often a disjointed and superficial use.
IV.A	Routine	Ongoing use with little preparation.
IV.B	Refinement	User varies use of the innovation to meet needs of clients/students.
V.	Integration	User combines own use of innovation with colleague's activities.
VI.	Renewal	User seeks to increase impact upon clients/students through major modifications of innovation.

The degree to which the innovation is used by the individual is termed the Level of Use (LoU). Eight levels of use have been operationally defined. The research to date indicates that most beginning users of an innovation are engaged in a mechanical Level of Use of the innovation (i.e., LoU III). Figure 21.2 shows the Level of Use of the Innovation.

It is apparent from Figure 21.2 that the 'isolation' – both psychologically and physically – of the individual teacher in his/her own classroom is likely to be the first barrier which must be overcome. The change facilitator should be concerned with the teacher's worries about the innovation and recognize that full implementation of the innovation will not be achieved immediately.

It is well known from the literature that innovations are unlikely to be adopted in their 'pristine' state. In practice, innovations are modified by the user for personal preference or the setting where they will be used. These modifications of the intended innovations are referred to as 'Innovation Configurations'. Hall *et al.* have devised analytical tools to describe these characteristic changes with the aim of distinguishing between what they see as an acceptable variation in the innovation from an unacceptable one. Such analytical tools involve interviews with both the developer and the facilitator, followed by interviews with the users and observation while they employ the innovation. These activities form the basis for a check-list for each user and the check-list is used to determine dominant configurations.

With the CBAM there are several dimensions that need to be borne in mind. Firstly, there are clearly policy matters; that is, the passage of a law does not automatically mean that change will occur. Secondly, change is viewed as a process and there is seen to be a significant gap between what policy-makers espouse and what teachers practice. Finally, there is the need to have someone at the 'grassroots' who is willing to fulfil the role of facilitator for the innovation.

Teaching Strategies: It is the way that you do it

The notion that there are different teaching 'styles' has a ready appeal to many people. It can be supported by casual observation if we enter a classroom and observe the teacher at work. After a while, we begin to 'see' a general mode of teacher behaviour and sense the resulting classroom climate. This general sense of how the teacher approaches classroom tasks we can call the teaching style. A number of authors have used this descriptive approach. Reissman (1967), for example, has classfied eight different teaching styles which include those he has labelled Maverick,

Boomer, Coach and Entertainer. In a similarly descriptive vein, Thelen (1954) coined the terms, Town Meeting, Boss-Employee Method, Guided-tour, and so on to indicate various styles. In these descriptive classifications one is struck mostly by the richness of the imagery in the terms used. However, as a basis for research, they leave a great deal to be desired. Nevertheless, recent British researchers (for example, Galton *et al.* 1980) have also used the idea of teaching 'styles' and they have tried to ground their descriptions in a more systematic view of the classroom. It would seem, however, that the notion of teaching style, because it has subsumed so many different elements of the classroom life, may have become unworkable as a research tool. Some researchers believe, therefore, that teaching strategy is more appropriate. In broad terms, a teaching strategy is a recurrent pattern of teacher behaviour, which is appropriate to a number of subjects in the curriculum. It is not unique to one teacher and aims at attaining a particular goal. Bruce Joyce has done much useful work in this area of teaching strategies. He argues that competence in teaching '. . . stems from the capacity to reach out to different children and to create a rich and multidimensional environment for them' (1980, p.xxiii). Joyce has examined much of the literature on teaching and he has rejected the idea that there can be 'one right way' of teaching which achieves the many objectives that teachers can set for their students. From the more than eighty teaching approaches that have been identified by Joyce, he has focused attention upon twenty of them which he described in his book *Models of Teaching*.

These models of teaching have been further categorized into four main groups or families of models: (1) information processing models; (2) personal models; (3) social interaction models; and (4) behavioural models. These four models represent distinct orientations toward teaching and views of how best to assist students' learning. For each model Joyce has provided its rationale, a series of steps which outline the behaviour to be taken by the teacher and the students, and a description of the required conditions for the model to be implemented. The orientation of two of the models and some examples of theorists who contribute to these particular models are provided below.

Information Processing Models (See Table I.)

These models are concerned with the ways students can improve their ability to master information.

Table 21.1   Information Processing Models

Model	Major Theorist	Objectives or Goal
Advanced Organizer Model	David Ausubel	To increase the efficiency of information-processing capacities and to absorb and relate bodies of knowledge.
Concept Attainment	Jerome Bruner	To develop inductive reasoning and concept development and analysis.
Cognitive Growth	Jean Piaget	To increase general intellectual development, especially logical reasoning.

Behavioural models (see table 21.2).

These models focus on a change in the overt behaviour of the individual, rather than on the covert behaviour.

Table 21.2   Behavioural Models

Model	Major Theorist	Objectives or Goal
Direct Training Contingency Management	Robert Gagne B.F. Skinner	To acquire a pattern of behaviour skills To acquire facts, concepts or skills.
Self-Control	B.F. Skinner	To acquire social behaviour and/or skills.

It is possible to discern three assumptions that form the basis of Joyce's theorizing: (i) that there are many different but valid approaches to teaching and learning; (ii) that teaching strategies make a difference to what is learned and how well it is learned; and (iii) that students respond differently to each different teaching strategy.

For Joyce, 'the entire approach rests on the thesis that we can learn to select and blend models of teaching in such a way as to increase different types of learning. Various models can produce more of certain kinds of learning, and blends or combinations can increase the probability of increasing learning even more' (p.11).

To implement a programme of teaching strategies in classrooms, what appears to be needed is a three-stage process. Firstly, teachers must be trained in the use and suitable selection of a number of teaching strategies. Secondly, someone skilled in the various teaching strategies should visit the teachers in their classrooms, say once a week, and observe them while they implemented the strategies. Then, there would be a post-lesson conference between the observer and the teacher to discuss the application of a particular teaching strategy and provide feedback on the congruence between the model which was intended to be used and its implementation. Finally, school principals should be trained in clinical supervision so that they could provide feedback on the use of the teaching strategy and make suggestions for how its use might be improved.

Relevant research in Australia

Introduction

The circumstances in which education presently finds itself were discussed long and often at the conference. For many participants one cause of the lack of public support for education was the development of a theory-practice gap, especially in teacher preparation courses. Consequently, when student teachers went into schools they were unable to implement the knowledge or skills they had learned in their preparation courses. In addition, many conference participants expressed the view that they were unable to assist their own students more in the school situation because they did not have the skills to do so, for example, to observe a lesson and provide feedback on it. The importance of these aspects of teacher preparation courses has been reiterated in recent reviews of Australian teacher education. An extensive investigation of the practicum conducted by Cliff Turney and his colleagues at the University of Sydney may provide some answers to the questions that were asked at the conference and as such it would repay consideration in the United Kingdom context.

In Australia, the movement into a more school-based curriculum development approach has meant that calls for greater accountability have become more frequent. A project directed by Phil Hughes and Neil Russell, which was designed to support evaluation by teachers within a school-based curriculum development and decision-making context, has provided ideas on the development of materials and so on that would be useful for many teachers.

In 1981 the Review of Commonwealth Functions – the so-called 'Razor Gang' – recommended that the two major education funding sources, the Curriculum Development Centre (CDC) and the Educational Research and Development Committee (ERDC), should be abolished or that their funding arrangements should be renegotiated. Subsequently, however, both the CDC and the ERDC were abolished. The two examples discussed below are excellent testimonials to both the CDC and the ERDC.

The practicum: Improve the initial practice to improve the profession

In the past two or three years in Australia, there have been published, not only a national report of the Inquiry into Teacher Education (Auchmuty 1980) but at least three state reports into teacher education (Asche 1980, Victoria; Corey 1980, New South Wales; Vickery 1980, Western Australia). In these reports there arises a consistent theme regardless of title; i.e., whether it is called the practicum, field experience or practice teaching, such a practical component is regarded as being of major importance in teacher preparation courses. As the reports of the various committees maintain, it is in this section of student teachers' professional development that they have a chance to apply much of the theory propounded in their courses. Students also attest to its importance. And yet, what is known of the practicum?

In Australia, Turney *et al.* have recently concluded an investigation into the practicum and its supervision. Turney (1980) observed that since the 1960s there has been a gradually increasing focus upon the centrality of the practicum. He asserted, '. . . there has been increasing recognition of the need to relate the theoretical aspects of teacher preparation to the practical experience of students. The purely academic study of the foundations of education has slowly begun to give way to the study of teaching – the study of what teachers do in classroom, school and community' (p.xii).

Certainly in the various reports there has been not only a reaffirmation of the importance of the practicum, but there have also been suggestions made as to how the practicum might be improved. In broad terms, these latter suggestions cover the following needs: (i) to develop more collaboration between the teacher education institutions and the schools in matters of planning, operating and evaluating the practicum, (ii) to bridge the so-called theory/practice gap, (iii) to design an ordered pattern of practical experience that reflects the developmental experience of the student teacher, and (iv) to provide a training programme for supervising teachers in the schools.

But is the job being well done, and will a few minor modifications result in an excellent series of supervised practical experiences? Consider the first of the suggestions relating to the need for more collaboration between the individuals and the institutions involved in the practicum and recall Eggleston's (1974) observation:

> Allegedly, the student arrives in the school full of college-inspired faith in the individual goodness and creativity of children with fanciful lesson plans suggested by lecturers who have not taught for many years, devoid of knowledge of how to control the turbulent and restive oversized classes and supervised by an unknown tutor. In such circumstances the student is in a double bind. Not only is his faith in the credibility of the college shattered by the school staff, he is also overwhelmed by their enthusiasm to help him 'really get to know the job'. Teaching practice becomes an undercover initiation into an alternative style of teaching unrelated to the work of the college. Problems may indeed arise when the college assessment takes place, but the school staff are loyal to their student and conspire with him to put on the sort of show that can be relied upon to satisfy the college. (p.97)

In such a situation, even if only partially true, the need for more collaboration and agreement on the objectives of the practicum, the role of co-operating teachers and so on, is apparent.

Obviously, part of the difficulty lies in the gap between what is intended and what is implemented in the practicum, and here part of the responsibility for the problem resides in the teacher education institutions. In this connection, Conant's (1963) comments, although referring to the situation in America just on twenty years ago, seem relevant in Australia now:

> Student teaching is one of the most casually conducted phases of the enterprise [teacher preparation]. Senior professors rarely want to fool with it; junior professors too often regard the supervision of teachers as a necessary evil to be endured only until promotion releases them from it. Too often, student teachers are turned over to co-operating teachers in the schools who are only vaguely aware of the program objectives (if any) and of what is expected of them by the college or university. (p.63)

Also, part of the difficulty is inherent in the task of supervision of the practicum. The supervisor must master such a complex series of roles that often he/she is unable to separate them effectively. On occasion, therefore, the roles may overlap and create potentially conflicting responsibilities as, for example, in the situation which arises when the supervisor must not only provide feedback of an advisory kind but must also evaluate the student. In such a situation, it is unwarranted to assume that success as a classroom teacher or lecturer in a tertiary institution will automatically guarantee success as a supervisor. There must be a programme of preparation for the practicum supervisors and the development of the supervision programme must be based upon a more detailed understanding of the practicum and its various phases. Turney and other researchers have developed a vocabulary for the practicum and in doing so have identified its constituent parts. This vocabulary of the practicum should form the basis of a programme to achieve a systematic, collegial supervision of the student teacher. The programme of training for supervisors that best fits these requirements is called 'clinical supervision' and Goldhammer (1980) states that it: '. . . draws its data from first-hand observation of actual teaching events, and involves face-to-face (and other associated) interaction between the supervisor and the [student] teacher in the analysis of teaching behaviours and activities for instructional improvement' (p.15).

Goldhammer *et al.* have devised procedures for assisting student teachers and their supervisors to achieve a rational understanding of teaching behaviour. In the sequence of stages that has been identified, the role of supervisor is no longer taken to mean just that of an evaluator. Rather, the role of the supervisor is more properly viewed as that of consultant, who has a wider involvement in the student's professional development.

Teachers as evaluators: What have we learned?

In Australia during the past decade, there has been a steady movement toward devolution of authority for much of the curriculum decision making. In terms of visibility, this shift is particularly apparent in Australia, because previously there were very centralized state education systems which devised and sent out the curricula and syllabus statements. It is not the intention here to trace the reasons for this devolutionary movement. However, it represents the view that the school is responsive to its local community and has the concern to improve the teaching and learning which occurs within it. Also in Australia, it is possible to discern another body of opinion which views current educational practices as being less rigorous than they were in the past.

In the *Teachers as Evaluators* project (Hughes *et al.* 1979) it is possible to see the convergence of these two approaches. The Teachers as Evaluators project was established with the following objectives: a) to develop an understanding of and a commitment to the role of evaluation processes as a means of curriculum improvement; b) to involve and train teachers in evaluation processes directed toward curriculum improvement; c) to develop materials designed to help teachers towards this end; d) to involve curriculum officers and in-service personnel at the system level in the evaluation process directed towards assisting teachers to develop their own evaluation processes and to evaluate their own procedures and programmes.

Taken together, these objectives address the central question of how educational programmes might be improved particularly in the context of curriculum decisions being made by the school community.

As in many countries, the pre-eminent model of curriculum development in Australia in the 1960s was Ralph Tyler's objectives model of curriculum development. With the benefit of hindsight one can follow the changes that have been made to this model by other American writers. Cronbach (1967), for instance, drew attention to the *use* of evaluation data; and Stufflebeam (1971) identified a number of different types of evaluation in addition to formal evaluation. A similar development could be shown in the United Kingdom (for example, see Hamilton *et. al* 1978).

The discussion in Australia has not been entirely at the theoretical level. The Australian Schools Commission in its *Report for the Triennium 1979-81* stated:

> The term evaluation is being used to include all those means through which members of a school community can participate in a co-operative examination of what the school is doing, set particular targets for improvement, plan action to advance towards them and evaluate that action in terms of the

objectives they have set for it, changing course in the light of experience. It accepts the developmental model of school change which begins from looking at what is being done, not from debate about aims. (p.6)

Clearly, evaluation must be based upon valid data, rather than just on a pooling of staff intuitions or on organizational reactions to a community pressure group. It is also possible to deduce from the report's statement that evaluation should be collegial rather than hierarchical; that evaluation should be an integral part of the curriculum and curriculum development; and that evaluation should involve the pupils of the school and the members of the local community.

Many teachers are anxious about the change to a situation where they must assume more responsibility for class, year group or grade, or whole school evaluation. The project team has prepared a number of statements about school level evaluation and these are shown in Table.

Table 21.3   School Level Evaluation

What it is	What it is not
– an activity for improvement	a final assessment
– something you have been doing	something new
– teacher-initiated	an inspection by an external authority
– school-based	imposed
– an expression of our professional concern	assessment of teachers
– a team effort	unco-ordinated
– informing of ourselves to make good judgements	an imposed accountability

Once they are involved in the evaluation teachers do not adhere to a single theorist or follow a particular dominant evaluation approach (Fraser 1982). Rather, the teachers are more concerned to have a pragmatic approach to evaluation and to amend whatever procedures are in use in light of their local circumstances.

To facilitate the introduction and conduct of an evaluation Hughes et al. have produced a number of reports, which show in detail how to prepare for an evaluation, how to plan for an evaluation, how to gather relevant information, and how to report and use this information. In addition they have also produced a number of reports which provide case studies of evaluations.

In *Giving an Account* (Part IV) (1981), for example, there is a report of the first attempt at a kindergarten-based evaluation.

This case study illustrates the nature of first attempts at evaluation. The teachers and director of the kindergarten were keen to find out certain kinds of information, for instance: i) if parents of the children wished to participate in the kindergarten, and ii) what types of parent participation were evident in the kindergarten. The teachers formulated a rationale for seeking parental participation in the kindergarten and then deliberately set about encouraging this participation. Data on the degree to which parents wished to be involved was gathered through the use of a questionnaire that the teachers had devised. This enabled the teachers to find out that most parents wished to be involved in the kindergarten. To determine how parents were currently involved in the kindergarten the teachers kept diaries, took still photographs and made video-recordings during the second term of the 1980 kindergarten year. From these data a list of the various ways parents were involved in the kindergarten was developed.

The reports were written for teachers, and grapple with such methodological concerns as how best to prepare and present reports. The reports, perhaps for the first time, also allow teachers to present to the community the educational situation as they perceive it.

Overview

In the preceding sections six research and/or development activities were presented. While each is unique, they all had as a major concern the improvement of educational practice. The Cambridge Accountability Project and the Teachers as Evaluators project indicate that teachers – as professionals – must be competent to, and vitally involved in, the conduct of a self- or school evaluation so that they and their schools can respond more positively to the needs of their community. Both of these projects provide important information for staff and schools who are just beginning, or are already engaged in, this process. Hall *et al.* show us how to recognize the process of change and how to nurture curricula or instructional change. Joyce in the United States and Turney *et al.* in

Australia, in complementary ways, are concerned with classroom practice and the learning environments that teachers provide for their students. Finally, Armstrong provides some of the good sense which binds all educational research together, when he writes of the sensitive teachers who begin to examine the thoughts and the actions of the children whom they are teaching.

References

Angus, M., Evans, K., and Parkin, B. (1975) *An observational study of selected pupil and teacher behaviour in open plan and conventional design classrooms*, Australian Open Area Project, Technical Report No 4, Education Department of Western Australia, Perth, Australia.

Armstrong, M. (1980) *Closely Observed Children: the diary of a primary classroom*, Writers and Readers Publishing Co-operative Society Ltd, London.

Asche, A. (Chairman) (1980) *Teacher Education in Victoria*, Interim Report of the Committee of the Victorian Enquiry into Teacher Education Melbourne, Government Printer, Melbourne.

Auchmuty, J. (Chairman) (1980) *Report of the National Inquiry into Teacher Education*, AGPS, Canberra.

Christensen, C. (1981) *Giving An Account (Part IV): Evaluation of Parent Participation at Springbrook Kindergarten, South Australia*, CDC, Canberra, Australia.

Conant, J.B. (1963) *The Education of American Teachers*, McGraw-Hill, New York.

Corey, S.M. (1954) 'Action research in education', *Journal of Educational Research* Vol 47, pp. 375-380.

Correy, P. (Chairman) (1980) *Teachers for Tomorrow*, Report of the Committee to Examine Teacher Education in New South Wales, Government Printer, Sydney.

Cronbach, L.J. (1963) 'Course improvement through evaluation', *Teachers College Record*, Vol 64, pp. 672-683.

Eggleston, S.J. (1974) 'United Kingdom: innovative trends to teacher training and retraining', in *New Patterns of Teacher Education and Tasks: Country Experience – Belgium, France, United Kingdom*, OCED, Paris.

Elliott, J., Bridges, D., Ebbutt, D., Gibson, R. and Nias, J. (1981) *School Accountability: The SSRC Cambridge Accountability Project*, Grant McIntyre, London.

Fisher, C.W., Berliner, D., Filby, N., Marliave, R., Cahen, L., Dishaw, M., and Moore, J. (1978) *Teaching and Learning in Elementary Schools: summary of the beginning teacher evaluation study*, Far West Laboratory for Educational Research and Development, San Francisco, California.

Fisher, C.W., Berliner, D., Filby, N., Marliave, R., Cahen, L., and Dishaw, M. (1980) 'Teaching behaviours, academic learning time and student achievement: an overview', in Denham, C. and Lieberman, A. (eds) (1980) *Time to Learn*, US Department of Education, National Institute of Education, Washington, DC.

Fraser, B. and Smith, D. (1980) 'Application of a change agent strategy in dissemination of an Australian innovation', *Australian Journal of Teacher Education*, Vol 5, No 1, pp. 9-20.

Fraser, B.J. (1982) *Annotated Bibliography of Curriculum Evaluation Literature*, School of Education, Macquarie University, Sydney.

Fuller, F. (1969) 'Concerns of teachers: A developmental conceptualization', *American Research Journal*, Vol 6, No 2, pp. 207-226.

Galton, M., Simon, B., and Croll, P. (1980) *Inside the Primary Classroom*, Routledge & Kegan Paul, London.

Good, T. (1979) 'Teacher effectiveness in the elementary school', *Journal of Teacher*

Education, Vol 30, pp. 52-64.

Hall, G. (1979) 'The concerns-based approach to facilitating change', *Educational Horizons*, Vol 57, No 4, pp. 202-208.

Hall, G., Loucks, S., Rutherford, W. and Newlove, B. (1975) 'Levels of use of the innovation: A framework for analyzing innovation adoption', *Journal of Teacher Education*, Vol 26, No 1, pp. 52-56.

Hall, G. and Loucks, S. (1977) 'A developmental model for determining whether the treatment is actually implemented', *American Educational Research Journal*, Vol 14, No 3, pp. 263-276.

Hamilton, D. *et al.* (eds) (1978) *Beyond the Numbers Game*, Macmillan, London.

Hughes, P., Russell, N., and McConachy, D. (1979) *Curriculum Evaluation in Australia: a new challenge for teachers*, CDC, Canberra.

Joyce, B. and Weil, M. (1980) *Models of Teaching* (2nd edition), Prentice-Hall, Inc, Englewood Cliffs, New Jersey.

Karmos, A. and Jacko, C. (1977) 'The role of significant others during the student teaching experience', *Journal of Teacher Education*, Vol 28, pp. 51-55.

Kuhn, T.S. (1962) *The Structure of Scientific Revolutions*, University of Chicago Press, Chicago.

McDonald, F.J. (1976) *Research on teaching and its implications for policy making: Report on phase II of the Beginning Teacher Evaluation Study*, Educational Testing Service, Princeton, New Jersey.

Patton, M.Q. (1978) *Utilization – Focussed Evaluation*, Sage Publications, Beverley Hills, California.

Plowden Report (1967) *Children and Their Primary Schools* (2 vols) Report of the Central Advisory Council for Education in England, HMSO, London.

Reissman, F. (1967) 'Teachers of the poor: a five-point plan', *Journal of Teacher Education*, Vol 18, pp. 326-336.

Schmuck, R.A. and Schmuck, P.A. (1975) *Group Processes in the Classroom* (2nd edition), William C. Brown, Dubuque, Iowa.

School Commission Report for the Triennium 1979-81 (1978), AGPS, Canberra.

Seperson, M. and Joyce, B. (1973) 'Teaching styles of student teachers as related to those of co-operating teachers', *Educational Leadership*, Vol 31, pp. 146-157.

Shulman, L.S. (1974) 'The psychology of school subjects: A premature obituary?', *Journal of Research on Science Teaching*, No 11, pp. 319-339.

Stake, R. (1967) 'The countenance of educational evaluation', *Teachers College Record*, Vol 68, pp. 523-580.

Stufflebeam, D. *et al.* (1971) *Educational Evaluation and Decision-making*, F.E. Peacock, Itasca, Illinois.

Teachers as Evaluators Project (1980) *Evaluation Network*, No 4, Canberra.

Turney, C., Cairns, L., Eltis, K., Hatton, N., Thew, D., Towler, J., and Wright, R. (1982) *The Practicum in Teacher Education: Research, Practice and Supervision*, Sydney University Press, Sydney.

Tyler, R. (1949) *Basic Principles of Curriculum and Instruction*, University of Chicago Press, Chicago.

Tyler, R. (1967) *Perspectives on Curriculum Evaluation*, AERA Monograph Series on Curriculum Evaluation, No 1, Rand McNally, Chicago.

Vickery, R. (Chairman) (1980) *Teacher Education in Western Australia*, Report of the Committee of Inquiry into Teacher Education, appointed by the Minister for Education in Western Australia, Government Printer, Perth.

PART V

THE LEGACY OF THE CURRICULUM MOVEMENT

PERSONAL REFLECTION

MAURICE GALTON

Strangely enough, Lawrence Stenhouse was not present at the inaugural conference which led to the founding of the Association for the Study of the Curriculum. He did, however, attend the second conference at Manchester and hosted the third at Norwich where he had set up the Centre for Applied Research in Education. Thereafter, in spite of heavy demands on his time and energies, as his fame grew, he remained a regular attender. More than anyone else among the membership he personified the aim of the association, to pursue the practical applications of curriculum theory. Over the years he was asked to give keynote lectures at many of the association's conferences and it was a fitting choice that he should have been asked at the tenth conference to assess the contribution of the curriculum movement as it had developed within the association. The text of his address which follows remains exactly in the same form that it was given at the conference, except for minor alterations which Lawrence made shortly before his untimely death.

In assessing the achievements of the curriculum movement in Britain over the past decade, one is doing no more than assessing the contribution of Lawrence Stenhouse. His was the dominant figure. His curriculum textbook, the first to bring together the various strands of the arguments of the 'new wave' of curriculum workers, by its powerful advocacy, established school-based development as a legitimate research activity. Anyone travelling to other English-speaking parts of the world would continually come across teachers who were unmistakably influenced by his thinking. Like the Jesuits of old, giving him a teacher for one year resulted in their being imbued with his philosophy for life. If at times such teachers appeared, collectively, somewhat indifferent to researchers outside their own orbit, they could usually be found where the action was toughest, displaying a passionate concern to improve the quality of teaching and learning in the classroom. At a time when financial cutbacks continue to put enormous pressures on schools and stress on teachers, the existence of these dedicated followers remains an important legacy of the man.

CHAPTER 22

THE LEGACY OF THE CURRICULUM MOVEMENT

LAWRENCE STENHOUSE

I want to begin by reminding you of the context in which we are working. This country has two educational systems running in parallel – the private system and the state system – and although they are not the same size, it is difficult to decide which carries more weight.

The first of these two systems has its origins in an ideal of education for leadership, and it is an education of privilege that empowers those who receive it. The Clarendon Report of 1864, which was concerned with the public schools, remarked on the great service that these schools performed in

> the creation of a system of government and discipline for boys, the excellence of which has been universally recognized, and which is admitted to have been most important in its effects on national character and on social life.

And the commissioners continued:

> It is not easy to estimate the degree in which the English people are indebted to these schools for the qualities on which they pride themselves most – for their capacity to govern others and control themselves, their aptitude for combining freedom with order, their public spirit, their vigour and manliness of character, their strong but not slavish respect for public opinion, their love of healthy sports and exercise. These schools have been the chief nurseries of our statesmen; in them, and in schools modelled after them, men of all the various classes that make up English society, destined for every profession and career, have been brought up on a footing of social equality, and have contracted the most enduring friendships, and some of

the ruling habits of their lives; and they have had perhaps the largest share in moulding the character of an English gentleman.

The picture of these schools is still recognizable; and there is a sense in which they have provided a model of schooling for an education of privilege all over the Western and the colonial world.

The second of the two English systems of education, the state system, was far different in its origins both from the private system and from those systems like the Scots or the Scandinavian which were conceived against the background of the enormous responsibilities shouldered by the individual in protestant theology. The Newcastle Commission, which was set up in 1858 and reported in 1861 – just three years before the Clarendon Commission – was concerned with 'the extension of sound and cheap elementary instruction to all classes of the people'. It interpreted its concern as 'the independent poor', 2,655,767 children of the poorer classes, and in this sector of education, England trailed rather than led. The commissioners remarked that:

Without entering into general considerations of the duty of the state with regard to the education of the poorer classes of a community, they think it sufficient to refer to the fact that all the principal nations of Europe, and the United States of America, as well as British North America, have felt it necessary to provide for the education of the people by public taxation; . . .

But the temper of the times was one of accountability and, following the Newcastle Commission, the Revised Code of 1862 introduced payment by results. Robert Lowe told the House of Commons:

I cannot promise the House that this system will be an economical one and I cannot promise that it will be an efficient one, but I can promise that it shall be one or the other. If it is not cheap, it shall be efficient; if it is not efficient, it shall be cheap.

I attended an elementary school in Manchester from 1931 to 1937. Some children, like me, 'won' scholarships into the private – then the direct-grant – day schools. Some 'won' scholarships to Manchester Corporation Secondary Schools – still called 'winning', though lower down on the honours board as I remember. When I first went to the elementary school, it was an all-age school to fourteen. By the time I left in 1937, the progressive Manchester Education Committee under W.O. Lester Smith had established 'central schools' for the losers. But twenty years later, in the years 1957 to 1960, as a tutor in Durham Institute of Education, I was still visiting all-age, unreorganized elementary schools in the Northeast. We have only so recently achieved secondary education for all, and it was achieved in the context of the long climb of postwar reconstruction.

By 1960, reorganization was almost achieved and a new system of grammar and secondary modern schools – with a few technical schools here and there – had been set up. There were even experiments with comprehensive schools.

In 1961 the heads of mathematics of four public schools together with Bryan Thwaites, then Professor of Theoretical Mechanics in the University of Southampton, started the School Mathematics Project as a private venture with financial support from industry. It was not very long before four state grammar schools joined, and later the enterprise mushroomed. It is still in existence, sustained financially by its royalties.

The British curriculum movement – and it is not the American movement that concerns me here – thus began in the private sector, but it spread rapidly into the state grammar schools. Although it started in a private venture initiated by schools in collaboration with universities and drawing on financial support from industry, the Nuffield Foundation soon came in to support the enterprise. Initially, it was concerned with the modernization of science and mathematics teaching in the grammar school sector – there was concern for the literacy and numeracy of the leadership of the country in those subjects which were the foundation of technological progress. Subsequently, as we turned more towards Europe, it took up the problem of the more effective teaching of foreign languages. Its instrument was the 'project' and the 'working party'.

It is difficult to conceive now how novel the idea of a 'project' was in education. It had two aspects: a core in which a number of people were discussing curriculum issues, generally in a particular subject area, and trying to represent ideas about teaching and about knowledge in forms, such as teachers' handbooks and teaching materials, that were directly addressed to practice. This is what is crucial about curriculum work: it is about the presentation of ideas disciplined by the fact that they have to be presented to teachers in schools in forms of practice.

Round the core group of a project would always grow a constituency of schools in critical dialogue with the central team; and that constituency gradually expanded. The expansion later came to be known as diffusion and later still as dissemination. And successful dissemination means for me dissemination of the ideas discussed in the project.

Now, consider the kind of background that those early projects came into. I taught for five years in schools without hearing the word *curriculum* mentioned, and with the exception of short meetings at the beginning of each term when the head welcomed us back, without staff or departmental meetings. What I taught and how I taught it was a matter for negotiation between my head of department and myself.

So the first legacy of the curriculum movement had a dual aspect. First, it declared curriculum and teaching to be problematic and introduced curriculum as an area of discourse within schools. Second, it suggested that the problem was one for professional discussion and collaboration in schools, rather than an individualistic professional matter for each teacher, or for the head or head of department. This idea that curriculum as a concern is a focus for professional discussion across the board is celebrated in this association, and it is, I suppose, now so taken for granted that we may readily forget that it is a legacy of the curriculum movement.

The curriculum movement was transformed by ROSLA, comprehensivization and extension to the primary school. The raising of the school-leaving age was seen as setting acute problems for secondary schools, and comprehensivization as presenting those problems to teachers often quite ill-prepared by experience to solve them. How and what were the average and below average in academic ability to be taught now that they were to be detained in school during the years in which it must become apparent to them that they were to be excluded from GCE 'O' level, the notional objective of a completed secondary education? And at the primary level, how were the foundations of modern languages, of science and of mathematics to be introduced?

It was in the face of such problems that the so-called 'Nuffield model' of curriculum research and development was handed over from the Nuffield Foundation to the newly founded quango, the Schools Council. Curriculum renewal became much more clearly associated with policy through an organization financed jointly by central and local government. Large sums of money became available.

Four reactions to this situation have left us with different legacies: in managerialism; in evaluation and accountability; in the educational academy; and in classroom research.

I mean by managerialism the idea that education can be improved by curricular reform or innovation implemented in the school system by the influence or the power of the management hierarchy. Managerialism was the natural reaction to the expansion of the new field of curriculum on the part of the LEAs, of HM Inspectorate and of UNESCO and other international agencies. On the whole, it was resisted by those working in research and development in the curriculum movement, who saw the situation in terms of development rather than reform, and dissemination rather than innovation; but the framework of managerialism was often imposed upon them by the assumptions and expectations with which they were surrounded.

It could be argued that curriculum projects in this country attempted to appeal to the judgement of teachers and found themselves constrained to address the judgement of administrators. Thus the legacy here is represented by a tension: school-based curriculum development associated with teacher participation leading to staff development; or centralization of curricular prescription with monitoring or accountability as the principle underlying staff development – a matter of keeping up to the mark. The intellectual and the structural resources supporting both sides of this tension were inherited from the curriculum movement.

So much for the managerial strand. Let me now interpret the evaluation strand.

There is in this country a research community that relies on financial support by way of commissions. Historically that research community has overwhelmingly been concerned, not with scientific problems such as might elucidate the educational enterprise by coherent theory, but with the technical problems of so-called 'mental testing'. The National Foundation for Educational Research and Godfrey Thomson's Moray House testing unit dominated the field. Universities – or individuals within them – had a smaller, but significant, share of the cake. We had a strong and relatively powerful community of psychometrists with highly developed skills in which much toil had been invested.

Let me read to you from Sir Walter Scott's *Guy Mannering*:

> Grave and studious men were loth to relinquish the calculations which had early become the principal objects of their studies, and felt reluctant to descend from the predominating height to which a supposed insight into futurity, by the power of consulting abstract influences and conjunctions ['correlations', we call them in our jargon] had exalted them over the rest of mankind.

What was true of astrologers was true too of psychometrists.

They could look with yearning eyes towards the United States, whose parallel curriculum movement, far more prodigal of money, had set up their colleagues in a strong position. Robert Kennedy had mandated evaluation as a condition of grants for research and development, and the American foundations had for the most part followed suit. You couldn't do curriculum research and development in America without having an evaluation tied on to you, and that evaluation for the most part staffed by members of the psychometric community. Managerial assumptions had united with the input-output model of curriculum development, whose tablet of stone was Ralph Tyler's *Basic Principles of Curriculum and Instruction* – a more sensitive book than most interpreters made it seem – to produce a psycho-statistical pattern of evaluation by pre- and post-testing with parallel control groups, which swept the board, rang the bell and collected the money.

In a Schools Council working party on evaluation the psychometrists, who were being robbed of substantial monies by the decline of eleven-plus testing in the face of comprehensivization, made their bid to collect the British jackpot in curriculum evaluation. They lost. Wiseman and Pidgeon had to publish their views on evaluation from the NFER, not under the Schools Council imprint.

The Schools Council never made evaluation mandatory, and generally, when it occurred, it involved the close study of schools and classrooms in addition to some testing. That close study of schools and classrooms increasingly aimed to evoke self-monitoring and self-evaluation on the part of teachers. The curriculum movement coined the slogan: teacher as researcher.

It provided a strong stimulus to classroom action-research, though it must be said that a minority tradition in such research had existed earlier. One of the pioneers must have been my colleague in Newcastle, Ronald Morris, who made available to teachers a cumbersome early tape recorder so that they could record their work in classrooms, and then gave them tutorial support in the analysis of their own teaching. He published four remarkable books, all written by teachers as diploma dissertations, in a series which he called *Achievements in Teaching*.

About the same time, Reg Revans, who has been a remarkably innovative, and until recently under-recognized, researcher in management, undertook some educational research in Manchester schools, and introduced to this country Ned Flanders' interaction analysis schedule, which was conceived as a self-monitoring device.

However, classroom research did not thrive until the curriculum movement gave it new life. Particularly notable has been the work of John Elliott in a particular tradition of classroom research in which the logic of teaching rather than the social psychology is to the fore. This involves the analysis of one's teaching against some logic which one adopts as an intention: neutral chairmanship in the Humanities Project, the principle of inquiry in Ford T. And the specification of the logic of the teaching is, se, a curricular specification such as the teacher as artist might set elf to implement in the classroom and then evaluate and decide how ch of it to embody into the common currency of day-to-day teaching. It s that strand of classroom research that is the legacy of the curriculum movement, at any rate in its present form.

I opened this talk by describing the gap between the private and the public systems of education in this country. From 1902 to the advent of comprehensivization that gap was for those in the grammar school in certain respects closing. The state grammar schools modelled themselves on the public day schools and there was considerable interchange of staff between them. Comprehensive education set up a different educational ideal, and led to much sharper division between state and private sectors, partly because it seemed to ask that the state system might consider granting to the pupils of average and below-average ability something of the benefits available to their peers in the private system. The aspiration was to extend an education of some quality beyond the minority who had traditionally enjoyed sponsored mobility by scholarship in the state system. The task was enormous and no doubt underestimated by the policy-makers. The government – whether Labour under Callaghan or Conservative under Thatcher – clearly felt that the expense involved for slow returns could not in the end be sustained. The escape was through an accountability movement which now pushes the non-academic student back to the fare of the old elementary school. The crude training goals in basic skills favour a definition of efficiency after the style of Robert Lowe's principles of economy, and serve to justify testing rather than examining.

If the psychometrists had lost the battle for curriculum evaluation, they won at least the first round of the battle for accountability. Lean days were over for the NFER. Theirs was no longer a Slough of Despond. The APU's magic hand brought Excalibur forth from their Mere.

However, the proposals that looked towards a concept of accountability based purely on measures of output are not wholly uncontested or wholly victorious. The alternative suggested is school-based accountability through formal self-evaluation. And if I mention in this connection the names of John Elliott and Michael Eraut, Tony Becher and Helen Simons, then many of you will immediately recognize that school-based account-ability must be another legacy of the curriculum movement.

The movement did not leave the academy of education untouched either. By the academy I mean those in universities and colleges who, though they have research interests and pursue research activities, earn their living primarily through teaching and scholarship. Not a few of those recruited into colleges and departments of education primarily to supervise training in the teaching of specific subjects were products of the curriculum movement, but it is not of them that I am now thinking. In teacher education the main current of the 1960s and 1970s was towards a collection code teaching of education in terms of its so-called 'constituent disciplines'. This movement to place the teaching of education within the academic sphere of power of philosophy, psychology and sociology was spearheaded by R.S. Peters, Stephen Wiseman and – ironically perhaps in the light of his later work – Basil Bernstein. It corresponded with a huge expansion in teacher education, particularly initial teacher education, and it served to obtain jobs in higher education for a good proportion of the graduates from the academic diplomas and master's degrees offered by the universities – of which London Institute of Education was the leader.

Curriculum studies did not for the most part figure in initial training, nor was it as strong in in-service education as it has become. The Open University courses were important leaders in the in-service field. As late as 1975 I was publishing a textbook in curriculum research and development in a conscious bid to make curriculum central to the study of education in an integrated code. Even the work of the sociologists of curriculum may be seen as in a sense a legacy of the curriculum movement, though it is inclined towards a style of critique which is not often thought through in terms of curricular action.

Now, as the candidates for higher degrees in education see less and less career prospect in initial teacher education, and consequently less inducement to provide themselves with philosophy, psychology or sociology to teach to others, they turn to management courses that seem to hold promise for headship and administration, or counselling courses that open up avenues of promotion in the pastoral sector, or curriculum courses that offer prospects in academic deputy headships, the advisory service and the in-service area – and indeed classroom benefits if promotion is elusive or involves a deal of queuing. The tradition of curriculum studies which feeds these needs is another legacy of the curriculum movement.

Any diagnosis of a legacy is, of course, a controversial matter of historical interpretation – and in the context of a speech at a conference an interpretation not fully argued or even comprehensive in its claims. But for what it is worth I have claimed that what we wrought in that movement and now hand on is at least:

the notion of curriculum as problematic;

  the idea that this problematic may be the centre of a collegial discourse that strengthens teachers relative to those outside the school;

3 a tradition of classroom research in terms of a critique based upon analysis of classroom process in terms of the logics of teaching, which was there before, but has been greatly boosted by the curriculum movement;

4 a structuring of the managerialism/teacher-centred dichotomy that has sharpened and focused on the issues of centralization of curriculum prescription and school-based development of curriculum and teaching;

5 the school-based evaluation response to the pressure towards accountability;

6 a tradition of curriculum studies within the academy of education.

To these I want to add a seventh legacy, more tangible and sometimes more neglected, or even derided. The curriculum movement has left behind it materials and handbooks and the like produced in the age of plenty. These artefacts embody ideas, often of great power, that were masked from many teachers because the curriculum projects were shadowed by managerialism with its implication of direction from outside the classroom.

Schools need to develop as communities rather than at the hands of reformers, and the key to that development is a maturing in the art of teaching of members of staff: it is about professional biographies fertilized by a critical extension of ideas about teaching and curriculum. Discourse within a school, however, needs to be fertilized from outside: school-based development of curriculum and teaching is not well conceived as a Robinson Crusoe island affair. The often-derided packages of the curriculum movement are, I am prepared to argue, the best outside source of ideas about pedagogy and knowledge for teachers who will approach them as critical professionals who perceive ideas not as threats to their own professional autonomy, but as supports for it. The seventh legacy of the curriculum movement is in your store cupboards.

And make no mistake, we shall need our stores, for we are under siege. In education the rich are getting richer and the poor are getting poorer. The private sector continues to develop the individual's powers and confidence at a time when the public sector is being pushed back towards elementary competences. What is at stake is the relative benefit schools offer their pupils, *attainment in basic skills held constant*. Compare a non-academic school in the private sector – like Gordonstoun – with most schools in the state system in the light of that criterion. The Gordonstoun boy will become a merchant navy captain or director of a business and a confident citizen when too often the state schoolboy of comparable ability becomes a deckhand who would falter at the door of the Savoy even with the price of a Savoy lunch in his pocket because such places are not for the likes of him. And the disparity for girls is perhaps worse.

We are not going to erode the wall of privilege between the two nations in this country easily or soon, or by education only. But education is one important factor, and it is recognized as such by pupils themselves. This week's *Times Educational Supplement* carries under the headline, 'Schoolboys look across the great divide', a report of research by Miles Hewstone that bears witness to pupils' perception of that division. Teachers too recognize it. Recently, in conversation with me, the head of a public school and the head of a state comprehensive, each with experience of both systems, were deploring the way in which the two systems were drifting apart.

The years of the curriculum movement were years of good harvests for the state system. Now we face lean years of famine. There are ways through to continue to redress the inequalities of distribution of cultural resources and personal powers in our society, particularly through developments negotiated with pupils and students. These will be difficult ways to clear in hard times; but we have a stock in hand from which we can work in the legacy of the curriculum movement. Not least the ideas that were then abroad need to be brought down from the attic, dusted off, adapted, turned to good use. The legacy is by and large a rich one.

LIST OF CONTRIBUTORS

David Alexander is county inspector with responsibility for environmental studies in Bedfordshire. Recently he has been involved in the development of primary science and humanities for the age range 5–13. He is an active menber of the Shire Counties branch of the Association for Study of Curriculum.

Neville Bennett Professor of Education, Research Director of Centre for Educational Research and Development at University of Lancaster. He has written *Teaching Styles and Pupil Progress, Focus on Teaching, Open Plan School* and *Ability of Pupil Learning Experience* (forthcoming).

Tim Brighouse Chief Education Officer of Oxfordshire, taught in a grammar school, a secondary modern school and in community education before entering administration in Monmouthshire.

Peter Cornall has been Senior County Inspector in Cornwall since September 1981. He taught first in Oxfordshire and London comprehensives, and was an Assistant Education Officer in Wiltshire. In 1967 he became Head at West Bridgford, Nottingham, and in 1972 at Carisbrooke High School in the Isle of Wight. This school managed to combine a falling roll ("Keats" in the Briault Survey) with selection as U.K. representative school in a major Council of Europe study in 1980.

Jim Eggleston Professor of Education, Head of School of Education, University of Nottingham, Head of PGCE Division and Research and Higher Degree Division. Originally a marine zoologist, later taught biology and appointed Head of Science at Hinckley Upper School, then Research Fellow at University of Leicester and member of Nuffield Science 'mafia'. Interests, evaluation of teaching and teacher training.

John Elliott is currently Tutor in Curriculum Studies at the Cambridge Institute of Education. From 1972–1974 he directed the Ford Teaching Project while at the Centre for Applied Research in Education in the University of East Anglia. This teachers' based project was one of the early examples of educational action–research to appeear in the U.K. Subsequently John Elliott has directed funded action-research projects into School Accountability (1978–80) and Teacher-Pupil Interaction and the Quality of Learning (1980–83).

Maurice Galton holds a Chair in Education at the School of Education, University of Leicester and has co-directed the ORACLE project since its inception in 1975. He has contributed to a number of books concerning teaching methods in the primary classroom including *Inside the Primary Classroom* and his latest work, *Moving from the Primary Classroom*.

Peter Green is an English teacher; he has taught at Bosworth College, Leicestershire and Stantonbury Campus in Milton Keynes, where he was Head of the Faculty of European Studies; he is currently Vice-Principal of Countesthorpe College, Leicestershire.

Douglas Hamblin Honorary Research Fellow, University College of Swansea, recently Senior Lecturer responsible for M.Ed., B.Ed. and Diploma Courses in Pastoral care, Guidance and Counselling. Author of *Teacher and Counselling* (1974), *Teacher and Pastoral Care* (1978), *Teaching Study Skills* (1981). *Guidance for the 16-19 Age Group* (1983) and *Educational Problems and Practice of Pastoral Care* (1981).

John Isaac has taught in primary schools in Sussex and Nottingham and a Secondary School in the Solomon Islands. He has worked in a College of Education and Polytechnic Departments of Education since 1963 and is at present Head of the Department of Education at Oxford Polytechnic. His interests and experience include working on in-service courses and in initial teacher education.

Maurice Kogan is Professor of Government and Social Administration and Head of Department of Government at Brunel University. He is the author of several works on the politics and government of education. His most recent work includes *Directors of Education* (with Tony Bush) and *Government and Science* (forthcoming) (with Mary Henkel).

Peter Mann Educated Tavistock Grammar School and Merton College, Oxford, 1953–57 (History Postmaster); M.A., F.R.S.A. teaching appointments in West Riding, Bristol and Herts. 1957–71; Headmaster, The Cavendish School, Hemel Hempstead, 1971–81; Divisional Inspector of Secondary Schools (I.L.E.A.) 1981–83; Specialist Adviser to House of Commons Select Committee on Education (inquiry into the secondary school curriculum and examinations) 1981–82; Principal Adviser for Dorset from September 1983.

Bob Moon has taught in the I.L.E.A., Milton Keynes (Bucks) and Oxfordshire; formerly Head of Bridgewater Hall School on Stantonbury Campus he is now Head of the Peers School, Oxford. In addition to producing a number of publications for the Open University he is Deputy Editor of the Journal 'Curriculum' and he has recently edited *Comprehensive Schools: Challenge and Change* published by NFER/Nelson.

Peter Mortimore taught for nine years in London secondary schools before training in research and working with Michael Rutter and colleagues on the secondary schools study reported as 'Fifteen Thousand Hours'. He is currently Director of Research & Statistics for the ILEA.

Andrew Pollard Senior Lecturer in Education, Faculty of Educational Studies, Oxford Polytechnic took up his present post in 1981 having taught in first, infant and middle schools for the previous nine years. During that time he undertook various part-time research projects on sociological aspects of classroom processes.

Colin Richards was Lecturer in Education at the University of Leicester at the time of the Oxford Conference. He is now a member of Her Majesty's Inspectorate of Schools. His publications include *An Introduction to Curriculum Studies* (co–authored Philip Taylor, NFER 1979), *Curriculum Studies: a select annotated bibliography* (Nafferton, second edition 1983), *Power and the Curriculum* (Nafferton 1978) and *New Directions in Primary Education* (Falmer Press, 1982).

Stephen Rowland Having taught in primary schools, Stephen Rowland is now the co-ordinator of CRISES (Leicestershire Classroom Research Inservice Education Scheme). Supported by Leicestershire Education Department, this project aims to provide opportunities for primary and secondary school teachers to investigate the quality and development of children's understanding in their classrooms.

Ken Shaw taught in secondary modern and grammar schools before being appointed to the staff of St. Luke's College. He is now Senior Lecturer in the University of Exeter where he lectures on management, curriculum and sociology of education. He has contributed to many books and journals and lectured in Australia and Nigeria.

Marten Shipman is currently Professor of Education at the University of Warwick. He has written several books on the curriculum, the sociology of education and social research methods and served as an advisor on research to public and international organisations.

Lawrence Stenhouse Head of the Centre for Applied Research in Education and Professor of Education in the University of East Anglia until his death in August 1982. He was the outstanding figure of the curriculum development movement during the nineteen-seventies and will be best remembered for his pioneering work in developing new approaches to curriculum development through working collaboratively alongside teachers in their own classrooms.

Barry Taylor Chief Education Officer with Somerset LEA. Consultant to OECD on problems relating to transition from school to work. Member of the Schools Council Professional Committee. Chairman of the BBC Continuing Education Advisory Council. Member of the Technician Education Council. Governor of FE Staff College. Chairman of the Society of Education Officers International Committee.

David Walton Adviser for Microtechnology for Oxfordshire County Council, appointed in 1981. Responsible for promoting the good use of microcomputers, etc. in Primary and Secondary Schools in the County.

John Williamson is Head of Teaching Studies in the School of Education at the Western Australian Institute of Technology in Perth. He lectures on classroom research and is project director of a study concerned with teachers' decision-making.

Kay Wood taught in a variety of schools after graduating in sociology. She worked for several years in commerce in North Africa and Canada before undertaking Ph.D research into classroom teaching as Assistant to Professor Wragg. She then joined the Schools Council project at the conclusion of which she was appointed to the staff of Rolle College, Exmouth.

INDEX

Galton, Maurice 40, 85, 96, 152, 218, 255,
    256, 297, 299, 323, 333
Garfinkel, H. 277
Garland, R. 49
Garson, Y. 42
Geoffrey, W. 83
Geography 64, 65, 70
Gettinger, M. 265
Giddens, A. 230
Giving an Account 341
Glaser, B.G. 281
Goffree, F. 200
Godamer, H.G. 236
Goldhammer, 338
Good, T. 270
Goode, J. 50
Goodman, Paul 136
Gottman, J. 208
Government's Expenditure Plans, The 44
Grammar schools 68, 69, 73, 74
Gray, J. 258
"Great Debate" 8, 68, 253
Green, Peter 132, 133
Grundy, S. 230, 243, 244
Guidelines for Review and Institutional
    Development in Schools 247
Gump, P.V. 268

Habermas, Jurgen 244, 245
Hacker, R.J. 97
Hall, Gene 328-30, 332, 341
Hamblin, Douglas 8, 111
Hamilton, D. 339
Hammersley, M. 279
Handicap 18, 111, 112
Hargreaves, A. 279, 282
Hargreaves, David 5, 85
Harlen, W. 307
Harnischfeger, A. 259, 262
Harris, Chris 312
Hawkins, D. 319, 324
head teachers 28, 29, 305-8
health education 48, 64
Hencke, D. 76
H.M.I. Reports 22, 36, 37, 61, 70, 71, 80, 89,
    253, 258, 269, 272, 297, 301, 308
Hewstone, Miles 355
Hilsum, S. 261
Hirst, Paul 93, 226, 233
history 64, 65, 70
Holland, education in 182, 183, 198-201, 207

Holland Geoffrey 16, 17
Holt, Maurice 212, 220, 221
Hornsey College of Art 148, 149
"host" teachers 311, 312, 315, 316
Howson, G. 202
Hughes, Phil 336, 339, 340
Humanities Curriculum Project 85
Humanities Teaching Project 2, 298

Identity 113, 114
Illich, Ivan 136, 137
Impact and Take-up Project 251
*Implications of Classroom Research for
    Professional Development* 242, 243
Independent schools 69, 73, 74
information, acquiring 58-60
Information Processing Models 333, 334
Initial and In-Service B.Ed. Degrees 80
Initial teacher training 77-84, 93-110
Inner London Education Authority 215, 253
Innovation Configuration 332
inquiry-based courses 88
In-School Evaluation 213
in-service training 77, 78, 81-3, 305-9
Inside the Primary Classroom 83·
Institut National de Recherche Pedagogique
    183, 185, 209n.
Institut Ontwikkeling Wiskunde Onderwije
    199, 200, 206
"Intermittent workers" 297, 298, 302, 303
International Commission for Mathematics
    Education 202
Isaac, John 10
IT—Inset project 89, 305

Jackson, Brian 207
Jackson, Philip 272. 303, 304
James, William 266
Jasman, Anne 304
Jenkins, D. 250
Johnson, Daphne 139, 142
Johnston, David 307
Jones, M. 96
Journal of Curriculum Studies 255
Journal of Education for Teaching 86
Joyce, Bruce 328, 333, 335, 341

Kaskowitz, D.H. 277
Katz, R.L. 81
Keddie, N. 278
Keele Integrated Studies Project 251